Lecture Notes in Artificial Intelligence 3859

Edited by J. G. Carbonell and J. Siekmann

Subseries of Lecture Notes in Computer Science

W0230398

Frank Dignum   Rogier M. van Eijk
Roberto Flores (Eds.)

Agent
Communication II

International Workshops
on Agent Communication, AC 2005 and AC 2006
Utrecht, Netherlands, July 25, 2005
and Hakodate, Japan, May 9, 2006
Selected and Revised Papers

 Springer

Series Editors

Jaime G. Carbonell, Carnegie Mellon University, Pittsburgh, PA, USA
Jörg Siekmann, University of Saarland, Saarbrücken, Germany

Volume Editors

Frank Dignum
Department of Information and Computing Sciences
Universiteit Utrecht
3508 TB Utrecht, The Netherlands
E-mail: dignum@cs.uu.nl

Rogier M. van Eijk
Department of Information and Computing Sciences
Universiteit Utrecht
3508 Utrecht, The Netherlands
E-mail: rogier@cs.uu.nl

Roberto Flores
Department of Physics
Computer Science and Engineering
Chistopher Newport University
Newport News VA 23606, USA
E-mail: flores@pcs.cnu.edu

Library of Congress Control Number: 2006937885

CR Subject Classification (1998): I.2.11, I.2, C.2.4, C.2, D.2, F.3

LNCS Sublibrary: SL 7 – Artificial Intelligence

ISSN   0302-9743
ISBN-10   3-540-68142-6 Springer Berlin Heidelberg New York
ISBN-13   978-3-540-68142-7 Springer Berlin Heidelberg New York

Springer is a part of Springer Science+Business Media

springer.com

© Springer-Verlag Berlin Heidelberg 2006
Printed in Germany

Typesetting: Camera-ready by author, data conversion by Scientific Publishing Services, Chennai, India
Printed on acid-free paper   SPIN: 11947745   06/3142   5 4 3 2 1 0

Preface

Although everyone recognizes communication as a central concept in multi-agents, many no longer see agent communication as a research topic. Unfortunately there seems to be a tendency to regard communication as a kind of information exchange that can easily be covered using the standard FIPA ACL. However, the papers in this volume show that research in agent communication is far from finished. If we want to develop the full potential of multi-agent systems, agent communication should also develop to a level beyond parameter or value passing as is done in OO approaches!

In this book we present the latest collection of papers around the topic of agent communication. The collection comprises of the best papers from the agent communication workshops of 2005 and 2006, enriched with a few revised agent communication papers from the AAMAS conference. Due to some unfortunate circumstances the proceedings of the 2005 workshop were delayed, but it gave us the opportunity to join the best papers of the 2006 edition to this volume. Together these papers give a very good overview of the state of the art in this area of research and give a good indication of the topics that are of major interest at the moment.

The papers are divided into the following four topics:

- Semantics of Agent Communication
- Commitments in Agent Communication
- Protocols and Strategies
- Reliability and Overhearing

The research on the semantics of agent communication has shifted from concepts based on mental attitudes of the agents towards concepts based on social attitudes. However, FIPA ACL, the de facto agent communication standard language, still has an official semantics based on mental attitudes. The first paper in this volume by *V. Louis and T. Martinez* describes a first attempt to actually develop a tool to support verification of compliance to the FIPA ACL semantics, therefore giving an operational semantics to FIPA ACL. The paper of *U. Endriss* shows how conversation protocols can be described in terms of temporal logic. This allows model checking of the protocols and verifying their correctness with respect to a number of properties. The third paper on the semantics of agent communication by *G. Boello, R. Damiano, J. Hulstijn and L. van der Torre* is one of the first that tries to combine private and social mental attitudes to determine the semantics of the communication. Another effort to combine social commitments with the other attitudes of an agent can be found in the paper by *P. Pasquier and B. Chaib-draa*, which is placed under the second topic of social commitments, but could also have been placed under this heading. The last paper in this section of the volume by *S. Khan and Y. Lesperance* describes a possible semantics for conditional commitments. This is an important step

because since commitments are themselves used as semantics of the communication it is important to have some grasp of the characteristics of this concept
as well!

The second section of the volume is completely devoted to papers on social
commitments. The first paper in this section by *M. Verdicchio and M. Colombetti*
discusses how the concept of commitment can be used to build up a library of
speech acts to be used in agent communication. A similar topic is discussed in the
paper of *R. Kremer and R. Flores*. They add the idea of organizing the speech
acts according to a subsumption hierarchy to facilitate their processing. The paper of *G. Muller and L. Vercouter* discusses the use of social commitments that
follow from speech acts as constraints on subsequent communication, therefore
truly utilizing the intuitions that come with the "commitment" concept. Once
commitments are seen as constraints on the behavior of the agents, one should
also consider what should be done if the agents do not comply to these constraints. This aspect is discussed in the paper of *J. Heard and R. Kremer*. The
last paper in the section on commitments by *A. Mallya and M. Singh* discusses
a more advanced aspect of commitments. It looks at preferences with respect to
different commitment protocols which can be used to solve potential conflicts
between different commitments.

The third section of this volume is devoted to protocols and strategies for
communication. It starts with a paper by *L. Amgoud and S. Kaci* on strategies
for agents to be used during negotiation. The idea is to make these strategies
less restrictive such that good compromises are not discarded too quickly. The
second paper in this section by *J. van Diggelen, E. de Jong and M. Wiering* also
discusses strategies for communication, but in the domain of ontology alignment.
What is the influence of the strategies that agents use to adopt concepts on
the convergence to the use of one or more concepts? An important question in
order to see what will happen if thousands of agents with different ontologies on
the Web start communicating. The next paper by *J. van Diggelen, R-J. Beun,
F. Dignum, R. van Eijk and J-J. Meyer* actually continues this discussion. It
describes how agents can align their ontologies on the fly using some extensions
of normal communication protocols. Instead of learning complete ontologies the
agents just learn enough about the concepts to be able to use them properly.

The paper of *Pinar Yolum* discusses the important topic of designing protocols and shows some tools that can support this process. Whereas most approaches see protocols as a kind of finite state machine or Petri net, *F. Fischer,
M. Rovatsos, and G. Weiss* see protocols as patterns that can be adapted. The
semantics follows from the use rather than the use from the semantics. It is thus
a perfect example of the use of a bottom approach for creating semantics to
communication.

The last two papers in this section discuss communication in relation to the
beliefs of the agents. The first paper, by *H-J. Lebbink, C. Witteman and J-J.
Meyer*, discusses conversations about changing one's beliefs. When can an agent
conclude that it should retract some beliefs based on information it hears from
another agent? Preferably this only happens in a way that keeps the beliefs of

the agents "consistent" as far as possible. The paper by *I. Letia and R. Vartic* discusses the different consequences of basing communication on firm beliefs and on defeasible beliefs. Making this distinction allows for more subtle conversations that also seem to resemble human conversations more closely.

The last section of this volume contains papers that deal with multi-party communication. The paper of *S. Cranefield* discusses group communication in which a reliable shared perception of the order of the messages can be very important. This leads to a design of a type of synchronous group communication. The second paper by *N. Dragoni, M. Gaspari and D. Guidi* discusses the very important issue of communication breakdowns. Especially communication over the Internet should be fault-tolerant in order to work for large applications. They discuss a fault-tolerant ACL and illustrate its use on the Web. The final paper of this volume also discusses reliability of communication. In the approach of *G. Gutnik and G. Kaminka* this is achieved by selective overhearing of communication by other agents. Because trying to monitor all communication is prohibitively expensive they propose a hierarchical organization of the agents that can perform a selective overhearing.

We want to conclude this preface by extending our thanks to the members of the Program Committee of the ACL workshops that were willing to review the papers in a very short time span, to the external reviewers that probably even had less time to review their papers and also of course to the authors that were willing to submit their papers to our workshops and the authors that revised their papers for this book.

September 2006

Frank Dignum (Utrecht, Netherlands)
Rogier van Eijk (Utrecht, Netherlands)
Roberto Flores (Newport News, USA)

Workshop Organization

Organizing Committee

Rogier van Eijk   Universiteit Utrecht, Utrecht, Netherlands
Roberto Flores   Christopher Newport University, USA
Marc-Philippe Huget   University of Savoie, Annecy, France
Frank Dignum   Universiteit Utrecht, Netherlands, (**2006**)

Program Committee

L. Amgoud   IRIT,France
J. Bentahar   Laval University, Canada
B. Chaib-draa   Laval University, Canada
P. Cohen   Oregon Health and Science University, USA
M. Colombetti   Politecnico di Milano, Italy
M. Dastani   Utrecht University, Netherlands
F. Dignum   Utrecht University, Netherlands
R. van Eijk   Utrecht University, Netherlands, (**2006**)
A. El Fallah-Seghrouchni   University of Paris 6, France
R. Flores   Christopher Newport University, USA, (**2006**)
F. Guerin   University of Aberdeen, UK
M.-P. Huget   University of Savoie, France, (**2006**)
M. d'Inverno   Westminster University, UK
A. Jones   King's College, London, UK
F. Lin   Athabasca University, Canada, (**2006**)
N. Maudet   University of Paris 9, France
P. McBurney   University of Liverpool, UK
S. Parsons   City University of New York, USA
P. Pasquier   University of Melbourne, Australia, (**2006**)
S. Paurobally   University of Liverpool, UK
J. Pitt   Imperial College, UK
N. Roos   Maastricht University, Netherlands
D. Traum   University of California Los Angeles, USA
G. Weiss   Technical University Munich, Germany
M. Wooldridge   University of Liverpool, UK, (**2006**)
P. Yolum   Bogazici University, Turkey

External Reviewers

D. Grossi	Universiteit Utrecht, Netherlands, (**2005**)
M. Nickles	Technical University of Munich, Germany, (**2005**)
P. Pasquier	Laval University, Canada, (**2005**)
M. Rovatsos	University of Edinburgh, UK, (**2005**)
J. Saunier	University of Paris 9, France, (**2006**)

Table of Contents

Section III: Protocols and Strategies

Section IV: Reliability and Overhearing

An Operational Model for the FIPA-ACL Semantics

Vincent Louis and Thierry Martinez

France Telecom Research & Development
2, avenue Pierre Marzin
22307 Lannion Cedex, France
{vincent.louis, thierry.martinez}@francetelecom.com

Abstract. Despite the effort made to standardize agent communication languages, almost no tool has been developed to implement agents' conformance to their semantics. In this paper, we review the formal principles supporting the FIPA-ACL semantics and propose an operational model facilitating their implementation. This model has been implemented upon the JADE platform, resulting in more flexible agents, avoiding intensive use of rigid protocols.

1 Introduction

Many research and industrial actors in the field of multi-agent systems have identified the need for a shared agent communication language (ACL) long ago. The most enthusiastic ones consider such a language as the counterpart of human natural languages for agents. In particular, ACLs should make it possible to convey meanings instead of "simple" objects with no semantics like in classical object middlewares [1]. At least, ACLs should let heterogeneous agents communicate and interact with each other [2]. This trend resulted in late nineties in mainly two initiatives to come to a standard language: KQML (Knowledge Query and Manipulation Language) from the ARPA knowledge sharing project [3] and FIPA-ACL from the Foundation for Intelligent Physical Agents consortium [4, 5]. Although the usefulness of such languages in building open, heterogeneous and interoperable agent systems is generally acknowledged, ACLs have also often been criticized because of their formal semantics, which make them generally difficult to implement and hence seldom implemented [6, 7].

On the one hand, a commonly pointed out difficulty in using these ACLs is that they assume a mental state-based model for agents. While such mentalistic approaches are well suited to specify the meaning of communicative acts from the subjective viewpoint of the participants, they cannot ensure any global objective property of the system. Along this line, a recent stream in the multi-agent community has proposed to use so-called social approaches (as opposed to mentalistic or individual ones) [2]. These approaches model interactions through public structures, generally based on the notion of (social) commitment. They lead to recent concrete alternatives for defining ACLs [8, 9].

On the other hand, because the formal semantics of ACLs rely on complex logical theories of agency (mixing reasoning on several concepts such as beliefs, intentions and actions), they require a high level of understanding to design conforming agents. This matter of fact is not only pointed out at a theoretical level but also at a concrete

F. Dignum, R. van Eijk, and R. Flores (Eds.): AC 2005/2006, LNAI 3859, pp. 1 – 14, 2006.

development level [10]. Consequently, even if some recent work attempts to simplify this kind of models [11], designers often prefer protocol-based approaches (such as [12]). In these cases, they do not benefit from the original semantics of ACLs, which only account for an intuitive meaning of the communicative acts. As a resulting drawback, the use of rigid interaction protocols often results in decreasing the flexibility and therefore the autonomy of agents.

A third possible working direction consists in making available proper tools in order to encompass these difficulties. To our knowledge, little work has investigated this area. For example, in the FIPA community, most of the existing platforms that claim to be FIPA-compliant (among the most famous ones, JADE [13], FIPA-OS [14], Zeus [15]) implement the middleware-related specifications but provide no concrete support regarding the ACL semantics-related specifications. In order to promote such tools, this paper proposes an operational model for implementing the theory of agency that underlies the FIPA-ACL semantics. This model, which is obviously missing today, aims at both helping developers to soundly conform to the FIPA-ACL semantics and leading to the development of proper tools to be integrated into FIPA-compliant platforms. Actually, this model provides a design framework that ensures consistency with the theory principles. Interestingly, it is flexible enough to customize agents' behaviors, while the built agents also benefit from generic capabilities for interpreting and generating communicative acts. This paper only focuses on the interpretation part.

The next section reviews some formal principles of the theory of agency underlying the FIPA-ACL semantics, which are relevant to the interpretation of communicative acts. Section 3 describes the main concepts and mechanisms of the model from which these principles can be implemented. Section 4 illustrates the resulting model with a simple example. Finally, section 5 concludes and discusses some perspectives.

2   Reviewing FIPA-ACL Semantics

The FIPA Agent Communication Language is defined through a set of communicative acts [5]. Their precise meaning results from their interpretation as particular actions within a more general theory of agency, namely the theory of rational interaction proposed by Sadek [16]. Thus, the semantics of FIPA communicative acts is formally defined by the generic principles of Sadek's theory that apply to actions. Although the FIPA specifications list most of these principles [5, Informative Annex A], some significant ones are unfortunately missing. This section reviews the essential principles formalizing the interpretation of FIPA-ACL communicative acts and identifies a general template in the perspective of implementing them.

All formal properties described in this paper are written in FIPA-SL [17], which is the modal logic language that sustains the theory of agency defining the FIPA-ACL semantics.

2.1   Mental Attitudes and Actions

First of all, the underlying theory formally specifies agents' behaviors through mental state notions describing internal agents' features that must be interpreted subjectively, i.e. from their point of view. Mental states are classically described using beliefs and intentions (according to the widely acknowledged Belief-Desire-Intention paradigm [18]). Beliefs are formalized by two logical modal operators: $(B \underline{i} \underline{p})$[1] expresses that agent $\underline{i}$ believes that $\underline{p}$ holds and $(U \underline{i} \underline{p})$ expresses that agent $\underline{i}$ is uncertain about $\underline{p}$, that is, s/he does not believe that $\underline{p}$ holds but s/he believes that $\underline{p}$ is more probably true than $(not \underline{p})$. The B operator satisfies a KD45 model and is semantically defined by a Kripke possible world structure, whereas the semantics of the U operator is defined in probabilistic terms upon the accessible possible worlds supporting the B operator.[2] Intentions are mainly formalized by one logical operator, $(I \underline{i} \underline{p})$, which expresses that agent $\underline{i}$ intends that $\underline{p}$ holds. Sadek's theory actually provides several degrees of intention (similar, to some extent, to Cohen and Levesque's approach [20]), including choice, achievement goal (agent $\underline{i}$ does not believe that $\underline{p}$ holds), persistent goal (agent $\underline{i}$ will drop her/his goal $\underline{p}$ until it is satisfied or s/he comes to believe it is unachievable) and intention itself (agent $\underline{i}$ commits to perform, individually or collectively with other cooperative agents, any action s/he believes that can reach the goal $\underline{p}$), each one being defined upon a more primitive choice concept [21]. Within the scope of the FIPA specifications, the intention operator is considered to be primitive.

A property of agents' mental attitudes, which is worth mentioning, is that they must be consistent with their beliefs: agents always believe the mental attitudes they actually have. Formally, the following property is valid within the theory, for both primitive (expressed with the previous operators of belief, uncertainty and intention) and composite mental attitudes (expressed by combining these operators with logical connectors):

$$(equiv (B \underline{i} \underline{PHI}(\underline{i})) \underline{PHI}(\underline{i})) \qquad (1)$$

where $\underline{i}$ denotes an agent and $\underline{PHI}(\underline{i})$ a mental attitude of $\underline{i}$

Consequently, agents' internal states (including all their mental attitudes) can be exclusively described by their beliefs. An important corollary is that agents cannot be uncertain (with the meaning of the U operator) of any of their mental attitudes (since they fully believe it). The following property is valid within the theory:

$$(not (U \underline{i} \underline{PHI}(\underline{i}))) \qquad (2)$$

where $\underline{i}$ denotes an agent and $\underline{PHI}(\underline{i})$ a mental attitude of $\underline{i}$

In order to describe temporal facts, the theory supports two other modalities: $(done \underline{a} \underline{p})$ expresses that action $\underline{a}$ has just occurred and that $\underline{p}$ held just before its occurrence (past-oriented), and $(feasible \underline{a} \underline{p})$ expresses that action $\underline{a}$ may possibly occur and that $\underline{p}$ will hold just after its occurrence, if it actually occurs (future-oriented). Both these operators are possible normal modal operators that satisfy a K model and are semantically defined by a Kripke possible world structure. Their accessibility relations classically define a branching future (several different actions

---

[1] In this paper, the underlined terms in logical formulas denote schematic variables. Here, $\underline{i}$ and $\underline{p}$ may be respectively replaced with references to agents and formulas.

[2] Sadek originally proposed a set of logical properties satisfied by the U operator. More recent work investigates an axiomatic system for this operator, but without proving its completeness with respect to the semantic model [19].

may occur in a given possible world) and a linear past (exactly one action has just occurred in a given possible world).

The resulting framework is a homogeneous multimodal logic powerful enough to account for very subtle nuances. For example, (exists ?X (B i (feasible ?X p))) expresses that agent i knows an action ?X (which is not explicit) that may bring about p (e.g. "Mary knows a recipe to cook a cake"), whereas (B i (exists ?X (feasible ?X p))) expresses that agent i believes that there are some ways of reaching p, without necessarily knowing how to reach it (e.g. "Mary knows cakes can be cooked").

2.2 Formally Interpreting Incoming Communicative Acts

FIPA-ACL defines four primitive (Inform, Confirm, Disconfirm and Request) and eighteen composite communicative acts [5]. Each of them (primitive or composite) is defined by two semantic features, namely its feasibility precondition and its rational effect. We now review the formal principles embedded in the theory of agency that specify how agents should interpret received communicative acts based on their semantic features.

Feasibility Precondition
The feasibility precondition of a communicative act states the condition that must necessarily hold for this act to be sent. This classical notion of action precondition is formalized by the following axiom within the theory[3]. It means that any agent observing a communicative act performance (left part of the implication) necessarily believes that its feasibility precondition held just before its performance (right part, in the scope of the done operator):

$$(B \ i \ (implies \ (done \ \underline{a} \ true) \quad (done \ \underline{a} \ FP(\underline{a})))) \tag{3}$$

where $\underline{a}$, FP(a) and i respectively denote a communicative act, its feasibility precondition and an agent

This principle is particularly useful to check the consistency of incoming communicative acts. For example, agents should reject received Inform acts about one of their own mental attitudes (e.g. when they are told "you intend to jump out the window") because applying property (2) to the corresponding propositional content makes the feasibility precondition inconsistent. Actually, the informative annex of [5] mentions no property that formally deals with feasibility precondition interpretation, so that a specification of inconsistent communicative acts is clearly missing.

Rational Effect
The rational effect of a communicative act states what the result expected by agents performing this act is. It underlies a unique classical actual postcondition of the communicative act, namely its "intentional effect", which is formalized by the following axiom within the theory. It means that agents observing an act performance (left part of the implication) believe that the sender intends each receiver believes the sender intends the rational effect of this act (right part):

---

[3] This axiom, which was actually proposed by Louis [19], generalizes Sadek's original formalization: (B i (implies (feasible a true) FP(a))).

$$
\begin{aligned}
&\texttt{(B \underline{i} (implies (done \underline{a} true)} \\
&\qquad\qquad\texttt{(I \underline{j} (B \underline{k} (I \underline{j} \underline{RE}(\underline{a})))))} \\
&\quad\texttt{))}
\end{aligned} \tag{4}
$$

where $\underline{a}$, $\underline{RE}(\underline{a})$, $\underline{i}$, $\underline{j}$ and $\underline{k}$ respectively denote a communicative act, its rational effect, an agent, the author of $\underline{a}$ and a receiver of $\underline{a}$

Actually, [5, Property 4] only considers the following weaker principle:

$$
\begin{aligned}
&\texttt{(B \underline{i} (implies (done \underline{a} true)} \\
&\qquad\qquad\texttt{(I \underline{j} \underline{RE}(\underline{a})))))}
\end{aligned} \tag{5}
$$

where $\underline{a}$, $\underline{RE}(\underline{a})$, $\underline{i}$ and $\underline{j}$ respectively denote a communicative act, its rational effect, any agent and the author of $\underline{a}$

The consequent is simplified, assuming that most agents receiving a message (whether they be cooperative or not with the sender) adopt the primary intention expressed by the intentional effect, that is, believe the sender intends the rational effect. Anyway, the important feature of both of these expressions is the surrounding B operator, which makes the intentional effect relative to each observing agent. It means the intentional effect is not an absolute effect, but rather a subjective one that has to be interpreted individually (and possibly differently) by each agent. Thus, it is up to the receiver of a communicative act to satisfy the author's intention (recognized through the principles (4) or (5)), depending on her/his specified behavior.

Cooperation Principles

Contrary to some criticisms expressed against FIPA-ACL [22], agents conforming to the semantics of this language are not necessarily cooperative. Since interpreting the intentional effect of a received message should be specific to each agent (resulting in customized behaviors), the informative annex of [5] gives no recommendation about this process. However, the underlying theory provides some formal principles that should be made explicit. For instance, we accommodate two principles of Sadek's theory that guide the agents' behaviors in the perspective of implementing FIPA agents.

The belief transfer principle states the condition under which an agent comes to believe what another agent intends s/he believes. It is formally expressed by the following axiom schema:

$$
\begin{aligned}
&\texttt{(implies (and (B \underline{i} (I \underline{j} (B \underline{i} \underline{p}))) (B \underline{i} \underline{COND_B(j,p)}))} \\
&\qquad\texttt{(B \underline{i} \underline{p}))}
\end{aligned} \tag{6}
$$

where $\underline{i}$, $\underline{j}$ and $\underline{p}$ respectively denote two agents and a formula

Sadek's original principle only applies to facts $\underline{p}$ denoting a mental attitude of agent $\underline{j}$. We have extended it to any kind of facts by adding a condition $\underline{COND_B(j,p)}$ that has to be customized depending on the expected behavior of agent $\underline{i}$. Note that this condition appears under the scope of an $\underline{i}$'s belief operator, so that it can be differently specified (i.e. customized) for each agent. For example, if agent i_0 does not trust agent i_1 at all, the i_0-related condition can simply be specified to be `false` for $j=i_1$ and any $\underline{p}$.

Similarly, the intention transfer principle states the condition under which agents adopt intentions of other agents. In other words, it sets the extent to which agents are cooperative with other agents. It can be formally expressed by an axiom schema of the following form:

$$
\begin{array}{l}
\text{(implies (and (B \underline{i} (I \underline{j} \underline{p})) (B \underline{i} \underline{COND_T(j,p)}))} \\
\qquad \text{(I \underline{i} \underline{p}))}
\end{array} \tag{7}
$$

where $\underline{i}$, $\underline{j}$ and $\underline{p}$ respectively denote two agents and a formula that is not a mental attitude of $\underline{i}$

Here, the agents' cooperative inclination can be customized by specifying the condition $\underline{COND_T(j,p)}$ (which, as above, is specific to each agent $\underline{i}$). Note that the schematic variable $\underline{p}$ is constrained not to denote a mental attitude of $\underline{i}$, so that the application of (6) and (7) is mutually exclusive. Actually, we only provide an example of what could be an intention transfer principle in the perspective of implementing FIPA agents and we do not claim giving a complete set of axioms in the scope of this paper. For further interest, [16] and [23] propose extended cooperation principles that could easily be adapted to this framework in order to get more specific agents' behaviors.

Identifying a General Template for Formal Principles

As (B $\underline{i}$ (implies $\underline{p}$ $\underline{q}$)) logically entails (implies (B $\underline{i}$ $\underline{p}$) (B $\underline{i}$ $\underline{q}$)) within the modal logic supporting the theory of agency, the following template can be easily identified as matching the reviewed principles that formally characterize the semantic interpretation of communicative acts:

$$
\text{(implies (and \underline{A} \underline{COND}) \underline{C})} \tag{8}
$$

$\underline{A}$ denotes the antecedent to recognize for applying the corresponding principle, $\underline{COND}$ denotes a condition that must be checked before applying it and $\underline{C}$ denotes the consequent resulting from its application. For example, instantiating $\underline{A}$ with (B $\underline{i}$ (done $\underline{a}$ true)), $\underline{COND}$ with true (i.e. no additional condition to check) and $\underline{C}$ with (B $\underline{i}$ (done $\underline{a}$ FP($\underline{a}$))) soundly represents the feasibility precondition principle (3).

Casting all formal principles of the theory into this template provides a sound but not necessarily complete set of axioms with respect to this theory. In the perspective of implementing agents, the soundness ensures the consistency of their behaviors; the completeness loss is not a problem provided the inferences that are relevant to their behaviors are preserved. Anyway, as the underlying theory of agency is intrinsically not decidable, a trade-off must be found in order to implement it.

The next section develops an operational model for implementing a set of such templates and therefore a significant part of the FIPA-ACL semantics.

3   Operationalizing the FIPA-ACL Semantics

As previously argued, implementing agents that comply with and thus take full advantage of the FIPA-ACL semantics requires a suitable mechanism. This section describes the main constituents of a FIPA-ACL operational model that can lead to the implementation of such a mechanism. These elements can be refined into two main categories: the first one includes classical constituents BDI-style agents must hold, whereas the second one introduces new specific elements in order to reify the general template identified in the previous section for the formal principles defining the FIPA-ACL semantics. As a prerequisite, we first expose three major constraints a FIPA-ACL implementation has to deal with.

Firstly, agents conforming to FIPA-ACL are supposed to receive and send communicative acts according to their mental states (i.e., their beliefs). As a direct consequence, the aimed mechanism should make it possible to program agents through these mental states. For example, in order to inform another agent about the value of a property, an agent is required to have this value among her/his beliefs, as well as the fact that the receiver does not already believe this value.

Secondly, the aimed mechanism should efficiently handle FIPA-SL expressions, since the semantics of FIPA-ACL is defined using the terms of this language. For example, the feasibility precondition and the rational effect of communicative acts are specified by SL formulas.

Lastly, parts of agents' behaviors, such as their cooperation abilities, are not imposed by the FIPA-ACL semantics and should be customizable. Thus, that the aimed mechanism should provide flexibility hooks. For example, extending these hooks should make it possible to setup which requested actions an agent should perform.

3.1 Classical Agent Constituents

Two basic concepts at least are needed to handle the FIPA-ACL semantics: activities and beliefs.

Activities
By activity, we mean an agent's performing some course of action, such as issuing a communicative act, sending an email, switching on a light, ... Most of the time, interpreting incoming messages results in adding one or several activities to the receiving agent. For example, handling Query-if communicative acts typically results in an activity consisting in issuing an Inform act, and handling Request acts typically results in an activity consisting in performing the requested action. Activities are generally either primitive or compound, resulting from a planner computation. In an implementation perspective, the JADE platform provides a "Behaviour" mechanism that could support the concept of activity.

Beliefs
Agents need to perform some reflexive operations both to access and update their own beliefs. Interpreting or sending communicative acts indeed intensively refers to the author's and receiver's beliefs, according to their semantic features. For example, in order to inform another agent about a fact, agents should select the proper act (Inform, Confirm or Disconfirm) depending on their beliefs about the receiver's beliefs regarding this fact. Moreover, after issuing this act, they should come to believe the other agent henceforth believes this fact. Typically, the `COND` part of the template (`implies (and A COND) C`) refers to agents' beliefs.

Such reflexive operations should at least support an Assert operation to add new believed facts, a Query-if operation to query believed facts, and a Query-ref operation to query the believed values of identifying expressions. Here are some examples of invocation of such operations:

```
1. Assert("(temperature 20)");
2. Query-if("(temperature 21)");
3. Query-if("(temperature-greater-than 10)");
4. Query-ref("(any ?x (temperature ?x))");
```

The first invocation asserts the agent believes the temperature is 20. The second one queries whether the agent believes the temperature is 21. The third one queries whether the agent believes the temperature is greater than 10. The last one queries for a temperature value believed by the agent.

Considering this example, several issues may generally influence the whole mechanism implementation. The first issue is the need for a mechanism that ensures the consistency of the stored beliefs. For example, assuming a classical semantics for the temperature predicate (i.e., it satisfies exactly one value), an agent should not believe at the same time (temperature 20) and (temperature 21). The second issue is the practical need for inference capabilities. In this example, an agent that believes (temperature 20) should also believe (temperature-greater-than 10). Finally, the real semantics of the Query operations is worth highlighting. Query-if returns true for a given fact if the agent believes this fact (whether the truth value of this fact actually be). It returns false if this fact does not belong to her/his beliefs (s/he does not necessarily believe it is false). This characterizes the agent subjectivity.

3.2 Additional Constituents

Beyond the two basic concepts of activity and belief, we introduce two key additional concepts to build our operational model: semantic representations (SRs) and semantic interpretation principles (SIPs).

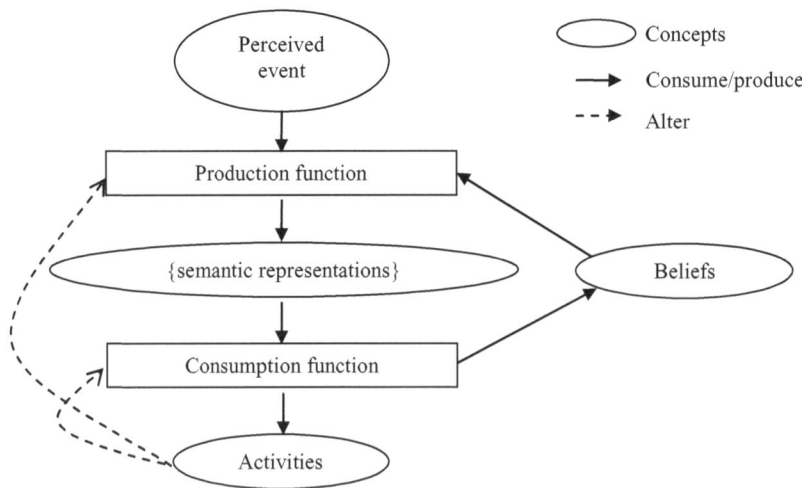

Fig. 1. Interpretation abstract process

Semantic Representation (SR)

A semantic representation is a FIPA-SL formula representing a part of the meaning of an event perceived by the agent, for instance, an incoming message. As SRs refer to *perceived* events, they are necessarily expressed as beliefs of the corresponding agent, ranging from simple beliefs (about the state of the world, her/his own intentions, other agents' beliefs, ...) to combined ones.

SR is the central concept supporting the general process for interpreting incoming messages (and more generally perceived events). This process is refined into two main functions, which can take place simultaneously: the first one consists in producing SRs while the second one consumes them (see Fig. 1):

1. The production function computes from an input perceived event an output consisting of all SRs expressing the agent understanding of this event. For example, assuming agent j perceives the following communicative act:

```
(Inform
        :sender i
        :receiver j
        :content "((p))")
```

The production function implemented by j generates the following SRs:
  - (B j (done (action i (Inform ...): this SR means j believes that i has just issued the Inform act, it is the direct representation of the perceived event;
  - (B j (B i p)): this SR means j believes that i believes the content of the Inform act is true. It represents the interpretation of part of the feasibility precondition of this act (namely, the fact that the sender should believe the informed content) and can be formally derived using the formal principle (3) applied to the Inform act;
  - Other SRs may represent the interpretation of the intentional effect of the Inform act, the intentions derived applying cooperation principles, and so on.
2. The consumption function computes from the previously produced SRs new activities and beliefs within the perceiving agent. In the previous example, the consumption function implemented by j adds (B i p) to j's beliefs from the second produced SR. The global interpretation process ends when all SRs are consumed.

In this general interpretation process, the formal principles defining the FIPA-ACL semantics can be directly connected to the production function. This connection is detailed in the next subsection about "SIPs". Another point worth mentioning is the requirement for a normal form mechanism to ensure that two logically equivalent FIPA-SL formulas lead to the same SR, resulting in the same understanding of the agent. Finally, this model provides a natural support to proactive behaviors: internally generated events (sensor events, activity-triggered events, ...) viewed as particular perceived events are interpreted through the same process.

Semantic Interpretation Principle (SIP)

Semantic interpretation principles provide the basic means to produce and consume SRs (see Fig. 2). A SIP is closely related to a particular instantiation of the general template (implies (and A COND) C) corresponding to one formal principle of the theory:

- It accepts as input the SR representing the A part of the formal principle,
- If the COND part is satisfied (this generally requires accessing the agent's beliefs), then:
  - It produces as output a set of SRs, representing the C part,
  - It consumes the input SR,
  - It may add new activities to the agent,
  - It may update the agent's beliefs.

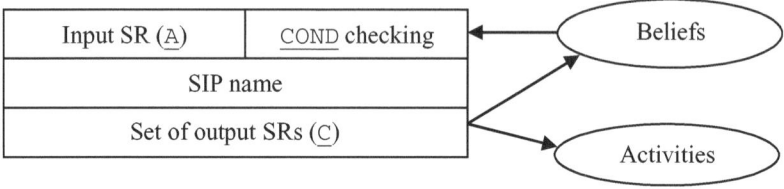

Fig. 2. Representation of a SIP

Practically, implementing the FIPA-ACL semantics using our operational model generally consists in:

- Reusing SIPs that implement generic formal principles of the underlying theory, such as the intentional effect interpretation (5) or the feasibility precondition checking (3),
- Customizing SIPs that implement customizable cooperation principles of the theory, such as the belief transfer (6) or the intention transfer (7) principle,
- Defining agent- or application-specific SIPs, providing our model with flexibility hooks.

This operational model has been implemented as an add-on upon the JADE multi-agent platform [13]. The following table sums up the main SIPs that have been explicitly implemented.

Table 1. List of implemented SIPs on the JADE platform

This SIP...	Consists in
ActionFeatures	Applying the principles (3) and (5)
BeliefTransfer	Applying the principle (6)
IntentionTransfer	Applying the principle (7)
ActionPerformance	Adding an activity that performs an action intended by the agent
RationalityPrinciple	Adding an activity that brings about an effect intended by the agent (rationality principle [5, Property 1])
Planning	Invoking a planning computation (if available)
Subscribe	Adding an observer mechanism on the belief base of the agent to monitor the truth of a given belief

The ActionPerformance, RationalityPrinciple and Planning SIPs actually implement three (customizable) principles of the underlying agent theory dealing with the planning of actions with respect to the agent's intentions. The first one applies to SRs of the form (`I` `i` (`done` `a` `true`)) and directly performs the action `a`, by adding a proper activity to the agent. The rationality principle applies to SRs of the form (`I` `i` `p`) and performs an action, the rational effect of which matches the formula `p`, if the agent knows such an action (the set of known actions include all FIPA communicative acts as well as all application-specific actions). Last, the Planning SIP applies to SRs of the same form and makes it possible to call an external planning algorithm. Its result must be an activity to be added into the agent in order to reach the goal `p`.

The Subscribe SIP makes it possible to properly handle subscription-related FIPA communicative acts, such as Request-When, Request-Whenever or Subscribe. It applies to SRs representing the belief of the receiver about the conditional intention of the sender of a subscription-related act. Such a conditional intention actually states the sender (or subscriber) adopts a certain "regular" intention (of performing the subscribed action) as soon as a condition becomes true. These regular intention and condition depend on the content of the subscription-related act. The Subscribe SIP then sets up a special mechanism onto the belief base of the receiver. This mechanism consists in monitoring the condition and producing a new SR representing the regular intention as soon as the condition is believed by the receiver. This new SR is in turn processed by the general interpretation algorithm and, in particular, by the cooperation- and planning-related SIPs.

4 Example

Fig. 3 partially shows the interpretation process applied by an agent `j` to two almost equivalent incoming messages from agent `i`. The first one is an Inform act stating that `i` intends `j` to perform action `a`. The second one is a Request act requiring `j` to perform `a`.

The Inform act is interpreted by applying four SIPs:

1. The first SIP produces an SR representing the intentional effect of the act, which states `j` believes `i` intends the rational effect of the Inform act to hold,
2. The second SIP produces an SR stating `j` believes `i` intends `a` to be done, by applying a belief transfer principle,
3. The third SIP produces an SR stating `j` intends `a` to be done, by applying an intention transfer principle,
4. Then the last SIP creates the activity to perform `a`.

The Request act is interpreted by applying three SIPs:

1. The first SIP is the same one as the previous 1., except that it applies to a Request instead of an Inform act,
2. The second and the third SIPs are respectively the same as the previous 3. and 4., resulting in the same behavior of `j`.

This simple example illustrates how agents can react to incoming messages in respect to their meaning rather than their syntax.

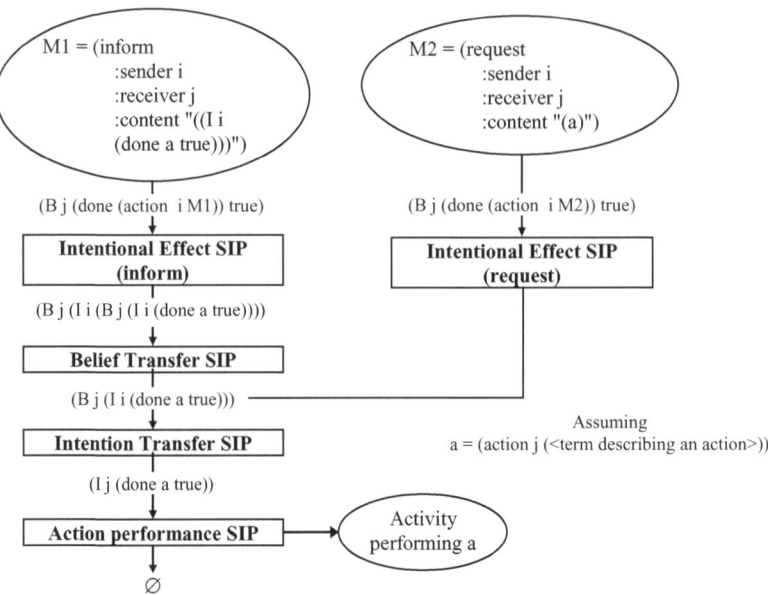

Fig. 3. Interpreting Inform and Request messages

5 Concluding Remarks

We have identified a recurrent template for the formal principles of the theory of agency that defines the FIPA-ACL semantics. Considered as a general primitive inference rule, this template can be thought of as the basis of a global interpretation process. We define the concepts of "semantic interpretation principle" (SIP) and "semantic representation" (SR) to implement such a template. These notions, together with proper mechanisms and classical agent-related notions like beliefs and activities, result in an operational model that makes it possible to implement the FIPA-ACL semantics.

Agents built upon this operational model, which relies on the identified template, comply with the formal principles defining the semantics of FIPA-ACL. For example, these agents reject inconsistent incoming messages, such as Inform messages about their own mental states. Moreover, they naturally interpret incoming messages according to their semantic meaning and not to their syntactic form (see the example in section 4). Finally, the operational model provides enough flexibility to support specific behaviors by customizing or specifying additional SIPs.

Considering the effective implementation of our proposed model, we see at least three solutions: the first one consists in using a dedicated inference engine for the modal logic theory of agency supporting the FIPA-ACL semantics. In this case, each instance of SIP is implemented as a particular axiom schema within this engine. For example, the ARTIMIS technology, which currently supports the deployment of real agent-based dialogue applications [24,25], relies on this approach. However, it requires a complex inference engine, which is not available on the market, to our knowledge. The second solution consists in using a rule engine, each instance of SIP being a rule itself. The anticipated difficulty is to setup the proper data structures to handle logical formulas and their normal forms. Finally, we have actually considered a direct ad-hoc implementation of our operational model into the JADE FIPA compliant platform, a first release of which is publicly available since July 2005.

In any case, our operational model is expected to give rise to new reliable software tools that will make it possible to develop "semantic" agents. Such challenging agents, which intrinsically work on the meaning of the messages, would no longer explicitly need interaction protocols. The flexibility and therefore the autonomy of these agents would thus be significantly improved. For example, an agent expecting an answer to her/his query from another agent could perfectly deal with an unplanned sub-query from this other agent before getting the actual answer, which is currently not possible by implementing protocols like FIPA-Query with finite state machines.

Finally, our operational model provides novel perspectives regarding the often criticized problem of FIPA compliance testing. Obviously, it remains not possible to externally check agents' conformance to the FIPA-ACL semantics because there is no means to access their private mental states. Anyway, we argue that future complex systems (disappearing computing, ambient intelligence and so on) will mix both artificial and human agents and so make illusory any usual conformance test. In this spirit, our operational model provides a kind of "weak" compliance framework that ensures that the designed agents at least conform to a subset of a standardized formal semantics by directly implementing some principles of the corresponding theory.

References

1. Labrou, Y., Finin, T., Peng, Y.: Agent Communication Languages: The Current Landscape. IEEE Intelligent Systems, Volume 14(2) (1999) 45–52
2. Singh, M.: Agent Communication Languages: Rethinking the Principles. Computer, Volume 31(12). IEEE Computer Society Press (1998) 40–47
3. Labrou, Y., Finin, T.: A Proposal for a New KQML Specification. Technical Report TR-CS-97-03, Computer Science and Electrical Engineering Dept., Univ. of Maryland, USA (1997)
4. Foundation for Physical Intelligent Agents (FIPA), Geneva, Switzerland, http://www.fipa.org
5. FIPA: FIPA Communicative Act Library Specification. FIPA00037, http://www.fipa.org/specs/fipa00037/ (2002)
6. Pitt, J., Mamdani, A.: Some Remarks on the Semantics of FIPA's Agent Communication Language. Autonomous Agents and Multi-Agent Systems, Volume 2 (1999) 333–356
7. Chaib-Draa, B., Dignum, F.: Trends in Agent Communication Language. Computational Intelligence, Volume 18(2) (2002) 89–101
8. Bergeron, M., Chaib-draa, B.: ACL: Specification, Design and Analysis All Based on Commitments. This Volume (2005).
9. Verdicchio, M., Colombetti, M.: A Commitment-based Communicative Act Library. This Volume (2005)
10. Willmott, S. (ed.): Technical Input and Feedback to FIPA from Agentcities.RTD and the Agentcities Initiative. Agentcities Task Force Technical Note 00003, http://www.agentcities.org/note/00003/ (2003)

11. Paurobally, S., Cunnigham, J., Jennings, N.: A Formal Framework for Agent Interaction Semantics. This Volume (2005)
12. Pitt J., Bellifemine, F., A Protocol-Based Semantics for FIPA '97 ACL and its implementation in JADE. CSELT internal technical report (1999). Part of this report has been also published in Proceedings of AI*IA'99
13. Bellifemine, F., Caire, G., Poggi, A., Rimassa, G.: JADE A White Paper. exp in search of innovation, Volume 3(3), Telecom Italia Lab (2003) 6–19
14. emorphia: FIPA-OS, http://fipa-os.sourceforge.net/index.htm
15. Nwana, H., Ndumu, D., Lee, L., Collis, J.: ZEUS: A Tool-Kit for Building Distributed Multi-Agent Systems. Applied Artifical Intelligence Journal, Volume 13(1) (1999) 129–186
16. Sadek, D.: Attitudes mentales et interaction rationnelle : vers une théorie formelle de la communication, PhD thesis, Rennes I university, France (1991)
17. FIPA: FIPA SL Content Language Specification. FIPA00008, http://www.fipa.org/specs/fipa00008/ (2002)
18. Rao, A., Georgeff, M.: Modeling rational agents within a BDI-architecture. Proceedings of KR'91 (1991) 473–484
19. Louis, V.: Conception et mise en œuvre de modèles formels du calcul de plans d'action complexes par un agent rationnel dialoguant, PhD thesis, Caen university, France (2002)
20. Cohen, P., Levesque, H.: Intention is choice with commitment. Artificial Intelligence, Volume 42(2–3) (1990) 213–262
21. Sadek, D.: A Study in the Logic of Intention. Proceedings of KR'92 (1992) 462–473
22. McBurney, P., Parsons, S., Locutions for argumentation in agent interaction protocols. Revised Proceedings of the International Workshop on Agent Communication (AC2004), New York, NY, USA. Lecture Notes in Artificial Intelligence, Volume 3396. Springer, Berlin, Germany (2004) 209–225
23. Bretier, P., Panaget, F., Sadek, D.: Integrating linguistic capabilities into the formal model of a rational agent : Application to cooperative spoken dialogue. Proceedings of the AAAI'95 Fall Symposium on Rational Agency (1995)
24. Bretier, P., Sadek, D.: A Rational Agent as the Kernel of a Cooperative Spoken Dialogue System: Implementing a Logical Theory of Interaction. Proceedings of the ECAI'96 3rd ATAL Workshop (1997)
25. Sadek, D.: Design Considerations on Dialogue Systems: From Theory to Technology — The Case of ARTIMIS. Proceedings of the ESCA TR Workshop on Interactive Dialogue for Multimodal Systems, Germany (1999)

Temporal Logics for Representing Agent Communication Protocols

Ulle Endriss

Institute for Logic, Language and Computation
University of Amsterdam, 1018 TV Amsterdam, The Netherlands
ulle@illc.uva.nl

Abstract. This paper explores the use of temporal logics in the context of communication protocols for multiagent systems. We concentrate on frameworks where protocols are used to specify the conventions of social interaction, rather than making reference to the mental states of agents. Model checking can be used to check the conformance of a given dialogue between agents to a given protocol expressed in a suitable temporal logic. We begin by showing how simple protocols, such as those typically presented as finite automata, can be specified using a fragment of propositional linear temporal logic. The full logic can also express concepts such as future dialogue obligations (or commitments). Finally, we discuss how an extended temporal logic based on ordered trees can be used to specify nested protocols.

1 Introduction

Communication in multiagent systems is an important and very active area of research [15,29,37]. While much work has been devoted to so-called mentalistic models of communication (see in particular [15]), where communicative acts are specified in terms of agents' beliefs and intentions, recently a number of authors have argued for a *convention-based* approach to agent communication languages [9,23,29,31]. Mental attitudes are useful to explain *why* agents may behave in certain ways, but (being non-verifiable for an outside observer) they cannot serve as a basis for specifying the *norms* and *conventions* of interaction required for building open systems that allow for meaningful communication. In the convention-based approach, *protocols* specifying the rules of interaction play a central role.

This paper explores the use of temporal logics in the context of agent communication protocols. Rather than using a form of deontic logic to specify what agents *ought* to do, we use temporal logic formulas to specify the class of all dialogues (sequences of utterances) that are *legal* according to a given protocol. The notion of what an agent ought to do is then implicit: the social conventions of communication are fulfilled, if the generated dialogue satisfies the protocol specification. In particular, we propose to use *propositional linear temporal logic* [16,18] to specify protocols and *generalised model checking* [7] to decide whether an actual dialogue conforms to such a protocol.

F. Dignum, R. van Eijk, and R. Flores (Eds.): AC 2005/2006, LNAI 3859, pp. 15–29, 2006.
© Springer-Verlag Berlin Heidelberg 2006

Checking conformance *at runtime*, which is what we are concerned with here, can be distinguished from *a priori* conformance checking which addresses the problem of checking whether an agent can be guaranteed to always conform to a given protocol, on the basis of its specification [12,19]. Being able to check conformance at runtime is a minimal requirement for systems that operate with a convention-based communication protocol; if violations cannot be detected then the use of such a protocol will be of little use (but how to react to an observed violation is an issue that lies outside the scope of this paper).

The remainder of the paper is structured as follows. Section 2 provides an introduction to agent communication protocols and Section 3 covers the necessary background on temporal logic. In Section 4 the basic ideas of representing dialogues as models, using formulas to specify protocols, and applying (generalised) model checking to verify conformance are introduced. These ideas are then applied to protocols that can be represented as *finite automata* (in Section 5) and to the modelling of *dialogue obligations* (in Section 6). Section 7 discusses ideas on the specification of *nested protocols* using an extended temporal logic based on ordered trees, and Section 8 concludes with a brief discussion of related work.

2   Background on Protocols

An agent communication protocol lays down the conventions (or norms, or rules) of communicative interaction in a multiagent system. Agents communicate with each other by sending messages, which we refer to as *dialogue moves* (or communicative acts, or simply utterances). A *dialogue* is a sequence of such moves. A dialogue move will typically have, at least, the following components: a *sender*, a (list of) *receiver(s)*, a *performative* determining the type of move, and a *content* item defining the actual message content [12,15,37]. An example for a performative would be *inform*; an example for a content item would be "the city of Utrecht is more than 1300 years old". Indeed, the *content language* may be highly application-dependent, which means we cannot hope to be able to develop general tools for dealing with this particular aspect of communication. In addition, a dialogue move may also include a time-stamp.

The role of a protocol is to define whether a dialogue is *legal*, *i.e.* whether it conforms to the social rules governing the system to which the protocol in question applies. A variety of mechanisms for the specification of protocols have been put forward in the literature. Pitt and Mamdani [28], for instance, discuss several protocols based on deterministic finite automata. One of these, the *continuous update protocol*, is shown in Figure 1. This protocol may be used to regulate a dialogue where an agent A continuously updates another agent B on the value of some proposition. In each round, B may either acknowledge the information or end the dialogue. Figure 1 only specifies the performative (*inform*, *ack*, or *end*) and the sender (A or B) for each move. In fact, to keep our examples simple, throughout this paper we are going to abstract from the other components of a dialogue move. In the context of automata-based protocols, the definition of legality of a dialogue reduces to the definition of acceptance of a language by an

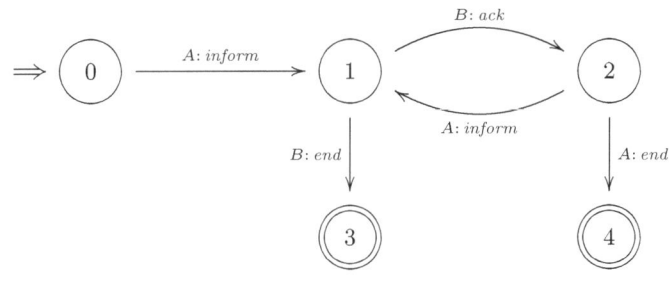

Fig. 1. The continuous update protocol

automaton in the usual sense [26]: A dialogue is legal according to a protocol iff it would be accepted by the automaton corresponding to the protocol.

Protocols defined in terms of finite automata are *complete* in the sense of clearly specifying the range of legal follow-up moves at every stage in a dialogue. This need not be the case, however [1]. In general, any set of rules that put some constraints on a dialogue between agents may be considered a protocol (although complete protocols may often be preferred for practical reasons). Typical examples for protocol rules that constrain a dialogue without necessarily restricting the range of legal follow-ups at every stage are conversational commitments (e.g. to honour a promise) [9], which require an agent to perform a certain communicative act at *some* point in the future. We are going to consider the specification of dialogue obligations like this in Section 6.

3   Background on Temporal Logic

Temporal logic has found many applications in artificial intelligence and computer science. In fact, over the years, a whole family of temporal logics have been developed. In this paper, we are mostly going to use *propositional linear temporal logic* (PLTL), which is probably the most intuitive of the standard temporal logics [16,18].

We briefly review the syntax and semantics of this logic. The language of PLTL builds on a countable set $\mathcal{L}$ of propositional letters. The set of well-formed *formulas* is the smallest set such that propositional letters are formulas and, whenever φ and ψ are formulas, so are $\neg\varphi$, $\varphi \wedge \psi$, and φ UNTIL ψ. Formulas are evaluated over a *frame* (also known as the *flow of time*). As we are going to identify the points in a frame with the turns in a dialogue (which, for all practical purposes, may be assumed to be finite), we define the semantics of PLTL over finite frames only. A (finite) frame is a pair $\mathcal{T} = (T, <)$ where $T = [0, \ldots, n]$ is an initial segment of the non-negative integers and $<$ is the usual ordering over integers. The elements of T are called *time points*. A *model* is a pair $\mathcal{M} = (\mathcal{T}, V)$ where $\mathcal{T}$ is such a frame and V (called the *valuation*) is a mapping from propositional letters in $\mathcal{L}$ to subsets of T. Intuitively, $V(p)$ defines the set of points at which an atomic proposition $p \in \mathcal{L}$ is true.

We write $\mathcal{M}, t \models \varphi$ to express that the formula φ is *true* at time point t in the model $\mathcal{M}$. This notion of truth in a model is defined inductively over the structure of formulas:

- $\mathcal{M}, t \models p$ iff $t \in V(p)$ for propositional letters $p \in \mathcal{L}$;
- $\mathcal{M}, t \models \neg\varphi$ iff $\mathcal{M}, t \not\models \varphi$;
- $\mathcal{M}, t \models \varphi \wedge \psi$ iff $\mathcal{M}, t \models \varphi$ and $\mathcal{M}, t \models \psi$;
- $\mathcal{M}, t \models \varphi$ UNTIL ψ iff there exists a $t' \in T$ with $\mathcal{M}, t' \models \psi$ and $t < t'$, and $\mathcal{M}, t'' \models \varphi$ for all $t'' \in T$ with $t < t''$ and $t'' < t'$.

Propositional connectives other than negation and conjunction can be defined in the usual manner; e.g. $\varphi \vee \psi = \neg(\neg\varphi \wedge \neg\psi)$. We also use $\top$ as a shorthand for $p \vee \neg p$ for some propositional letter p, *i.e.* $\top$ is true at any point in a model. The symbol $\bot$ is short for $\neg\top$. Further temporal operators can be defined in terms of the UNTIL-operator:

$$\bigcirc\varphi = \bot \text{ UNTIL } \varphi$$
$$\Diamond\varphi = \top \text{ UNTIL } \varphi$$
$$\Box\varphi = \neg\Diamond\neg\varphi$$

The first of these is called the next-operator: $\bigcirc\varphi$ is true at t whenever φ is true at a future point t' and there are no other points in between t and t' (as they would have to satisfy $\bot$), *i.e.* φ is true at the *next* point in time. The eventuality operator $\Diamond$ is used to express that a formula holds at *some* future time, while $\Box\varphi$ says that φ is true *always* in the future (it is not the case that there exists a future point where φ is not true). Alternatively, in particular if we are working with a fragment of PLTL that may not include the UNTIL-operator, these modalities can also be defined directly.

4   Dialogues as Models

Given a model $\mathcal{M}$ and a formula φ, the *model checking* problem is the problem of deciding whether φ is true at every point in $\mathcal{M}$. In the sequel, we are going to formulate the problem of checking conformance of a dialogue to a protocol as a (variant of the) model checking problem. The extraordinary success of model checking in software engineering in recent years is largely due to the availability of very efficient algorithms, in particular for the branching-time temporal logic CTL [8]. Given that the reasoning problems faced in the context of agent communication will typically be considerably less complex than those encountered in software engineering, efficiency is not our main concern. Instead, clarity and simplicity of protocol specifications must be our main objective.

We are going to use a special class of PLTL models to represent dialogues between agents and PLTL formulas to specify protocols. For every agent A referred to in the protocol under consideration, we assume that the set $\mathcal{L}$ of propositional letters includes a special proposition $turn(A)$ and that there are no other propositions of this form in $\mathcal{L}$. Furthermore, we assume that the set of performatives in our communication language is a subset of $\mathcal{L}$, and that $\mathcal{L}$ includes the special proposition INITIAL. We say that a model *represents* a dialogue iff it meets the following conditions:

- INITIAL is true at point 0 and at no other $t > 0$;
- exactly one proposition of the form $turn(\_)$ is true at any point $t > 0$;
- exactly one performative is true at any point $t > 0$.

Note that we do not allow for concurrent moves. The following is an example for such a model representing a dialogue (conforming to the protocol of Figure 1):

$$\begin{array}{ccccccccc}
 & turn(A) & & turn(B) & & turn(A) & & turn(B) & \\
\bullet & \longrightarrow & \bullet & \longrightarrow & \bullet & \longrightarrow & \bullet & \longrightarrow & \bullet \\
\text{INITIAL} & inform & & ack & & inform & & end &
\end{array}$$

An actual dialogue determines a *partial* model: It fixes the frame as well as the valuation for INITIAL and the propositions in $\mathcal{L}$ corresponding to turn-assignments and performatives, but it does not say anything about any of the other propositional letters that we may have in our language $\mathcal{L}$ (e.g. to represent dialogue states; see Section 5). We can *complete* a given partial model by arbitrarily fixing the valuation V for the remaining propositional letters. Every possible way of completing a dialogue model in this manner givens rise to a different PLTL model, *i.e.* a dialogue typically corresponds to a whole classes of models. This is why we cannot use standard model checking (which applies to single models) to decide whether a given dialogue satisfies a formula encoding a protocol. Instead, the reasoning problem we are interested in is this:

> Given a partial model $\mathcal{M}$ (induced by a dialogue) and a formula φ (the specification of a protocol), is there a full model $\mathcal{M}'$ completing $\mathcal{M}$ such that φ is true at every point in $\mathcal{M}'$?

In other words, we have to decide whether the partial description of a model can be completed in such a way that model checking would succeed.

The above problem is known as the *generalised model checking* problem and has been studied by Bruns and Godefroid [7]. In fact, the problem they address is slightly more general than ours, as they do not work with a fixed frame and distinguish cases where all complete instances of the partial model validate the formula from those where there exists at least one such instance. Generalised model checking may be regarded as a combination of satisfiability checking and model checking in the usual sense. If there are no additional propositions in $\mathcal{L}$, then generalised model checking reduces to standard model checking. If we can characterise the class of all models representing a given dialogue by means of a formula ψ, then φ and ψ can be used to construct a formula that is satisfiable (has got a model) iff that dialogue conforms to the protocol given by φ.

Note that the generalised model checking problem is EXPTIME-complete for both CTL and PLTL [7], *i.e.* there would be no apparent computational advantages in using a branching-time logic.

Before we move on to show how PLTL can be used to specify protocols in Sections 5 and 6, one further technical remark is in order. While we have defined the semantics of PLTL with respect to *finite* frames, the standard model checking algorithms for this logic are designed to check that all *infinite* runs through a given Kripke structure satisfy the formula in question. This is a crucial feature of these algorithms as they rely on the translation of temporal logic formulas into Büchi automata [21,34] and acceptance conditions for such automata are defined in terms of states that are being visited infinitely often. We note here that the problem of (generalised) model checking for finite models admitting only a single run is certainly not more difficult than (generalised) model checking for structures with infinite runs. Furthermore, to directly exploit existing algorithms, our approach could easily be adapted to a representation of dialogues as structures admitting only infinite runs. Because our main interest here lies in representing communication protocols and highlighting the potential of automated reasoning tools in this area, rather than in the design of concrete algorithms, in the remainder of the paper, we are going to continue to work with finite models.

5 Automata-Based Protocols

A wide range of communication protocols studied in the multiagent systems literature can be represented using deterministic finite automata (see e.g. [12,27,28,29]). As we shall see, we can represent this class of protocols using a fragment of PLTL where the only temporal operator required is the next-operator $\bigcirc$.

Consider again the protocol of Figure 1, which is an example for such an automaton-based protocol. If our language $\mathcal{L}$ includes a propositional letter of the form $state(i)$ for every state $i \in \{0, \ldots, 4\}$, then we can describe the *state transition function* of this automaton by means of the following formulas:

$$state(0) \wedge \bigcirc inform \rightarrow \bigcirc state(1)$$
$$state(1) \wedge \bigcirc ack \rightarrow \bigcirc state(2)$$
$$state(1) \wedge \bigcirc end \rightarrow \bigcirc state(3)$$
$$state(2) \wedge \bigcirc inform \rightarrow \bigcirc state(1)$$
$$state(2) \wedge \bigcirc end \rightarrow \bigcirc state(4)$$

To specify that state 0 is the (only) initial state we use the following formula:

$$\textsc{initial} \leftrightarrow state(0)$$

For automata with more than one initial state, we would use a disjunction on the righthand side of the above formula.

Next we have to specify the range of legal follow-up moves for every dialogue state. Let us ignore, for the moment, the question of turn-taking and only consider performatives. For instance, in state 1, the only legal follow-up moves would be *ack* and *end*. The seemingly most natural representation of this legality condition would be the following:

$$state(1) \rightarrow \bigcirc(ack \vee end)$$

This representation is indeed useful if we want to verify the legality of a *complete* dialogue. However, if we also want to use (generalised) model checking to establish whether an *unfinished* dialogue conforms to a protocol, we run into problems. Take a dialogue that has just begun and where the only event so far is a single *inform* move uttered by agent A, *i.e.* we are in state 1 and the dialogue should be considered legal, albeit incomplete. Then the next-operator in the above legality condition would *force* the existence of an additional time point, which is not present in the dialogue model under consideration, *i.e.* model checking would fail.

To overcome this problem, we use a *weak* variant of the next-operator. Observe that a formula of the form $\neg \bigcirc \neg \varphi$ is true at time point t iff φ is true at the successor of t or t has no successor at all. For the non-final states in the protocol of Figure 1, we now model *legality conditions* as follows:

$$state(0) \rightarrow \neg \bigcirc \neg inform$$
$$state(1) \rightarrow \neg \bigcirc \neg (ack \lor end)$$
$$state(2) \rightarrow \neg \bigcirc \neg (inform \lor end)$$

Next we specify that states 3 and 4 are *final* states and that a move taking us to a final state cannot have any successors:

$$\text{FINAL} \leftrightarrow state(3) \lor state(4)$$
$$\text{FINAL} \rightarrow \neg \bigcirc \top$$

Automata-based protocols regulating the communication between pairs of agents will typically implement a strict *turn-taking policy* (although this need not be so; see [27] for an example). This is also the case for the continuous update protocol. After a dialogue has been initiated, it is agent A's turn and after that the turn changes with every move. This can be specified as follows:

$$\text{INITIAL} \rightarrow \neg \bigcirc \neg turn(A)$$
$$turn(A) \rightarrow \neg \bigcirc \neg turn(B)$$
$$turn(B) \rightarrow \neg \bigcirc \neg turn(A)$$

Alternatively, these rules could have been incorporated into the specification of legality conditions pertaining to performatives given earlier. Where possible, it seems advantageous to separate the two, to allow for a modular specification.

Now let φ_{cu} stand for the conjunction of the above formulas characterising the continuous update protocol (*i.e.* the five formulas encoding the transition function, the formulas characterising initial and final states, the three formulas specifying the legality conditions for non-final states, and the formulas describing the turn-taking policy). Then a (possibly incomplete) dialogue is legal according to this protocol iff generalised model checking succeeds for φ_{cu} with respect to the partial model induced by the dialogue.

If we want this check to succeed only if the dialogue is not only legal but also complete, we can add the following formulas, which specify that any non-final state requires an additional turn:

$$\text{NON-FINAL} \leftrightarrow state(0) \lor state(1) \lor state(2)$$
$$\text{NON-FINAL} \rightarrow \bigcirc \top$$

While our description of how to specify automata-based protocols in PLTL has been example-driven, the general methodology is clear: It involves the specification of both the state transition function (including the identification of initial, final, and non-final states) and the range of legal follow-ups for any given state.

A special class of automata-based protocols, so-called *shallow* protocols, have been identified in [12]. A shallow protocol is a protocol where the legality of a move can be determined on the sole basis of the previous move in the dialogue. Many automata-based protocols in the multiagent systems literature, including the continuous update protocol and those proposed in [27,28,29], are shallow and allow for an even simpler specification than the one presented here. In fact, these protocols can be specified using a language $\mathcal{L}$ including *only* the special symbol INITIAL and propositions for performatives and turn-assignment (along the lines of the rules for the turn-taking policy given earlier), *i.e.* for this class of protocols standard model checking may be used to check conformance. Where available, a shallow specification may therefore be preferred.

6   Modelling Future Obligations

For many purposes, purely automata-based protocols are not sufficient. For instance, they do not support the specification of general *future obligations* on the communicative behaviour of an agent. This is an important feature of many classes of protocols proposed in the literature. Examples are the *discourse obligations* of Traum and Allen [33], the *commitments* in the work of Singh [31] and Colombetti [9], or the *social expectations* of Alberti et al. [1].

We should stress that we use the term *obligation* in rather generic a manner; in particular, we are not concerned with the fine distinctions between, say, obligations and commitments discussed in the literature [9,30].

In the context of an auction protocol, for example, we may say that, by opening an auction, an auctioneer acquires the obligation to close that auction again at some later stage. Suppose these actions can be performed by making a dialogue move with the performatives *open-auction* and *end-auction*, respectively. Again, to simplify presentation, we abstract from the issue of turn-taking and only write rules pertaining to performatives. The most straightforward representation of this protocol rule would be the following:

$$open\text{-}auction \rightarrow \Diamond end\text{-}auction$$

However, in analogy to the problematic aspects of using the next-operator to specify legal follow-ups in the context of automata-based protocols, the above rule forces the existence of future turns in a dialogue once *open-auction* has been performed. If we were to check an incomplete dialogue against this specification before the auction has been closed, model checking would fail and the dialogue would have to be classified as illegal. To be able to distinguish between complete dialogues where the non-fulfilment of an obligation constitutes a violation of the protocol and incomplete dialogues where this may still be acceptable, we have to move to a slightly more sophisticated specification.

To this end, we first define a weak version of the UNTIL-operator, which is sometimes called the UNLESS-operator:

$$\varphi \text{ UNLESS } \psi = (\varphi \text{ UNTIL } \psi) \vee \Box\varphi$$

That is, the formula φ UNLESS ψ is true at point t iff φ holds from t onwards (excluding t itself) either until a point where ψ is true or until the last point in the model.

We now use the following formula to specify that opening an auction invokes the obligation to end that auction at some later point in time:

$$open\text{-}auction \rightarrow \text{PENDING} \wedge (\text{PENDING UNLESS } end\text{-}auction)$$

The new propositional letter PENDING is used to mark time points at which there are still obligations that have not yet been fulfilled. A model representing a dialogue where *open-auction* has been uttered, but *end-auction* has not, will satisfy this protocol rule. However, in such a model, PENDING will be true at the very last time point. If we want to check whether a dialogue does not only not violate any rules but also fulfils all obligations, we can run generalised model checking with a specification including the following additional formula:

$$\text{PENDING} \rightarrow \bigcirc\top$$

No finite model satisfying this formula can make PENDING true at the last time point. That is, unless *end-auction* has been uttered, generalised model checking will now fail.

In a slight variation of our example, we may require our agent to end the auction not just at some point in the future, but by a certain deadline. Reference to concrete time points ("by number") is something that is typically not possible (nor intended) in temporal logic. However, if we can model the invocation of the deadline by means of a proposition *deadline* (which could be, say, the logical consequence of another agent's dialogue moves), then we can add the following formula to our specification to express that *end-auction* has to be uttered before *deadline* becomes true:

$$open\text{-}auction \rightarrow (\neg deadline \text{ UNLESS } end\text{-}auction)$$

The examples in this section suggest that PLTL is an appropriate language for specifying dialogue obligations. Due to Kamp's seminal result on the expressive completeness of PLTL over Dedekind-complete flows of time (which include our finite dialogue frames), we know that we can express *any* combination of temporal constraints over obligations expressible in the appropriate first-order theory also in PLTL [16,25].

Of course, protocol rules that constrain the *content* item in a dialogue move (e.g. "the price specified in a bid must be higher than any previous offer") cannot be represented in PLTL, nor in any other general-purpose logic. Arguably, while (temporal) logic is a suitable tool for modelling conversational conventions, reasoning about application-specific content requires domain-specific reasoners (even in simple cases such as the comparison of alternative price offers).

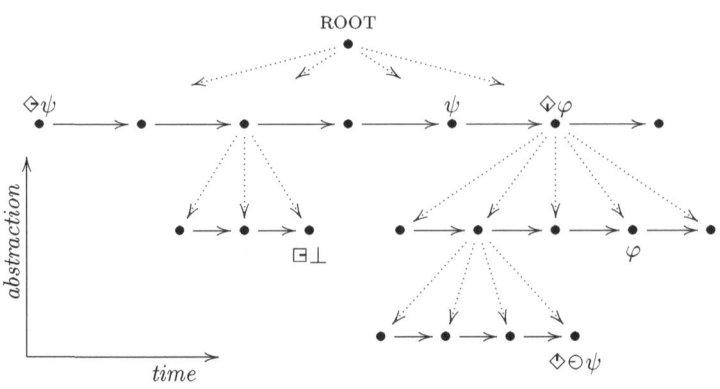

Fig. 2. An ordered tree model

7 Nested Protocols

In practice, a multiagent system may specify a whole range of different inter-action protocols, and agents may use a combination of several of these during a communicative interaction [28,36]. For instance, there may be different proto-cols for different types of auctions available, as well as a meta-protocol to jointly decide which of these auction protocols to use in a given situation. Such *nesting* of protocols could also be recursive.

We propose to use OTL [10,11], a *modal logic of ordered trees* (see also [4,5]), to specify nested protocols. This is an extended temporal logic based on frames that are ordered trees, *i.e.* trees where the children of each node form a linear order. In the context of modelling dialogues, again, we may assume that such trees are finite. OTL is the modal logic over frames that are ordered trees. The logic includes modal operators for all four directions in an ordered tree. The formula $\ominus\varphi$, for instance, expresses that φ is true at the immediate righthand sibling of the current node, while $\boxdot\psi$ forces ψ to be true at all of its children.

We briefly summarise the syntax and semantics of OTL; details may be found in [10]. The set of *formulas* of OTL is the smallest set extending the language of classical propositional logic such that. whenever φ is a formula, so are $\circlearrowleft\varphi$, $\diamondsuit\varphi$, $\ominus\varphi$, $\diamondsuit\varphi$, $\ominus\varphi$, $\diamondsuit\varphi$, $\diamondsuit\varphi$ and $\diamondsuit^{+}\varphi$ (we omit the discussion of *until*-style oper-ators from this short introduction [4,10]). Formulas are evaluated over ordered trees. An ordered tree $\mathcal{T}$ defines the relations of being a *parent*, *child*, *ances-tor*, *descendant*, *lefthand* and *righthand sibling* over a set of nodes T. The first sibling to the left of a node is also called that node's *lefthand neighbour* (and *righthand neighbours* are defined analogously). An *ordered tree model* is a pair $\mathcal{M} = (\mathcal{T}, V)$ where $\mathcal{T}$ is such an ordered tree an V is a valuation function from propositional letters to subsets of T. The truth conditions for atomic formulas and the propositional connectives are defined as for PLTL. Furthermore:

- $\mathcal{M}, t \models \bigcirc\varphi$ iff t is not the root of $\mathcal{T}$ and $\mathcal{M}, t' \models \varphi$ holds for t's parent t';
- $\mathcal{M}, t \models \diamondsuit\varphi$ iff t has got an ancestor t' such that $\mathcal{M}, t' \models \varphi$;
- $\mathcal{M}, t \models \ominus\varphi$ iff t has got a righthand neighbour t' such that $\mathcal{M}, t' \models \varphi$;
- $\mathcal{M}, t \models \diamondsuit\varphi$ iff t has got a righthand sibling t' such that $\mathcal{M}, t' \models \varphi$;
- $\mathcal{M}, t \models \diamondsuit\varphi$ iff t has got a child t' such that $\mathcal{M}, t' \models \varphi$;
- $\mathcal{M}, t \models \diamondsuit^{+}\varphi$ iff t has got a descendant t' such that $\mathcal{M}, t' \models \varphi$.

The truth conditions for $\diamondsuit$ and $\ominus$ are similar. Box-operators are defined in the usual manner: $\Box\varphi = \neg\diamondsuit\neg\varphi$, etc. The semantics explains our choice of a slightly different notation for the downward modalities: because there is (usually) no *unique* next node when moving down in a tree, we do not use a next-operator to refer to children. Figure 2 shows an example for an ordered tree model.

This logic can be given a *temporal interpretation*. Time is understood to run from left to right, along the order declared over the children of a node (*i.e. not* from top to bottom as in branching-time logics such as CTL), while the child relation provides a means of "zooming" into the events associated with a node. In the context of dialogues and nested protocols, the righthand sibling relation is used to model the passing of time with respect to a single protocol, while the child relation is used to model the relationship between a dialogue state and the subprotocol being initiated from that state.

Our example for a nested protocol is inspired by work in natural language dialogue modelling [13,17]. When a question is asked, besides answering that question, another reasonable follow-up move would be to pose a clarification question related to the first question. This latter question would then have to be answered before the original one. This protocol rule may, in principle, be applied recursively, *i.e.* we could have a whole sequence of clarification questions followed by the corresponding answers in reverse order. In addition, we may also ask several clarification questions pertaining to the same question (at the same level). The corresponding protocol is shown in Figure 3. The edge labelled by CLAR(B, A) represents a "meta-move": this is not a dialogue move uttered by one of the agents involved, but stands for a whole subdialogue following the rules of the clarification protocol with B (rather than A) being the agent asking the initial question. That is, the clarification protocol of Figure 3 does *not* belong to the class of automata-based protocols discussed in Section 5. Indeed, this kind of protocol cannot be specified by a simple finite state automaton. Instead we would require a pushdown automaton [26]. The stack of such a pushdown automaton would be used to store questions and every answer would cause the topmost question to be popped again [13].

Suppose INITIAL, FINAL, and NON-FINAL states have been specified as in Section 5 (using $\ominus$ in place of $\bigcirc$). If we treat CLAR in the same way as we would treat a simple performative, then the transition function for the clarification protocol can be specified as follows:

$$state(0) \wedge \ominus ask \rightarrow \ominus state(1)$$
$$state(1) \wedge \ominus\text{CLAR} \rightarrow \ominus state(1)$$
$$state(1) \wedge \ominus answer \rightarrow \ominus state(2)$$

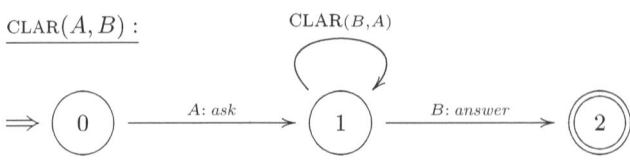

Fig. 3. A clarification protocol

Abstracting from turn-taking issues, the legality conditions for this protocol are given by the following formulas:

$$state(0) \rightarrow \neg \ominus \neg ask$$
$$state(1) \rightarrow \neg \ominus \neg (\text{CLAR} \vee answer)$$

The next formula says that a node corresponding to a final state in a subdialogue cannot have any righthand siblings:

$$\text{FINAL} \rightarrow \neg \ominus \top$$

That CLAR requires a subdialogue to take place can be specified by a formula that says that every node satisfying CLAR has to have a child satisfying INITIAL:

$$\text{CLAR} \rightarrow \Diamond \text{INITIAL}$$

The next formula specifies that a subdialogue must be completed before the dialogue at the next higher level may continue. This is expressed by postulating that, if a node has got a righthand sibling, then its rightmost child (if any) cannot satisfy NON-FINAL:

$$\ominus \top \rightarrow \Box (\text{NON-FINAL} \rightarrow \ominus \top)$$

To characterise dialogues that have been completed in their entirety, we may again add the following rule:

$$\text{NON-FINAL} \rightarrow \ominus \top$$

We hope that this very simple example gives some indication of the options available to us when specifying nested protocols using OTL. Our example has been special in the sense that it only uses a single protocol that can be nested arbitrarily. In general, there may be several different protocols, each associated with its own propositions to identify initial, final, and non-final states. Observe that, for OTL, deriving the partial (ordered tree) model induced by an observed dialogue is not as straightforward as for PLTL. However, if the moves used to initiate and terminate subdialogues following a particular protocol clearly identify that protocol (which seems a reasonable assumption), then constructing an ordered tree from a sequence of utterances is not difficult.

For OTL, to date, no model checking algorithms (or algorithms for generalised model checking) have been developed. However, it seems likely that such algorithms could be designed by adapting well-known algorithms for other temporal logics. And even without the availability of tools for model checking, we believe that the specification of nested protocols in OTL can be useful to give a precise semantics to the intuitive "operation of nesting".

8   Conclusion

In this paper, we have argued that temporal logic can be used to specify convention-based agent communication protocols in a simple and elegant manner. In particular, we have seen how to use *propositional linear temporal logic* to specify both very simple *automata-based protocols* and protocols involving *dialogue obligations*. Of course, using this logic to express the kinds of properties we have considered in our examples is not new, but the application of this technique to the specification of conversational conventions is both novel and, we believe, very promising. We have then outlined how *nested protocols* can be specified using the *ordered tree logic* OTL, which is an extension of propositional linear temporal logic, but also permits reasoning about different levels of abstraction within a single model.

We have also identified *generalised model checking* as a tool for checking protocol conformance at runtime. For simple protocol representation formalisms (such as finite automata), this is not a difficult problem and to resort to sophisticated tools such a model checking may seem inappropriate. However, for richer formalisms, in particular those that allow for the definition of complex dialogue obligations, the problem is certainly not trivial (witness the work of Alberti et al. [1], who develop a complex abductive proof procedure to address conformance checking). Computational issues aside, being able to define the conformance problem in clear logical terms already constitutes an important advantage in its own right.

Our aim for this paper has been to promote the use of simple temporal logics in the context of agent communication. Most of our presentation has been based on examples, but we hope that the generality of the approach shines through. As argued already at the end of Section 6, linear temporal logic is very expressive and can specify a rich class of protocols. Our concrete examples merely highlight some of the most important features of typical protocols.

The idea of using temporal logic for the representation of convention-based agent interaction protocols is not new [32,35]. The two cited works both use a form of the branching-time temporal logic CTL to give semantics to the notion of *social commitment*, but they do not attempt to exploit existing automated reasoning tools developed for these logics. The logic of Verdicchio and Colombetti [35] also incorporates some, albeit very restricted, first-order features. In our view, this is unfortunate as it trades in much of what is attractive about using temporal logics (decidability, low complexity, simple semantics).

Although there has been a growing interest in model checking for multiagent systems in recent years (examples include [3,6,24]), only little work has specifically addressed issues of communication. An exception is the work of Huget and Wooldridge [22], which studies model checking as a tool for verifying conformance to the semantics of an agent communication language in a mentalistic framework. There has also been a certain amount of work on *deductive* approaches to verification in multiagent systems [14], but again without special focus on communication protocols or conversational conventions.

In our future work, we hope to cover a wider range of protocol features and show how they may be specified using a suitable temporal logic. For instance, it would be interesting to explore the use of past-time operators to specify protocol rules relating to the content of a *commitment store* (e.g. only challenge arguments that have previously been asserted), as used in the context of argumentation-based communication models [2,13,20].

References

1. M. Alberti, M. Gavanelli, E. Lamma, P. Mello, and P. Torroni. Specification and verification of agent interactions using social integrity constraints. In *Workshop on Logic and Communication in Multi-Agent Systems*, 2003.
2. L. Amgoud, N. Maudet, and S. Parsons. Modelling dialogues using argumentation. In *4th International Conference on MultiAgent Systems*. IEEE, 2000.
3. M. Benerecetti, F. Giunchiglia, and L. Serafini. Model checking multiagent systems. *Journal of Logic and Computation*, 8(3):401–423, 1998.
4. P. Blackburn, B. Gaiffe, and M. Marx. Variable-free reasoning on finite trees. In *Mathematics of Language 8*, 2003.
5. P. Blackburn, W. Meyer-Viol, and M. de Rijke. A proof system for finite trees. In *Computer Science Logic*. Springer-Verlag, 1996.
6. R. H. Bordini, M. Fisher, C. Pardavila, and M. Wooldridge. Model checking AgentSpeak. In *2nd International Conference on Autonomous Agents and Multiagent Systems*. ACM Press, 2003.
7. G. Bruns and P. Godefroid. Generalized model checking: Reasoning about partial state spaces. In *11th International Conference on Concurrency Theory*. Springer-Verlag, 2000.
8. E. M. Clarke, O. Grumberg, and D. Peled. *Model Checking*. MIT Press, 1999.
9. M. Colombetti. A commitment-based approach to agent speech acts and conversations. In *Workshop on Agent Languages and Conversation Policies*, 2000.
10. U. Endriss. *Modal Logics of Ordered Trees*. PhD thesis, King's College London, Department of Computer Science, 2003.
11. U. Endriss and D. Gabbay. Halfway between points and intervals: A temporal logic based on ordered trees. In *ESSLLI Workshop on Interval Temporal Logics and Duration Calculi*, 2003.
12. U. Endriss, N. Maudet, F. Sadri, and F. Toni. Protocol conformance for logic-based agents. In *18th International Joint Conference on Artificial Intelligence*. Morgan Kaufmann, 2003.
13. R. Fernández and U. Endriss. Towards a hierarchy of abstract models for dialogue protocols. In *Proceedings of the 5th International Tbilisi Symposium on Language, Logic and Computation*. ILLC, 2003.
14. M. Fisher. Temporal development methods for agent-based systems. *Journal of Autonomous Agents and Multi-agent Systems*, 10:41–66, 2005.
15. Foundation for Intelligent Physical Agents (FIPA). *Communicative Act Library Specification*, 2002.

16. D. Gabbay, I. Hodkinson, and M. Reynolds. *Temporal Logic: Mathematical Foundations and Computational Aspects*, volume 1. Oxford University Press, 1994.
17. J. Ginzburg. Interrogatives: Questions, facts, and dialogue. In *Handbook of Contemporary Semantic Theory*. Blackwell, 1996.
18. R. Goldblatt. *Logics of Time and Computation*. CSLI, 2nd edition, 1992.
19. F. Guerin and J. Pitt. Guaranteeing properties for e-commerce systems. In *Agent-Mediated Electronic Commerce IV*. Springer-Verlag, 2002.
20. C. L. Hamblin. *Fallacies*. Methuen, London, 1970.
21. G. J. Holzmann. The model checker SPIN. *IEEE Transactions on Software Engineering*, pages 279–295, 1997.
22. M.-P. Huget and M. Wooldridge. Model checking for ACL compliance verification. In *Advances in Agent Communication*. Springer-Verlag, 2004.
23. A. J. I. Jones and X. Parent. Conventional signalling acts and conversation. In *Advances in Agent Communication*. Springer-Verlag, 2004.
24. M. Kacprzak, A. Lomuscio, and W. Penczek. Verification of multiagent systems via unbounded model checking. In *3rd International Conference on Autonomous Agents and Multiagent Systems*. ACM Press, 2004.
25. J. A. W. Kamp. *Tense Logic and the Theory of Linear Order*. PhD thesis, University of California at Los Angeles, Department of Philosophy, 1968.
26. H. R. Lewis and C. H. Papadimitriou. *Elements of the Theory of Computation*. Prentice-Hall International, 2nd edition, 1998.
27. S. Parsons, N. Jennings, and C. Sierra. Agents that reason and negotiate by arguing. *Journal of Logic and Computation*, 8(3):261–292, 1998.
28. J. Pitt and A. Mamdani. Communication protocols in multi-agent systems. In *Workshop on Specifying and Implementing Conversation Policies*, 1999.
29. J. Pitt and A. Mamdani. A protocol-based semantics for an agent communication language. In *16th International Joint Conference on Artificial Intelligence*. Morgan Kaufmann, 1999.
30. M. J. Sergot. A computational theory of normative positions. *ACM Transactions on Computational Logic*, 2(4):581–622, 2001.
31. M. P. Singh. Agent communication languages: Rethinking the principles. *IEEE Computer*, 31(12):40–47, 1998.
32. M. P. Singh. A social semantics for agent communication languages. In *Issues in Agent Communication*. Springer-Verlag, 2000.
33. D. R. Traum and J. F. Allen. Discourse obligations in dialogue processing. In *32nd Annual Meeting of the Association for Computational Linguistics*, 1994.
34. M. Y. Vardi and P. Wolper. An automata-theoretic approach to automatic program verification. In *1st Symposium on Logic in Computer Science*. IEEE, 1986.
35. M. Verdicchio and M. Colombetti. A logical model of social commitment for agent communication. In *2nd International Conference on Autonomous Agents and Multiagent Systems*. ACM Press, 2003.
36. B. Vitteau and M.-P. Huget. Modularity in interaction protocols. In *Advances in Agent Communication*. Springer-Verlag, 2004.
37. M. Wooldridge. *An Introduction to MultiAgent Systems*. Wiley, 2002.

ACL Semantics Between
Social Commitments and Mental Attitudes

Guido Boella[1], Rossana Damiano[1], Joris Hulstijn[2], and Leendert van der Torre[3]

[1] Università di Torino, Italy
{guido, rossana}@di.unito.it
[2] VU Amsterdam, The Netherlands
jhulstijn@feweb.vu.nl
[3] University of Luxembourg, Luxembourg
leendert@vandertorre.com

Abstract. There are two main traditions in defining a semantics for agent communication languages, based either on mental attitudes or on social commitments. In this paper, we translate both traditions in a different approach in which the dialogue state is represented by the beliefs and goals publicly attributed to the roles played by the dialogue participants. On the one hand, this approach avoids the problems of mentalistic semantics, such as the unverifiability of private mental states. On the other hand, it allows to reuse the logics and implementations developed for FIPA compliant approaches.

1 Introduction

Communication in multi-agent systems is often associated with the roles agents play in the social structure of the systems [1,2]. In contrast, most approaches to the semantics of agent communication languages (ACL) do not take roles into account. The semantics of speech acts in mentalistic approaches like FIPA [3] is specified in terms of plan operators whose preconditions refer to the beliefs, goals and intentions of agents, without considering the notion of role. Social semantics approaches are based on the idea that a speech act publicly commits the agents, regardless of the role of roles in communication.

A role-based semantics advances the idea that communication can be described in terms of beliefs and goals, but that those beliefs and goals must be maintained in public. The solution is to attribute beliefs and goals to roles played by the participants in the dialogue, rather than referring to the participants' private mental states, which are kept separate from the dialogue model. The roles' beliefs and goals are public and are constructed by the introduction or removal of beliefs and goals by the speech acts. The public beliefs and goals of a dialogue participant in a particular role may differ in interesting ways from his private beliefs and goals.

Thus, in this paper, we answer the following research questions:

– How to set up a role-based semantics for agent communication languages?
– How to translate the two traditional approaches into a role-based approach?

In [4] we started proposing a role-based semantics for ACL. However, that paper addresses the problem in a partial way and is focussed on persuasion dialogues and

F. Dignum, R. van Eijk, and R. Flores (Eds.): AC 2005/2006, LNAI 3859, pp. 30–44, 2006.

assertive speech acts only. The approach in [4] is based on our normative multi-agent systems framework [5,6]; it describes roles via the agent metaphor and is formalized in Input/Output logic. In this paper, we refer to a commonly known framework, the FIPA formal language, to translate the traditional ACL semantics to a role-based semantics. Moreover, we model additional categories of speech acts, like commissives and directives, that we apply in negotiation dialogues between cooperative agents.

The paper is structured as follows. In Section 2 we present our role model followed by the translation of FIPA-ACL and social semantics [7] into role-based semantics (Sections 3 and 4). In Section 5 we translate the Propose interaction protocol from FIPA and from social semantics to our role model, in order to be able to compare the two different approaches. Conclusions end the paper.

2   The Role Model

Communication among agents in a MAS is often associated with the roles agents play in the social structure of the systems. The GAIA methodology [1] proposes interaction rules to specify communication among roles, the ROADMAP methodology [8] specifies in the Social model the relations among roles, and in AALAADIN [2] interaction is defined only between the roles of a group: "The communication model within a group can be more easily described by an abstracted interaction scheme between roles like the 'bidder' and the 'manager' roles rather than between individual, actual agents".

Role names, like 'speaker' and 'addressee' or 'buyer' and 'seller' are often mentioned in the definition of agent communications languages. However, these terms only serve the function to bind individual agents to the speech acts in the protocol, but they are not associated with a state which changes during the conversation as a result of the performed speech acts. In our approach the notion of roles is interpreted as role instances, sometimes also called *qua individuals* or Role Enacting Agents [9]. The function played by roles in dialogue is similar to the function they play in an organization, where they define the power of agents to create commitments. As in organizations, it is possible that different roles are filled in by the same agent, thus determining ambiguities and conflicts (e.g., a command issued by a friend may not be effective, unless the friend is also the addressee's boss).

In [4] we propose to use the notion of role as a basis for a semantics of agent communication languages. The basic idea is that speech acts can be modelled as plan operators with preconditions and effects which can refer to beliefs, goals and intentions, but the mental attitudes they refer to are not the private inaccessible ones of the agents. Rather, the beliefs, goals and intentions to which speech acts refer are attributed to a public image of the participants in the dialogue representing the role they play.

The advantage of this approach is that it overcomes the unverifiability problem of mental attitudes approaches, since the role's mental attitudes are publicly attributed by the rules of the dialogue according to the moves performed. Roles represent expectations, but the model remains neutral with respect to the motivations that agents have when they play a role: the agents can adopt the mental attitudes attributed to roles as a form of cooperation, or they can be publicly committed to their roles in more formal contexts. To play a role, an agent is expected to act *as if* the beliefs and goals of the role were its own, and to keep them coherent, as it does for its own mental attitudes. It should adopt his role's goals and carry them out according to his role's beliefs.

Note that our model keeps apart the motivations for playing a role from the rules of the game which affect the state of the roles. In this way, we keep separate the public character of dialogue from the private motivations of the agents involved in a dialogue. The roles' attitudes represent what the agent is publicly held responsible for: if the agent does not adhere to his role, he can be sanctioned or blamed. So, an agent may be sincere (i.e., he really acts as expected from his role) for pure cooperativity, or for the fear of a sanction. Here, we focus on the relation between the role-based semantics and the existing approaches to ACL semantics, and we are not concerned with the way the obligation to play a role consistently can be enforced. The introduction of obligations requires the reference to an explicit multi-agent normative system, as described in [10].

The only thing agents have to do when communicating is to respect the rules of the dialogue or they are out of the game. The agents thus have to respect the cognitive coherence of the roles they play or they get into a contradictory position. We adopt Pasquier and Chaib-draa [11]'s view that dialogue arises from the need of maintaining coherence of mental states: "two agents communicate if an incoherence forces them to do so. [...] Conversation might be seen [...] as a generic procedure for attempting to reduce incoherence". An agent engaged in the dialogue tries to avoid contradictions, not with its private mental states, but with the public image which its role constitutes. As long as an agent plays a game following its constitutive rules, it cannot refuse that what it has said will be considered as a public display of its position in the game, according to its role. Consider the example of a liar, who once he starts lying, has to continue the dialogue consistently with what he said before, independently of his real beliefs.

In order to make the translation possible we need the following formal system:

Definition 1. *A dialogue game is composed of* $\langle A, R, PL, B, G, RL, CR \rangle$ *where*

- A *is a set of agents involved in the interaction, e.g.,* x, y.
- RN *is a set of role names, like* $r_1, r_2, ...$
- R *is a set of role enacting agents, e.g.,* $a = x : r_1$, $b = y : r_2$. *We denote with* i, j *variables over role enacting agents.*
- SA *is a set of speech act types, e.g.,* $inform, request,$ *etc.*
- $PL : A \times RN \mapsto R$ *is a role playing function* $a = PL(x, r_1)$ *is a role* r_1 *enacting agent played by agent* $x \in A$. *We will write* $a = x : r_1$ *for* $a = PL(x, r_1)$.
- RL *is a set of axioms on the role model.*
- CR *are the constitutive rules of the dialogue game: they are common beliefs specifying how speech acts affect the roles' mental attitudes.*
- B *and* G *are the agents' and roles' beliefs and goals, respectively.*

We can now define the formal language, inspired by FIPA's specification language.

Definition 2 (Language)
Given a set of propositions L *and basic actions* ACT:
$q := p \mid \neg q \mid q \vee q \mid B(m, q) \mid G(n, q) \mid done(act) \mid done(i, act) \mid$
$\quad message(x, y, SA(i, j, q)) \mid SA(i, j, q) \mid a = x : r_1$
$act := action \mid act; act$

where $p, q \in L$, $x, y \in A$, $i, j \in R$, $m, n \in A \cup R$, $r_1 \in RN$ and action $\in ACT$. B and G represent the beliefs and goals.

Note that according to this definition also roles can have beliefs and goals. For simplicity here we do not distinguish goals from intentions.

The $done(act)$ and $done(i, act)$ expressions denote the execution of an action, specifying or not the agent of the action. We will use $done(act)$ later when act is a joint action, for example, $sell(i, j) = give(i); pay(j)$. Here we use a minimal definition of actions which allows us to cover the examples.

Is it possible that roles have mental attitudes? What we are modelling are public mental states of the same kind as the ones associated to role enacting agents in the model of [9]. A similar solution is proposed also by [12] where beliefs (but not goals) can be publicly attributed to agents by means of a grounding operator. The right perspective should be always $B(x, B(i, p)) \wedge B(y, B(i, p))$, where x and y play a role in the dialogue, rather than $B(i, p)$ when $i \in R$. However, for convenience we will use the latter formula $B(i, p)$. Preconditions and postconditions of speech acts will refer to beliefs and goals of the roles. The difference is that roles' mental attitudes have different properties with respect to those of their players. In particular, they are public: a role knows what the other role believes and wants, because speech acts are public.

We add the following axioms RL in a dialog game, representing rationality constraints; they are mostly inspired by FIPA, apart from those concerning public mental states and distribution of goals in joint plans. For all roles i, j:

- Each role has correct knowledge about its own mental states, in particular, its beliefs about its goals are correct. This axiom corresponds to FIPA's [3] schema $\phi \leftrightarrow B_i \phi$, where ϕ is governed by an operator formalising a mental attitude of agent i:

$$(B(i, G(i, p)) \rightarrow G(i, p)) \wedge (B(i, \neg G(i, p)) \rightarrow \neg G(i, p)) \tag{RL1}$$
$$(B(i, B(i, p)) \rightarrow B(i, p)) \wedge (B(i, \neg B(i, p)) \rightarrow \neg B(i, p)) \tag{RL2}$$

- Since the beliefs of the roles are public, each role has the complete knowledge about the other roles' beliefs and goals:

$$(B(j, p) \leftrightarrow B(i, B(j, p))) \wedge (\neg B(j, p) \leftrightarrow B(i, \neg B(j, p))) \tag{RL3}$$
$$(G(j, p) \leftrightarrow B(i, G(j, p))) \wedge (\neg G(j, p) \leftrightarrow B(i, \neg G(j, p))) \tag{RL4}$$

- Forwarding a message is a way to perform a speech act:

$$B(m, message(x, y, SA(i, j, p)) \rightarrow SA(i, j, p)) \tag{RL5}$$

where $SA \in \{inform, request, propose, \dots\}$, for all $x, y \in A$ and $m \in \{i, j\}$. Note that the sender of the message x is an agent playing the role i in the speech act and the receiver agent y plays the role j.

- Each agent is aware of which speech acts have been performed, where $i = x : r_1$, $j = y : r_2$ and $m \in \{i, j\}$:

$$message(x, y, SA(i, j, p)) \rightarrow B(m, message(x, y, SA(i, j, p))) \tag{RL6}$$

- A rationality constraint concerning the goal that other agents perform an action: if agent i wants that action act is done by agent j, then agent i has the goal that agent j has the goal to do act:

$$G(i, done(j, act)) \rightarrow G(i, G(j, done(j, act))) \tag{RL7}$$

- Some FIPA axioms like Property 1 $(G(i, p) \rightarrow G(i, a_1|\dots|a_n)$, where $a_1|\dots|a_n$ are feasible alternatives to achieve p) [3] concern the execution of complex actions. In a similar vein, we add two axioms concerning the distribution of tasks. Taking inspiration from [13], we add an axiom to express that if an agent intends a joint action, then it intends that each part is done at the right moment. If $act = act_1; ...; act_n$, where ";" is the sequence operator, act is a joint action and $k < n$:

$$G(i, done(act)) \rightarrow$$
$$(done(act_1(i_1); \ldots; act_k(i_k)) \rightarrow G(i, done(act_{k+1}(i)))) \tag{RL8}$$

If $act_{k+1}(j)$ and $i \neq j$, then by axiom RL7:

$$G(i, done(act)) \rightarrow$$
$$(done(act_1(i_1); \ldots; act_k(i_k)) \rightarrow G(i, G(j, done(act_{k+1}(j))))) \tag{RL9}$$

Each agent in the group wants that the others do their part.

Note that in the role model it is not assumed that the role's mental attitudes correspond to the mental attitudes of their players. This assumption can be made only when an agent is sincere, and can be expressed as:

$$(B(i, p) \wedge i = x : r \wedge sincere(x, r)) \rightarrow B(x, p)$$
$$(G(i, p) \wedge i = x : r \wedge sincere(x, r)) \rightarrow G(x, p)$$

In the next two sections, we show how the semantics of speech acts defined by FIPA and by social semantics can be expressed in terms of roles.

3   From FIPA to Roles

The semantics of agent communication languages provided by FIPA [3] are paradigmatic of the models based on mental attitudes. In FIPA, communicative acts are defined in terms of the mental state of the BDI agent who issues them. The bridge between the communicative acts and the behavior of agents is provided by the notions of rational effect and feasibility preconditions. The rational effect is the mental state that the speaker intends to bring about in the hearer by issuing a communicative act, and the feasibility preconditions encode the appropriate mental states for issuing a communicative act. To guarantee communication, the framework relies on intention recognition on the part of the hearer.

The main drawback of FIPA resides in the fact that mentalistic constructs cannot be verified [14,15]. So, they are not appropriate in situations in which agents may be insincere or non cooperative, like in argumentation or negotiation. In contrast, meaning should be public as Singh [16], Walton and Krabbe [17], Fornara and Colombetti [7] claim.

In the following, we provide a role-based semantics for FIPA communicative acts by proposing a translation using constitutive rules CR of our dialogue game. Note, however, that the beliefs and goals of roles resulting from the translation have different properties than the beliefs and goals of the agents referred to by FIPA semantics.

The structure of the constitutive rules of dialogue reflects the structure of FIPA operators: the speech act is mapped to the antecedent, while feasibility preconditions and rational effects are mapped to the consequent. This methodology relies on some FIPA axioms according to which, when a speech act is executed, its feasibility preconditions and its rational effects must be true. So, after a speech act, its preconditions and its rational effect are added to the roles' beliefs and goals:

$B(i, done(act) \wedge agent(j, act)) \rightarrow G(j, RE(act)))$ (Property 4 of FIPA)   (RL10)

$B(i, done(act) \rightarrow FP(act))$ (Property 5 of FIPA)   (RL11)

where FP stands for feasibility preconditions, RE for rational effects, and i and j are the role enacting agents in the conversation. Since in the role-based semantics these axioms apply to roles, the belief that the preconditions of the speech act hold is publicly attributed to the role of the speaker, abstracting from the actual beliefs of the agent who plays the role.

For space reasons, we do not report here preconditions concerning uncertain beliefs (the modal operator Uif in FIPA), but the extension to them is straightforward.

Here is FIPA definition of the $inform$ communicative act (CA):

$< i, inform(j, p) >$
   FP: $B(i, p) \wedge \neg B(i, B(j, p) \vee B(j, \neg p))$
   RE: $B(j, p)$

- The first precondition $B(i, p)$ is modelled by the rule:
   $B(i, inform(i, j, p) \rightarrow B(i, p))$ (CR12)
   The second precondition $\neg B(i, B(j, p) \vee B(j, \neg p))$ is modelled by
   $B(i, inform(i, j, p) \rightarrow \neg B(i, B(j, p) \vee B(i, \neg p)))$ (CR13)
   Remember that $B(j, p) \rightarrow B(i, B(j, p))$, so now this precondition can be verified on the public state of the dialogue.
- The effect is accounted for by
   $B(i, inform(i, j, p) \rightarrow G(i, B(j, p)))$ (CR14)

To model FIPA's remark that "Whether or not the receiver does, indeed, adopt belief in the proposition will be a function of the receiver's trust in the sincerity and reliability of the sender" we need the following rule:

$B(j, (G(i, B(j, p)) \wedge reliable(i, p)) \rightarrow B(j, p))$ (CR15)

We do not want to comment further on this issue here: see e.g., [18,19,20] for the subjects of reliability and trust. As illustrated in the previous section, we keep separate reliability and sincerity: sincerity is not part of the game, but it refers to the relation between the role's beliefs and the player's private beliefs.

Concerning the $request$ CA :

$< i, request(j, act) >$
   FP: $\neg B(i, G(j, done(act))) \wedge agent(j, act)$
   RE: $done(act)$

- The precondition is modelled as follows:
   $B(i, request(i, j, done(j, act)) \rightarrow \neg B(i, G(j, done(j, act))))$ (CR16)
- The effect is modelled by
   $B(i, request(i, j, done(j, act)) \rightarrow G(i, done(j, act)))$ (CR17)

Analogously to *inform*, a rule expresses that only a cooperative receiver adopts a speaker's goal:

$B(j, (G(i, done(j, act)) \wedge cooperative(j, i)) \rightarrow G(j, done(j, act)))$ (CR18)

Note that $B(j, G(i, done(j, act))$ is not the result of an intention reconstruction by j about i's goals, but part of the state of the conversation. So only goals which are publicly stated are adopted in a cooperative dialogue.

Since it is of particular importance for our running example, we illustrate how the propose speech act is defined in FIPA and explain how we model it. Since propose is an *inform* act in FIPA, its definition in role-based semantics derives from the definition of the *inform* provided above, yielding the following definition:

$< i, propose(j, act) >$

FP: $B(i, G(j, done(act)) \rightarrow G(i, done(act)))$
$\quad \neg B(i, B(j, G(j, done(act)) \rightarrow G(i, done(act))) \lor$
$\quad B(j, \neg G(j, done(act)) \rightarrow G(i, done(act))))$

RE: $B(j, G(j, done(act)) \rightarrow G(i, done(act)))$

Where act is an action of i or a joint action, otherwise we call it a request and not a propose.

Since an agent is *reliable* concerning its own mental states (it has a correct view of what he believes and intends) from rule CR15 it follows that:

$$B(j, propose(i, j, done(act)) \rightarrow (G(j, done(act)) \rightarrow G(i, done(act)))) \qquad (CR19)$$

We illustrate how the accept and reject speech acts are modelled even if they are defined as *inform* acts in FIPA:

$< i, accept\ proposal(j, act) >$

FP: $B(i, G(i, done(act))) \land$
$\quad \neg B(i, B(j, G(i, done(act))) \lor \neg B(j, G(i, done(act))))$

RE: $B(j, G(i, done(act)))$

Since an agent is accounted *reliable* about its own mental state:

$$B(j, accept\ proposal(i, j, done(act)) \rightarrow G(i, done(act)))) \qquad (CR20)$$

$< i, reject\ proposal(j, done(act)) >$

FP: $B(i, G(i, done(act))) \neg B(i, B(j, G(i, done(act))) \lor \neg B(j, G(i, done(act))))$

RE: $B(j, \neg G(i, done(act)))$

4 From Commitments to Roles

Agent communication languages based on social commitment constitute an attempt to overcome the mentalistic assumption of FIPA by restricting the analysis to the public level of communication (Singh [16], Verdicchio and Colombetti [21]). Communicative acts are defined in terms of the social commitments they publicly determine for the speaker and the hearer. According to Singh [22], describing communication using social commitment has the practical consequence that "[...] one can design agents independently of each other and just ensure that their S-commitment would mesh in properly when combined".

The use of social commitments to model communication does not explain how the social dimension of commitment affects the behavior of the individual agents. While this approach is mostly appropriate in competitive environments, like negotiation, its advantages are less clearcut in cooperative ones, like information seeking dialogues. The reference to obligations to bridge this gap brings into social semantics the controversial issue of obligation enforcement [23].

Here, we show how to define a particular social semantics presented by Fornara and Colombetti [7] in the role-based semantics (from now on, SC). In the SC model, speech acts introduce commitments in the dialogue state or manipulate them. A commitment

$C(i, j, p \mid q)$ has a *debtor* i, a *creditor* j, i.e., respectively, the agent which has the commitment, and the agent to which the commitment is made, a content p and a condition q. A commitment can have different states: unset (i.e., to be confirmed), pending (i.e., confirmed, but its condition is not true), active (i.e., confirmed and its condition is true), fulfilled (i.e., its content is true), violated (i.e., the content is false even if the commitment was active), cancelled (e.g., the debtor does not want to be committed to the action). A commitment instance is set by a speech act, with a certain state. This state can be modified by actions of the participants to the dialogue or by events, like the execution of an action fulfilling the new commitment state.

In order to perform the translation, we adopt the following methodology: we map each commitment state to a specific configuration of roles' beliefs and goals, then we define how speech acts change those beliefs and goals in such a way to reflect the changes in the commitment state.

In Fornara and Colombetti's model [7], the difference between propositional and action commitment lies only in their content. As a result, the difference between an inform and a promise is reduced to the fact that the content of the commitment they introduce is a proposition or an action respectively. By contrast, according to Walton and Krabbe [17], propositional commitment is an action commitment to defend one's position. In the mapping between SC and the role model a new distinction emerges: rather than having commitment stores, we model propositional commitments as beliefs of the role and action commitments as goals. How roles' beliefs capture the idea of a commitment to defend one's position is the topic of [4]. In this paper we focus on action commitment only.

Here, we represent conditionals commitment $C(i, j, p \mid q)$ in a simplified way, as a conditional goal p of role i in case q is true: $B(i, q \rightarrow G(i, p))$. Conditional attitudes can be better accounted for in a conditional logic, like the Input/Output logic we used in [4]. Here, we stick to FIPA's solution for the sake of clarity, while aware of its limitations.

An unset commitment corresponds to a goal of the creditor. We translate this in the CR of a dialogue game in this way:

$$C(unset, i, j, done(i, act) \mid q) \equiv q \rightarrow G(j, G(i, done(i, act))) \qquad \text{(CR21)}$$

In the antecedent of this rule, the commitment condition q becomes a condition on the goal assumed by the creditor of the commitment. At this stage of the commitment life-cycle, no mental attitude is attributed to the debtor: it has not publicly assumed any actual goal, but has only been publicly requested to.

A commitment is pending when it is a conditional goal of the creditor and the debtor of the commitment conditionally wants to perform the action if the associated condition q is true, and the creditor has this as a belief:

$$C(pending, i, j, done(i, act) \mid q) \equiv q \rightarrow G(j, G(i, done(i, act))) \wedge$$
$$B(i, q \rightarrow G(i, done(i, act))) \wedge B(j, q \rightarrow G(i, done(i, act))) \qquad \text{(CR22)}$$

A commitment is active when it is both a goal of the debtor and of the creditor, and the pending condition is true:

$$C(active, i, j, done(j, act) \mid \top) \equiv G(i, done(i, act)) \wedge G(j, done(i, act)) \qquad \text{(CR23)}$$

Note that to make active a pending commitment, it is sufficient that the condition q is believed true, since from

$$B(i, q \wedge q \rightarrow G(i, done(i, act))) \tag{CR24}$$

we can derive $G(i, done(i, act))$ with axiom RL1.

Commitments are violated or fulfilled when they are goals of the creditor and the content of the commitment is respectively true or false according to the beliefs of the creditor (abstracting here from temporal issues):

$$C(fulfilled, i, j, done(i, act) \mid \top) \equiv B(j, done(i, act)) \wedge G(j, done(i, act)) \tag{CR25}$$
$$C(violated, i, j, done(i, act) \mid \top) \equiv B(j, \neg done(i, act)) \wedge G(j, done(i, act)) \tag{CR26}$$

Since roles are public, fulfilment and violation are not dependent on what the agents subjectively believe about the truth value of the content of the commitment, but on roles' public beliefs.

A commitment is cancelled if the creditor does not want the goal to be achieved anymore, no matter if the debtor still wants it:

$$C(cancelled, i, j, done(i, act) \mid q) \equiv \neg G(j, done(i, act)) \tag{CR27}$$

Given the definition of the commitment state in terms of the mental states of the roles, we can provide the following translation of the speech acts semantics define by Fornara and Colombetti [7].

A *promise* introduces a pending commitment of the speaker (rule CR22):

$$promise(i, j, done(i, act), q) \rightarrow (q \rightarrow G(j, G(i, done(i, act)))) \wedge$$
$$B(i, q \rightarrow G(i, done(i, act))) \wedge B(j, q \rightarrow G(i, done(i, act)))) \tag{CR28}$$

A *request* introduces an unset commitment with the receiver as debtor, i.e., the agent of the requested action (Rule CR21):

$$request(i, j, done(j, act), q) \rightarrow (q \rightarrow G(i, G(j, done(j, act)))) \tag{CR29}$$

Accept and *reject* change the state of an existing unset commitment to pending and cancelled respectively. In order to account for this fact, we insert in the antecedent of the rules for accept and reject the reference to the configuration of beliefs and goals that represent an existing commitment.

$$(B(i, (q \rightarrow G(j, G(i, done(i, act))))) \wedge accept(i, j, done(i, act), q)) \rightarrow$$
$$(B(i, q \rightarrow G(i, done(i, act))) \wedge B(j, q \rightarrow G(i, done(i, act)))) \tag{CR30}$$

$$(B(i, q \rightarrow G(j, G(i, done(i, act)))) \wedge reject(i, j, done(j, act), q)) \rightarrow$$
$$(B(i, \neg G(i, done(i, act))) \wedge B(j, \neg G(i, done(i, act)))) \tag{CR31}$$

A *propose* is a complex speech act composed by a *request* and a conditional *promise*; it introduces an unset commitment with the receiver as debtor and a pending commitment with the speaker as debtor. Since a *propose* is used in a negotiation, q and p refer respectively to an action of the speaker and of the receiver.

$$propose(i, j, done(j, p), done(i, q)) \equiv$$
$$request(i, j, done(j, p), done(i, q)) promise(i, j, done(i, q), s) \tag{CR32}$$

where $s \equiv B(i, done(i, q) \rightarrow G(j, done(j, p))) \wedge B(j, done(i, q) \rightarrow G(j, done(j, p)))$, i.e., p is a pending commitment of the receiver.

propose is expressed by the following constitutive rules:

$$propose(i, j, done(j, p), done(i, q)) \rightarrow$$
$$B(i, (done(i, q) \rightarrow G(i, G(j, done(j, p))))) \wedge B(i, s \rightarrow G(i, done(i, q))) \wedge$$
$$B(j, s \rightarrow G(i, done(i, q))) \tag{CR33}$$

CA	Seller a (FIPA)	Buyer b (FIPA)
propose	BELIEFS $G(b, sell(a,b)) \rightarrow G(a, sell(a,b))$	BELIEF $G(b, sell(a,b)) \rightarrow G(a, sell(a,b))$
	GOALS $B(b, G(b, sell(a,b)) \rightarrow G(a, sell(a,b)))$	GOALS
accept	BELIEFS $G(b, sell(a,b)) \rightarrow G(a, sell(a,b))$ $G(b, sell(a,b))$ $G(a, sell(a,b))$ $G(a, give(a))$ $give(a) \rightarrow G(a, pay(b))$ $give(a) \rightarrow G(b, pay(b))$	BELIEF $G(b, sell(a,b)) \rightarrow G(a, sell(a,b))$ $G(b, sell(a,b))$ $G(b, give(a))$ $give(a) \rightarrow G(b, pay(b))$
	GOALS $give(a)$	GOALS $B(a, G(b, sell(a,b)))$
give(a)	BELIEFS $G(b, sell(a,b)) \rightarrow G(a, sell(a,b))$ $give(a) \rightarrow G(b, pay(b))$ $give(a) \rightarrow G(a, pay(b))$ $G(a, give(a))$ $give(a)$ $G(b, pay(b))$ $G(a, pay(b))$	BELIEFS $G(b, sell(a,b)) \rightarrow G(a, sell(a,b))$ $give(a) \rightarrow G(b, pay(b))$ $G(b, give(a))$ $give(a)$ $G(b, pay(b))$
	GOALS	GOALS $pay(b)$
pay(b)	BELIEFS $G(b, sell(a,b)) \rightarrow G(a, sell(a,b))$ $give(a) \rightarrow G(b, pay(b))$ $give(a) \rightarrow G(a, G(b, pay(b)))$ $G(b, pay(b))$ $pay(b)$	BELIEFS $G(b, sell(a,b)) \rightarrow G(a, sell(a,b)))$ $give(a) \rightarrow G(b, pay(b))$ $G(b, pay(b))$ $pay(b)$
	GOALS	GOALS
reject	BELIEFS $G(b, sell(a,b)) \rightarrow G(a, sell(a,b))$ $\neg G(b, sell(a,b))$	BELIEF $G(b, sell(a,b)) \rightarrow G(a, sell(a,b))$ $\neg G(b, sell(a,b))$
	GOALS	GOALS $B(a, \neg G(b, sell(a,b)))$

Fig. 1. The example with FIPA. Note that for space reasons $done(i, act(i))$ is abbreviated in $act(i)$.

5   Example: The Propose Protocol

In this section we propose an example of comparison between FIPA and SC using our role semantics, as a means to assess the feasibility of the role semantics as an intermediate language. We choose as example the Propose interaction protocol of FIPA [3]. This simple protocol consists of a *propose* followed by an acceptance or a refusal, and does not refer to group coordination or group action (differently from [24]).

In the following, we illustrate how the speech acts in the two approaches introduce and modify the beliefs and goals of the roles a and b. Eventually, we compare the set of beliefs and goals produced by the translation of FIPA and SC into the role-based semantics to assess whether the goals concerning executable actions are the same in the two approaches (i.e., the agents would act at the same moment), and whether it is possible to find in FIPA the same commitments as in SC.

The main difficulty in mapping FIPA onto SC concerns the FIPA *propose* communicative act. In SC it is viewed as a way to negotiate a joint plan: "If I do q, then you do p". This models for example auctions [7]. Instead, FIPA definition of *propose* refers to one action only. Here, we are inspired by the example reported in FIPA documentation [3], which reports the action of selling an item for a given amount of money: we explicit the fact that the action of selling is a joint plan composed of the proponent's action of giving the item and the receiver's subsequent action of giving the money: $sell(i, j) = give(i); pay(j)$.

In this way, the FIPA *propose* act becomes an act of proposing a plan to be performed by both agents. Once the goals of both agents to perform the plan have been formed, the plan is distributed between the agents according to axioms RL8 and RL9, and the goals concerning the steps of the plan are formed.

Apart form the mapping of *propose* the translation of FIPA and SC semantics to the role-based semantic is straightforward: at each turn, the constitutive rules for translating the semantics of FIPA and SC into the role-based semantics are applied (see the definition of the rules in Sections 3 and 4). Then, modus ponens and the axioms are applied. Beliefs and goals which are not affected by subsequent speech acts persist.

In FIPA (see Figure 1, where a simplified notation is used), the *propose* to sell ($propose(a, b, done(sell(a, b)))$) is an *inform* that introduces in the role a the belief that the precondition $G(b, done(sell(a, b)))) \rightarrow G(a, done(sell(a, b)))$ is true. We skip for space reasons the other feasibility precondition, but the reader can easily check that it is true and consistent with the state of the dialogue. The rational effect is a goal of the speaker, but since the speaker is reliable (it has correct beliefs about its own mental states), after the proposal, the receiver believes $G(b, done(sell(a, b))) \rightarrow G(a, done(sell(a, b)))$ too, by rule CR15.

The acceptance of the proposal by b in FIPA is an *inform* that b has the goal $G(b, done(sell(a, b))$: $acceptproposal(a, b, done(sell(a, b)))$

Again, the receiver believes the content of the accept proposal speech act because an agent is reliable about its own mental states. Since the speaker believes $G(b, done(sell(a, b)))$, $G(a, done(sell(a, b)))$ and $G(b, done(sell(a, b))$, it believes also to have $done(sell(a, b))$ as a goal (by modus ponens) and, by axiom RL1, it actually has the goal to sell. Most importantly, if an agent has the goal to make the joint plan, by the axiom RL8, then it has the goal to do its part at the right moment (and the other knows this) and the goal that the other does its part. The result of the distribution is: $B(a, give(a) \rightarrow G(a, done(pay(b))))) \land B(b, give(a) \rightarrow G(b, done(pay(b))))$.

Thus, when $done(give(a))$ is true, from $done(give(a)) \rightarrow G(a, done(pay(b))))$, we derive that a wants that b does its part $G(b, done(pay(b)))$.

CA	Seller a (SC)	Buyer b (SC)
propose	BELIEFS $give(a) \rightarrow G(a, G(b, pay(b)))$	BELIEFS
	GOALS	GOALS
accept	BELIEFS $give(a) \rightarrow G(a, G(b, pay(b)))$ $(give(a) \rightarrow G(b, pay(b))) \rightarrow$ $G(a, give(a)))$ $give(a) \rightarrow G(b, pay(b))$ $G(a, give(a))$	BELIEFS $(give(a) \rightarrow G(b, pay(b))) \rightarrow$ $G(a, give(a)))$ $give(a) \rightarrow G(b, pay(b))$ $G(a, give(a))$
	GOALS $give(a)$	GOALS
give(a)	BELIEFS $give(a) \rightarrow G(a, G(b, pay(b)))$ $(give(a) \rightarrow G(b, pay(b))) \rightarrow$ $G(a, give(a)))$ $give(a) \rightarrow G(b, pay(b))$ $G(a, give(a))$ $give(a)$ $G(b, pay(b))$	BELIEFS $(give(a) \rightarrow G(b, pay(b))) \rightarrow$ $G(a, give(a)))$ $give(a) \rightarrow G(b, pay(b))$ $G(a, give(a))$ $give(a)$ $G(b, pay(b))$
	GOALS	GOALS $pay(b)$
pay(b)	BELIEFS $G(b, pay(b))$ $pay(b)$	BELIEFS $G(b, pay(b))$ $pay(b)$
	GOALS	GOALS
reject	BELIEFS $give(a) \rightarrow G(a, G(b, pay(b)))$ $(give(a) \rightarrow G(b, pay(b))) \rightarrow$ $G(a, give(a)))$ $\neg G(b, pay(b))$	BELIEF $(give(a) \rightarrow G(b, pay(b))) \rightarrow$ $G(a, give(a)))$ $\neg G(b, pay(b))$
	GOALS	GOALS

Fig. 2. The example with commitments. Note that for space reasons $done(i, act)$ is abbreviated in $act(i)$.

The translation from SC ACL semantics to the role-based semantics is accomplished by applying the rules defined in the previous section (see Figure 2). Given the FIPA *propose* CA, the corresponding speech act in SC ACL is $propose(a, b, done(give(a)),$ $done(pay(b)))$. By applying the rule that translates this speech act in the role-based ACL semantics, we get to the state in which both a and b have the belief that $done(give(a)) \rightarrow G(a, G(b, done(pay(b))))$ representing an unset commitment of b. Moreover, a pending commitment by a is represented by $done(give(a)) \rightarrow$ $G(b, done(pay(b)))) \rightarrow G(a, done(give(s)))$.

The *accept proposal* is modelled by $accept(b, a, C_i(unset, b, a, pay(b) \mid give(a))$ in SC. This speech act, whose precondition is true, results in b's act of creating the belief of a that b believes $done(give(a)) \rightarrow G(b, done(pay(b)))$. The application of modus ponens to the belief $done(give(a)) \to G(b, done(pay(b)))) \to G(a, done(give(s))))$ and this new belief results in the introduction of an active commitment whose debtor is role a: $G(a, done(give(a))) \wedge G(b, done(give(a)))$.

When $give(a)$ is executed, then the commitment of a to do $give(a)$ is fulfilled and the commitment of b to do $pay(b)$ is active: its condition $done(give(a))$ is satisfied.

The *reject proposal* communicative act in FIPA in SC corresponds to the speech act $reject(b, a, C_i(unset, b, a, pay(r) \mid give(a)))$. The reject speech act attributes to both a and b the belief that b does not have the goal $done(pay(a))$, thus retaining a's pending commitment from becoming active and cancelling the unset commitment from b role.

Which are the main differences between these approaches? By comparing the two tables in Figures 1 and 2, it is possible to observe that, once translated in the role-based semantics, the actual commitments and their state coincide in the two approaches, with a significant exception. The difference can be observed in the first row, where after the *propose* speech act there is no equivalent in FIPA of the belief - publicly attributed to the proponent - that it has the goal that the addressee forms a conditional goal to pay the requested amount of money for the sold item, where the condition consists of the proponent giving the item.

This difference is to be ascribed to the definition of the act of proposing in FIPA. In practice, FIPA does not express the advantage of the proponent in proposing the plan. For example, in the selling case, there is no clue of the fact that reason why the proponent proposes the joint plan is that it wants to receive the specified amount of money. However, this is implicit in the definition of the selling plan. In SC, reciprocity is expressed by the fact that a *propose* is composed by a conditional *promise* together with a *request* (see also the model in [25]), thus providing a way to express any kind of arrangements, even non conventional ones. In SC, the subsequent accept speech act presupposes the existence of an unset commitment having as debtor the role to which the proposal has been addressed. However, the *accept proposal* act in the second turn fills the gap in FIPA: when the addressee displays the goal to take part in the joint plan, the distribution of the tasks of giving and paying takes place, generating the appropriate goals in the two roles.

6   Conclusions

In this paper we propose a role-based semantics for agent communication languages. In this approach, the state of a dialogue is represented by beliefs and goals publicly attributed to the roles played by the participants in the dialogue. These beliefs and goals are added and removed by the speech acts performed by the roles and are distinct - and potentially different - from the agents' private ones. The role-based semantics opens the way to the possibility that they diverge, so that a wide range of cooperative and non-cooperative situations can be modelled.

We show that both the mentalistic and the social commitment approach to the semantics of agent communication languages, can be translated into a role-based semantics, showing their differences and similarities. The translation makes it possible to re-use logics and implementations of the FIPA-style mentalistic approach, while avoiding the unverifiability of the mental states.

In addition, a role-based semantics makes it possible to represent and study the way in which mental states attributed to agents in a role, may differ from the private mental states. Thus a wide range of cooperative and non-cooperative situations can be modelled. As a first example, consider a teacher who is teaching Darwinism to a class of pupils. Teachers are considered to be reliable. So according to rule RL15, when a teacher makes an inform speech act, the pupils will publicly adopt the information. But privately the pupils may not believe the information, for example because of religious objections against Darwinism. As a second example, reconsider the proposal in Figure 2. As a result of the acceptance by a of the joint action $give(a); pay(b)$, b publicly adopts the goal $pay(b)$. But clearly, this is only a means to get the good, as part of the joint action. It is quite possible that the agent y enacting b, does not have the individual goal to give the object away.

References

1. Zambonelli, F., Jennings, N., Wooldridge, M.: Developing multiagent systems: The Gaia methodology. IEEE Transactions of Software Engineering and Methodology **12(3)** (2003) 317–370
2. Ferber, J., Gutknecht, O., Michel, F.: From agents to organizations: an organizational view of multiagent systems. In: LNCS n. 2935: Procs. of AOSE'03, Springer Verlag (2003) 214–230
3. FIPA: FIPA ACL specification. Technical Report FIPA00037, Foundation for Intelligent Physical Agents, http://www.fipa.org/specs/fipa00037/SC00037J.html (2002)
4. Boella, G., Hulstjin, J., van der Torre, L.: A synthesis between mental attitudes and social commitments in agent communication languages. In: Procs. of IAT'05, IEEE Press (2005)
5. Boella, G., van der Torre, L.: A game theoretic approach to contracts in multiagent systems. IEEE Transactions on Systems, Man and Cybernetics - Part C **36(1)** (2006)68–79
6. Boella, G., van der Torre, L.: Security policies for sharing knowledge in virtual communities. IEEE Transactions on Systems, Man and Cybernetics - Part A **36(3)** (2006) 439–450
7. Fornara, N., Colombetti, M.: A commitment-based approach to agent communication. Applied Artificial Intelligence **18(9-10)** (2004) 853–866
8. Juan, T., Sterling, L.: Achieving dynamic interfaces with agents concepts. In: Procs. of AAMAS'04. (2004) 688–695
9. Dastani, M., Dignum, V., Dignum, F.: Role-assignment in open agent societies. In: Procs. of AAMAS'03. (2003) 489–496
10. Boella, G., van der Torre, L.: Organizations as socially constructed agents in the agent oriented paradigm. In: LNAI n. 3451: Procs. of the Workshop Engineering Societies in the Agents World (ESAW), Berlin, Springer Verlag (2004) 1–13
11. Pasquier, P., Chaib-draa, B.: The cognitive coherence approach for agent communication pragmatics. In: Procs. of AAMAS'03 (2003) 544–551
12. Gaudou, B., Herzig, A., Longin, D.: A logical framework for grounding-based dialogue analysis. In van der Hoek, W., Lomuscio, A., de Wink, E., eds.: ENTCS: Procs. of LCMAS'05. **157(4)** (2005) 117–137
13. Grossi, D., Dignum, F., Dastani, M., Royakkers, L.: Foundations of organizational structures in multiagent systems. In: Procs. of AAMAS'05. (2005)
14. Maudet, N., Chaib-draa, B.: Commitment-based and dialogue-game based protocols–news trends in agent communication language. Knowledge Engineering **17(2)** (2002) 157–179
15. Wooldridge, M.J.: Semantic issues in the verification of agent communication languages. Journal of Autonomous Agents and Multi-Agent Systems **3(1)** (2000) 9–31

16. Singh, M.P.: A social semantics for agent communication languages. In Dignum, F., Greaves, M., eds.: LNCS n 1916: Issues in Agent Cmmunication: Procs. of the IJCAI Workshop on Agent Communication Languages. Springer-Verlag, (2000) 31 – 45

17. Walton, D.N., Krabbe, E.C.: Commitment in Dialogue: Basic Concepts of Interpersonal Reasoning. State University of New York Press (1995)

18. Dastani, M., Herzig, A., Hulstijn, J., Van der Torre, L.: Inferring trust. In: LNAI n. 3487: Procs. of Fifth Workshop on Computational Logic in Multi-agent Systems (CLIMA V), Springer Verlag (2004) 144– 160

19. Demolombe, R.: To trust information sources: a proposal for a modal logical framework. In Castelfranchi, C., Tan, Y.H., eds.: Trust and Deception in Virtual Societies. Kluwer (2001) 111 – 124

20. Liau, C.J.: Belief, information acquisition, and trust in multi-agent systems – a modal formulation. Artificial Intelligence **149** (2003) 31–60

21. Verdicchio, M., Colombetti, M.: A logical model of social commitment for agent communication. In: Procs. of AAMAS'03. (2003) 528–535

22. Singh, M.P.: Social and psychological commitments in multiagent systems. In: AAAI Fall Symposium in Knowledge and Action at Social and Organizational Level. (1991)

23. Pasquier, P., Flores, R., Chaib-draa, B.: Modeling flexible social commitments and their enforcement. In Gleizes, M.P., Omicini, A., Zambonelli, F., eds.: LNAI n. 3451: Procs. of the Workshop Engineering Societies in the Agents World (ESAW), Springer Verlag (2004) 153–165

24. Busetta, P., Merzi, M., Rossi, S., Legras, F.: Intra-role coordination using group communication: a preliminary report. In: LNAI n. 2922: Procs. of AAMAS'03 Workshop on Agent Communication Languages and Conversation Policies, Springer Verlag (2003)

25. Yolum, P., Singh, M.P.: Flexible protocol specification and execution: applying event calculus planning using commitments. In: Procs. of AAMAS'02. (2002) 527–534

26. Kumar, S., Huber, M., Cohen, P., McGee, D.: Toward a formalism for conversational protocols using joint intention theory. Computational Intelligence **18(2)** (2002)

27. Endriss, U., Maudet, N., Sadri, F., Toni, F.: Protocol conformance for logic-based agents. In: Procs. of IJCAI'03, Morgan Kaufmann (2003) 679–684

28. Weiss, G., Nickles, M., Rovatsos, M.: Formulating Agent Communication Semantics and Pragmatics as Behavioral Expectations In: LNCS n. 3396: Procs. of Agent Communication workshop (AC'04) Springer Verlag (2005) 153–172

On the Semantics of Conditional Commitment

Shakil M. Khan and Yves Lespérance

Dept. of Computer Science and Engineering,
York University, Toronto, ON, Canada M3J 1P3
{skhan, lesperan}@cs.yorku.ca

Abstract. In this paper, we identify some problems with current formalizations of conditional commitments, i.e. commitments to achieve a goal if some condition becomes true. We present a solution to these problems. We also formalize two types of communicative actions that can be used by an agent to request another agent to achieve a goal or perform an action provided that some condition becomes true. Our account is set within ECASL [8], a framework for modeling communicating agents based on the situation calculus.

1 Introduction

In recent years, the importance of agent communication in multiagent systems has been widely recognized. As a result, many researchers have developed communicative multiagent frameworks [3,5,7,16,20,24,26] and attempted to formalize various types of communicative actions in these frameworks. One important concept in these is the notion of *conditional commitment*. A conditional commitment is a commitment to achieve some goal if some condition becomes true (e.g. a commitment to ship some goods when payment of an agreed to amount arrives). Conditional requests are requests that seek to have the addressee acquire a conditional commitment. Any multiagent framework that deals with negotiation and cooperation ought to handle conditional commitments. Unfortunately, most definitions found in the literature (in [5,29,24,1], for example) are inadequate: they either define conditional commitments as disjunctive goals, which makes the agents under-committed to the conditional goal, or define them as conjunctive goals, which renders the agent over-committed.

We will go over some examples to point out the problems associated with the disjunctive and the conjunctive accounts of conditional commitment. In these, we use the following modal operators: $\Diamond\phi$, i.e. ϕ eventually holds, Happens(α), i.e. the action α is performed next, ϕ Until ψ, i.e. eventually ψ becomes true, and as long as ψ is false, ϕ holds, and Before(ψ, ϕ), i.e. if ψ eventually becomes true, then ϕ becomes true before ψ does. The formal semantics of these operators are given in Section 2.

In the *disjunctive account*, a conditional commitment to achieve some goal provided that some condition holds is modeled as a commitment to achieve the goal if the condition holds, i.e. as a simple material implication. For example, consider an online marketplace domain. Suppose that there are two agents, a

F. Dignum, R. van Eijk, and R. Flores (Eds.): AC 2005/2006, LNAI 3859, pp. 45–60, 2006.

seller agent *slr*, and a buyer agent *byr*. If we use a disjunctive account, *slr*'s conditional commitment to ship some goods to *byr* on the condition that *byr* pays can be modeled as follows:

$$\text{CondInt}_{\text{dis}}(slr, GetPaid, \text{Happens}(shipGoods(slr, byr)))$$
$$\doteq \text{Int}(slr, \neg\Diamond GetPaid \vee$$
$$[\neg GetPaid \text{ Until}$$
$$(GetPaid \wedge \text{Happens}(shipGoods(slr, byr)))]).$$

This says that *slr*'s conditional commitment to ship the goods when *byr* pays amounts to *slr* having the intention that *byr* eventually pays and after that she ships the goods, if *byr* eventually pays (as mentioned earlier, the Until construct in the goal above implies that $\Diamond GetPaid$ and $\Diamond\text{Happens}(shipGoods(slr, byr))$). One problem with this account of conditional intention is that there is a counter-intuitive way to satisfy the conditional intention, namely, the agent may commit to the triggering condition remaining false and deliberately perform some action that makes it remain false. Thus, in the example, to satisfy her conditional intention, *slr* may intentionally perform some action to stop *byr* from paying her, such as blocking debits from *byr*. In other words, there is nothing in this formalization of conditional intention that stops *slr* from intending not to get paid and not to send the goods. However, this is counter-intuitive and a model of conditional commitment should not support this. Thus, with the disjunctive account of conditional commitment, the agent seems under-committed to the goal. Examples of accounts in the literature that formalize conditional commitments as disjunctive goals are [24] and [1].

In the *conjunctive account*, a conditional commitment to achieve a goal provided that a condition holds is modeled as a temporally ordered conjunctive commitment to the triggering condition and the conditional goal, where the triggering condition is achieved first. Although this model may seem appropriate in many cases, it often leads to problems. For example, suppose that *slr* has the conditional commitment to ship a replacement unit provided that *byr* reports and returns a defective good. If we use a conjunctive account, this can be modeled as follows:

$$\text{CondInt}_{\text{con}}(slr, DefGoodRet, \text{Happens}(shipRepl(slr, byr))) \doteq$$
$$\text{Int}(slr, \text{Before}(\text{Happens}(shipRepl(slr, byr)), DefGoodRet)$$
$$\wedge \Diamond\text{Happens}(shipRepl(slr, byr))).$$

This says that *slr*'s conditional commitment to ship a replacement unit provided that *byr* returns a defective good can be modeled as *slr*'s intention that *byr* returns a defective good before *slr* ships a replacement unit, and eventually *slr* ships a replacement unit. Note that, according to this definition, since *slr* has the intention that the defective product is returned before she ships the replacement unit, and that she eventually ships the replacement unit, it follows that *slr* has the intention that *byr* eventually returns a product, i.e. $\text{Int}(slr, \Diamond DefGoodRet)$. So *slr* may deliberately perform some action, such as shipping a defective good in the first place, to achieve this intention. Thus, the conjunctive account of conditional commitment results in over-committed agents. Both [5] and [29] formalize conditional commitments as conjunctive goals.

In this paper, we propose a solution to these problems (the *under/over-commitment problems*, henceforth). Our solution involves using an additional constraint with the disjunctive account to eliminate the under-commitment problem. We use the Extended Cognitive Agent Specification Language (ECASL) [8] as our base formalism for this. Our account is formulated for internal/mental states semantics for communication acts. Nevertheless, the same issues arise for public/social-commitment semantics (as discussed in Section 5). In this paper, we will use the terms 'intention' and 'commitment' interchangeably.

The paper is organized as follows: in the next section, we outline the ECASL framework. In Section 3, we present our model of conditional commitment and discuss some of its properties. In Section 4, we present some communicative acts that allow agents to make requests that result in conditional commitments. In Section 5, we compare our approach to previous work on conditional commitments. Finally in Section 6, we summarize our results and discuss possible future work.

2   ECASL

The Extended Cognitive Agent Specification Language (ECASL) [8], an extension of CASL [23,25], is a framework for specifying and verifying complex communicating multiagent systems that incorporates a formal model of means-ends reasoning. In this section, we outline the part of ECASL that is needed for our formalization of conditional commitment.

In ECASL, agents are viewed as entities with mental states, i.e., knowledge and goals, and the specifier can define the behavior of the agents in terms of these mental states. ECASL combines a declarative action theory defined in the situation calculus with a rich programming/process language, ConGolog [4]. Domain dynamics and agents' mental states are specified declaratively in the theory, while the agents' behavior is specified procedurally in ConGolog.

In ECASL, a dynamic domain is represented using an action theory [17] formulated in the situation calculus [13], a (mostly) first order language for representing dynamically changing worlds in which all changes are the result of named actions. ECASL uses a theory D that includes the following set of axioms:

- action precondition axioms, one per action,
- successor state axioms (SSA), one per fluent, that encode both effect and frame axioms and specify exactly when the fluent changes [18],
- initial state axioms describing what is true initially including the mental states of the agents,
- axioms identifying the agent of each action,
- unique name axioms for actions, and
- domain-independent foundational axioms describing the structure of situations [10].

Within ECASL, the behavior of agents is specified using the notation of the logic programming language ConGolog [4], the concurrent version of Golog [11]. A typical ConGolog program is composed of a sequence of procedure declarations, followed by a complex action. Complex actions can be composed using constructs that include primitive actions, waiting for a condition, sequence, nondeterministic branch, nondeterministic choice of arguments, conditional branching, while loop, procedure call, nondeterministic iteration, concurrent execution with and without priorities, and interrupts. To deal with multiagent processes, primitive actions in ECASL take the agent of the action as argument.

The semantics of the ConGolog process description language is defined in terms of *transitions*, in the style of structural operational semantics [15]. The overall semantics of a program is specified by the $Do(\delta, s, s')$ relation, which holds if and only if s' can be reached by performing a sequence of transitions starting with program δ in s, and the remaining program may legally terminate in s'.[1]

The situation calculus underlying ECASL is a branching time temporal logic, where each situation has a linear past and a branching future. In the framework, one can write both state formulas and path formulas. A state formula $\phi(s)$ takes a single situation as argument and is evaluated with respect to that situation. On the other hand, a path formula $\psi(s_1, s_2)$ takes two situations as arguments and is evaluated with respect to the interval (finite path) $[s_1, s_2]$. A state formula ϕ may contain a placeholder constant *now* that stands for the situation in which ϕ must hold. $\phi(s)$ is the formula that results from replacing *now* by s. Similarly, a path formula ψ may contain the placeholder constants *now* and *then* that stand for the situations that are the endpoints of the interval $[now, then]$ over which ψ must hold. $\psi(s_1, s_2)$ denotes ψ with s_1 substituted for *now* and s_2 substituted for *then*. Where the intended meaning is clear, we sometimes suppress the placeholder(s).

ECASL allows the specifier to model agents in terms of their mental states by including operators to specify agents' information (i.e., their knowledge), and motivation (i.e., their goals or intentions). We use state formulas within the scope of knowledge, and path formulas within the scope of intentions. Following [14,21], ECASL models knowledge using a possible worlds account adapted to the situation calculus. $K(agt, s', s)$ is used to denote that in situation s, agt thinks that she could be in situation s'. s' is called a *K-alternative situation* for agt in s. Using K, the knowledge or belief of an agent, $Know(agt, \phi, s)$, is defined as $\forall s'(K(agt, s', s) \supset \phi(s'))$, i.e. agt knows ϕ in s if ϕ holds in all of agt's K-accessible situations in s. In ECASL, K is constrained to be reflexive, transitive, and Euclidean in the initial situation to capture the fact that agents' knowledge is true, and that agents have positive and negative introspection. As shown in [21], these constraints then continue to hold after any sequence of actions since they are preserved by the successor state axiom for K.

---

[1] Since we have predicates that take programs as arguments, we need to encode programs and formulas as first-order terms as in [4]. For notational simplicity, we suppress this encoding and use formulas and programs as terms directly.

ECASL supports knowledge expansion as a result of sensing actions [21] and some *informing* communicative actions. Here, we restrict our discussion to knowledge expansion as a result of *inform* actions. The preconditions of *inform* are as follows:

$$Poss(inform(inf, agt, \phi), s) \equiv \text{Know}(inf, \phi, s)$$
$$\land \neg\text{Know}(inf, \text{Know}(agt, \phi, now), s).$$

In other words, the agent *inf* can inform *agt* that ϕ, iff *inf* knows that ϕ currently holds, and does not believe that *agt* currently knows that ϕ. The successor state axiom (SSA) for K can be defined as follows:

$$K(agt, s^*, do(a, s)) \equiv \exists s'.\ K(agt, s', s) \land s^* = do(a, s') \land Poss(a, s').$$

This says that after an action happens, every agent learns that it was possible and has happened. Moreover, if the action involves someone informing *agt* that ϕ holds, then *agt* knows this afterwards. This follows from the fact that it is a precondition of $inform(inf, agt, \phi)$ that *inf* knows that ϕ, that what is known must be true (i.e. K is reflexive), and that the SSA for K requires the agent to know that $Poss(a, s)$ after a happens in s. Note that this axiom only handles knowledge expansion, not revision.

ECASL also incorporates goal expansion and a limited form of goal contraction. Goals or intentions are modeled using an accessibility relation W over possible situations. The W-accessible situations for an agent are the ones where she thinks that all her goals are satisfied. W-accessible situations may include situations that the agent thinks are impossible, unlike Cohen and Levesque's [2] G-accessible worlds. But intentions are defined in terms of the more primitive W and K relations so that the intention accessible situations are W-accessible situations that are also compatible with what the agent knows, in the sense that there is a K-accessible situation in their history. This guarantees that agents' intentions are realistic, that is, agents can only intend things that they believe are possible. Thus we have:

$$\text{Int}(agt, \psi, s) \doteq \forall s', s^*.[W(agt, s^*, s) \land K(agt, s', s) \land s' \leq s^*] \supset \psi(s', s^*).$$

This means that the intentions of an agent in s are those formulas that are true for all intervals between situations s' and s^* where the situations s^* are W-accessible from s and have a K-accessible situation s' in their past. Intentions are future oriented, and any goal formula will be evaluated with respect to a finite path defined by a pair of situations, a current situation *now* and an ending situation *then*. This formalization of goals can deal with both achievement goals and maintenance goals. An achievement goal ϕ is said to be eventually satisfied if ϕ holds in some situation between *now* and *then*, i.e., if $\diamond(\phi, now, then)$, which is defined as $\exists s'.\ (now \leq s' \leq then \land \phi(s')).$[2] In [22], Shapiro showed

---

[2] We sometimes use $\diamond$ with a path formula ψ argument, in which case, we mean that ψ holds over some interval $[s, then]$ that starts at some situation s between *now* and *then*; see Table 1 for the formal definition.

how positive and negative introspection of intentions can be modeled by placing some constraints on K and W. To make sure that agents' wishes and intentions are consistent, W is also constrained to be serial.

ECASL provides an intention transfer communication action, *request*, which is defined in terms of *inform*. This is similar to Herzig and Longin's account [7], where a request is defined as informing about one's intentions, and the requested goals are adopted via cooperation principles. The *request* action can be used by an agent to request another agent to achieve some state of affairs. Formally, we have:

$$request(req, agt, \phi) \doteq inform(req, agt, \text{Int}(req, \phi, now)).$$

The SSA for W which handles intention change in ECASL, has the same structure as a SSA for a domain dependent fluent. In the following, $W^+(agt, a, s^*, s)$ ($W^-(agt, a, s^*, s)$, resp.) denotes the conditions under which s^* is added to (dropped from, resp.) W as a result of the action a in s:

$$W(agt, s^*, do(a, s)) \equiv W^+(agt, a, s^*, s) \vee$$
$$(W(agt, s^*, s) \wedge \neg W^-(agt, a, s^*, s)).$$

An agent's intentions are expanded when it is requested something by another agent. After the $request(req, agt, \psi)$ action, agt adopts the goal that ψ, unless she has a conflicting goal or is not willing to serve req for ψ. Therefore, this action should cause agt to drop any paths in W where ψ does not hold. This is handled in W^-:

$$W^-(agt, a, s^*, s) \doteq [\exists req, \psi. \, a = request(req, agt, \psi)$$
$$\wedge Serves(agt, req, \psi, s) \wedge \neg \text{Int}(agt, \neg \psi, s)$$
$$\wedge \exists s'. \, K(agt, s', s) \wedge s' \leq s^* \wedge \neg \psi(do(a, s'), s^*)].$$

A limited form of intention contraction is also handled in ECASL. Agents intentions are contracted as a result of a *cancelRequest* action. ECASL also incorporates a formal model of means-ends reasoning and commitment to rational plans to achieve intentions. See [8] for the details of these.

Table 1 shows some abbreviations that will be used throughout the paper.

3   Conditional Commitments

Having presented our framework, we now return to our discussion about conditional commitments. Informally, an agent agt has a conditional commitment or intention that ψ on the condition that ϕ if agt intends to achieve ψ as soon as the condition ϕ holds. In our specification, we assume that ϕ is a state formula, whereas ψ is a path formula and can represent any kind of goal (achievement, maintenance, etc.). In other words, the trigger condition ϕ of a conditional intention takes a single situation *now* as argument, unlike the goal formula ψ,

Table 1. Some Definitions of Temporal Operators

1. $\Diamond(\psi, now, then) \doteq \exists s'.\ now \leq s' \leq then \wedge \psi(s', then)$,
2. $\Box(\psi, now, then) \doteq \neg\Diamond(\neg\psi, now, then)$,
3. $[\phi\ \mathrm{Until}\ \psi](now, then) \doteq \exists s'.\ now \leq s' \leq then$
   $\wedge\ \psi(s', then) \wedge \forall s''.\ now \leq s'' < s' \supset \phi(s'')$,
4. $\mathrm{Before}(\psi, \phi, now, then) \doteq \exists s'.\ now \leq s' \leq then$
   $\wedge\ \psi(s', then) \supset \exists s''.\ now \leq s'' < s' \wedge \phi(s'')$,
5. $\mathrm{E}_\Diamond(\phi, now) \doteq \exists s.\ now \leq s \wedge \phi(s)$,
6. $\mathrm{A}_\Box(\phi, now) \doteq \neg\mathrm{E}_\Diamond(\neg\phi, now)$,
7. $\mathrm{Happens}(a, now, then) \doteq do(a, now) \leq then$,
8. $\mathrm{Happens}_C(\delta, now, then) \doteq \exists s'.\ s' \leq then \wedge Do(\delta, s', then)$.

which takes two situations *now* and *then* as arguments.[3] If one wishes to use an achievement goal ϕ' for ψ, one can use $\Diamond(\phi', now, then)$, i.e. eventually ϕ'. For simplicity, we also assume that the trigger condition ϕ is a one-time goal, i.e. once ϕ becomes true, it remains true forever.

So we now propose a formalization of conditional intentions that avoids the under/over-commitment problem:

$$\mathrm{CondInt}(agt, \phi, \psi, s) \doteq$$
$$\mathrm{Int}(agt, DisjGoal(\phi, \psi, now, then)$$
$$\wedge\ NoUnderComm(agt, \phi, now, then), s),$$
$$DisjGoal(\phi, \psi, now, then) \doteq$$
$$[\neg\phi\ \mathrm{Until}\ (\phi \wedge \psi)](now, then) \vee \neg\Diamond(\phi, now, then),$$
$$NoUnderComm(agt, \phi, now, then) \doteq$$
$$\Box([\mathrm{Int}(agt, \Box(\neg\phi, now, then), now) \supset$$
$$\mathrm{Know}(agt, \mathrm{A}_\Box(\neg\phi, now), now)], now, then).$$

That is, *agt* conditionally intends that ψ provided that ϕ, iff *agt* intends that the following conditions hold:

1. either (a) ϕ eventually holds, and ψ holds immediately from the time ϕ comes to hold, or (b) ϕ never holds, and
2. if in any situation *agt* intends that ϕ never comes to hold, she must also know in that situation that it can never become true.

Intuitively, this says that one way to fulfill an agent's conditional intention is to (1a) satisfy ψ after ϕ comes to hold, and a second way is that (1b) ϕ never comes to hold in the future. This part of our account is as in the disjunctive approach. However, we add to this that (2) the agent does not intend that

---

[3] We could also handle trigger conditions that are not state formulas. However, in these cases, since the trigger condition holds over a time interval, it is not always clear when exactly the triggering of the commitment to the conditional goal should occur. To avoid these complications, we stick to state formulas as triggers.

ϕ never comes to hold unless she knows that it can never hold. Thus we require that if at some situation, agt intends that ϕ never comes true, it must be the case that she knows in that situation that ϕ can never become true, and she only intends this because it has become inevitable. So the additional constraint that $NoUnderComm(agt, \phi, now, then)$ ensures that agt will not do anything intentionally to make the triggering condition ϕ remain false. One might be tempted to define $NoUnderComm(agt, \phi, now, then)$ as $\Box(\neg Int(agt, \Box(\neg\phi, now, then), now), now, then)$, i.e. agt never intends that ϕ never holds. However, since some event may make ϕ impossible to achieve, there is a possibility that agt may come to intend that ϕ always be false, if this becomes inevitable. The only case in which agt intends that ϕ always be false is when she knows that it can never become true.

Consider once again our online marketplace example given in Section 1 for the disjunctive account. Using this definition of conditional commitment, a seller slr's intention to send the goods when a buyer byr pays, CondInt(slr,-$GetPaid(byr, slr)$, Happens($shipGoods(slr, byr)$,$now, then$), s) can be formalized as follows:

$$Int(slr, DisjGoal(GetPaid(byr, slr),$$
$$Happens(shipGoods(slr, byr), now, then), now, then)$$
$$\wedge NoUnderComm(slr, GetPaid(byr, slr), now, then), s).$$

slr's intention can be further expanded to:

$$Int(slr, [GetPaidAndThenSendGoods(byr, slr, now, then)$$
$$\vee \neg\Diamond(GetPaid(byr, slr), now, then)] \wedge$$
$$[\Box((Int(slr, \Box\neg GetPaid(byr, slr), now) \supset$$
$$Know(slr, A_\Box(\neg GetPaid(byr, slr), now), now)), now, then)], s),$$

where,

$$GetPaidAndThenSendGoods(byr, slr, now, then) \doteq$$
$$[\neg GetPaid(byr, slr) \text{ Until}$$
$$(GetPaid(byr, slr) \wedge$$
$$Happens(shipGoods(slr, byr), now, then))](now, then).$$

From this, we can see that there are only two ways by which slr can satisfy this conditional intention: either at some future or current situation byr pays slr and then slr sends the goods to byr, or, byr never pays slr, and as long as slr does not know that byr will never pay her, she does not intend not to get paid. Since slr cannot intend not to get paid, she cannot deliberately perform anything (for example block payments from byr) to make the triggering condition remain false. If at a later situation, slr learns that it has become impossible for byr to ever pay her, slr will inevitably intend that byr never pays her, but otherwise she cannot acquire this intention. Thus, our formalization of conditional commitment does not suffer from the under-commitment problem.

Moreover, since we use the disjunctive approach, our account does not suffer from the over-commitment problem associated with the conjunctive approach. Consider the second example given in Section 1, where *slr* has the intention to ship a replacement unit when *byr* returns a defective good. Using our definition, this can be expanded to *slr*'s intention that either *byr* never returns a defective product, or *byr* returns a defective product and *slr* ships the replacement unit after that. Thus *slr* is not over-committed and will not perform something deliberately so that *byr* returns a product. The additional constraint that *slr* never intends that *byr* never return a product unless she knows that *byr* will never return a product does not seem to lead to any over-commitment. Thus our formalization of conditional intention is also free from the over-commitment problem.

Note that our account allows the agent who has a conditional intention to intend not to know whether the condition holds. We could easily strengthen the definition to rule this out, but it is not clear that this is always appropriate.

Next, we show two simple properties of conditional intention. Assume that the domain theory D (as discussed in Section 2) includes our definition of conditional commitment given above. Then we have the following theorem that says that if an agent *agt* conditionally intends that ψ provided that ϕ in situation s, and if she knows that ϕ holds in s, then *agt* intends that ψ in s.

Theorem 1

$$D \models \mathrm{CondInt}(agt, \phi, \psi, s) \wedge \mathrm{Know}(agt, \phi, s) \supset$$
$$\mathrm{Int}(agt, \psi, s).$$

So when the agent knows that the condition has become true, a conditional intention reduces to an ordinary intention. The second property states that agents are able to introspect their conditional intentions:

Theorem 2

$$D \models [\mathrm{CondInt}(agt, \phi, \psi, s) \supset$$
$$\mathrm{Know}(agt, \mathrm{CondInt}(agt, \phi, \psi, now), s)] \wedge$$
$$[\neg\mathrm{CondInt}(agt, \phi, \psi, s) \supset$$
$$\mathrm{Know}(agt, \neg\mathrm{CondInt}(agt, \phi, \psi, now), s)].$$

Thus, if an agent has a conditional intention (does not have a conditional intention, resp.) that ψ provided that ϕ, then she knows that she has (does not have, resp.) this conditional intention.

It would be interesting to prove additional results about conditional intentions, for instance, that a conditional intention persists as long as its condition is known to remain false and not known to have become impossible. We leave this for future work.

4   Conditional Requests

We now discuss two communicative acts, *requestWhen* and *reqActWhen*, that can be used by an agent to request someone to achieve ψ or to execute a program δ respectively, on the condition that ϕ becomes true. Recall that, in ECASL the SSA for W determines whether an agent adopts a goal when requested; the requested goal is adopted by the requestee via cooperation principles encoded in the SSA for W. Thus, we model requests as informing about intentions, rather than as primitives. In the following, we use $CondIntCont(agt, \phi, \psi)$ as an abbreviation for the content of a conditional intention $DisjGoal(\phi, \psi, now, then) \wedge NoUnderComm(agt, \phi, now, then)$. Now, one simple way to model a requester req's request to requestee agt to achieve ψ on the condition that ϕ is as follows:

$$requestWhen_{sim}(req, agt, \phi, \psi) \doteq$$
$$request(req, agt, CondIntCont(req, \phi, \psi)).$$

This says that, req's conditional request to agt to achieve ψ provided that ϕ amounts to req's request to agt to fulfill the content $CondIntCont(req, \phi, \psi)$ of her own conditional intention. Using the definition of *request*, this conditional request amounts to req informing agt that she currently intends to achieve ψ provided that ϕ. However, note that the content $CondIntCont(req, \phi, \psi)$ of this conditional intention includes mental attitudes that refer to req, rather than agt. Since the SSA for W does not automatically replace the agent parameters of mental state operators used in a goal formula, if we model conditional requests as above, given appropriate conditions (i.e., when agt agrees to serve req on $CondIntCont(req, \phi, \psi)$ and does not currently have the intention that $\neg CondIntCont(req, \phi, \psi)$), agt will adopt the intention that $CondIntCont(req,\phi, \psi)$, but not that $CondIntCont(agt, \phi, \psi)$. Thus she will not have the conditional intention to achieve ψ provided that ϕ after the conditional request is performed, and this simple definition is not quite correct.

For example, suppose that the manager agent mgr wants to conditionally request the seller slr in situation s to ship the goods when the buyer byr pays her. So mgr can do this by performing the following action in s:

$$requestWhen_{sim}(mgr, slr, GetPaid(byr, slr),$$
$$Happens(shipGoods(slr, byr), now, then)),$$

which can be expanded to:

$$request(mgr, slr,$$
$$CondIntCont(mgr, GetPaid(byr, slr),$$
$$Happens(shipGoods(slr, byr), now, then))).$$

After the request is performed, if slr agrees to serve mgr on $CondIntCont(mgr,- GetPaid(byr, slr),$ $Happens(shipGoods(slr, byr), now, then))$, and does not intend that $\neg CondIntCont(mgr, GetPaid(byr, slr), Happens(shipGoods(slr, byr), now, then))$, the SSA for W will ensure that:

$$\text{Int}(slr, CondIntCont(mgr, GetPaid(byr, slr),$$
$$\text{Happens}(shipGoods(slr, byr), now, then)), s_r),$$

which can be expanded to:

$$\text{Int}(slr, DisjGoal(GetPaid(byr, slr),$$
$$\text{Happens}(shipGoods(slr, byr), now, then), now, then)$$
$$\land NoUnderComm(mgr, GetPaid(byr, slr), now, then), s_r),$$

where s_r is the situation that results from performing the $requestWhen$ action in s. Now, using the definition of conditional intention, we can see that in s_r, slr does not have the conditional intention of sending the goods provided that byr pays her. The problem is with the mental state operators in the $NoUnderComm(mgr, \ldots)$ part of slr's intention: they say that mgr will not intend that the payment not occur unless she knows it can never occur. What we need is for this constraint to hold for slr.

To deal with this problem, we propose the following model of conditional requests:

$$requestWhen(req, agt, \phi, \psi) \doteq request(req, agt, CondIntCont(agt, \phi, \psi)).$$

This says that req's request to agt to conditionally achieve ψ provided that ϕ amounts to req's request to agt to fulfill the content of agt's conditional intention to achieve ψ provided that ϕ, i.e., $CondIntCont(agt, \phi, \psi)$. Using the definition of $request$, this can be further expanded to:

$$requestWhen(req, agt, \phi, \psi) \doteq$$
$$inform(req, agt, \text{Int}(req, CondIntCont(agt, \phi, \psi), now)).$$

That is, req can request agt to achieve ψ on the condition that ϕ by informing agt that she intends that $CondIntCont(agt, \phi, \psi)$. Note that, the agent parameter of $CondIntCont(agt, \phi, \psi)$ is now the requestee agt, rather than the requester req. This guarantees that given that agt serves req and does not have the opposite intention, she will conditionally intend to achieve ψ provided that ϕ after req conditionally requests her this. Thus this formalization of conditional request does not suffer from the above mentioned problem.

We also define a special type of conditional request, namely, a request to perform an action when some condition holds:

$$reqActWhen(req, agt, \phi, \delta) \doteq$$
$$requestWhen(req, agt, \phi, Happens_C(\delta, now, then)).$$

This states that req's conditional request to agt to execute the program δ provided that ϕ amounts to req's conditional request to agt to execute δ starting in the situation where ϕ holds.

Now consider what happens when mgr conditionally requests slr to ship the goods when byr pays her, that is, when mgr performs the $reqActWhen(mgr, slr,$ $GetPaid(byr, slr), shipGoods(slr, byr))$ action. Given that slr agrees to serve *mgr* and does not have the opposite intention, the SSA for W will make *slr* adopt the following intention:

$$\text{Int}(slr, CondIntCont(slr, GetPaid(byr, slr),$$
$$\text{Happen}_C(sendGoods(slr, byr), when, then)), s_r),$$

and thus, by the definition of conditional intention, she will conditionally intend to send the goods when *byr* pays her. Thus, our formalization of conditional requests allows the proper transfer of conditional intention from the requester to the requestee.

We next present a theorem that shows how agents' intentions are affected by the *requestWhen* action. Assume that the domain theory D includes our definition of these new communicative actions. We can show that:

Theorem 3

$$D \models [\neg\text{Int}(agt, \neg CondIntCont(agt, \phi, \psi), s)$$
$$\wedge Serves(agt, req, CondIntCont(agt, \phi, \psi), s)$$
$$\wedge Poss(requestWhen(req, agt, \phi, \psi), s)] \supset$$
$$\text{CondInt}(agt, \phi, \psi, do(requestWhen(req, agt, \phi, \psi), s)).$$

This says that if in some situation s, an agent *agt* does not intend not to fulfill the content of a conditional intention to achieve ψ provided that ϕ, and if she serves another agent *req* on the content of this conditional commitment in s, then she will have the conditional intention to achieve ψ given that ϕ after *req* conditionally request her this in s, provided that the request is possible in s.

It would be useful to extend our framework with a communication act that allows a conditional commitment created as a result of a *requestWhen* to be cancelled. We believe that the existing ECASL *cancelRequest* action can be used to define such a conditional commitment cancelling act. We leave this for future work.

5   Related Work

The under-commitment problem that we pointed out in Section 1 is related to another problem involving intentions discussed by Cohen and Levesque [2]. In that paper, they consider a robot who drops the intention of bringing a bottle of beer by breaking the last available bottle and thus making the intention impossible to achieve. Their solution was twofold: (1) they formalize intentions as persistent goals and (2) they assume that existing intentions act as a screen of admissibility over new intentions. In their framework, an agent's intentions persist until she knows that they have been achieved, or knows that it has become impossible to achieve them. Since the robot intends to bring a bottle of beer, she will not drop this goal until she achieves it or gets to know that it has become impossible to achieve. However, the robot can break the last available bottle to make her goal unachievable. But since an agent's current intentions provide a screen of admissibility for adopting new intentions, she cannot have these two conflicting intentions at the same time. Thus since she intends to bring a bottle, she cannot adopt the intention to break the only available bottle. Note that while this problem has similarities with the one addressed here, it does not involve conditional intentions.

In the literature, there has been some work on conditional intention. However, as mentioned earlier, all of the proposed treatments that we are aware of seem to suffer from the under- or over-commitment problems. Although it does not explictly address conditional intentions, the FIPA agent communication language specification [5] defines a type of communication act that leads to conditional intentions. In that framework, an agent can conditionally request another agent to execute an action when some condition holds. This is modeled as follows: req's conditional request to agt to perform act when ϕ holds amounts to req informing agt that she has the intention that agt execute act and that ϕ be true just before that. Note that req's intention amounts to the conjunction that ϕ be true at some point and agt executes act right after that. Thus, this treatment of conditional intention can be viewed as a conjunctive account where the intention is to first achieve the triggering condition ϕ, and then to achieve the conditional goal. As discussed in Section 1, this leads to the over-commitment problem.

Yolum and Singh [29] present a different model of conditional commitment that relies on a social obligation-based semantics rather than a traditional one based on mental states. Their main concern was the study of communication protocols that accommodate exceptions and take advantage of opportunities. They model interaction protocols using *commitment machines* that supply a content to protocol states and actions in terms of the social commitments of the participating agents. In their formal semantics, which is only briefly described, they adopt a branching time temporal model. The semantics for commitments involves a modal accessibility relation for commitments C that relates a state of the protocol (i.e. a time-point) s, a debtor agent x, and a creditor agent y to a set of paths P. Intuitively, x is responsible to y for satisfying ϕ in state s iff ϕ holds at time-point s along all paths p that are C-accessible from (x, y, s). To model conditional commitment, they introduce a strict implication operator (denoted by $\rightsquigarrow$) that requires the consequent to hold when the antecedent holds. The strict implication is false when the antecedent is false. Their semantics says that $\phi \rightsquigarrow \phi'$ holds in a state s iff ϕ holds in s and for all s' that satisfy ϕ, every s'' that is similar to s' (i.e. $s \approx s'$) also satisfies ϕ'. What they mean by the similarity relation $\approx$ is not explained. Thus for them, a conditional commitment $C(x, y, \phi \rightsquigarrow \phi')$ holds in state s iff on all C-accessible paths p, ϕ holds at s, and whenever some s' satisfies ϕ, every s'' that is similar to s' satisfies ϕ'. Since they model conditional commitments using the $\rightsquigarrow$ operator, which behaves like a conjunction with some additional constraints, it appears that their formalization suffers from the over-commitment problem. It is also not clear how their formalization ensures that the goal is achieved *after* the condition along the paths.

Both [1] and [24] model conditional commitment as a disjunctive goal. In their social commitment and argument network based framework, Bentahar et al. [1] define conditional commitments as a simple implication. Their semantics of conditional commitment goes as follows: $M, s \models \text{CondInt}_{Ben}(agt_1, agt_2, \phi, \psi)$ iff $M, s \models \text{EF}^+ \phi \Rightarrow M, s \models \text{ABC}(agt_1, agt_2, \psi)$, where s, E, F^+, and ABC denotes a timepoint, there exists a path, sometime in the future, and absolute commitment, respectively. This says that agt_1 is committed to agt_2 to achieve ψ on the condition that ϕ means that agt_1 is unconditionally committed to agt_2 to achieve ψ if ϕ holds at some timepoint over some path in the future. Besides suffering from the under-commitment problem associated with disjunctive accounts, this seems to require commitment to the goal too early, before the condition becomes true.

In [24], Shapiro et al. describe a framework for specifying communicative multiagent systems using ConGolog [4] within the situation calculus, an early version of CASL. Since they were lacking a goal-revision mechanism at that point, they introduced a type of conditional request, the *requestUnless* action, in an attempt to avoid the need for goal-revision. *requestUnless*(req, agt, ϕ, ψ) means that *req* is requesting *agt* to adopt the goal that ψ unless ϕ is obtained. The execution of *requestUnless*(req, agt, ϕ, ψ) makes *agt* adopt the goal that $\phi \vee \psi$. This amounts to modeling conditional intentions as disjunctive goals, and hence the account suffers from the under-commitment problem.

6   Conclusion

In this paper, we identified some problems with many existing formalizations of conditional commitments. These seem to either have the agents over-committed, intending to achieve the condition under which the goal would have to be achieved, or under-committed, possibly intending that this condition remain false forever. We could not find any problem-free account in the literature. We presented a definition of conditional intentions that does not suffer from these problems. We then formalized two types of communicative actions that allow agents to make requests that lead to conditional commitments. We also proved some properties of conditional commitments and conditional requests. Finally, we discussed previous work on conditional commitments.

Note that, our framework allows an agent with a conditional intention to not intend that the trigger condition eventually becomes true. However, it does not allow her to intend that the trigger condition never comes to hold, without also knowing that it can never become true. In other words, in our framework, an agent's conditional intention that ψ provided that ϕ is not consistent with her intention that $\Box \neg \phi$, unless she already knows that this must be the case. This might be problematic in some cases. For instance, in our example where a seller has a conditional intention to ship a replacement unit when a buyer returns a defective product, we might want to say that the seller has the intention that the buyer never returns a defective good. However, it is not possible for an agent to consistently have both of these intentions in our framework. One way to overcome this limitation might be to adopt a richer semantic model of intention, where one allows different degrees of preferability, similar to the levels of plausibility in traditional belief revision frameworks such as [6]. Such semantic models and the resulting logics are more expressive, but much more complex to specify and reason in.

The theory presented here is a part of our ongoing research on the semantics of speech acts and agent communication in the situation calculus. In [9], we present an extended version of this work where we model some simple communication protocols that deal with conditional requests. Much work remains. In the future, we would like to prove other properties of conditional commitments, for example, about the persistence and revision of such commitments. We also plan to formalize complex interaction protocols, such as the Contract Net protocol [28] and the Net Bill protocol [27], using our formalization of conditional intention. It would also be interesting to try to use this formalization to implement flexible communication agents and to develop tools to support multiagent programming as in [19,12].

Acknowledgements

We thank Hector Levesque and the reviewers for useful comments on this work.

References

1. J. Bentahar, B. Moulin, J.-J. Ch. Meyer, and B. Chaib-draa. A logical model of commitment and argument network for agent communication. In *Proc. of AAMAS-04*, pages 792–799, 2004.
2. P. Cohen and H. Levesque. Intention is choice with commitment. *Artificial Intelligence*, 42(2-3):213–361, 1990.
3. P. Cohen and H. Levesque. Rational interaction as the basis for communication. In P. Cohen, J. Morgan, and M. Pollack, editors, *Intentions in Communication*, pages 221–255. MIT Press, Cambridge, Mass., 1990.
4. G. De Giacomo, Y. Lespérance, and H. Levesque. ConGolog, a concurrent programming language based on the situation calculus. *Artificial Intelligence*, 121:109–169, 2000.
5. Foundations for Intelligent Physical Agents. FIPA communicative act library specification, document 37. 1997-2002.
6. P. Gardenfors. *Knowledge in Flux: Modeling the Dynamics of Epistemic States*. MIT Press, Cambridge, Massachusetts, 1988.
7. A. Herzig and D. Longin. A logic of intention with cooperation principles and with assertive speech acts as communication primitives. In *Proc. of AAMAS-02*, pages 920–927, 2002.
8. S. Khan and Y. Lespérance. ECASL: A model of rational agency for communicating agents. In *Proc. of AAMAS-05*, pages 762–769. Utrecht, The Netherlands, July 2005.
9. S. Khan. A situation calculus account of multiagent planning, speech acts, and communication, MSc Thesis (in preparation), 2005.

10. G. Lakemeyer and H. Levesque. AOL: A logic of acting, sensing, knowing, and only-knowing. In *Proc. of KR-98*, pages 316–327, 1998.
11. H. Levesque, R. Reiter, Y. Lespérance, F. Lin, and R. Scherl. Golog: A logic programming language for dynamic domains. *J. of Logic Programming*, 31:59–84, 1997.
12. V. Louis and T. Martinez. An operational model for the FIPA-ACL semantics. In R. van Eijk, R. Flores, and M.-P. Huget, editors, Proc. of International Workshop on Agent Communication. LNCS, 2005
13. J. McCarthy and P. Hayes. Some philosophical problems from the standpoint of artificial intelligence. *Machine Intelligence*, 4:463–502, 1969.
14. R. Moore. A formal theory of knowledge and action. *Formal Theories of the Commonsense World*, pages 319–358, 1985.
15. G. Plotkin. A structural approach to operational semantics. Technical Report DAIMI-FN-19, Computer Science Dept., Aarhus University, Denmark, 1981.
16. A. Rao and M. Georgeff. Modeling rational agents within a BDI-architecture. In R. Fikes and E. Sandewall, editors, *Proc. of KR&R-91*, pages 473–484, 1991.
17. R. Reiter. *Knowledge in Action. Logical Foundations for Specifying and Implementing Dynamical Systems*. MIT Press, 2001.
18. R. Reiter. The frame problem in the situation calculus: A simple solution (sometimes) and a completeness result for goal regression. In V. Lifschitz, editor, *Artificial Intelligence and Mathematical Theory of Computation: Papers in the Honor of John McCarthy*. Academic Press, 1991.
19. D. Sadek and P. Bretier. ARTIMIS: Natural dialogue meets rational agency. In *Proc. of IJCAI-97*, pages 1030–1035, 1997.
20. D. Sadek. Communication theory = rationality principles + communicative act models. In *Proc. of AAAI-94 Workshop on Planning for Interagent Comm.*, 1994.
21. R. Scherl and H. Levesque. Knowledge, action, and the frame problem. *Artificial Intelligence*, 144(1-2), 2003.
22. S. Shapiro. *Specifying and Verifying Multiagent Systems Using CASL*. PhD thesis, Dept. of C.S., U. of Toronto, 2005.
23. S. Shapiro and Y. Lespérance. Modeling multiagent systems with the Cognitive Agents Specification Language - a feature interaction resolution application. In C. Castelfranchi and Y. Lespérance, editors, *Intelligent Agents Vol. VII - Proc. of ATAL-00*, volume LNAI 1986, pages 244–259, 2001.
24. S. Shapiro, Y. Lespérance, and H. Levesque. Specifying communicative multi-agent systems. *Agents and Multi-Agent Systems – Formalisms, Methodologies, and Applications*, LNAI 1441:1–14, 1998.
25. S. Shapiro, Y. Lespérance, and H. Levesque. The Cognitive Agents Specification Language and verification environment for multiagent systems. In *Proc. of AAMAS-02*, pages 19–26, 2002.
26. M. Singh. *Multiagent Systems: A Theoretical Framework for Intentions, Know-How, and Communications*. LNAI 799, 1994.
27. M. Sirbu. Credits and debits on the internet. *Readings in Agents*, pages 299–305, 1998.
28. R. Smith. The contract net protocol: High level communication and control in a distributed problem solver. *IEEE Transactions on Computers*, C-29(12):1104–1113, 1980.
29. P. Yolum and M. Singh. Commitment machines. In J.-J. C. Meyer and M. Tambe, editors, *Intelligent Agents VIII : 8th Intl. Workshop, ATAL-01*, volume LNAI 2333, pages 235–247, 2002.

A Commitment-Based
Communicative Act Library

Mario Verdicchio[1,2] and Marco Colombetti[2,3]

[1] University of Bergamo, Bergamo, Italy
`Mario.Verdicchio@UniBG.It`
[2] Politecnico di Milano, Milano, Italy
`{Mario.Verdicchio, Marco.Colombetti}@PoliMi.It`
[3] University of Lugano, Lugano, Switzerland
`Marco.Colombetti@Lu.UniSi.CH`

Abstract. The Agent Communication Language (ACL) proposed by
the Foundation for Intelligent Physical Agents (FIPA) is the most complete attempt to create a universally accepted standard so far. Nevertheless, this standard shows some shortcomings which are probably hin-
dering an even greater impact upon the scientific research dealing with
multiagent systems. Although agreeing with the mainstream view that
analyzes agent communication in terms of communicative acts, we part
from FIPA's assumptions about the semantics, as we shift the focus from
affecting communicating agents' mental states to modifying the commitments binding them to each other. We show that our commitment-based
framework is powerful enough to allow for the main FIPA communicative acts and provides a semantics which overcomes some of the problems
that are currently affecting the standard.[1]

1 Introduction

Agent Communication Languages (ACLs) play a very important role in the context of open multiagent systems, which must provide a standard communication
framework that allows all participating agents to interact. The fact that we do
not have an established standard yet has lead us to research for some unre-
solved issues that may have hindered the universal acceptance of the proposals
put forward so far. Our analysis focuses on the proposal by the Foundation for
Intelligent Physical Agents (FIPA) [2] because it has recently emerged as the
best candidate to become an established standard. Some works in the literature,
like [16], aimed at showing that several critical issues rise from expressing the
language's semantics in terms of mental states and that instead turning to social
states (i.e. commitments) would provide a way to solve some of these issues. We
aim to show that this approach is a real alternative to mentalistic semantics,
and we consider as a fundamental step to rewrite FIPA's Communicative Act

---

[1] This paper appears also in the Proceedings of the Fourth International Joint Conference on Autonomous Agents and Multi-Agent Systems (AAMAS 05).

F. Dignum, R. van Eijk, and R. Flores (Eds.): AC 2005/2006, LNAI 3859, pp. 61–75, 2006.

Library [3] according to this perspective, that is, express FIPA communicative acts in terms of commitments between agents. Such a task has led us to classify them into four different categories, as follows:

1. the acts in this category (i.e. *inform* and *request*) are such that even if they are given a new semantics in terms of commitments, their illocutionary force (their point, i.e. informing and requesting, respectively) is not affected by such change;
2. the semantics of the acts that fall in this category (e.g. *propose*) is slightly changed when they are described in terms of commitments (for instance, a *propose* act is not defined as informing about one's intentions to perform a certain action, but as creating a proposal of a commitment to such action);
3. we put into this category those acts, like *request-when*, that do not express an illocutionary force, but a compound of illocutionary force and content; we suggest a way to redefine such acts (e.g. we define a *request-when* act as a *request* act with a temporal conditional content);
4. this last category is comprised of those acts, like *confirm* and *disconfirm*, that are not considered necessary in an approach which does not take mental states into account; enriching our model to include such acts is beyond the scope of this work.

This paper is organized as follows: Section 2 provides the formal apparatus our model is based upon; Section 3 illustrates a way to formalize commitments in a multiagent system; Section 4 defines FIPA communicative acts belonging to the first three categories above in terms of commitments; Section 5 finally draws our conclusions and illustrates the future directions of this work.

2   The Formal Model

As commitments deal with certain states of affairs that occur in time, we first need to provide some formal definitions about time, events, and actions. To do so, we provide new definitions which extend the temporal logic that is illustrated in [16] with a different notation to increase readability. Our starting point is $CTL^{\pm}$, a temporal language close to CTL*, which is a branching temporal logic including only future-directed temporal operators [1]. Past-directed operators do not increase the logic's expressiveness [8], but nevertheless they allow us to express some properties of computational systems in a far more succinct way [11]. In $CTL^{\pm}$, time is assumed to be discrete, with no start or end point, and branching only in the future. In the literature we can find temporal logic proposals that involve branching also in the past [14], but we prefer to rely on the idea of "historical necessity" [15], according to which agents have no possibility of changing the past, so that they are enabled to reason about alternatives or indeterminacy only with respect to the future.

2.1   The Syntax

We call *sort set* a finite, nonempty set of elements, called *sorts*; a finite, possibly empty sequence of sorts is called a prototype. A $CTL^{\pm}$ language is a sextuple

$\langle \Sigma, V, C, \Xi, \Pi, \theta \rangle$, where Σ is a sort set, V is a denumerable set of (individual) variables, C is an arbitrary set of (individual) constants, Ξ is an arbitrary set of functors, Π is an arbitrary set of predicates, and θ is a function that assigns a sort to every variable and every constant, and a prototype to every functor and every predicate. The set V of variables includes denumerable many variables for every sort.

For every sort σ, we define the set T_σ of *terms* of sort σ as follows:

- $x \in T_\sigma$ if $x \in V$ and $\theta(x) = \sigma$;
- $a \in T_\sigma$ if $a \in C$ and $\theta(a) = \sigma$;
- $f(t_1, ..., t_n) \in T_\sigma$ if $f \in \Xi$ and
  $\theta(f) = \langle \sigma, \theta(t_1), ..., \theta(t_n) \rangle$;
- nothing else belongs to T_σ.

The set A of *atomic formulae* is defined as follows:

- $(t_1 = t_2) \in A$ if $t_1, t_2 \in T_s$ for some $s \in \Sigma$;
- $P(t_1, ..., t_n) \in A$ if $P \in \Pi$, $\theta(P) = \langle \sigma_1, ..., \sigma_n \rangle$ and
  $t_i \in T_{\sigma_i}$ for $1 \le i \le n$;
- nothing else belongs to A.

The set Φ of CTL$^\pm$ *formulae* is such that:

- $A \subseteq \Phi$;
- $\neg\phi \in \Phi$ if $\phi \in \Phi$;
- $(\phi \wedge \psi) \in \Phi$ if $\phi, \psi \in \Phi$;
- $\forall x \phi \in \Phi$ if $x \in V$ and $\phi \in \Phi$;
- $\mathsf{Next}\phi$, $\mathsf{Pre}\phi \in \Phi$ if $\phi \in \Phi$;
- $(\phi\mathsf{Until}\psi)$, $(\phi\mathsf{Since}\psi) \in \Phi$ if $\phi, \psi \in \Phi$;
- $\mathsf{A}\phi$ if $\phi \in \Phi$;
- nothing else belongs to Φ.

The temporal operators Next (at the next state), Pre (at the previous state), Until, Since, and A (on all paths), are primitive. The formulae *true, false*, $(\phi \vee \psi)$, $(\phi \rightarrow \psi)$, $(\phi \leftrightarrow \psi)$, and $\exists x \phi$ respectively abbreviate $\forall x(x = x)$, $\neg true$, $\neg(\neg\phi \wedge \neg\psi)$, $(\neg\phi \vee \psi)$, $((\phi \rightarrow \psi) \wedge (\psi \rightarrow \phi))$, and $\neg\forall x\neg\phi$. As usual, $\phi[t/x]$ denotes the result of replacing all free occurrences of variable x in ϕ with term t. Formula $\mathsf{E}\phi$ abbreviates $\neg\mathsf{A}\neg\phi$. We also introduce these temporal operators, $\mathsf{SomeFut}$ (sometimes in the future), $\mathsf{SomePast}$ (sometimes in the past), AlwFut (always in the future), $\mathsf{AlwPast}$ (always in the past), Some (sometimes), and Alw (always) as abbreviations, as follows:

$\mathsf{SomeFut}\phi =_{def} true\mathsf{Until}\phi$; $\mathsf{SomePast}\phi =_{def} true\mathsf{Since}\phi$;
$\mathsf{AlwFut}\phi =_{def} \neg\mathsf{SomeFut}\neg\phi$; $\mathsf{AlwPast}\phi =_{def} \neg\mathsf{SomePast}\neg\phi$;
$\mathsf{Some}\phi =_{def} \mathsf{SomeFut}\phi \wedge \mathsf{SomePast}\phi$;
$\mathsf{Alw}\phi =_{def} \mathsf{AlwFut}\phi \wedge \mathsf{AlwPast}\phi$.

2.2   The Semantics

A CTL$^\pm$ frame is a structure $F = \langle S, \pi \rangle$, where S is a set of states, and $\pi : S \to S$ is an injective function that associates to every state a unique predecessor. Function π is such that every state is the predecessor of at least one state. A *path* in F is an infinite sequence $p = \langle p_0, ..., p_n, ... \rangle$ of states, in which every element p_n of the sequence is the predecessor of p_{n+1} in F. The subsequence of p starting from element p_n is itself a path, which we denote with p^n; for every $n > 0$, we say that p^n is a *subpath* of p.

A *multidomain* $D = \{D_\sigma\}_{\sigma \in \Sigma}$ is a collection of mutually disjoint, nonempty domains of individuals. A *model* for CTL$^\pm$ is a triple $M = \langle F, D, i \rangle$, where F is a CTL$^\pm$ frame, D is a multidomain, and i is an interpretation function assigning:

- an individual $i(c) \in D_{\theta(c)}$ to every constant c;
- a function $i(s, f) : D_{\sigma_1} \times ... \times D_{\sigma_n} \to D_\sigma$ to every state s and every function f such that $\theta(f) = \langle \sigma, \sigma_1, ..., \sigma_n \rangle$;
- a relation $i(s, P) \subseteq D_{\sigma_1} \times ... \times D_{\sigma_n}$ to every state s and every predicate P such that $\theta(P) = \langle \sigma_1, ..., \sigma_n \rangle$.

An assignment of individuals to variables is a function $v : V \to D$ such that $v(x) \in D_{\theta(x)}$. Given assignment v, an assignment v' is an *x-variant* of v ($v \approx_x v'$, in symbols) if $v(y) = v'(y)$ for all $y \neq x$. The denotation of term t under an assignment v is defined as follows:

- $\delta_{M,v}(t) = v(t)$ if $t \in V$;
- $\delta_{M,v}(t) = i(t)$ if $t \in C$;
- $\delta_{M,v}(f(t_1, ..., t_n)) = i(s, f)(\delta_{M,v}(t_1), ..., \delta_{M,v}(t_n))$.

Denotations do not depend on paths, so that constants are rigid.

Let us define the conditions under which a formula is true in model M on path p under assignment v:

$M, p, v \models (t_1 = t_2)$ iff $\delta_{M,v}(t_1) = \delta_{M,v}(t_2)$;

$M, p, v \models P(t_1, ..., t_n)$ iff $\langle \delta_{M,v}(t_1), ..., \delta_{M,v}(t_n) \rangle \in i(p_0, P)$;

$M, p, v \models \neg \phi$ iff   not $M, p, v \models \phi$;

$M, p, v \models (\phi \wedge \psi)$ iff $M, p, v \models \phi$ and $M, p, v \models \psi$;

$M, p, v \models \forall x \phi$ iff $M, p, v' \models \phi$ for all v' such that $v \approx_x v'$;

$M, p, v \models \mathsf{Next}\ \phi$ iff $M, p^1, v \models \phi$;

$M, p, v \models \mathsf{Pre}\ \phi$ iff   for some path q, $q^1 = p$ and $M, q, v \models \phi$;

$M, p, v \models (\phi\ \mathsf{Until}\ \psi)$ iff   for some n, $M, p^n, v \models \psi$ and
                              for all m s.t. $0 \leq m \leq n$, $M, p^m, v \models \phi$;

$M, p, v \models (\phi\ \mathsf{Since}\ \psi)$ iff   for some path q and for some n, $q^n = p$ and
                              $M, q \models \psi$ and for all m s.t. $0 \leq m \leq n$, $M, q^m \models \phi$;

$M, p, v \models \mathsf{A}\phi$ iff   for all q s.t. $q_0 = p_0$, $M, q, v \models \phi$.

Please note that the definitions of Until and Since deviate from the classical ones, in that they are inclusive of both states at the boundaries of the relevant interval. A formula is true in model M on path p if it is true in M on path p under all assignments:

$M, p \models \phi$ iff $M, p, v \models \phi$ for all v.

If ϕ is a closed formula (i.e. it contains no free occurrences of variables), then its truth value does not depend on variable assignments. Thus, ϕ is true in M on p under v if, and only if, it is true in M on p. Finally, a formula is valid if it is true on all paths of every model:

$$\models \phi$$

if and only if $M, p \models \phi$ for all models M and all paths p in the frame of M.

3   Commitments and Their Manipulation

To define a logic of commitments we have to deal with agents, typed events that agents bring about, and sentences of a content language (CL) that are the content of their commitments. Thus, we need to introduce the relevant sorts in our language.

3.1   Events and Actions

We assume that the set Σ of CTL$^{\pm}$ sorts contains at least the elements *event* (the sort of events), *agent* (the sort of agents), *eventtype* (the sort of event types), and *sentence* (the sort of CL sentences), and that the set P of predicates contains at least the elements *Happ*, *Actor*, *Type*, *Comm*, and *Prec*. To indicate that predicate *Happ*'s prototype is $\theta(Happ) = \langle event \rangle$, we write $Happ(event)$, and we use a similar notation for the other predicates:

- *Actor(event,agent)*;
- *Type(event,eventtype)*;
- *Comm(event,agent,agent,sentence)*;
- *Prec(event,agent,agent,sentence)*.

Intuitively, $Happ(e)$ means that event e has just happened, $Actor(e, x)$ means that event e, if it happened at all, has been brought about by agent x (we also say that x is the actor of e), and $Type(e, t)$ means that e is an event of type t. We assume that an event cannot happen more than once on the same path. This assumption is captured by the following event uniqueness axiom:

(EU) $Happ(e) \rightarrow \mathsf{PreAlwPast} \neg Happ(e) \wedge \mathsf{ANextAlwFut} \neg Happ(e)$.

Here we define the predicate *Done(event,agent,eventtype)*:

(DD) $Done(e, x, t) =_{def} Happ(e) \wedge Actor(e, x) \wedge Type(e, t)$.

The intuitive meaning of $Done(e, x, t)$ is that agent x has just brought about an event e of type t, or, that x has performed an action e of type t. We thus define actions as events that have an actor.

3.2   Commitments and Precommitments

In our approach, we analytically define communicative acts (a special type of actions) in terms of changes at the level of social relations among agents. We take commitment to be a primitive concept that underlies the social structure of a multi-agent system, and describe communicative acts as actions brought about by an agent to affect the network of commitments that binds it to other agents. We thus introduce the *Comm* predicate: to state that a commitment holds at a state in which agent x (the debtor) is bound, relative to agent y (the creditor), to the fact that some proposition (the content) is true, we write

$$M, p, v \models Comm(e, x, y, s).$$

The first argument of the *Comm* predicate, e, is the event that has brought about the state of affairs in which the commitment holds. The content of the commitment is a formula of a content language represented as a first-order term s of sort *sentence*, which is the fourth parameter of the *Comm* predicate. The semantics of CL sentences is provided by translating them into formulae of Φ. More formally, we define a function $\lfloor \ \rfloor : D_{sentence} \rightarrow \Phi$ such that, given a *sentence term* s, $\lfloor s \rfloor$ is the Φ formula it corresponds to. We also introduce a function $\lceil \ \rceil : \Phi \rightarrow D_{sentence}$ which, given a formula $\phi \in \Phi$, returns the relevant term $\lceil \phi \rceil \in D_{sentence}$.

Commitments that have been proposed but not yet accepted nor rejected are defined as *precommitments*. They are represented in the same way as commitments: the following formula holds when e has brought about a precommitment between two agents (the potential debtor x and the potential creditor y) to the truth of a sentence represented by s:

$$M, p, v \models Prec(e, x, y, s).$$

In our approach, agent communication is brought about by means of message exchanges that under specific conditions count as commitment manipulation actions. We suppose that the set $D_{eventtype}$ contains the following event types, corresponding to five basic actions for manipulating commitments:

1. make-commitment: $mc(x, y, s)$;
2. make-precommitment: $mp(x, y, s)$;
3. cancel-commitment: $cc(e, x, y, s)$;
4. cancel-precommitment: $cp(e, x, y, s)$;
5. accept-precommitment: $ap(e, x, y, s)$.

The mc and mp event types have three parameters, x, y, and s, that correspond to the debtor, the creditor, and the content of the (pre)commitment that is being created. The cc, cp, and ap event types have one more parameter e, that refers to the event that has brought about the (pre)commitment that is being cancelled or accepted. These are types of actions that agents can perform. For instance, to state that agent x has brought about an event e of making a commitment towards agent y with content s, we write as follows:

$M, p, v \models Done(e, x, mc(x, y, s))$.

We may use the 'm-dash' character to express existential quantification, as follows:

$Done(e, -, t) =_{def} \exists x Done(e, x, t)$;
$Done(-, -, t) =_{def} \exists e \exists x Done(e, x, t)$;
$Done(e, -, -)$ corresponds to the primitive $Happ(e)$.

Here are the axioms that describe the above mentioned types of commitment manipulation events in terms of their constitutive effects, that is, the state of affairs that are the case after a token of the given event type is performed.

These axioms feature the Z temporal operator, which represents the intuitive concept of "until and no longer" and is defined as follows:

ϕ Z $\psi =_{def} \phi$ WeakUntil$\psi \wedge$ AlwFut$(\psi \rightarrow$ NextAlwFut$\neg\phi)$,
where
ϕ WeakUntil $\psi =_{def}$ AlwFut $\phi \vee \phi$ Until ψ.

ϕ Z ψ is true if and only if in the future ψ never becomes true and ϕ is always true, or ϕ is true until ψ eventually becomes true and since then ϕ is no longer true.

(MC) $Done(e, -, mc(x, y, s)) \rightarrow$
        A $(Comm(e, x, y, s)$ Z $Done(-, -, cc(e, x, y, s)))$;
(MP) $Done(e, -, mp(x, y, s)) \rightarrow$
        A $(Prec(e, x, y, s)$ Z $(Done(-, -, ap(e, x, y, s)) \vee$
                                $Done(-, -, cp(e, x, y, s))))$;
(AP) $Done(e', -, ap(e, x, y, s)) \rightarrow$
        A$(Comm(e', x, y, s)$ Z $Done(-, -, cc(e', x, y, s)))$.

Axiom MC (Make Commitment) states that if an agent (not necessarily x or y) performs an action of making a commitment with x as the debtor, y as the creditor, and s as the content, then on all paths x is committed, relative to y, to the truth of s, until an agent possibly cancels such a commitment, after which the commitment no longer exists. Axiom MP (Make Precommitment) is analogous to MC, and it deals with the creation of a precommitment. Axiom AP (Accept Precommitment) entails that if an agent performs the action of accepting a precommitment brought about by event e with x, y, and s respectively as debtor, creditor, and content, then such acceptance brings about on all paths a commitment of x, relative to y, to the truth of s, which will hold until it is possibly cancelled. There are no specific axioms for the actions of cancelling a precommitment (cp) or a commitment (cc), because the analytical effects of these commitment manipulations are already illustrated in the axioms dealing with other actions.

Commitments are said to be *fulfilled* and *violated* when their content is *settled true* and *false*, respectively. Before dealing with the truth conditions of formulae, we must take the following considerations into account. Firstly, the truth of a sentence including temporal qualifications at a given state (namely, the *point of reference* [10]) can be evaluated only if we know the state at which the sentence has been uttered (the *point of speech*). Moreover, branching time brings in a phenomenon known as *contingent future*, which means that at a given point of reference it may be still undetermined if a sentence is going to be true or false (e.g., "it will rain until 6:00", stated while it is raining at 4:00). In such a case, a formula is said to be *unsettled*, and the relevant commitment is *pending*. The truth conditions of CL sentences are thus formalized as follows:

(DT) $True(e, s) =_{def}$ ASomePast$(Happ(e) \land \lfloor s \rfloor)$,
(DF) $False(e, s) =_{def}$ ASomePast$(Happ(e) \land \neg \lfloor s \rfloor)$,
(DU) $Unset(e, s) =_{def}$ ASomePast$Happ(e) \land \neg True(e, s) \land \neg False(e, s)$.

The truth conditions of sentence s are given with respect to an event e, which does not necessarily correspond to the event of uttering s. As event e is used to set a well-defined temporal reference by which we can evaluate the truth of s, all these definitions rely on the event uniqueness axiom. We then have the following definitions:

(DL) $Fulf(e, x, y, s) =_{def} Comm(e, x, y, s) \land True(e, s)$,
(DV) $Viol(e, x, y, s) =_{def} Comm(e, x, y, s) \land False(e, s)$,
(DP) $Pend(e, x, y, s) =_{def} Comm(e, x, y, s) \land Unset(e, s)$.

3.3   Action Expressions

So far, we have dealt with commitments with a generic content term s, but we may want to focus on more specific contents, dealing with future actions performed by agents. To do so, let us first introduce some derived temporal operators, which will enable us to write more synthetic formulae:

ϕ Before ψ $=_{def}$ $\neg(\neg\phi$ WeakUntil $\psi)$;
ϕ AsSoonAs ψ $=_{def}$ $(\psi \rightarrow \phi)$ WeakUntil ψ.

Formula ϕ AsSoonAs ψ holds when at the first state at which ψ is true, also ϕ is the case. In other words, ϕ is true as soon as ψ is (possibly) true. We define a subdomain $D_{action} \subseteq D_{sentence}$ of *action expressions*, that is, terms corresponding to a particular subset of CL sentences. We have identified two action expression schemata, which are expressive enough to allow for a vast range of formulae dealing with action performances. Let d, s_λ, s_ω, and s_χ be terms of $D_{sentence}$. In particular, let d correspond to a formula representing the performance of an action of a certain type by an agent: $\lfloor d \rfloor = Done(-, t_1, t_2)$, where $t_1 \in T_{agent}$ and $t_2 \in T_{eventtype}$. We then define the first action expression schema $\alpha_\forall$ as follows:

$\alpha_\forall = [s_\lambda, s_\omega | s_\chi]d$
$\lfloor \alpha_\forall \rfloor = ((\lfloor s_\chi \rfloor \rightarrow \lfloor d \rfloor)$WeakUntil$\lfloor s_\omega \rfloor)$AsSoonAs$\lfloor s_\lambda \rfloor$.

We have $M, p, v \models \lfloor \alpha_\forall \rfloor$ if and only if in the sequence of states on path p which begins at the first occurrence of $\lfloor s_\lambda \rfloor$ and ends at the subsequent state at which $\lfloor s_\omega \rfloor$ is the case, every time $\lfloor s_\chi \rfloor$ holds, then $\lfloor d \rfloor$ is true. The notation with square brackets has already been adopted in [18], and it was originally inspired by [9]. We define the other action expression schema, $\alpha_\exists$, as follows:

$$\alpha_\exists = \langle s_\lambda, s_\omega | s_\chi \rangle d$$
$$\lfloor \alpha_\exists \rfloor = ((\lfloor s_\chi \rfloor \text{Before} \lfloor s_\omega \rfloor) \to ((\lfloor s_\chi \rfloor \wedge \lfloor d \rfloor) \text{Before} \lfloor s_\omega \rfloor)) \ \text{AsSoonAs} \ \lfloor s_\lambda \rfloor.$$

If $\alpha_\forall$ is loosely based on the idea of universal quantification, $\alpha_\exists$ deals with existential quantification, in that $\lfloor \alpha_\exists \rfloor$ is true on a path where, in the interval identified by the subsequent occurrences of $\lfloor s_\lambda \rfloor$ and $\lfloor s_\omega \rfloor$, $\lfloor d \rfloor$ is true at a state at which $\lfloor s_\chi \rfloor$ holds, if it is ever the case. We will refer to a generic action expression, whether universal or existential, by α. Given an action expression α, we denote with $agent(\alpha)$ the agent that is designated as the actor of the action to be performed.

4   Communicative Acts

An institutional action is defined within the context of an artificial institution, a set of shared rules that regulate the management of a fragment of social reality [13,7], including multiagent systems. It is performed through the execution of some lower level act that *conventionally* counts as a performance of the institutional action; an example is provided by communicative acts, which are performed by executing lower level acts of message exchange. Institutional actions thus require a set of conventions for their execution. We adopt the view according to which the commitment manipulation actions described in the previous section are institutional actions that are conventionally realized by the exchange of messages.

4.1   Basic Communicative Acts

In our approach, we call *basic* those communicative acts that map directly onto a commitment manipulation action. For every kind of message we introduce a functor that specifies the type of the action that an agent performs when exchanging such a message. This approach is illustrated by the following example. Suppose that a message is sent to agent y to inform y that $\lfloor s \rfloor$ is the case. The exchange of such a message is an event of type $inform(y, s)$, where $inform$ is a two-place functor denoting the type of the message, y denotes the receiver of the message, and s is its content. When event e is an exchange of a message of type $inform$ and content s, sent by agent x to agent y, the following formula holds:

$Done(e, x, inform(y, s))$.

This event, under given conditions which we illustrate later on, implies the performance of a commitment manipulation action. The semantics of the message is defined as the effect that exchanging such a message has on the network of commitments binding the sender and the receiver. The correspondence between the message exchange event type and the commitment manipulation action type relies on a relation that is formally described by the formula below,

$Conv(x, t, t')$,

which means that an action of type t performed by agent x corresponds to an action of type t' in accordance to a convention established in the communication framework. Here we define a basic set of communicative acts by means of which agents carry out the commitment manipulation actions. Each communicative act is accompanied by a possibly empty set of conditions that must hold to make the message exchange count as a commitment manipulation. These conditions deal with the agent designated to perform an action (e.g., if x makes a request to y, y must be the performer of the requested action), with the creators of precommitments (e.g., if x accepts a proposal by exchanging a message with y, y must be the issuer of such proposal), and with some presuppositions about the existence of precommitments (i.e., x cannot reject a proposal that has not been made). This is formally stated by the following axiom:

(CO) $Done(e, x, t) \wedge Conv(x, t, t') \wedge \Psi \rightarrow Done(e, x, t')$,

where Ψ is to be understood as the conjunction of the formulae indicated in the fourth column of the table in Figure 1 for each communicative act type. A comparison between our approach and another work dealing with the notion of convention [6] can be found in [17].

message type	$Conv(x,t,t')$		additional conditions
	t	t'	
inform	$inform(y,s)$	$mc(x,y,s)$	
request	$request(y, a)$	$mp(y,x,a)$	$y=agent(a)$
agree	$agree(y,(e,x,y,a))$	$ap(e,x,y,a)$	$x=agent(a)$ $Actor(e,y)$ Pre $Prec(e,x,y,a)$
propose	$propose(y,a)$	$mp(x,y,a)$	$x=agent(a)$
accept-proposal	$accept$-$proposal(y,(e,y,x,a))$	$ap(e,y,x,a)$	$y=agent(a)$ $Actor(e,y)$ Pre $Prec(e,y,x,a)$
refuse	$refuse(y,(e,x,y,a))$	$cp(e,x,y,a)$	$x=agent(a)$ $Actor(e,y)$ Pre $Prec(e,x,y,a)$
reject-proposal	$reject$-$proposal(y,(e,y,x,a))$	$cp(e,y,x,a)$	$y=agent(a)$ $Actor(e,y)$ Pre $Prec(e,y,x,a)$
cancel	$cancel(y,(e,y,x,a))$	$cc(e,y,x,a)$	$y=agent(a)$ Pre $Comm(e,y,x,a)$

Fig. 1. FIPA communicative acts as conventions to perform commitment manipulations

4.2   Derived Communicative Acts

Derived communicative acts are defined in terms of the above mentioned basic communicative acts. We can distinguish two kinds of derivation. In the case of the *request-when* and *request-whenever* acts, we deal with derivation by *content specialization*, in that we define them as a *request* act with a specialized content. We thus part from FIPA's specifications, which define these acts in terms of an inform act. "Request-when allows an agent to inform another agent that a certain action should be performed as soon as a given precondition... becomes true [3]." A very similar description is provided for the request-whenever act. We avoid defining a request-like act in terms of a basic act of informing since we keep in mind a fundamental concept from Speech Act Theory (i.e. the *direction of fit* [12]), according to which a request has a *world-to-word* direction (we want the world to be like what we ask) while an inform act has a *word-to-world* direction (what we state must reflect the current state of affairs). Besides, we think that these definitions clash with the fact that the simple request is considered as a primitive act in FIPA's specification. If specialized requests can be defined in terms of an inform act, we should also be able to define the simple request in such terms. In our model, the *request-when* and *request-whenever* acts are formally defined as follows:

$$request\text{-}when(y, t_1, s_1) =_{def} request(y, \alpha_1),$$
$$\alpha_1 = \langle \lceil true \rceil, s_1 | s_1 \rangle \lceil Done(-, y, t_1) \rceil;$$
$$request\text{-}whenever(y, t_2, s_2) =_{def} request(y, \alpha_2),$$
$$\alpha_2 = [\lceil true \rceil, \lceil false \rceil | s_2] \lceil Done(-, y, t_2) \rceil.$$

As it can be easily shown that

$$\lfloor \langle \lceil true \rceil, s_1 | s_1 \rangle \lceil Done(-, y, t_1) \rceil \rfloor \leftrightarrow Done(-, y, t_1) \text{ AsSoonAs } \lfloor s_1 \rfloor,$$

by performing a message exchange of type *request-when*(y, t_1, s_1), an agent requests y to perform an act of type t_1 as soon as $\lfloor s_1 \rfloor$ holds. Similarly, as we have

$$\lfloor [\lceil true \rceil, \lceil false \rceil | s_2] \lceil Done(-, y, t_2) \rceil \rfloor \leftrightarrow \text{AlwFut}(\lfloor s_2 \rfloor \rightarrow Done(-, y, t_2)),$$

a *request-whenever*(y, t_2, s_2) act consists of a request to y to perform a t_2 action every time $\lfloor s_2 \rfloor$ is the case.

Following the FIPA specifications, we define the *inform-if* act as a 'macro' act to inform whether a sentence is true or not. In this case, we deal with derivation by *macro composition*, as we define an *inform-if* act as a disjunction of mutually exclusive *inform* acts, as follows.

$$Done(e, x, inform\text{-}if(y, s)) =_{def}$$
$$Done(e, x, inform(y, s)) \veebar Done(e, x, inform(y, \lceil \neg \lfloor s \rfloor \rceil)),$$

where $\phi \veebar \psi =_{def} (\phi \vee \psi) \wedge \neg(\phi \wedge \psi)$. We then define a *query-if* act by content specification as a *request* for an *inform-if* act, as follows:

$$Done(e, x, query\text{-}if(y, s)) =_{def} Done(e, x, request(y, \alpha)),$$
$$\alpha = \langle \lceil true \rceil, \lceil false \rceil | \lceil true \rceil \rangle \lceil Done(-, y, inform\text{-}if(x, s)) \rceil,$$

where the temporal qualification $\langle \lceil true \rceil, \lceil false \rceil | \lceil true \rceil \rangle \phi$, which is equivalent to SomeFutϕ, may be specified in order to introduce deadlines for the *inform-if* act, as we have $\langle \lceil true \rceil, \lceil \psi \rceil | \lceil true \rceil \rangle \phi \leftrightarrow \phi$ Before ψ.

Failure and *not-understood* are two more acts that can be defined as *inform* acts with a specific content, expressed in terms of predicates dealing with *attempts* and *message decoding* whose definition lies beyond the scope of this work.

4.3   Communicative Acts with Referential Operators

Following FIPA's specifications [5], we introduce three *referential operators*, *any*, *iota*, and *all*, to create referential terms like $(any\ x\ f)$, $(iota\ x\ f)$, and $(all\ x\ f)$ (with $f \in D_{sentence}$) which are to be read as "any x", "the x", and "all the x" such that $\lfloor f \rfloor$ is true . We will not provide a formal definition of such terms, in that in our approach they are used only as a notation to distinguish one referential act from another. We assume that there exists a sort *URI* of *uniform resource identifiers*, which identify every object in multidomain D with a unique name, and a function $uri : D \rightarrow D_{URI}$ that returns the URI of every element in D. URIs are assumed to be self-referential. Given a referential term r, we define the *inform-ref* act as a specialization of an *inform* act, as follows:

$$inform\text{-}ref(y, r) =_{def} inform(y, s),$$

where s corresponds to a specific formula in accordance with r, as follows:

if $r = (any\ x\ f)$, then
$\lfloor s \rfloor = \lfloor f \rfloor [k/x] \wedge uri(k) = n;$
if $r = (the\ x\ f)$, then
$\lfloor s \rfloor = \lfloor f \rfloor [k/x] \wedge uri(k) = n \wedge \forall z(\lfloor f \rfloor [z/x] \rightarrow z = k);$
if $r = (all\ x\ f)$, then
$\lfloor s \rfloor = \bigwedge_i (\lfloor f \rfloor [k_i/x] \wedge (uri(k_i) = n_i)) \wedge$
$\quad \forall z(\lfloor f \rfloor [z/x] \rightarrow \bigvee_i (z = k_i)).$

We then define the *query-ref* act as a *request* for an *inform-ref* act, as below:

$$Done(e, x, query\text{-}ref(y, r)) =_{def} Done(e, x, request(y, \alpha)),$$
$$\alpha = \lceil \mathsf{SomeFut} Done(-, y, inform\text{-}ref(x, r)) \rceil.$$

As stated before, we have that:

$$\mathsf{SomeFut}\phi \leftrightarrow \langle \lceil true \rceil, \lceil false \rceil | \lceil true \rceil \rangle \phi.$$

4.4   The Call for Proposal Act

Let us have a closer look at the logical model (and at the advantages of an approach based on commitments rather than on mental states) while illustrating the *cfp* (call for proposal) act. Like FIPA, we define a *cfp* act as a *query-ref* act with a specific content, as follows:

$$Done(e, x, cfp(y, \tau)) =_{def} Done(e, x, query\text{-}ref(y, any\ w\ \alpha)),$$
$$\alpha = \langle \lceil Done(-, x, pay(y, w)) \rceil, \lceil Deadline \rceil | \lceil true \rceil \rangle \lceil Done(-, y, \tau) \rceil.$$

Considering also the *query-ref* act definition, we can see that a *cfp* act boils down to x asking y what is the sum w that x has to pay to y to have service τ done by y before a certain deadline (the $Done(-, x, pay(y, w))$ formula can be easily generalized or adapted to different application domains). Let us analyze how the commitments between two agents exchanging such a message evolve on a path p of a model M under an assignment v:

1. $M, p, v \models Done(e, x, cfp(y, \tau))$ (hypothesis)
2. $M, p, v \models Done(e, x, query\text{-}ref(y, any\ w\ \alpha))$ (1, *cfp* def)
3. $M, p, v \models Done(e, x, request(y, \alpha'))$ (2, *query-ref* def)
3°. $\lfloor \alpha' \rfloor = \mathsf{SomeFut}Done(-, y, inform\text{-}ref(x, any\ w\ \alpha))$
4. $M, p, v \models Done(e, x, mp(e, y, x, \alpha'))$ (3, CO)
5. $M, p, v \models Prec(e, y, x, \alpha')$ (4, MP)

A *cfp* act to y by x thus leads to the creation of a precommitment of y towards x to perform an *inform-ref* act (we could also specify a deadline for such performance). Let us first suppose that y refuses such a precommitment (on a path p' that is a subpath of p, $\exists n(p' = p^n)$):

6'. $M, p', v \models Done(e', y, refuse(x, (e, y, x, \alpha')))$ (hyp)
7'. $M, p', v \models Done(e', y, cp(e, y, x, \alpha'))$ (6', CO)
8'. $M, p', v \models \mathsf{AAlwFut}\neg Prec(e, y, x, \alpha')$ (7', MP)

As a result, the call for proposal has been turned down, and the relevant precommitment does not exist anymore. Let us show an alternative course of events on another subpath p'':

6''. $M, p'', v \models Done(e'', y, agree(x, (e, y, x, \alpha')))$ (hyp)
7''. $M, p'', v \models Done(e'', y, ap(e, y, x, \alpha'))$ (6'', CO)
8''. $M, p'', v \models \neg Prec(e, y, x, \alpha') \wedge Comm(e'', y, x, \alpha')$ (7'', AP)

An *agree* act by y turns the precommitment into a commitment. Let us suppose that later on, on a subpath p''' ($\exists m(p''' = p''^m)$), y informs x about the sum k that y requires for service τ (we omit the *uri* function in the content of the *inform* message):

9''. $M, p''', v \models Done(e''', y, inform(x, \lceil \lfloor \alpha \rfloor [k/w] \rceil))$ (hyp)
10''. $M, p''', v \models Done(e''', y, inform\text{-}ref(x, any\ w\ \alpha))$ (9'', *inform-ref* def)
11''. $M, p''', v \models \mathsf{ASomePast}(Happ(e'') \wedge \lfloor \alpha' \rfloor)$ (3°, 6'', 10'')
12''. $M, p''', v \models True(e'', \alpha')$ (11'', DT)
13''. $M, p''', v \models Fulf(e'', y, x, \alpha')$ (8'', 12'', DL)

By performing an *inform-ref*, y fulfills a commitment, but such act, as it consists of an *inform* message exchange, also creates another commitment, as follows:

14''. $M, p''', v \models Done(e''', y, mc(y, x, \lceil \lfloor \alpha \rfloor [k/w] \rceil))$ (9'', CO)
15''. $M, p''', v \models Comm(e''', y, x, \lceil \lfloor \alpha \rfloor [k/w] \rceil)$ (14'', MC)

Agent y is thus committed to provide service τ before a specific deadline as soon as x pays k.

5 Conclusions and Future Work

The *cfp* example illustrates the advantages of our approach with respect to FIPA's. The FIPA standard does not provide any mechanism to verify the fulfillment of the agents' commitments, if not relying on *inform* messages by the agents themselves, as in the FIPA Contract Net protocol [4]. Such *inform* acts do not entail the completion of a requested task, but provide only a snapshot of some of the *beliefs* of the messages' sender. Such beliefs reflect an actual state of affairs in which the task has been carried out only under specific assumptions about the agents' internal architecture, which we cannot afford if we aim at creating *open* multiagent systems. On the contrary, in our model every message brings about changes in the social reality that underlies the multiagent system: precommitments are created, cancelled, turned into commitments throughout the message exchange process. As (pre)commitments are public and reflect an objective state of affairs between agents, our model naturally provides a method to verify whether every agent has fulfilled its own duties.

In this work, we have treated referential operators simply as a matter of notation, making *inform-ref*, *query-ref*, and *cfp* acts rely on fairly complex content language sentences. We think that this solution may be changed in the future, when we tackle the *proxy* and *propagate* acts, whose definition seems to require some further investigation about the topic of *reference*.

References

1. E. A. Emerson. Temporal and modal logic. In J. van Leeuwen, editor, *Handbook of Theoretical Computer Science*, volume B, chapter 16, pages 995–1072. MIT Press, Cambridge, MA, 1990.
2. FIPA. Agent Communication Language Specifications. Specification, Foundation for Intelligent Physical Agents, http://www.fipa.org/repository/aclspecs.html, 2002.
3. FIPA. Communicative Act Library Specification. Specification, Foundation for Intelligent Physical Agents, http://www.fipa.org/specs/fipa00037/, 2002.
4. FIPA. FIPA Contract Net Interaction Protocol Specification. Specification, Foundation for Intelligent Physical Agents, http://www.fipa.org/specs/fipa00029/, 2002.
5. FIPA. FIPA SL Content Language Specification. Specification, Foundation for Intelligent Physical Agents, http://www.fipa.org/specs/fipa00008/, 2002.
6. A. Jones and X. Parent. Conventional signalling acts and conversation. In F. Dignum, editor, *Advances in Agent Communication, International Workshop on Agent Communication Languages, ACL 2003, Melbourne, Australia, July 14, 2003*, volume 2922 of *Lecture Notes in Computer Science*. Springer, 2004.
7. A. Jones and M. J. Sergot. A formal characterisation of institutionalised power. *Journal of the IGPL*, 4(3):429–445, 1996.
8. F. Laroussinie and P. Schnoebelen. A hierarchy of temporal logics with past. *Theoretical Computer Science*, 148(2):303–324, 1995.
9. A. U. Mallya, P. Yolum, and M. P. Singh. Resolving commitments among autonomous agents. In F. Dignum, editor, *Advances in Agent Communication, Proceedings of the Interbational Workshop on Agent Communication Languages (ACL 2003)*, volume 2922 of *Lecture Notes in Artificial Intelligence*, pages 166–182. Springer, 2004.

10. H. Reichenbach. *Elements of Symbolic Logic*. MacMillan, New York, NY, 1947.
11. M. Reynolds. More past glories. In *Proceedings of the 15th Annual IEEE Symposium on Logic in Computer Science (LICS'00)*, pages 229–240. IEEE Comp. Soc. Press, 2000.
12. J. R. Searle. *Speech Acts*. Cambridge University Press, Cambridge, UK, 1969.
13. J. R. Searle. *The construction of social reality*. Free Press, New York, 1995.
14. C. Stirling. Modal and temporal logics. In S. Abramsky, D. Gabbay, and T. Maibaum, editors, *Handbook of Philosophical Logic, Volume 2*, pages 477–563. Oxford University Press, Oxford, England, 1992.
15. R. Thomason. Combinations of tense and modality. In D. Gabbay and F. Guenthner, editors, *Handbook of Philosophical Logic, Vol II: Extensions of Classical Logic*, pages 135–165. Reidel, Dordrecht, The Netherlands, 1984.
16. M. Verdicchio and M. Colombetti. A logical model of social commitment for agent communication. In J. S. Rosenschein, T. Sandholm, M. J. Wooldridge, and M. Yokoo, editors, *Proceedings of the 2nd International Joint Conference on Autonomous Agents and Multiagent Systems (AAMAS 03)*, pages 528–535. ACM Press, 2003.
17. M. Verdicchio and M. Colombetti. A logical model of social commitment for agent communication. In F. Dignum, editor, *Advances in Agent Communication, International Workshop on Agent Communication Languages, ACL 2003, Melbourne, Australia, July 14, 2003*, volume 2922 of *Lecture Notes in Computer Science*. Springer, 2004.
18. M. Verdicchio and M. Colombetti. Dealing with time in content language expressions. In R. M. van Eijk, M.-P. Huget, and F. Dignum, editors, *Agent Communication, International Workshop on Agent Communication, AC 2004, New York, NY, USA, July 19, 2004, Revised Selected and Invited Papers*, volume 3396 of *Lecture Notes in Computer Science*. Springer, 2005.

Integrating Social Commitment-Based Communication in Cognitive Agent Modeling

Philippe Pasquier[1] and Brahim Chaib-draa[2]

[1] AgentLab, University of Melbourne, Department of Information Systems, Australia
[2] DAMAS lab., Laval University, Computer Science Department, Canada
{pasquier, chaib}@iad.ift.ulaval.ca

Abstract. In this paper, we extend the classical BDI architecture for the treatment of social commitments based communication by: (1) linking social commitments and individual intentions, (2) providing a model of the cognitive aspect of communication pragmatics in order to automatize social commitment based communication. In particular, we introduce a general decision-making process leading to attitude change in the appropriate cases.

1 Introduction

Cognitive agent modelings rest on the isolation and formalization of private mental states such as beliefs, desires and intentions exemplified by the classic BDI [Beliefs, Desires and Intentions] model. However, social commitments as a way to capture interagent dependencies has founded improved agent communication frameworks.

In this paper, we try to narrow the gap between those two paradigms by proposing an extension of the classic BDI agent model (Section 2), enabling the resulting deliberative-normative agent to communicate using an agent communication language based on the manipulation of social commitments: the DIAlogues Games Agent Language (DIAGAL) (Section 3). This extension involves: refining intention typology, linking individual intention with social commitments (Section 4), and advancing a model of the cognitive aspects of pragmatics (Section 6) that leads to communication moves or attitude change (Section 5).

2 The Classic BDI Model

Various formulations of the BDI model can be found. The model has been expressed in multimodal logics [18,22], in first order specification languages [12] or in procedural/algorythmic notation [27, Chapter 4]. In this paper, we will focus on the procedural specifications.

BDI architecture rests on two main processes: deliberation and means-end reasoning. Deliberation is the process by which an agent generates its intentions on the basis of its beliefs and desires, while means-end reasoning consists in planning a sequence of actions to execute as an attempt at satisfying its intentions. The BDI control algorithm (presented in Figure 1) makes a compromise

F. Dignum, R. van Eijk, and R. Flores (Eds.): AC 2005/2006, LNAI 3859, pp. 76–92, 2006.

Procedure. BDICycle(B_0,I_0)

1: **Inputs:** B_0, set of initial beliefs;
$\quad\quad\quad\quad$ I_0, set of initially accepted intentions;
2: **Outputs:** *none*, this is not a function!
3: **Local:** $B := B_0$, object that store the agent's beliefs;
$\quad\quad\quad$ $I := I_0$, object that stores the agent's intentions;
$\quad\quad\quad$ D, object that stores the agent's desires;
$\quad\quad\quad$ List ρ, stores both internal and external percepts;
$\quad\quad\quad$ List $\pi := null$, current plan, sequence of actions;
4: **Body:**
5: **while** *true* **do**
6: $\quad$ Get new percepts ρ;
7: $\quad$ Update B on the basis of ρ;
8: $\quad$ **if** Reconsider(I,B) **then**
9: $\quad\quad$ $D :=$ Options(B,I);
10: $\quad\quad$ $I :=$ Deliberate(B,D,I); // deliberate if necessary
11: $\quad$ **end if**
12: $\quad$ **if** Empty(π) or Succeeded(I,B) or Impossible(I,B)) **then**
13: $\quad\quad$ $\pi :=$ Plan(B,I); // replan if necessary
14: $\quad$ **else**
15: $\quad\quad$ $\alpha :=$ Head(π);
16: $\quad\quad$ Execute(α); // execute an action
17: $\quad\quad$ $\pi :=$ Tail(π);
18: $\quad$ **end if**
19: **end while**

Fig. 1. BDI agent's control loop

between deliberation (a time consuming cognitive activity), means-end reasoning and acting activities through the Reconsider() function.

At each cycle of the algorithm, the BDI agent updates his beliefs according to its percepts (lines 6 and 7). If necessary (according to the boolean function Reconsider(), line 8), the agent (re)deliberates in order to update his desires and intentions (line 9 et 10). Then, if the current plan is empty or has become invalid or if the pursued intention has been achieved, has become impossible or has changed (line 11), the agent (re)plans (line 12). Otherwise (if all the preceding conditions are false), the agent executes an action from the current plan (lines 14-16). Notice that this action can be of a complex type.

As stated in [7], intentions are choices to which the agent commits. One of the main characteristics of individual intentions is that they are associated with what has been called an individual action commitment for which resources have been allocated [2,25]. It means that when an agent has accepted an intention, he is individually committed to achieving particular actions as an attempt to reach the wanted state (described by the intention). This individual commitment should not be confused with social commitments.

These individual commitments are not represented explicitly and it's the intention reconsideration process that ensures intentions' temporal persistence. The mechanism used by an agent in order to decide when and how to reject a formerly accepted intention is called *individual commitment strategies*. One usually distinguishes three main individual commitment strategies [18,22]:

- *Blind commitment (fanatical)*: agent continues to maintain intention until it has been achieved;
- *Single-minded commitment*: agent will continue to maintain intention until it has been achieved or it is impossible to achieve;
- *Open-minded commitment*: agent will maintain intention as long at it believes it is possible.

Communication in the BDI Model. In philosophy of language, Grice introduced the fundamental link that lies between intention and communication through the definition of non-natural meaning. This accounts for the fact that literal meaning of a statement does not cover its whole meaning. According to Levinson's formulation [13], non natural meaning can be defined as follows. The locutor A wanted to say z by uttering e, if and only if:

1. A has the intention that e yield to the effect z on B;
2. A has the intention that the previous intention will be achieved by B through its recognizing of it.

Intention is involved twice in that definition considering the locutor's prior intention as well as his communicative intention, i.e. that the interlocutor recognizes his prior intention and react cooperatively. Consequently, strong *cooperativity* and *sincerity* assumptions are assumed in agent models that use these mentalistic trends. For example, if the agent A wants to know if p holds and believes that B has these pieces of information, he will ask B and hope that B will recognize its intention and answer cooperatively and sincerely according to his own knowledge. Even for assertive speech acts, cooperativeness is present. For example, an assertion involves a belief change as a cooperative answer to it in a context where sincerity is trusted.

Furthermore, computational complexity of the multi-modal logics used for specifying speech-act based ACLs with mentalistic semantics forbids their use by MAS designers (see [8,16] for discussions on that subject). In practical systems, the communicative behavior of an agent is designed as a simplified reification of the afore-mentioned concepts. For example, in the JACK-BDI agent frameworks [11] (based on dMARS [12]), the agent's communicative behavior is part of its means-end reasoning, which is implanted as follows. Each plan consists of: an invocation condition, which is the event that the plan responds to, a context condition, stating conditions under which to use the plan, and a body that specifies a sequence of actions or subgoals to achieve. Each intention raises a particular internal event type (goal events). Planning consists in selecting one plan with that event as the triggering condition and with a context condition that is believed true. The choice between competitive plans is generally based on meta-plans or hardwired strategies (for efficiency). For example, in the JACK-BDI agent architecture the first eligible plan is chosen by default.

In that setting, dialogical actions are hard-coded in plans as other actions. Dialogue initiative is hard-coded as the primitive action of sending an ACL message that initiates a dialogue. Messages received from other agents are interpreted as external events of a particular type (message events) that are treated in the event queue by updating beliefs and trigger the appropriate plan in order to pursue (or cancel) the conversation.

Social commitment based communication frameworks allow leaving down these cooperativity and sincerity assumptions by providing a treatment of the social aspects of communication that is absent in previously proposed purely mentalistic approaches. The next section will both introduce social commitment based communication and discuss this point.

3   Social Commitment Based Communication

Social commitment has been introduced as a first class concept to represent socially established (and grounded) interagent dependencies. In particular, social commitments can model the semantics of agents' interactions. In that context being able to cancel or modify commitments is a key feature that allows agents to reassess the consequences of past dialogues in the context of dynamic environments. This *semantical flexibility* should not be confused with the commonly considered structural flexibility of dialogues.

Since [17] discusses our modelling of flexible social commitments and their enforcement through sanctions, we simply re-introduce the basic of it here. Conceptually, commitments are oriented responsibilities contracted towards a partner or a group. Following [26], we distinguish *action commitments* from *propositional commitments*. Commitments are expressed as predicates with an arity of 6. Thus, an *accepted* action commitment takes the form:

$$C(x, y, \alpha, t, s_x, s_y)$$

meaning that agent x is committed towards agent y to α since time t, under the sanctions sets s_x and s_y. An accepted propositional commitment would have propositional content p instead α. *Rejected* commitments, meaning that x is not committed toward y to α, takes the form $\neg C(x, y, \alpha, t, s_x, s_y)$. This notation for commitments is inspired from [21], and allows us to compose the actions or propositions involved in the commitments: $\alpha_1 | \alpha_2$ classically stands for the choice, and $\alpha_1 \Rightarrow \alpha_2$ for the conditional statement that α_2 will occur in case of the occurrence of the event α_1. Finally, agents keep track of each commitment in which they are debtor or creditor in their *agendas*, which constitutes a kind of distributed "Commitment Store".

In previous work, we proposed a DIAlogue Games Agent Language (DIAGAL) [14] for which our social commitment model offers a complete and valid operational semantics. DIAGAL dialogue games are composed of entry conditions (E), success condition (S), failure conditions (F), all expressed in terms of social commitments and dialogue rules (R) which are expressed in terms of dialogical commitments (C_g) that allow capturing the conventional level of communication. For example, here is DIAGAL's *Request* game (sanctions are avoided for the sake of clarity):

$$
\begin{array}{l|l}
E_{rg} & \neg C(y, x, \alpha, t_i) \text{ and } \neg C(y, x, \neg \alpha, t_i) \\
S_{rg} & C(y, x, \alpha, t_f) \\
F_{rg} & \neg C(y, x, \alpha, t_f) \\
R_{rg} & 1)\ C_g(x, y, request(x, y, \alpha), t_j) \\
& 2)\ C_g(y, x, request(x, y, \alpha)) \Rightarrow \\
& \quad C_g(y, x, accept(y, x, \alpha)|refuse(y, x, \alpha), t_k), t_j) \\
& 3)\ C_g(y, x, accept(y, x, \alpha)) \Rightarrow C(y, x, \alpha, t_f), t_j) \\
& 4)\ C_g(y, x, refuse(y, x, \alpha)) \Rightarrow \neg C(y, x, \alpha, t_f), t_j)
\end{array}
$$

DIAGAL dialogue based communication is grounded and structured through a so-called *contextualisation game* that allows the agents to enter and leave games as well as to structure complex dialogues. All together, our model of flexible social commitment and their enforcement [17] and the DIAGAL [14] language provides a complete agent communication framework that introduces a layered model of agent communication (also formally described in [10]):

1. At the *signal level* (sometimes called attentional level): the contextualisation game allows grounding dialogue games as well as their eventual structuration;
2. At the *message level*: messages (dialogue or speech act) allow fulfilling dialogical commitments and advancing the state of opened dialogue games;
3. At the *dialogic level*: dialogue games allow advancing the state of the social layer of social commitments;
4. At the *social level*: social commitments, if they are respected (which is the case with our model of the enforcement of social commitments) advance the state of activities;
5. At the *activity level*: activities advance the state of the environment in a way that should satisfy the agents or their designers.

According to the principle of *information asymmetry*, what is said does not convey anything about what is actually believed. However, what is said socially commits the locutors toward one another. Social commitments raise action expectations and the enforcement of social commitments through various social control mechanisms take place instead of the sincerity and the cooperativeness assumptions. Social commitments, when modelled with their enforcement mechanism (as in [17]), are not necessarily sincere and don't require the agents to be cooperative. From this perspective, communication serves to coordinate the agents whether or not they are cooperative and whether or not they are sincere.

These social commitment based frameworks, enhancing the social aspects of agents' communications, entail a change of paradigm: agents do not necessarily have to reason on others' intentions anymore but rather they must reason on taken and to be taken social commitments. However, it has not been indicated how agents should dynamically use social commitment based communication and social commitments were not taken into account in previous cognitive agents theory.

In order to fill this gap, we will extend the presented BDI model by: (1) linking private cognitions with social commitments, (2) providing a model of the cognitive aspect of communication pragmatics in order to automatize social commitment based communication. In particular, we will introduce a general decision-making process leading to attitude change in the appropriate cases.

4 Linking Public Cognition and Social Commitments

According to the classic practical reasoning scheme, private cognitions end up in intentions through deliberation and we make the usual distinction between *intention to* (do something or that someone do something) and *intention that* (a proposition holds) [2]. The *intention to* relates to a particular course of action (eventually of a complex and structured type), while *intention that* refers to a propositional statement that the agent wants to became true. Intentions are either accepted ($I_A(p)$) or rejected ($\neg I_A(p)$).

In order to address communication, we will further distinguish between *internal individual intentions* and *social individual intentions*. Internal individual intentions are intentions that the agent can try to achieve alone while social individual intentions are the intentions that relate to other agents' actions. Social individual intentions are intentions concerning goals which require other agents to be worked on. More generally, any intention that is embedded in a somewhat collective activity would be considered as a social individual intention except if it is part of an already socially accepted collective plan. Those social intentions are intentions about a (even indirectly) collective state of affairs indicating that those intentions will be part of a social activity (a problem requiring action, permission or opinion of the others: commerce, exchange, joint action, delegated actions,...). A classic example is delegation where an agent A has the social intention that an agent B achieves a particular action α, $I_A(\alpha_B)$.

Among internal individual intentions, we will also consider *failed individual intentions* which are the intentions that the agent failed to find an individual plan for or for which the available plans failed. This last type matches the case where the agent faces an individual problem he cannot solve alone or he failed to solve alone.

In our framework, failed individual intentions as well as the social individual intentions will be treated through dialogue. The phase of identifying intentions involving a social dimension appears to be crucial for integrating social commitment based approaches with existing cognitive agent architectures. In our approach, all intentions that are not achievable internal intentions will be selected as such. Filtering those failed and social intentions from the other ones is achieved by selecting the intentions for which the mean-end reasoning failed. In particular, in the JACK-BDI framework, intentions that don't match any individual plans or for which all available individual plans have failed fall into those categories. Notice that this implantation implies that trying to achieve individual action (through execution of individual plans) is the prioritized behavior of the agent. Figure 2 sums up this intention typology.

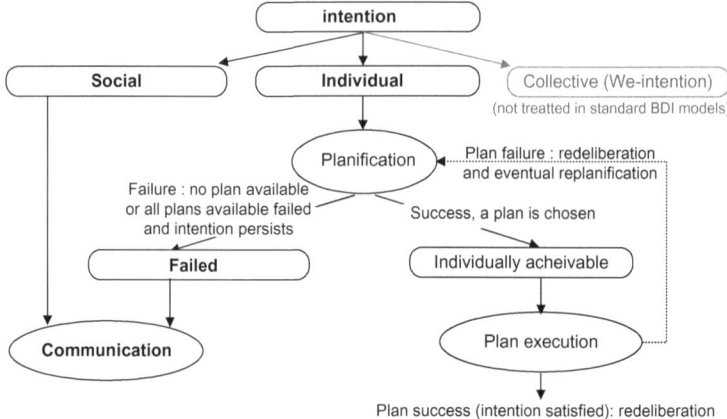

Fig. 2. Operational typology of intentions

In this context, we can return to the general question: what are the links between social commitments and private mental states? As a first answer, we propose linking private and public cognitions as follows. Ideally, an accepted social commitment is the socially accepted counterpart of an accepted intention. Commitments in action are the counterparts of "intentions to" while propositional commitments are the counterparts of "intentions that". In our approach, those links are taken into account by positive and negative binary constraints that link the agents intentions and social commitments. Positive constraints take into account the correspondence relation introduced above while negative constraints model the incompatibility relations that hold between incompatible intentions or/and social commitments.

Let's take an example to illustrate those relations. If an agent A has the accepted individual social "intention to" that another agent B achieves an action α (noted $I_A(\alpha_B)$), our links mean that the corresponding social commitment from B toward A to achieve α_B (noted $C(B, A, \alpha_B, t, s_B, s_A)$ must be socially accepted as part of this intention satisfaction. This ideal link between those two cognitions is captured with a positive constraint. For this constraint to be satisfied, both elements (the intention and the corresponding commitment) must be accepted or rejected. However, all other possibilities are also important to consider. Furthermore, incompatibility relations are modeled with negative constraints.

Those relations between the private and public cognitions are not completely new since many authors have already considered individual intentions as a special kind of individual commitment [2,25]. Our links extend this to reach the social level in the appropriate cases by saying that social individual intentions or failed individual intentions should ideally lead to the social acceptance of their social commitments counterparts through dialogue. Those links complement Singh's previous work [20], which introduces the idea of linking individual and social commitments. Comparable links have been introduced for so-called normative-deliberative cognitive agent architecture [6,1,4]. In particular, following [5], the following axioms have been introduced [19]:

$$S\text{-}COMM(i,j,\tau_i) \rightarrow I_j(\tau_i),^1 \text{ and}$$
$$S\text{-}COMM(i,j,\tau_i) \rightarrow I_i(\tau_i)$$

From which, one can deduce the following theorem: $\vdash \neg S\text{-}COMM(i,j,\tau) \vee (I_i(\tau) \wedge I_j(\tau))$, which clearly states that either the social commitment is rejected or both i and j have the intention that i achieves the action τ. This formalization is not compatible with the semantic flexibility of social commitments described in Section 3. For example, if i decides to violate or cancel the aforementioned commitment, it is probably because he does not have the corresponding intention accepted. In that case, we have the accepted commitment $S\text{-}COMM(i,j,\tau_i)$ and the rejected intention $\neg I_i(\tau_i)$ that holds which invalidates the second of the above axioms. Symmetrically, if the agent j tries to cancel the accepted commitment $S\text{-}COMM(i,j,\tau_i)$, it can be because he does not have the corresponding intention accepted. In that case, we have $S\text{-}COMM(i,j,\tau_i)$ and $\neg I_i(\tau_i)$ which invalidates the first of the above axioms. In other words, those axioms are not flexible enough to provide a good modelling of the links that lie between intentions and social commitments.

Constraints provide bidirectional and symmetric links that go behind the above mentioned axioms.[2] This is why we used constraints in order to model those links. Examples where a commitment is accepted and the corresponding intention is not or the reverse are very common and just mean that the positive constraint linking those two elements is not satisfied. As a consequence, not only those bidirectional links are more correct than the previously criticized axioms but they allow for a new question to be asked. When such a constraint is not satisfied, the agent has to decide which elements' acceptance state he will try to change in order to satisfy this positive constraint: his intention or the corresponding social commitment. This is the basic question of the attitude change process. Since this notion of attitude change has not been yet modelled in the context of AI, we will introduce it here.

5   Attitude Change

In cognitive sciences, cognitions gather together all cognitive elements: perceptions, propositional attitudes such as beliefs, desires and intentions, feelings and emotional constituents as well as social commitments. From the set of all private cognitions result *attitudes* which are positive or negative psychological dispositions towards a concrete or abstract object or behavior.

For contemporary psychologists, attitudes are the main components of cognition. These are the subjective preliminary to rational action [9]. Theoretically, an

---

[1] Sometimes formulated : $S\text{-}COMM(i,j,\tau_i) \rightarrow Goal_j(Does_i(\tau))$.

[2] We refer the interested reader to [23] for a discussion about bidirectionality in cognitive modelling.

agent's behavior is determined by his attitudes. The basic scheme highlighted by those researches is that beliefs (cognition) and desires (affect) lead to intentions which could lead to actual behaviors or dialogical attempts to get the corresponding social commitments depending on their nature. From another point of view, it could happen (due to hierarchies, power relations, negotiation, argumentation, persuasion dialogues,...) that an agent becomes socially committed to a counter-attitudinal course of action or proposition. In that case, *attitude change* can occur.

The links between private and public cognitions established in Section 4 allow defining the attitude change process in the way provided by cognitive psychology's classical studies [3]. Ideally, for each accepted or rejected social commitment, the corresponding intention should be accepted or rejected (respectively) in both the creditor and the debtor mental states. For example, we assume that $C(A, B, \alpha_A, t, s_A, s_B)$ holds, indicating that A is committed toward B, since time t, to achieve α_A under the sanction sets s_A and s_B. Then, A and B should ideally have the intention that A achieves α_A, noted $I(\alpha_A)$, accepted in their mental model. If, for example, A doesn't have $I(\alpha_A)$ accepted, he can: (1) revoke or violate the commitment and face the associated sanctions (2) try to modify the commitments through further dialogues or (3) he can begin an *attitude change*, i.e. adopt this intention and possibly reject incompatible ones.

6   Dialogue Pragmatics

6.1   The Cognitive Coherence Framework

All attitude theories, also called cognitive coherence theories appeal to the concept of homeostasis, i.e. the human faculty to maintain or restore some physiological or psychological constants despite the outside environment variations. All these theories share as a premise the *coherence principle* which puts coherence as the main organizing mechanism: *the individual is more satisfied with coherence than with incoherence*. The individual forms an opened system whose purpose is to maintain coherence as much as possible.

Our pragmatics theory (presented in [15]) follows from those principles by defining a formal theory of cognitive coherence. Here, elements are both failed or social intentions and social commitments. Elements are divided in two sets: the set $\mathcal{A}$ of *accepted elements* (accepted, failed or social, intentions and socially accepted social commitments) and the set $\mathcal{R}$ of *rejected elements* (rejected social intentions and socially rejected social commitments). Every non-explicitly accepted element is rejected. Two types of non-ordered binary constraints on these elements are inferred from the pre-existing relations that hold between them in the agent's cognitive model:

- *Positive constraints*: positive constraints are inferred from positive relations like the correspondence relation described in Section 4.
- *Negative constraints*: negative constraints are inferred from negative relations like mutual exclusion and incompatibility relations considered in Section 4.

These constraints can be satisfied or not: a positive constraint is satisfied if and only if the two elements that it binds are both accepted or both rejected. On the contrary, a negative constraint is satisfied if and only if one of the two elements that it binds is accepted and the other one rejected. For each of these constraints a weight reflecting the importance of the underlying relation can be attributed.[3]

Given a partition of elements among $\mathcal{A}$ and $\mathcal{R}$, one can measure the *coherence degree*, $\mathcal{C}(\mathcal{E})$, of a non-empty set of elements, $\mathcal{E}$, by adding the weights of constraints connected to this set (the constraints of which at least a pole is an element of the considered set) which are satisfied divided by the total weight of concerned constraints. The general coherence problem is then to find a partition between the set of accepted elements $\mathcal{A}$ and the set of rejected elements $\mathcal{R}$ that maximize cognitive coherence. It is a constraint optimization problem shown to be NP-complete by [24]. In our case the coherence problem is solved in an iterative manner by the local search algorithm.

6.2 Local Search Algorithm

Decision theories as well as micro-economical theories define utility as a property of some valuation functions. A function is a utility function if and only if it reflects the agent preferences. In the cognitive coherence theory, according to the afore-mentioned coherence principle, coherence is preferred to incoherence.

In order to try to maximize its coherence, at each step of his pragmatics' reasoning, an agent will search for a cognition's acceptance state change which maximizes the coherence increase, taking into account the resistance to change of that cognition (technically a 1-optimal move). If this attitude is a commitment, the agent will attempt to change it through dialogue and if it is an intention, it will be changed through attitude change. In that last case, we call the underlying architecture of the agent to spread the attitude change and re-deliberate.

In our implementation, an agent determines which is the most useful cognition's acceptance state change by exploring all states reachable from its current state and selects the cognition which can *in case of a successful change* be the most useful to change. A state is said to be reachable if it can be obtained from the current state by modifying only one cognition. A notion of cost has been introduced to advocate for the fact that all cognitions cannot be equally modified. All explored states are so evaluated through an *expected utility function*, g, expressed as below:

$$g(ExploredState) = \mathcal{C}(exploredState) - \mathcal{C}(currentState)$$
$$- r(cognitionChanged)$$

where *exploredState* is the evaluated state, *cognitionChanged* is the cognition we are examining the change, and r is a normalized cost function expressed as:

---

[3] This is a way of prioritizing some cognitive constraints as is done in the BOID architecture [4].

1. if *cognitionChanged* is an intention, its cost of change equals its resistance to change that reflects the underlying individual commitment strength;
2. if *cognitionChanged* is a rejected commitment, its cost of change equals its resistance to change, which is initially low but which could be increased at each unfruitful attempt to establish it;
3. if *cognitionChanged* is an accepted commitment, its cost of change is increased by its associated sanctions (which could be null, positive or negative).

The local search algorithm is an informed breath first search algorithm with the afore-mentioned expected utility measure as its greedy heuristics. We don't have a proof of correctness of this algorithm in regards to the general coherence problem but, as [24] (who used it in another context), it was shown to be optimal on tested examples.

6.3 Pragmatic Treatment Algorithm

The dialogic behavior of the agent is based on his cognitive coherence calculus involving failed and social intentions as well as social commitments. Social commitments and their state are memorized in the agent agenda which is maintained by the DIAGAL dialogue manager. Figure 3 presents the agent pragmatic treatment algorithm that integrates pragmatics reasoning and social commitments' treatment.

As seen in Section 3, we distinguish extra-dialogical commitments (assigned to a List on line 5) from dialogical commitments (assigned line 6). Dialogical commitments result from dialogue games' rules as well as from the contextualisation game. Extra-dialogical commitments are processed by TreatCommitments() (line 8) which consists in updating the agent representations of commitments by taking into account dialogical as well as extra-dialogical action of the agents that has been reported by the agent's dialogue manager in the agenda. Three cases are then distinguished:

1. *dialogue initiative*: there is no active dialogic commitment in the agenda and the *initiate* boolean is true (test, line 9), which means that the underlying BDI control loop just called the Pragmatic treatment algorithm. The InitiateDialogue() procedure is called (line 11);
2. *ending of a dialogue*: there is no more active dialogic commitment in the agenda and the *initiate* boolean is false (test, line 13), which means that the dialog segment is finished. The underlying BDI control loop is called again (ModifiedBDICycle(), line 14);
3. *pursuing a dialogue*: there are some dialogical commitments to process, the TreatDialogCommitment() (line 16) procedure is called.

In order to *initiate a dialogue*, InitiateDialogue(), generates the intentions and commitments network according to the principles of representation enunciated and argued in Section 4. Then, the local search algorithm is called and elements' acceptance states are changed until a social commitment is encountered and a

Procedure. CommunicationPragmatics(*initiate*)

1: **Inputs:** *initiate*, boolean variable (true when called by the
        underlying BDI architecture, false otherwise)
2: **Outputs:** *none*, this is not a function!
3: **Global:** *agenda*, object that stores the agent's agenda
4: **Local:**
5: List *commitments*:=*agenda*.GetCommitments();
6: List *dialogCommitments*:=*agenda*.GetDialogCommitments();
7: **Body:**
8: TreatCommitments(*commitments*);
9: **if** *dialogCommitments*.IsEmpty() and *initiate*=*true* **then**
10:    *initiate*:=*false*;
11:    InitiateDialogue(); // initiate a dialogue
12: **else**
13:    **if** *dialogCommitments*.IsEmpty() and *initiate*=*false* **then**
14:        ModifiedBDICycle(); // dialog finished
15:    **else**
16:        // pursue a dialogue
17:        TreatDialogCommitments(*dialogCommitments*);
18:    **end if**
19: **end if**

Fig. 3. Pragmatic treatment algorithm

dialogue is initiated as an attempt to realize the desired change.[4] The appropriate DIAGAL game is chosen by unifying *currentState* and the games entry conditions and *exploredState* with the success conditions of the game (see [14] for details). The different fields of the commitment indicate the partner and the subject of the dialogue.

In order to *pursue a dialogue*, TreatDialogCommitments(), consists in treating the remaining dialogical commitments. This is done by evaluating the consequences of all the outcomes allowed by the current dialogue games rules on the cognitive coherence. The resulting choice utility is compared to the local search choice utility. If the modification allowed by the current dialogue game is less usefull than the one proposed by local search, then the agent will imbricate a subjectively more appropriate sub-dialogue game.

In case a *dialogue ended*, control is given back to the underlying BDI control loop through the ModifiedBDICycle() (line 14) procedure call. The modified BDI control loop will take into account the eventual partial or complete attitude change and will deliberate again eventually generating new intentions that will be treated according to their nature as indicated by the algorithm of Figure 4.

---

[4] Notice that the local search can return nothing (e.g., if coherence is already maximal).

Procedure. ModifiedBDICycle(B_0, I_0)

1: **Inputs:** B_0, set of initial beliefs;
                I_0, set of initial intentions;
                Those inputs are optional (used for the first call)
2: **Outputs:** *none*, this is not a function!
3: **Global:** $B := B_0$, object that stores the agent's beliefs;
                $I := I_0$, stores the agent's accepted intentions;
                I_s, stores the agent's social or failed intentions;
                D, object that stores the agent's desires;
                List ρ, stores both internal and external percepts;
                List $\pi := null$, current plan, sequence of actions;
4: **Body:**
5: **while** *true* **do**
6:      ρ.GetNewPercepts(); // get new percepts ρ
7:      B.Update(ρ); // update B on the basis of ρ
8:      **if** Reconsider(I,B) **then**
9:          $D :=$ Options(B,I);
10:         $I :=$ Deliberate(B,D,I); // deliberate if necessary
11:     **end if**
12:     **if** Empty(π) or Succeeded(I,B) or Impossible(I,B)) **then**
13:         $\pi :=$ Plan(B,I); // replan if necessary
14:         $I_s :=$ Filter(B,I); // assign failed or social intentions
15:     **else**
16:         $\alpha :=$ Head(π);
17:         Execute(α); // execute an action
18:         $\pi :=$ Tail(π);
19:     **end if**
20:     **if** *agenda*.Modified()=*true* **then**
21:         CommunicationPragmatics(*false*); // pursue a dialogue or answer a new dialogue offer
22:     **end if**
23:     **if** not Empty(I_s) **then**
24:         CommunicationPragmatics(*true*); // initiate a dialogue
25:     **end if**
26: **end while**

Fig. 4. Modified BDI control loop

Finally, the CommunicationPragmatics() procedure is called each time:

- the underlying BDI control loop deliberation produces either social or failed intentions that the agent cannot fulfill by itself (and thus need to communicate).
- the DIAGAL dialogue manager modifies the agent agenda and this modification is not the fulfillment or violation of an extra-dialogical commitment (which are taken into account as specified in [17]). This ensures that: (1) the agent executes the CommunicationPragmatics() algorithm until all ongoing dialogue segments are closed and (2) the agent treats dialogues initiated by other agents.

7   Examples

Returning to the example of delegation, suppose the modified BDI control loop
of an agent A just generated the intention that B achieves an action α ($I_A(\alpha_B)$).
This intention is filtered (line 14) as a social intention and CommunicationPrag-
matics() (line 24) is called which in turn calls the InitiateDialogue() procedure
which produces the coherence framework of Figure 5,a. In these examples, we assume that constraints' weights are unitary and that elements rejected by default
have a lower default cost of change (0.05) than accepted elements' default resistance to change (which is 0.2, plus the eventual associated sanctions strength).
Update, reified by an increased by 0.2 of this resistance to change, occurs at each
attempt of change (according to Section 5).

The local search algorithm returns that the best change would be to have
a social commitment from B to A to $acheive(\alpha)$ accepted (as indicated by the
decision tree of Figure 5,b). The appropriate DIAGAL game is the *Request* game,
that is proposed by A through the contextualisation game. Suppose B refuses
A's request, the resistance to change of the still rejected commitment would
be updated and redeliberation will occur. If B accepts, the social commitment
would be marked as socially accepted and the enforcement mechanism would be
activated in order to foster its satisfaction.

In a more rich setting involving three agents, suppose that A is already committed toward a third agent F not to achieve β and has the corresponding intention accepted when an agent B orders him to achieve β (one can suppose that
there is a permanent commitment to accept B's request because of his authority
position, ...). Despite the fact that A has the intention to achieve β rejected,

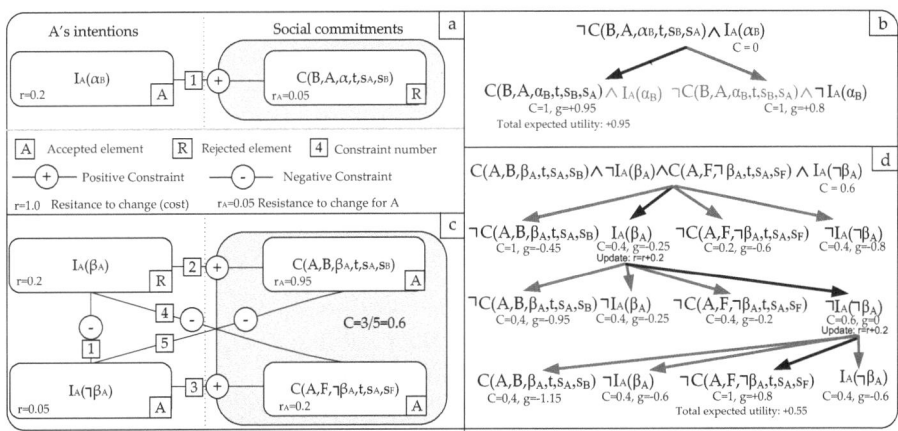

Fig. 5. Parts b and d indicate A's reasoning as computed by the local search algorithm
from the states described by in parts a and c respectively. For each reachable state,
the cognitive coherence and expected utility measures are indicated. The black path
indicates the change(s) returned by the local search algorithm (presented section 6.2).

the counter attitudinal commitment toward B to do so is accepted. This situation is presented by the coherence framework of Figure 5,c. The decision tree of Figure 5,d indicates that an attitude change occurred. Following our algorithms, agent A has rejected the intention not to achieve β and accepted the intention to achieve β and is now about to initiate a dialogue with F in order to cancel the previously accepted social commitment toward him.

Notice that the choice of the default resistances to change and update rules extends individual commitment strategies (presented in Section 1). In the proposed approach, intention persistence not only depends on the chosen default resistance to change (the higher it is, the more fanatic the agent is) but also on accepted commitments' resistance to change (reflecting sanctions and rewards). This models social pressure and allows to introduce the concept of attitude change that is central for the study and modelling of agent behavior changes.

8   Conclusion

In this paper, we unify – both at the theoretical (Section 4) and practical level (Section 5) – two important trends in MAS modelling: cognitive agents based on BDI models and social commitment based communication (a model of flexible social commitment and their enforcement [17] and the DIAGAL agent language [14]). Note that the resulting framework automatizes the agent pragmatic reasoning and communication behavior by giving him tools to measure himself the expected utility of possible communicative behaviors. The proposed model rests on solid cognitive sciences' results that allow to take into account the motivational aspects of agent communication. This approach models the persuasive dimension eventually present in all communications by reifying attitude change when necessary.

Notice that the proposed approach cumulates the advantages of past contributions. Resulting agents can be used in an open system (as long as the other agents use DIAGAL), no sincerity (of the others) is assumed, no hard-coded cooperation is needed. Notice that our pragmatic coherence approach includes the reasoning on sanctions (taken into account in the expected utility function) so that the chosen punishment strategy influences agent behavior as discussed in [14]. This is thus a major improvement over the hand written communication behavior of classical agent implantation (as those described in Section 2).

References

1. G. Boella and L. Lesmo. *Social Order in Multi-Agent Systems*, chapter Deliberative normative agents, pages 85–110. Kluwer Academic, 2001.
2. M. E. Bratman. What is intention? In P. R. Cohen, J. L. Morgan, and M. E. Pollack, editors, *Intentions in Communication*, pages 15–32. The MIT Press, 1990.
3. J. Brehm and A. Cohen. *Explorations in Cognitive Dissonance*. John Wiley and Sons, inc, 1962.
4. J. Broersen, M. Dastani, J. Hulstijn, Z. Huang, and L. Van der Torre. The BOID architecture: Conflicts between beliefs, obligations, intention and desires. In *Proceedings of the Fifth International Conference on Autonomous Agent*, pages 9–16. ACM Press, 2001.

5. C. Castelfranchi. Commitments: from individual intentions to groups and organizations. In *Proceedings of the First International Conference on Multi-Agent Systems (ICMAS-95)*, pages 41–48, San Francisco, CA, USA, 1995.

6. C. Castelfranchi, F. Dignum, C. Jonker, and J. Treur. Deliberative normative agents: Principles and architecture. In *Intelligent Agents V, Proceedings of the Internationnal Workshop on Agent Theories, Architectures, and Languages (ATAL)*, volume 1757 of *Lecture Notes in Artificial Intelligence (LNAI)*, pages 364–378. Springer-Verlag, 1999.

7. P. R. Cohen and H. J. Levesque. Intention is choice with commitment. *Artificial Intelligence*, 42:213–261, 1990.

8. F. Dignum and M. Greaves. Issues in agent communication: An introduction. In F Dignum and M. Greaves, editors, *Issues in Agent Communication*, volume 1916 of *LNAI*, pages 1–16. Springer-Verlag, 2000.

9. P. Erwin. *Attitudes and Persuasion*. Psychology Press, 2001.

10. R. A. Flores, P. Pasquier, and B. Chaib-draa. Conversational semantics with social commitments. *Journal of Autonomous Agent and Multiagent Systems, Special Issue on Agent Communication*, 2005. To appear.

11. N. Howden, R. Ronnquist, A. Hodgson, and A. Lucas. Jack intelligent agents: summary of an agent infrastructure. In *Proceedings of the Fifth International Conference on Autonomous Agents*. ACM Press, 2001.

12. M. Inverno, M. Luck, M. Georgeff, D. Kinny, and M. Wooldridge. The dmars architechure: A specification of the distributed multi-agent reasoning system. *Journal of Autonomous Agents and Multi-Agent Systems*, 1-2(9):5–53, 2004.

13. S. C. Levinson. Activity type and language. *Linguistics*, 17:365–399, 1979.

14. P. Pasquier, M. Bergeron, and B. Chaib-draa. DIAGAL: a Generic ACL for Open Systems. In *Proceedings of The Fifth International Workshop Engineering Societies in the Agents World (ESAW'04)*, volume 3451 of *Lecture Notes in Artificial Intelligence (LNAI)*, pages 139–152. Springer-Verlag, 2004.

15. P. Pasquier and B. Chaib-draa. The cognitive coherence approach for agent communication pragmatics. In *Proceedings of The Second International Joint Conference on Autonomous Agent and Multi-Agents Sytems (AAMAS'03)*, pages 544–552. ACM Press, 2003.

16. P. Pasquier and B. Chaib-draa. Modèles de dialogue entre agents cognitifs : un état de l'art. *In Cognito : Cahiers de Sciences Cognitive*, 1(4):77–135, 2004.

17. P. Pasquier, R. A. Flores, and B Chaib-draa. Modelling flexible social commitments and their enforcement. In *Proceedings of the Fifth International Workshop Engineering Societies in the Agents World (ESAW'04)*, volume 3451 of *Lecture Notes in Artificial Intelligence (LNAI)*, pages 153–165. Springer-Verlag, 2004.

18. A. S. Rao and M. P. Georgeff. Modeling rational agents within a BDI-architecture. In *Proceedings of Knowledge Representation and Reasoning (KR&R-91)*, pages 473–484. Morgan Kaufmann Publishers: San Mateo, CA, April 1991.

19. L. Royakkers and F. Dignum. No organisation without obligation: How to formalise collective obligation? In M. Ibrahim, J. Kung, and N. Revell, editors, *Proceedings of the 11th Internationnal Conference on Databases and Expert Systems Applications*, volume 1873 of *Lecture Notes in Computer Science (LNCS)*, pages 302–311. Springer-Verlag, 2000.

20. M. P. Singh. Social and psychological commitments in multiagent systems. In *AAAI Fall Symposium on Knowledge and Action at Social and Organizational Levels*, pages 104–106, 1991.

21. M. P. Singh. A social semantics for agent communication languages. In *Issues in Agent Communication*, Lecture Notes in Artificial Intelligence (LNAI), pages 31–45. Springer-Verlag, 2000.

22. M. P. Singh, S. Rao, and M. P. Georgeff. *Multiagent Systems : A Modern Approach to Distributed Artificial Intelligence*, chapter Formal Methods in DAI: Logic-Based Representation and Reasoning, pages 331–376. The MIT Press, 1999.

23. P. Thagard. *Coherence in Thought and Action*. The MIT Press, 2000.

24. P. Thagard and K. Verbeurgt. Coherence as constraint satisfaction. *Cognitive Science*, 22:1–24, 1998.

25. G. H. von Wright. *Freedom and determination*. North Holland Publishing, 1980.

26. D. N. Walton and E. Krabbe. *Commitment in Dialogue: Basic Concepts of Interpersonal Reasoning*. Suny Press, 1995.

27. M. Wooldridge. *An Introduction to MultiAgent Systems*. Wiley, 2001.

Flexible Conversations Using Social Commitments and a Performatives Hierarchy

Rob Kremer[1] and Roberto A. Flores[2]

[1] University of Calgary,
Department of Computer Science
Calgary, AB T2N 1N4, Canada
kremer@cpsc.ucalgary.ca
[2] Christopher Newport University,
Department of Physics, Computer Science & Engineering,
Newport News, VA 23606 USA
flores@pcs.cnu.edu

Abstract. In this research, we re-arrange FIPA's ACL performatives to form a subsumption lattice (ontology) and apply a theory of social commitments to achieve a simplified and observable model of agent behaviour. Using this model, we have implemented agent interaction through social commitments (or obligations) based solely on observation of messages passed between the agents (such observation is supported by the *cooperation domain* mechanism in our agent infrastructure system). Moreover, because the performatives are in a subsumption lattice, it is relatively easy for an observer to infer social commitment relationships even if the observer does not understand the details of messages or even the exact performatives used (so long as the observer has access to the performatives ontology).

Our social commitment model can be used in agent implementation to simplify the specification and observation of agent behaviour even if the agents themselves are *not implemented* using social commitments. This is accomplished through the use of *commitment operators* attached to the performatives (as policies) in the subsumption lattice.

In this work, we show how FIPA's performatives can be interpreted in a theory of social commitment to allow observable social behaviour and conformance to social norms.

1 Introduction

The FIPA standard SC00061G [8] has defined inter-agent messages in the envelope/letter pattern, where the "envelope" contains several standard fields which must be understood by all agents in the community, and the "letter" part may or may not be understood by other agents. FIPA further defines the contents of several envelope fields such as *performative* (the type of the communicative act), *sender, receiver, content, ontology, reply-with, in-reply-to, reply-by* and others.

We focus primarily on the performative field as the main means by which agents can choose their behaviour in reaction to a particular message.

F. Dignum, R. van Eijk, and R. Flores (Eds.): AC 2005/2006, LNAI 3859, pp. 93–108, 2006.
© Springer-Verlag Berlin Heidelberg 2006

Table 1. FIPA performatives

Performative	Description
accept-proposal	accepting a previous proposal
agree	agreeing to perform some action
cancel	inform another agent that it no longer need perform some action
call-for-proposal	call for proposals to perform an action
confirm	informs a given proposition is true
disconfirm	informs a given proposition is false
failure	an action was attempted but failed
inform	a given proposition is true
inform-if	inform whether a proposition is true
inform-ref	inform the object which corresponds to a descriptor
not-understood	did not understand what the receiver just did
propagate	pass a message on
propose	submit a proposal to perform an action
proxy	pass on an embedded message
query-if	asking whether a proposition is true
query-ref	asking for the object referred to
refuse	refusing to perform an action
reject-proposal	rejecting a proposal during negotiation
request	request to perform some action
request-when	request to perform an action when a proposition becomes true
request-whenever	request to perform an action each time proposition becomes true
subscribe	request to notify the value of a ref. whenever the object changes

Furthermore, we only focus on the behaviour relative to communication acts (speech acts) in conversation and do not delve into physical acts or domain-specific acts.

1.1 Performatives

The FIPA standard SC00037J [9] defines 22 "Communicative Act" names as values for the performative field (see Table 1).

In implementing our agent infrastructure, CASA [13], we have found that the FIPA performatives were very useful in that they include communicative acts that we would not have initially thought of ourselves. Unfortunately, it became obvious that they do not form a computationally useful set for our agents to decide on an action when they receive a message. When our agents used FIPA's flat classification, they had to switch behaviour in an ad-hoc manner for (almost) each of the 22 performatives. Our agents needed to perform a list of actions for each performative, and these actions were often duplicated among several of the performative behaviours. This lead to a complex and error-prone specification. Furthermore, we had to extend the list of performatives, and each of our agents had to constantly update the list.

We found that if we arrange the same performatives in a subsumption lattice (see Figure 1), we can succinctly glean the semantic information we need to clas-

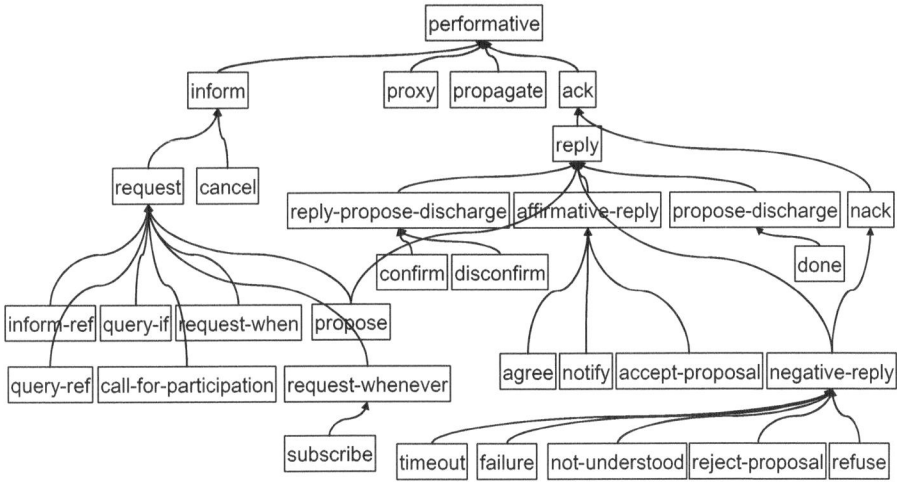

Fig. 1. The CASA performative subsumption lattice

sify the message and decide on a course of action. Because certain performatives are subtypes of others, we need only specify individual actions once for the parent performative type, and those actions are "inherited" by the child performative types. Thus, we eliminate the redundancies and simplify the specification significantly. We also eliminate the need for *every* agent to *always* be updated on the semantics of every extension to the performatives lattice: they can always interpret a new type of performative in terms of its parent type. (And for an agent to ask for the parentage of an unknown performative is a trivial operation which is supported by our infrastructure.)

1.2   The CASA Architecture

The CASA architecture [13] is an experimental infrastructure on which agents can be implemented. CASA agents work by exchanging messages (via TCP/IP or by local method calls) which consist of key/value pairs. The keys in the messages are the various FIPA message field names, but may also include other, extended keys, as appropriate.

The CASA architecture is a general purpose agent agent environment, but defines several specialized agents (see Figure 2). CASA defines computational *areas* (usually a single computer), and each area has exactly one *Local Area Coordinator* (LAC) agent. A LAC agent is a registry of agents for its area, and is responsible to act as a "white pages directory" for its area, to run agents on behalf of agents in its or other areas, as well as to perform several other duties. Another important type of agent is a *Cooperation Domain* (CD), which acts like a "meeting room" for agents. Agents may *join* and then send messages to a CD which, by default, re-broadcasts the message to all of its members. CDs are particularly useful for third-party observers of agent conversations. These

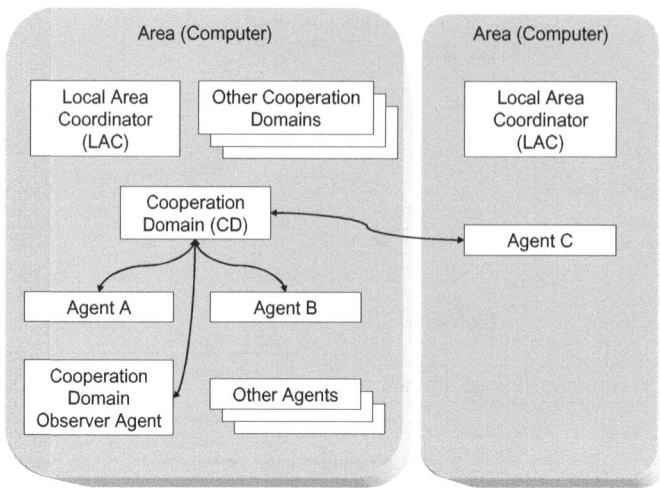

Fig. 2. The CASA architecture

observer agents can analyze agent behaviour on the behalf of the larger society of agents for various purposes such as analysis, possible sanctioning of rogue agents [11,16], or merely reporting unacceptable, malicious, or erroneous behaviour.

CASA is particularly concerned with agent behaviour and the observability of agents' behaviour. Unfortunately, the semantics behind FIPA's model is based on the BDI (Beliefs, Desired, Intensions) model, which has long been criticized as requiring "omniscient" knowledge of the internal workings of all agents in the environment [17]. Since the inner workings of agents is not typically available to an outside observer, the observer cannot predict expected behaviour of agents. Therefore, an observer has no formal bases on which to judge agent behaviour as "acceptable", "harmful", "malicious", "useful", etc. to the society of agents.

An alternate agent model is the commitment-based model [1]. Communicative acts between agents generate social commitments, which form a social "contract" among the agents. Assuming the communicative acts can be observed (as CASA is careful to support), an outside observer can infer social commitments among the observed agents. Our model is formally specified [3,4,5] and forms a clean formal basis on which an observer *can* decide whether or not a particular agent is fulfilling its social commitments, and therefore has a sound foundation on which to judge agents' behaviour.

2   Messages and Performatives

As stated in the introduction, we wish to simplify the specification of possible agent behaviour. As a step in that direction, we arrange our communicative acts, which we base on the FIPA standard, in a subsumption lattice of performatives as described in Figure 1. In the lattice, every child performative inherits the attributes of all of its ancestor performatives. In particular, we can associate *policies* with any performative, which will be inherited by all children of that performative. This is described in detail in Section 3.

Note that the performatives in Figure 1 are actually a superset of the performatives defined by FIPA. Some of the new performatives are classes of performative types which do not add any real semantic information to their children, but serve to enable our agents (and their observers) to more easily classify performatives into broader categories; thus allowing for more "superficial" specification where appropriate. For example, an observer, Carol, may note that an agent, Bob, sent a *request* to agent Alice, and that Alice replied with a *failure* performative. If Carol is tracking only social commitments, then she would not care if Alice had replied with a *failure*, a *non-understood*, a *reject-proposal*, a *refuse*, or some other descendent of *nack* and *reply*; in any of these cases, there is no social commitment entailed. Indeed, Carol need not understand the performative in the reply send by Alice, as long as she is aware (by looking it up in the appropriate ontology) that the performative in Alice's reply is subsumed by a *nack* (negative acknowledge).

Other extensions to the FIPA performatives include the addition of an *ack* (acknowledge) performative, which, in CASA, serves as an optional top-level method of checking receipt of messages. The use of *ack* will be be further explained in the light of social commitments in Section 3.

3   Commitments

We model agent communication as generating (or deleting) social commitments, thus allowing observation of the state of social commitments within a society of agents. More specifically, the performatives in agent communication acts (messages), are translated (by a set of *polices*) to a set of *social commitment operators*, which either add or delete a specific class of social commitments. We model a *social commitment* as the promise by a *debtor* agent to a *creditor* agent(s) to do some *action*:

$$(debtor, creditor, action)$$

and we model a *social commitment operator* as either an *add* or *delete* of a commitment (refer to [7] for a detailed view of the life cycle of commitments):

$$(add|delete, socialCommitment)$$

We have defined several *polices* (eg: *propose, accept, reject, counter,* and *inform*) [5] which can be *applied* to an agent's outgoing and incoming messages and set of social commitment operators:

apply: message $\times$ **P**policy $\times$ *ontology* $\rightarrow$ **P***socialCommitmentOperator*

Here, we mean that if we observe an agent's incoming or outgoing message, we can interpret it in the context of the agent's (or the society of agent's) policies and ontology. (The ontology is necessary to provide a semantics for the performatives.) Of course, not all the policies are *applicable* to a particular message;

Table 2. An informal description of the conversation policies as defined by Flores and Kremer. (The names of some of the policies have changed since the original work).

Policy	Description
P-inform	commits the addressee to acknowledge
P-ack	releases informed agents of the commitment to acknowledge
P-request	commits the proposed agents to reply
P-counteroffer	commits addressees to reply
P-reply	releases proposed agents of the commitment to reply and releases counteroffered agents of the commitment to reply
P-agree	an acceptance realizes the shared uptake of proposed/counteroffered commitments
P-done	releases accepted agents of the commitment earlier agree

a matching function (see Section 4.1) is used to choose the subset of applicable policies. The applicable polices are then *executed* to produce the set of social commitment operators.

Furthermore, we can *commit* this set of social commitment operators to an existing set of social commitments:

$$commit: \mathbf{P}socialCommitment \times \mathbf{P}socialCommitmentOperator$$
$$\rightarrow \mathbf{P}socialCommitment$$

Thus, it is easy to build up (or reduce) a set of social commitments based on observed messages. Note that this is just as easy for an individual agent to track its own social commitments (as in our implementation) or for a 3rd party observer to track all of the social commitments of a society of agents (as in Heard's study of sanctioning of rogue agents [11]).

Table 2 informally describes some of the fundamental polices we have defined so far. The policies are meant to be used by a community of agents as a description of "social norms". The policies are used to map our FIPA-based performatives to social commitments.

4   Using Social Commitments with Performatives

As already alluded to, we effectively use policies to annotate the performative lattice with social commitment operators to form expectations about agent behaviour (the "normative" behaviour of agents in a society of agents). Figure 3 illustrates some of the polices by describing the relationship between (part of) the performative lattice and commitments through policies and commitment operators. The performative lattice on the left, and the curved arrows originating on the performatives represent the policies that indicate the associated social commitment operators (center right column). The arrows originating in the commitment operators illustrate the type of the commitments' third parameter (an *action*) and terminate on the action subtype of the action. Since these particular policies are about conversational acts, all of these arrows (except the last two) terminate on subtypes of *communication-act*.

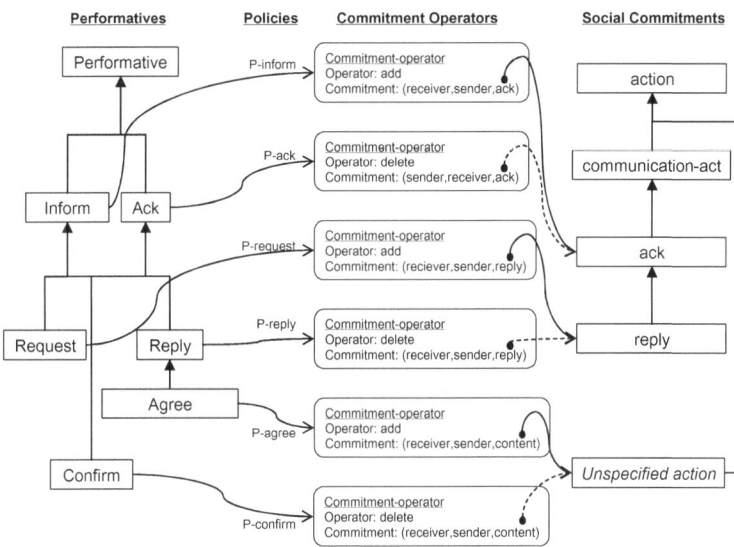

Fig. 3. Part of the CASA performative subsumption lattice together with their relationship via policies and performative operators to social commitments. The *policies* are labelled with the policy names from Table 2.

The curved arrows between the performatives and the social commitment operators in Figure 3 represent some of the policies described in [5] and informally described in Table 2. For example, the P-inform policy associated with the *inform* perforative would read "if Bob receives a message with an inform performative from Alice, then there exists a social commitment for Bob to send an acknowledgement to Alice ($\exists sc: socialCommitment, x: ack \bullet sc = (Bob, Alice, x))$".

The reading of the *request* performative's P-request policy is a bit more complex. Because *request* is a subtype of *inform*, not only do we have to apply the P-request policy, but also the P-inform policy as well (and likewise up the lattice for every ancestor performative). So we would read the P-request policy as "if Bob receives a message with a *request* performative from Alice, then there exists a social commitment for Bob to send an acknowledgement to Alice and another social commitment for Bob to send a reply to Alice, $(\exists sc_1, sc_2 : socialCommitment, x_1: ack, x_2: reply \bullet sc_1 = (Bob, Alice, x_1) \wedge sc_2 = (Bob, Alice, x_2))$".

This may seem somewhat redundant since a single conversational act (*request*) makes two (very similar) social commitments. But it makes sense and yields needed flexibility. If Alice were requesting Bob attend a meeting, Bob might not have his calendar with him, so might not be able to *reply* to Alice, but could *acknowledge* that he had received the request ("I'll check my calendar"). Alice would then know that Bob had received the request and the social commitment to acknowledge would be deleted (by policy *P-ack*), but the social commitment for Bob to reply to Alice would remain. Later, Bob would reply (affirmatively [*agree*] or negatively [by some reply that is subsumed by *nack*]), and that would remove the second social commitment (by policy P-reply). And that would end the conversation because there would exist no more conversational social commitments between the two. (Well, not quite: if Bob had replied affirmatively [using an *agree* performative], then Bob and Alice would uptake the social commitments for Bob to attend the meeting and to tell Alice about it [by policy P-agree] – but we will get into those details later in Section 5.)

On the other hand, if Bob *did* have his calendar with him when Alice requested he attend the meeting, then does Bob have to send an acknowledgement to Alice, and *then* send a reply to Alice? That wouldn't be very efficient. Fortunately, Bob doesn't have to respond twice: If Bob immediately sends a *reply* to Alice, then the social commitment to reply will be removed (by policy P-reply), *and so will the social commitment to acknowledge.* Why? Because, by virtue of *reply* being subsumed by *ack*, the *reply* will generate two commitment operators

$\exists delReply, delAck: socialCommitmentOperator \bullet$
   $\exists r: reply, a: ack \bullet$
      $delReply = (delete, (Bob, Alice, r)) \wedge delAck = (delete, (Bob, Alice, a))$

which will remove both of the commitments set up by the original request.

4.1   Implementation with Social Commitments

Thus, agents can be implemented by dealing with incoming messages by merely applying all the policies associated with the performative in the message and also those policies associated with all of the ancestors of the performatives in the message. These polices will either add or delete social commitments. It is important to note that this is also exactly what an observer does as well: The social commitments are in the context of the entire community of agents, so an observer's record of social commitments should always be consistent with (be a superset of) any observed agent's record of social commitments.

Agents do not have to be *implemented* using social commitments (as may have been implied by the previous paragraph). Observers can still use social commitments to formulate a model of agent behaviour regardless of *how* the agent is implemented. The policies merely form a codification of social norms. An agent that is not implemented using social commitments (who is well behaved) would still be regarded as not breaking any commitments by an observer using reasonable social commitment policies (like the ones in Table 2).

CASA implements its agents as either social commitment agents as listed above, or as *reactive* agents. Both kinds of agents use the same set of named policies, but the difference is that the policy *implementation* is different. When a social commitment-based agent "sees" an incoming or outgoing message, it merely applies it's policies to add or delete social commitments; later (during otherwise idle time) it will attempt to discharge any social commitments (for which it is the debtor) by executing them when it can. On the other hand, reactive agents will respond to a message immediately (without "thinking") whenever it "sees" an incoming message. Reactive agents do nothing in idle time, do nothing with outgoing messages, and don't keep a record of social commitments.

Both types of agents follow the same normative protocols, but the sequence of messages is usually quite different. For example, social commitment agents may easily and naturally choose to prioritize their tasks; reactive agents can't handle prioritized tasks easily.

4.2 Formal Model

It only remains to more formally describe how to apply social commitment operators to an agent's record of social commitments. If we assume an agent's record of social commitments is a set, SC, the operator op is applied as follows:

$\forall op$: $socialCommitmentOperator, sc$: $socialCommitment\bullet$
$op = (add, sc) \rightarrow SC' = SC \cup sc \wedge$
$op = (delete, sc) \rightarrow SC' = SC \backslash match(sc, SC)$

(In the above, we use SC' to represent the value of SC *after* the operation has taken place, *á la* Z [2].) That is, an add operator just inserts a new social commitment into the record, and a delete operator just removes any matching social commitments from the record. The *match* function takes a commitment and a set of commitments and returns a subset of the second argument as follows:

$\forall sc$: $socialCommitment, SC$: $\mathbf{P} socialCommitment \bullet match(sc, SC) \equiv$
$\{i \in SC | sc.debtor = i.debtor \wedge sc.creditor = i.creditor \wedge$
$typeOf(sc.action) \sqsubseteq typeOf(i.action)\}$

The reader may have noticed that there is no order specified on the application of several operators in response to a message, and, as a result, it is therefore possible that a delete operation may not remove any social commitments at all. In fact, this could be the case in Alice and Bob's meeting. If Bob were to reply to Alice (without first sending an acknowledgement) and the observer first applied the (delete,(Bob,Alice,reply)) operator, it would remove *both* the (Bob,Alice,reply) and the (Bob,Alice,ack) social commitments from the social commitments record. Then, when the observer applied the second operator, (delete,(Bob,Alice,ack)), there would be no change to the social commitments record. Our choice is not to worry about such null deletions, but other implementations may wish to avoid such empty applications either by applying the least specific deletions first if there is a subsumption relationship among operators, or by changing the match() function to only match on the most specific social commitment in the argument set.

Space limitations prohibit a detailed account of the formalization here, but a detailed formalization may be found in [3].

5 An Example

As a more formal example, we repeat the example of Bob and Alice's meeting using the more formal framework and tracking the conversation through to the end (signaled by there being no more social commitments left from the conversation). Figure 4 shows an interaction diagram of the conversation: Alice first

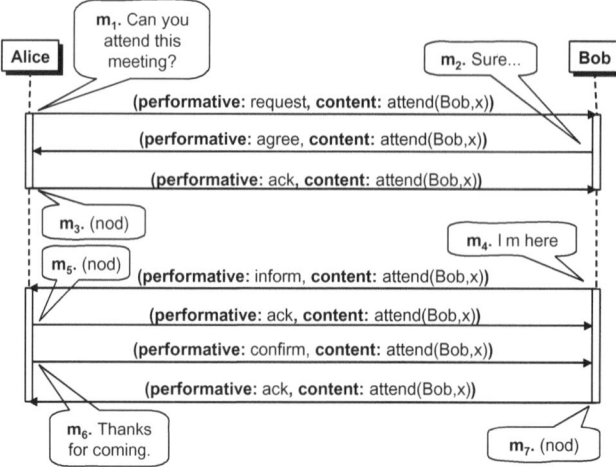

Fig. 4. Alice and Bob's conversation about a meeting

asks Bob to attend a meeting, "x" [1], by sending a message to Bob with a *request* performative and a contents describing the request, $(attend(Bob, x))$. Bob immediately confirms his acceptance to attend the meeting, by sending a message back to Alice with an agree performative and the same descriptive content. Alice acknowledges by sending an ack message back to Bob.

Later, Bob sends another message to Alice, informing him that the predicate, $attend(Bob, x)$, is true, that he is currently attending the meeting. Alice acknowledges. Alice then responds by sending a message to Bob with a confirm-complete performative, and the same contents. Bob acknowledges.

Does Alice and Bob's conversation conform to the social norms implied by the policies? Figure 5 describes the conversation in terms of the messages, policies, social commitment operators, and the constantly changing set of social commitments held by both Bob and Alice, and that would be held by an observer listening to the conversation.

Each row in Figure 5 represents the same message passing between the conversational participants as the corresponding cartoon balloons in Figure 4. In row m_1, Alice sends a message with a request performative to Bob and containing the content predicate $attend(Bob, x)$. Then Bob, Alice, and the observer can look up *request* in the policies in Figure 3 and see that there are two applicable policies (by searching up the lattice from the *request* node) representing policy P-inform and P-propose. To apply these policies, we need only apply the operators, which are $(add, (receiver, sender, reply))$ and $(add, (receiver, sender, ack))$. So we add these two social commitments to our set of social commitments.

Note that we have a slight notational difficulty here. We need to contextualize the reply and the *ack* social commitments with *what* to reply/acknowledge to. In

---

[1] The meeting is normally described by an expression, but we omit the details here for the sake of brevity.

Message					Policy	Operator	Social Commitments
Id	performative	sender	rec r	content			
m_1	request	Alice	Bob	attend(Bob, x)	P-request P-inform	(add,(Bob, Alice, reply(m_1))) (add,(Bob, Alice, ack(m_1)))	(Bob, Alice, reply(m_1)) (Bob, Alice, ack(m_1))

m_2	agree	Bob	Alice	attend(Bob, x)	P-reply
					P-ack
					P-agree
					
					P-inform
						(delete,(Bob, Alice, reply(m_1)))
						(delete,(Bob, Alice, ack(m_1)))
						(add,(Bob, Alice,
						      attend(Bob,x)))
						(add,(Bob, Alice, p-d(Bob,x)))
						(add,(Alice, Bob, ack(m_2)))
							~~(Bob, Alice, reply(m_1))~~
							~~(Bob, Alice, ack(m_1))~~
							(Bob, Alice,
							      attend(Bob,x))
							(Bob, Alice,p-d(Bob,x))
							(Alice, Bob, ack(m_2))

m_3	ack	Alice	Bob	attend(Bob, x)	 P-ack	 (delete,(Alice, Bob, ack(m_2)))	(Bob, Alice, attend(Bob,x)) (Bob, Alice,p-d(Bob,x)) ~~(Alice, Bob, ack(m_2))~~
m_4	propose-discharge	Bob	Alice	attend(Bob, x)	 P-prop-dis P-inform	 (delete,(Bob,Alice,p-d(Bob,x))) (add,(Alice,Bob,r-p-d(Bob,x))) (add,(Alice, Bob, ack(m_4)))	(Bob, Alice, attend(Bob,x)) ~~(Bob, Alice,p-d(Bob,x))~~ (Alice,Bob,r-p-d(Bob,x)) (Alice, Bob, ack(m_4))
m_5	ack	Alice	Bob	attend(Bob, x)	 P-ack	 (delete,(Alice, Bob, ack(m_4)))	(Bob, Alice, attend(Bob,x)) (Alice,Bob,r-p-d(Bob,x)) ~~(Alice, Bob, ack(m_4))~~
m_6	confirm	Alice	Bob	attend(Bob, x)	P-confirm P-reply-p-d P-inform	(delete,(Bob, Alice, attend(Bob,x)) (delete, (Alice,Bob,r-p-d(Bob,x))) (add,(Bob, Alice, ack(m_6)))	~~(Bob, Alice,~~ ~~ attend(Bob,x))~~ ~~(Alice,Bob,r-p-d(Bob,x))~~ (Bob, Alice, ack(m_6))
m_7	ack	Bob	Alice	attend(Bob, x)	P-ack	(delete,(Bob, Alice, ack(m_6)))	~~(Bob, Alice, ack(m_6))~~

Fig. 5. Alice and Bob's conversation about a meeting

the software, this is just done by attaching a copy of the message, which allows us to take advantage of FIPA's *reply-with* field and unambiguously mark the message as specifically in the context of the original inform/request message. However, here, we use the notation "*reply(message$_i$)*" to succinctly show the same thing.

The m_2 row of Figure 5 shows Bob immediately agreeing to go to the meeting. (He could have acknowledged receipt of the message first, which would have deleted the $(Bob, Alice, ack(m_1))$ commitment.) He replied with an *agree* performative, which isn't listed in Figure 3, but is a subtype of *affirmative-reply* (see Figure 1). Looking up the policies for *affirmative-reply* in Figure 3 shows that four policies are applicable (representing policies P-reply, P-ack, P-agree, and P-inform). These four policies can be applied in any order, but all sequences will yield the same end result (although intermediate results may differ). Applying these policies in the order given, $(delete, (Bob, Alice, reply(m_1)))$ will delete *both* social commitments $(Bob, Alice, reply(m_1))$ and $(Bob, Alice, ack(m_1))$.

$(delete, (Bob, Alice, ack(m_1)))$ will find nothing to delete (because the "target" has just been deleted), but this is fine. The $(add, (Bob, Alice, attend(Bob, x)))$ operator is parameterized with the action predicate in the contents of the m_2 message, and adds the $(Bob, Alice, attend(Bob, x))$ social commitment to the set of social commitments. Finally, the $(add, (Alice, Bob, ack(m_2)))$ operator adds the required commitment for Bob to acknowledge.

The m_3 row shows Bob acknowledging the previous *agree* message, and removing the social commitment for that acknowledgement.

Time passes, and the meeting commences. In row m_4, Bob informs Alice that he has fulfilled his commitment, $(Bob, Alice, attend(Bob, x))$, to attend the meeting, which invokes two policies, P-inform and P-propose-discharge. This message does *not* remove the $(Bob, Alice, attend(Bob, x))$ commitment. Intuitively, this is because Alice has not yet confirmed that Bob has attended the meeting and has satisfactorily fulfilled his commitment. If Alice were an agent that could sense her environment, and could "see" that Bob were in attendance, Bob would not have to send this message and we wouldn't have to include rows m_4 and m_5 in the table.

Row m_5 shows Alice acknowledging Bob's inform.

In row m_6, Alice has "seen" that Bob is in attendance at the meeting and sends a message with the confirm performative. This invokes three policies (P-done, P-reply-propose-discharge, and P-inform) which delete Bob's outstanding commitments to attend the meeting and to tell Alice about it and adds a commitment for Bob to acknowledge the confirm message.

Finally, in row m_7, Bob acknowledges Alice's last message, which removes the last of the social commitments. There being no more social commitments left, the conversation is over.

Just so the reader is not left with the impression that this work only applies to hypothetical human examples, we include a snapshot of the CASA system in the process of an actual agent conversation (see Figure 6). Here, we show a Cooperation Domain that has just fulfilled its obligations in three distinct (and interleaved) conversations: a request-to-join-CD conversation, a request-to-subscribe (to be updated on membership changes) conversation, and a request-for-a-membership-list conversation. The upper pane in the snapshot shows the recently discharged social commitments. The lower pane shows the message just received from another agent (called Jason) acknowledging successful completion of the get-members request (a *reply* performative).

5.1   Variations: Flexibility and Efficiency

As already mentioned, if Alice could sense her environment, she could notice on her own that Bob was attending the meeting, and messages m_4 and m_5 (rows m_4 and m_5 in Figure 5) could be omitted. If this were the case, and Bob sent the inform message anyway, the conversation would still not be harmed. The number of the messages in the conversation would drop from 7 to 5.

Our protocols, as defined in Table 2 and Figure 3, call for every message to be acknowledged. This is an option in our system, and can easily be "turned off" by merely deleting the policies in Figure 3 associated with P-inform and P-ack. If we do remove the P-inform policy, then messages m_3, m_5 and m_7 disappear and the number of messages drops from 7 to 4.

By combining both strategies in the previous two paragraphs, we can reduce the number of messages in the conversation from 7 to 3. The resulting conversation appears in Figure 7.

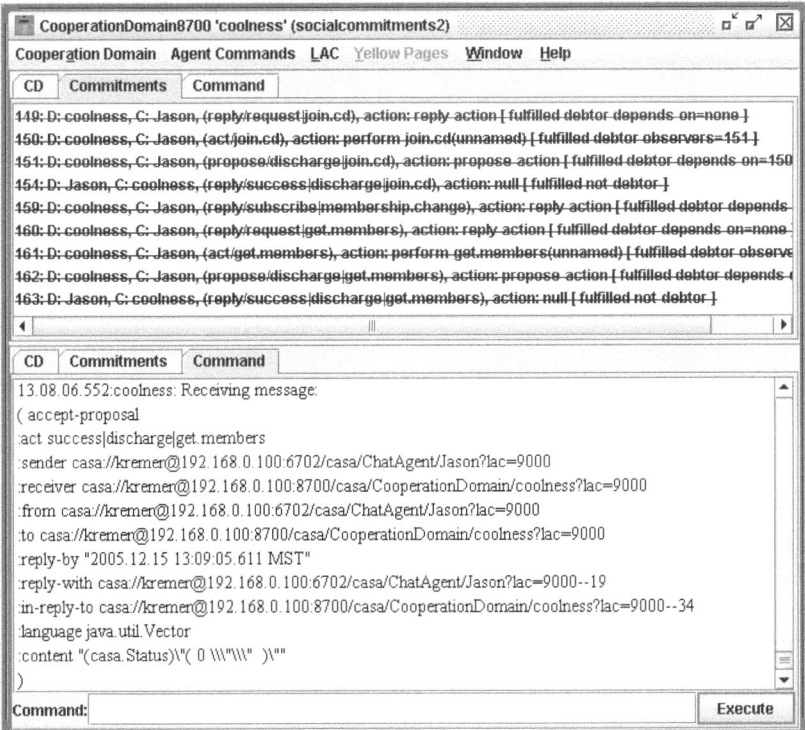

Fig. 6. A CASA CD conversing with another agent requesting to join the CD

5.2 Implementation Considerations

Figure 8 shows the conversational "schema" that arises from the polices involved in a typical *request* conversation, like the one between Alice and Bob or between the CD and another agent in Section 5. This figure is from the viewpoint of the actual implementation in CASA. The heavy vertical lines represent the two agents over time. The heavy horizontal arrows indicate messages, and the reader will no doubt notice that there are *eight* messages exchanged in this seemingly simple conversation. The reader should not be put off by this: this is only the worst case, and we have shown how this conversation can be dramatically simplified (optimized) earlier in this section. CASA can do this optimization.

Each of Figure 8's messages are labelled above with their possible performatives and their supertype sublattice. Arrows emerging from the performative names represent the applicable policies and social commitment operators (solid indicates *add*, and dashed indicates *delete*). The policy arrows terminate on shared (underscored) and private (grayed) social commitments. Some interesting details of the theory and implementation are shown in this diagram that aren't explicit elsewhere in this paper:

The lighter-colored (non-underscored) private social commitments in the figure form the method we use to attach agent executable code (usually a method

Message				Policy	Operator	Social Commitments
Id	performative	sender	rec r	content			
m_1	request	Alice	Bob	attend(Bob, x)	P-request	(add,(Bob, Alice, reply(m_1)))	(Bob, Alice, reply(m_1))
m_2	done	Bob	Alice	attend(Bob, x)	P-reply P-prop-dis	(delete,(Bob, Alice, reply(m_1))) (add,(Alice,Bob,r-p-d(Bob,x)))	~~(Bob, Alice, reply(m_1))~~ (Alice,Bob,r-p-d(Bob,x))
m_6	confirm	Alice	Bob	attend(Bob, x)	P-reply-p-d	(delete,(Alice,Bob,r-p-d(Bob,x)))	~~(Alice,Bob,r-p-d(Bob,x))~~

Fig. 7. Alice and Bob's conversation about a meeting, without Bob's inform to Alice, and without policy P-inform

call) to the policies: one needs to reference some bit of the agent's code to "wake" the agent to a particular event. These private social commitments are always bound to an *inform*, but are usually referenced from some subtype of of *inform á la* the *template method* design pattern [10]. These template references are represented in the figure by the light-colored curved arrows among the performatives in the sub-lattices at center.

The curved arrow on the extreme left and right of the diagram connecting social commitments are *dependencies* between social commitments. This is a powerful concept that is easily implemented by the *observer* design pattern [10], and arises naturally in the system. For example, naturally, one needs to actually *perform* an action before proposing to discharge it.

6   Related Work

Conversations and commitments have been studied in argumentation [19], where the evolution of conversations is motivated by the commitments they imply, and which are not necessarily made explicit. Others have looked into the mechanics of conversations using operations advancing the state of commitments, which is a view independent of the intentional motives behind their advancement [6,12,14,15,18]. We share these views, and aim at identifying public elements binding the evolution of conversations.

7   Conclusion

The main contribution of this paper is to show how the FIPA performatives can be mapped onto a social commitment theory framework to allow observable social behaviour. "Rules" (or policies), like those described in this paper, act as a codification of social norms, so can be easily used by an observer to judge whether an agent is well behaved relative to the social norms. Social commitments, and the ontology of performatives can be used to implement agents, but agents do not have be to implemented as social commitment-style agents to be observed and monitored by an observing agent using commitments as described here.

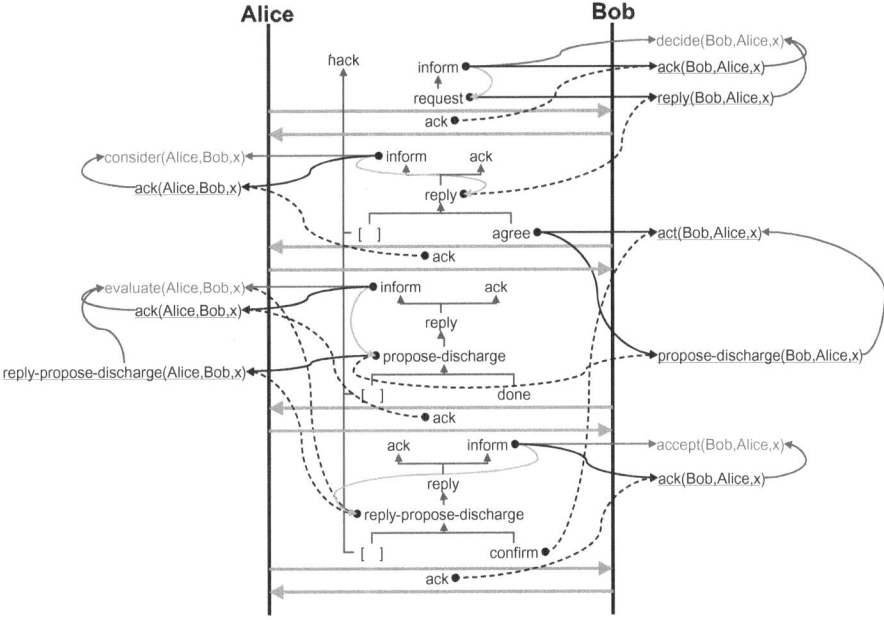

Fig. 8. An implementation view of the policies associated with a typical client-server *request* conversation

Acknowledgments

The authors thank the Canadian Natural Science and Engineering Research Council (NSERC) for their support.

References

1. C. Castelfranchi. Commitments: From individual intentions to groups and organizations. In *Proceedings of the First International Conference on Multi-Agent Systems*, pages 41–48, San Francisco, CA, June 1995.
2. A. Diller. *Z: An Introduction to Formal Methods.* John Wiley & Sons, Inc., Sussex, England, 1990.
3. R.A. Flores. *Modelling agent conversations for action.* Ph.D. thesis, Department of Computer Science, University of Calgary, June 2002.
4. R.A. Flores and R. Kremer. Formal conversations for the contract net protocol. In V. Marik, O. Stepankova, H. Krautwurmova, and M. Luck, editors, *Multi-Agent Systems and Applications II*, volume 2322 of *Lecture Notes in Artificial Intelligence*, pages 169–179. Springer Verlag, 2002.
5. R.A. Flores and R. Kremer. To commit or not to commit: Modelling agent conversations for action. *Computational Intelligence*, 18(2):120–173, 2003.
6. R.A. Flores and R. Kremer. Principled approach to construct complex conversation protocols. In A.Y. Tawfik, and S.D. Goodwin, editors, *Advances in Artificial Intelligence*, volume 3060 of *Lecture Notes in Artificial Intelligence*, pages 1–15. Springer Verlag, 2004.

108 R. Kremer and R.A. Flores

7. R.A. Flores, P. Pasquier, and B. Chaib-draa. Conversational semantic sustained by social commitments. In F. Dignum, and R. van Eijk, editors, *Autonomous Agents and Multi-Agent Systems*. To appear.
8. Foundation for Intelligent Physical Agents (FIPA). FIPA ACL message structure specification. document number SC00061G, FIPA TC communication. http://www.fipa.org/specs/fipa00061/SC00061G.html, Dec. 2003.
9. Foundation for Intelligent Physical Agents (FIPA). FIPA communicative act library specification. document number SC00037J, FIPA TC communication. http://www.fipa.org/specs/fipa00037/SC00037J.html, Dec. 2003.
10. E. Gamma, R. Helm, R. Johnson, and J. Vlissides. *Design Patterns: Elements of Reusable Object-Oriented Software*. Addison-Wesley Professional Computing Series. Addison-Wesley, Reading, Mass., 1994.
11. J. Heard and R. Kremer. Detecting broken social commitments. In this volume.
12. S. Khan and Y. Lesperance. On the semantics of conditional commitments. In this volume.
13. R. Kremer, R.A. Flores, and C. LaFournie. *Advances in Agent Communication*, chapter A Performative Type Hierarchy and Other Interesting Considerations in the Design of the CASA Agent Architecture. In F. Dignum, and R. van Eijk, and M-P. Huget, editors, *Advances in Agent Communication*, volume 2922 of *Lecture Notes in Computer Science*, pages 59–74. Springer Verlag, 2004. Available: http://sern.ucalgary.ca/ kremer/papers/-AdvancesInAgentCommunication_KremerFloresLaFournie.pdf.
14. A. Mallya and M. Singh. Introducing Preferences into Commitment Protocols. In this volume.
15. P. Pasquier, M. Bergeron, and B. Chaib-draa. Diagal: A generic ACL for open systems. In M.-P. Gleizes, A. Omicini, and F. Zambonelli, editors, *ESAW*, volume 3451 of *Lecture Notes in Artificial Intelligence*, pp 139–152. Springer Verlag, 2004.
16. P. Pasquier, R.A. Flores, and B. Chaib-draa. Modelling flexible social commitments and their enforcement. In M.-P. Gleizes, A. Omicini, and F. Zambonelli, editors, *ESAW*, volume 3451 of *Lecture Notes in Artificial Intelligence*, pages 153–165. Springer Verlag, 2004.
17. M. Singh. Agent communication languages: Rethinking the principles. *IEEE Computer*, 31(12):40–47, 1998.
18. M. Verdicchio and M. Colombetti. A commitment-based Communicative Act Library. In this volume.
19. D. Walton and E. Krabbe. *Commitment in Dialogue: Basic Concepts of Interpersonal Reasoning*. State University of New York Press, 1995.

Using Social Commitments to Control the Agents' Freedom of Speech

Guillaume Muller and Laurent Vercouter

SMA/G2I/ÉNS des Mines de Saint-Étienne
158 cours Fauriel,
42023 Saint-Étienne
France
{muller, vercouter}@emse.fr

Abstract. Communication is essential in multi-agent systems, since it allows agents to share knowledge and to coordinate. However, in open multi-agent systems, autonomous and heterogeneous agents can dynamically enter or leave the system. It is then important to take into account that some agents may behave badly, *i.e.* may not respect the rules that make the system function properly. In this article, we focus on communication rules and, especially, on the means necessary to detect when agents lie. Based on a model of the social semantics adapted to decentralised system, we first explicit the limits of the communicative behaviour of an agent, through the definition of obligations. Then, we propose a decentralised mechanism to detect situations where the obligations are violated. This mechanism is used to identify agents that exceed their rights and to build a representation of the honesty of the other agents by the way of a reputation value.

Introduction

Communication in multi-agent systems (MAS) is essential for the cooperation and coordination of autonomous entities. However, in open systems, some agents may not respect – voluntarily or not – the rules that govern a good communicating behaviour. In this paper, we focus on the detection of incoherent communicative behaviours.

Thanks to a formalism that comes from the social semantics approach of agent communication, agents are enabled to represent and reason on their communications. This paper first focuses on the adaptation of such a formalism (from [3]) to decentralised systems. Secondly, some norms are defined that explicit the limits of a good communicative behaviour. Then a decentralised process to detect lies is proposed. Finally the outcome of this process is used to update reputation values that, in turn, can be used in future interactions to trust only communication from highly reputed agents.

This paper is composed as follows: Section 1 presents the communicative framework and defines some contradictory situations that should be avoided in open and decentralised MAS. Section 2 shortly introduces the formalism of social commitments that is used, as well as its adaptation to open and decentralised MAS. This formalism is, then, used in Section 3 to define a process that allows an agent to locally detect liars. Finally, Section 4 shows how this process is integrated into a more general framework for the revision of reputation values.

F. Dignum, R. van Eijk, and R. Flores (Eds.): AC 2005/2006, LNAI 3859, pp. 109–123, 2006.

1   Motivations

The work presented in this paper takes place in decentralised and open multi-agents systems. In such systems, assumptions on the internal implementation of the agents are reduced to the minimum, in order to allow heterogeneous agents to enter or quit the system at any time. Some agents might therefore behave unpredictably and disturb the functioning of the overall system. This situation is particularly dangerous in open and decentralised systems since cooperation of the composing entities is required for the core components, like the transmission of communication, to function.

Some guarantees such as authentication, integrity, confidentiality, etc. can be obtained by the use of security techniques. However, there are also some threats upon the content of the messages.

1.1   Framework

In order to defend against such behaviours, the human societies created mechanisms based on social interactions. Recent works [16,4,15] suggest to use such mechanisms, like the calculation and the use of other agents reputation, as a solution to this problem in open and decentralised MAS. The reputation of an agent is usually evaluated based on its previous behaviour. The more an agent had bad behaviours, the lower its reputation is.

In such conditions, it is impossible to build a single reputation value stored in a central repository and shared by every agent: each agent computes locally its own subjective reputation toward a specific target. We propose [12] to enable agents with a trust model as shown in Figure 1, although agents built with completely different trust models, or with no trust model at all, may be present at the same time in the system. The

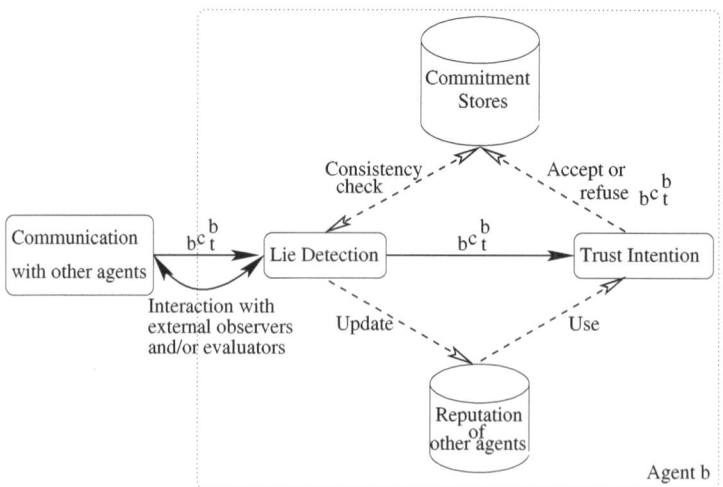

Fig. 1. General overview of the trust model

architecture of the trust model is composed of three main components: the communication module, the lies detection module and the trust intention module. When a communication is received from the communication module, as a social commitment, a first process is started that checks if it can identify a lie based on the current commitment stores and the incoming commitment. As a result, the process updates the reputation values associated to the utterer. If the module detects that the message is a lie, then it also updates its commitment stores according to the refusal of the message. If no lie is detected, it does not mean there is no lie. Therefore, to prevent a possible future deception, the commitment is transmitted to the trust intention module. This module uses the reputation values computed on earlier interactions to decide whether to trust or not the incoming commitment. We argue that this trust model, by increasing agents information regarding their peers will increase the efficiency of overall system.

In this paper, we focus on the lie detection module. The following sections first present the contradictory situations that constitute the basis of the decentralised lie detection process. Then, a model of communication which is well suited for external observation is presented. Finally, the decentralised process that agents use to detect lies by reasoning on their peers' communications is detailed.

1.2   Contradictory Situations

As an example, we use a scenario of information sharing in a peer-to-peer network of agents. Some peers have some information about the show times for some movie theaters. Others can query such information. Figure 2 shows such a situation with six agents. Agent 5 possesses the show times for the "Royal" movie theater. Agent 6 possesses he show times for the "Méliès" movie theater. Agent 3 has some parts of both show times. Agent 1 emits a query to know which theaters show the movie "Shrek" on Saturday evening. The arrows in Figure 2 show the spreading of the query by the means of the broadcasting mechanism used in peer-to-peer systems like Gnutella. Agent 1 sends this query to its neighbours, *i.e.* the agents to which it is directly connected. Then, these agents forward the query to their own neighbours. This process is only iterated a fixed number of times, in order not to overload the network. During this spreading process, each agent that receives the query can look if it locally has the queried information. If it has this information, it answers by using the same path as the query came from. Figure 3 shows the replies comming back to Agent 1 using this mechanism for the query considered in Figure 2. In this scenario, Agent 4 is in such a situation that it can hide and/or modify some answers for the Méliès theater show times. The case of simply hiding information is already solved in peer-to-peer systems thanks to the redundancy of information. In this paper we focus on the second and more difficult problem that consist in an agent sending an information that does not correspond to its beliefs. For instance, Agent 4, believes that the Méliès shows the movie "Shrek" on Saturday evening because of the message from Agent 6. However, it can modify Agent 6's answer so that it expresses that the Méliès does not show the movie "Shrek" on Saturday evening and send it back to Agent 1.

In such agentified peer-to-peer networks, two types of contradiction can be defined : contradiction in what is transmitted and contradiction in what is sent. The scenario presented above underlines the first kind of contradiction. An agent T can commits to

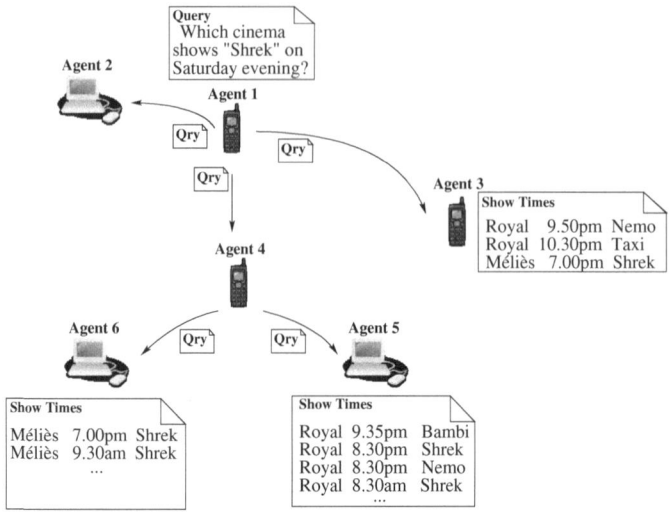

Fig. 2. Example of querying in a peer-to-peer theater show times sharing

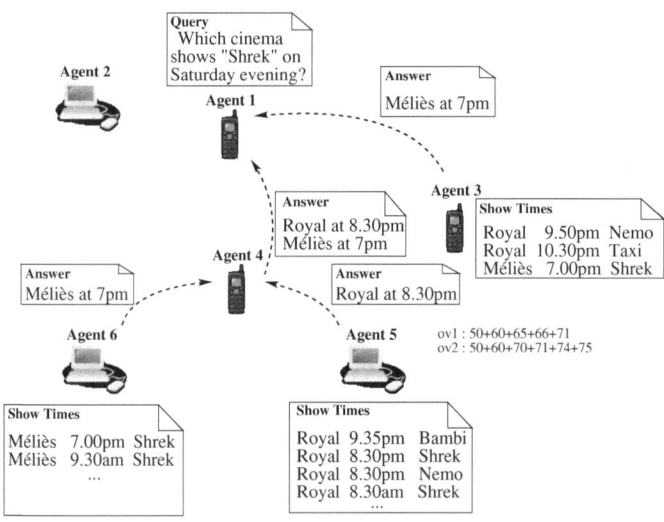

Fig. 3. Getting back the replies form a query in a peer-to-peer theater show times sharing

an agent B on a given content, whereas another agent A was previously committed to it with an inconsistent content (type of contradiction 4(b), figure 4). The contradiction in what is sent arises when an agent T commits to inconsistent contents, by sending a message with a certain content to an agent A and another message with an inconsistent content to another agent B (type of contradiction 4(a), figure 4).

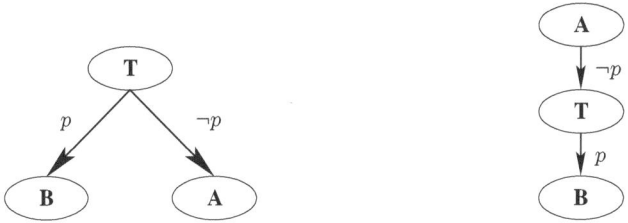

(a) An agent T should not contradict itself.   (b) An agent T should not contradict an accepted information.

Fig. 4. Contradictory behaviours that are not desirable in open and decentralised MAS

These types of contradiction are often the consequence of lie. In order to detect and sanction such behaviours, agents should be able to represent and reason about their peers' communications. Next section presents a model of communication that agents can use to detect such contradictory behaviours, in a decentralised system like described in this section.

2   Agent Communication

The scenario presented in the previous section emphasizes that agents should be able to reason about their communications in order to detect lies. This requires a formalism for inter-agent communications. There are three main approaches to communication modeling [7]: behavioural, mentalistic, and social. Most of those works inherits from the speech act theory [2,17].

2.1   Various Approaches to Agent Communication

The behavioural approach [14] defines the meaning of a speech act by its usage in interaction protocols. It is very effective for implementation, but too rigid and static for open MAS. The mentalistic approach is based on the agents' mental states [5,9]. This approach is unsuited for observations since, in open systems, agents may come from external designers and their internal implementation may remain inaccessible. An agent does not have access to the mental states of another and, therefore, cannot detect lies based on this representation. [18] discusses more limits to this approach. The social approach [18,6,3,13,19] associates speech acts with social commitments.

In the context of this work (detailed section 1) agents only have access to what they perceive. As far as communication is concerned, this implies that an agent only has access to the messages it sends, receives and observes (directly or that are transmitted by other agents). Therefore, agents need to represent communications based on their observations, using a formalism external from the agent. The social semantics therefore is well suited for observation of the communications by single agents, as it associates to the utterance of a speech act an object (the social commitment) that is external to the agent. It also does not consider any constraint on the actual language used in the messages. The lies detection process presented in this article is based on an operational semantics of the social approach from [3].

2.2 Decentralised Model of Social Commitments

In [3], a formalism is presented for social commitments. However, this model is centralised; commitment are stored in shared places that are publicly available. In open and decentralised MAS, it is not possible to make such an assumption. This model can be adapted to decentralised systems as follows:

$$c(\text{debt}, \text{cred}, \text{utterance\_time}, \text{validity\_time}, \text{state}(t), \text{content})$$

debt is the `debtor`, the agent which is committed.

cred is the `creditor`, the agent to which the `debtor` is committed. Here, we differ from [3], considering that if an agent has to commit to a set of agents, then it commits separately to each agent of the set.

utterance_time is the time when the message that created the commitment has been uttered.

validity_time is the *interval* of time associated with the commitment. When the current time is not in this interval, the commitment cannot be in the active state.

state(t) is *a function* of time. This function returns the state of the commitment object at time t, that can be either `inactive`, `active`, `fulfilled`, `violated` or `canceled`.

content is the content to which the `debtor` is committed. Its exact composition is out of the scope of this paper. However, we make two assumptions on this field: (i) inconsistency between two contents can be deduced and is defined by a function *inconsistent* : $\mathcal{C} \times \mathcal{C} \mapsto \{true, false\}$ where $\mathcal{C}$ is the domain of the contents; (ii) there should also be a function *context* : $\mathcal{C} \mapsto \mathcal{S}$ (where $\mathcal{S}$ is the overall set of topics that *cont* can be about) that returns the topic of the content *cont*. This latter is used to compute a reputation value for each possible context, e.g., providing weather informations, providing theater show times...

A commitment follows a life-cycle (as in [6]) that is composed of the following states:

- When the commitment is created, it is either in the `active` or `inactive` state, according to the current time being (resp. or not being) in between the validity time interval bounds.
- The commitment can be `fulfilled` (resp. `violated`) if the agent does (resp. does not) perform what it is committed to.
- The commitment can also be `canceled`.

However, in open and decentralised MAS, there is no shared and public place to store commitments. Therefore, we assume that each agent maintains its own local representation of the commitments. Consequently, we note $_x c_i^j$, a commitment from i (debtor) to j (creditor) as agent x represents it. Commitments are uniquely identified by the `creditor`, the `debtor`, the `utterance_time`, and the `content`.

As a consequence of the decentralization, one agent can observe a message, create the associated commitment (with the help of a mapping such as [6]) and then may be unable to observe another message that would have modified the commitment. Such situations may occur, for instance, if latter the message is cyphered or if the agent loses connection with a part of the peer-to-peer network... Therefore, according to the agent considered, the local representation of a commitment can differ. For instance, an agent can believe that a commitment is in the `violated` state and discover, with a message provided later by another agent, that it has been canceled before being violated. This is the kind of situation the processes described in the next sections deal with.

The decentralization of the commitments has another consequence: the commitment stores might be incomplete. A single agent does not have access to the overall set of commitments of the system since it can only observe some messages. As a consequence, it can build the commitments associated to the messages it has observed. The local commitment stores only contain commitments the agent has taken or that have been taken toward it, plus some commitments related to messages the agent may have observed, if it has the capacity to do so. We note by $_xCS_i^j$ agent x's representation of the commitment store from agent i toward agent j.

The detection of contradictions within these commitment stores constitute the basics of the detection of lies in our framework. The next section presents how we use such commitment stores to detect lies.

3   Lies Detection

The scenario presented in Section 1.2 emphasizes that a global result (such as fetching cinema timetables) is achieved by a collective activity of several agents. Therefore, agents that do not behave as expected, *i.e.* that do not respect the obligations that define a "good" behaviour, can prevent the success of the collective task. We focus here on communicative actions and on fraud detection within agent communications.

The general outline of the lies detection process is as follows:

1. An agent (that plays the role of detector) observes some messages between other agents.
2. This detector builds the commitments associated with the messages observed, using a mapping (e.g. [6]). It adds these commitments to its local representation of the commitment stores.
3. Based on its local representation of the commitment stores, the detector can detect violations of some obligations.
4. The detector suspects the target of a lie. It starts a process that aims to determine if a lie actually occurred or if there is another reason for the inconsistency (e.g. the detector's local representations of the commitment stores need to be updated, the target simply transmitted a lie, ...).

The process is decentralised due to the fact that the role of detector can be played by any agent of the system and may require the cooperation of other agents. This section first introduces the obligations we define, then presents the two processes. The first process consists in detecting the violations and the second process seeks for the source of the inconsistency.

3.1 Obligations in Communicative Behaviours

The good and bad communicative behaviours of agents can be defined according to the states of their commitment stores. We first need to define what is inconsistency between commitments in order to define what are the authorized and prohibited states for the commitment stores.

Inconsistent Commitments. We define the inconsistency of commitments as follows (where $\mathcal{T}$ is the domain of time):

$$\forall t \in \mathcal{T}, \forall c \in {}_b CS_x^y, \forall c' \in {}_{b'} CS_{x'}^{y'},$$
$$(inconsistent(c, c')$$

$$\equiv$$

$$((c.\texttt{state}(t) = \texttt{active}) \vee (c.\texttt{state}(t) = \texttt{fulfilled})) \wedge$$
$$((c'.\texttt{state}(t) = \texttt{active}) \vee (c'.\texttt{state}(t) = \texttt{fulfilled})) \wedge$$
$$inconsistent(c.\texttt{content}, c'.\texttt{content}))$$

Two commitments are inconsistent if they are, at the same time t, in a "positive" state (`active` or `fulfilled`) and if their contents are inconsistent.

Inconsistency in a set of commitments $\mathcal{U}$, is defined if there are two inconsistent commitents in it, more formally:

$$inconsistent(\mathcal{U})$$

$$\equiv$$

$$\exists c \in \mathcal{U} \wedge \exists c' \in \mathcal{U} \text{ s.a. } inconsistent(c, c')$$

By definition, a commitment store is a set of commitments. The formula above therefore also define inconsistency of a commitment store. Moreover, as a consequence of the definition of commitment stores, a union of commitment stores is also a set of commitments. Inconsistency of a union of commitment stores is also expressed in the formula above as the co-occurence of (at least) two inconsistent commitments in the union.

Obligations and Their Violations. With obligations, we define the limits of an acceptable communicative behaviour. These obligations are written using deontic logic [20]. The modal operator O is used to represent an obligation such that $O(\alpha)$ expresses that α is an obligatory state.

In the definition of the obligations we use $CS_x^y(t)$ instead of ${}_b CS_x^y(t)$ because obligations are defined in a system perspective, not for a single agent. However, each agent uses a local instanciation of the formulae during the process of detection of a violation.

In the scenario considered in this paper, communication between agents should respect the following obligations ($\Omega(t)$ is the set of the agents in the system at time t):

$$O(\forall t \in \mathcal{T}, \forall x \in \Omega(t), \neg inconsistent(\bigcup_{y \in \Omega(t)} CS_x^y(t)))$$

which is the contradiction of the debtor. In the example shown by Figure 5, Agent 4 is the debtor of inconsistent commitments (it commits both on the fact that the "Méliès"

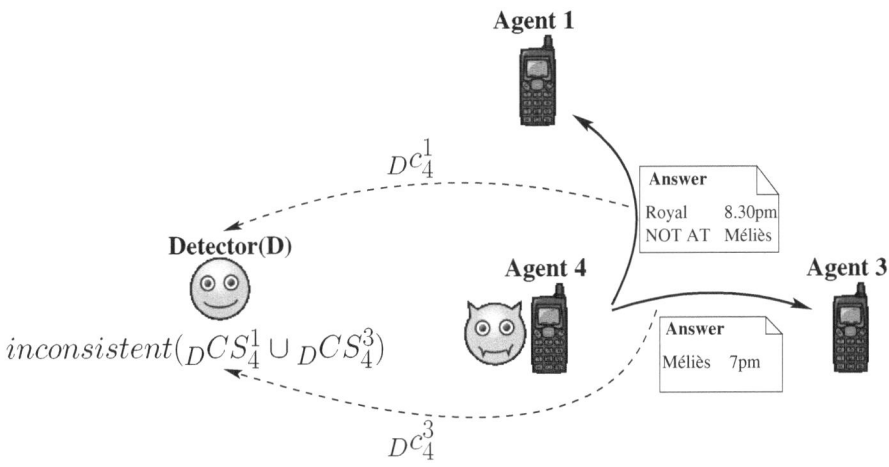

Fig. 5. Contradiction of the debtor

shows the movie and that it does not show the movie) and is in a situation of contradiction of the debtor. When such a situation is observed, we consider that Agent 4 has lied. We assume that the messages have the non-repudiation [1] property to prevent an agent from claiming that it did not send an observed message.

It is important to note that this obligation does not prevent an agent from changing its beliefs. It only constrains an agent to cancel its previous commitments, that are still active, about a given content α, if the agent wants to create a commitment about a content β that would be inconsistent with α. Then, the only way for Agent 4 to give evidence that it did not lie in the example of Figure 5 is to provide a message proving it has canceled one of the two inconsistent commitments before creating the other.

We also define a contradiction in transmission:

$$O(\forall t \in \mathcal{T}, \forall x \in \Omega(t), \forall c \in \bigcup_{y \in \Omega(t)} CS_x^y, \forall c' \in \bigcup_{y' \in \Omega(t)} CS_{y'}^x,$$

$$(c.\texttt{utterance\_time} > c'.\texttt{utterance\_time}) \wedge \neg inconsistent(c, c'))$$

This contradiction (figure 6) only appears if Agent 4 sent its message to Agent 1 after it received the message from Agent 6. If Agent 4 wants to send its message to Agent 1, it has to cancel explicitly the commitments for which it is creditor and that are inconsistent with the message to send.

However, a violation of the obligation is not always a lie. The agent that detects the violation of the obligation may have a local representation of some commitment stores that needs to be updated. For instance, the agent might have missed a message that canceled one of the commitments involved in the inconsistency. The detection of inconsistencies is therefore only the first step of the detection of lies. When a violation of one of the obligations is detected, it begins a process that leads either to such an update or to the evidence that a lie was performed.

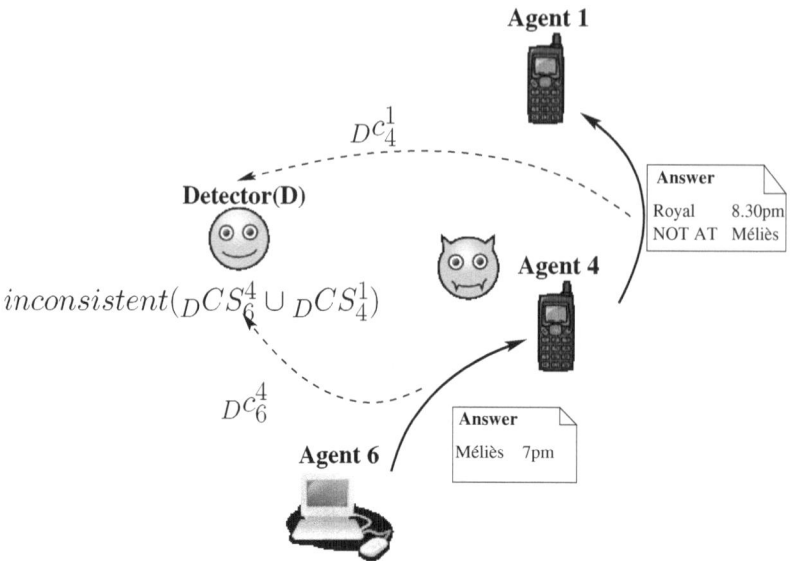

Fig. 6. Contradiction in transmission

3.2   Asking for Justification

The detector asks the agent suspected of a lie to provide a "proof" that, at least, one of the commitments involved in the inconsistency has been canceled. In the communication framework, a "proof" is a digitally signed message with the non-repudiation property [1]. If the suspected agent cannot give a proof that it has canceled one of the commitments, then the detector considers that it lied and sets the state of one of the commitments for which it is debtor in the `violated` state. How the detector chooses its local representation of the commitment to change is free. In the remaining of the paper, we consider it bases its decision on its trust model.

Previous sections show that there are several cases where the lies detection module is weak and cannot conclude that a lie occured. That's the reason why it is used in conjunction with a trust intention module that estimates the honesty of an agent based on its past behaviours. Next section presents this trust intention module.

4   Reasoning About Lies

Each time a lie is detected, the beneficiary of this detection should use this information to update its representation of the target. The information is usually merged in an evaluation of the honesty of the target: its reputation. Figure 1 (page 110) shows how an agent links lies detection with reputation: the *lies detection* module implements the processes described in Section 3.1. During these processes the beneficiary may have to communicate with other agents (observers and evaluators) and uses its *local beliefs* to check if an inconsistency occurs. This process can result in an update of the reputation attached to some agents. Then, if the commitment $_bc_t^x$ (commitment from t to x as perceived by b) has not been detected as a lie, it is transmitted to the *trust intention* module that decides whether to accept the message (trust the sender) or refuse it (distrust the sender).

In this section we focus on and present briefly the *reputation of other agents* and the *trust intention* module. First, we describe different ways to use the detection of a lie in order to update reputations. We then show how an agent can use the reputation attached to other agents to avoid being deceived in the future.

4.1 Using Different Kinds of Reputation

Even if a target has lied to another agent, it is not always a systematic liar. In the same way, an agent that has not yet lied may become dishonest in its future communications. Then, it may be useful to estimate the honesty of the target by a degree rather by a boolean value. We represent reputation as a real number in the interval $[-1, +1]$. An agent which reputation is -1 is considered as a systematic liar whereas an agent with a reputation of $+1$ would be always honest. In addition to this interval, an agent's reputation can take the value unknown if there is too few information about it.

There exists different kinds of trust [10]. For instance, there are trusts related to the perceived environment, trust related to the presence of institution, trust between two specific agents, etc. Here, we focus on the latter: trust between two specific agents based on their experiences.

An agent maintains a trust model about another agent by the way of reputation values. An agent can compute a reputation value based on its direct experiences, or based on external information, therefore there are various kinds of reputation [11]. In the processes of building those reputations, CONTE *et al.* [4] distinguish different roles that agents can fulfill in a trust framework. In the case of a lie detection process, we identified a few roles:

A target is an agent that is judged.

A beneficiary is an agent that maintains the reputation value.

An observer is an agent that observes some commitments from the target.

An evaluator is an agent that transforms a set of commitments into a reputation value.

A gossiper is an agent that transmits a reputation value about the target to the beneficiary.

Depending on the agents that play these roles, a reputation value is more or less reliable. It is then important to identify different kinds of reputations that can have different values. From the notions of observation and detection introduced in the previous section, we define four kinds of reputation:

Direct Experience based Reputation (DEbRp) is based on direct experiences between the beneficiary and the target. A direct experience is a message that has been sent by the target to the beneficiary and that has either been detected as a lie or as an honest message.

Observation based Reputation (ObRp) is computed from observations about commitments made by the target toward agents other than the beneficiary. The beneficiary uses these observations to detect lies and to compute a reputation value.

Evaluation based Reputation (EbRp) is computed by merging recommendations (reputation values) transmitted by gossipers.

General Disposition to Trust (GDtT) is not attached to a specific target. This value is not interpersonal and it represents the inclination of the beneficiary to trust another agent if it does not have any information about its honesty.

For instance, the ObRp can use the accumulation of observations gathered during the justification process described in section 3.2. As far as the EbRp is concerned, it can be computed based on recommendations requested to gossipers when needed.

The functions used to compute reputation values based on aggregation of several sources are out of the scope of this paper. However, the functions for DEbRp, ObRp and EbRp can be found in [12]. In essence, reputation values are computed based on the number of positive, neutral or negative experiences, therefore, each time a lie is detected, the reputation value decreases and each time a correct behaviour is detected, the reputation value increases. Next section shows how an agent can use these various reputation values to decide whether to trust or not another agent.

4.2   Preventing Future Deceptions

The aim of the *trust intention* module is to decide whether the agent should trust or not a given target regarding a particular information. We consider here the specific case of communications where this information is a message sent by the target and where the decision process leads the agent to accept the message or refuse it. However, we think that this decision mechanism is general and can handle other situations where an agent

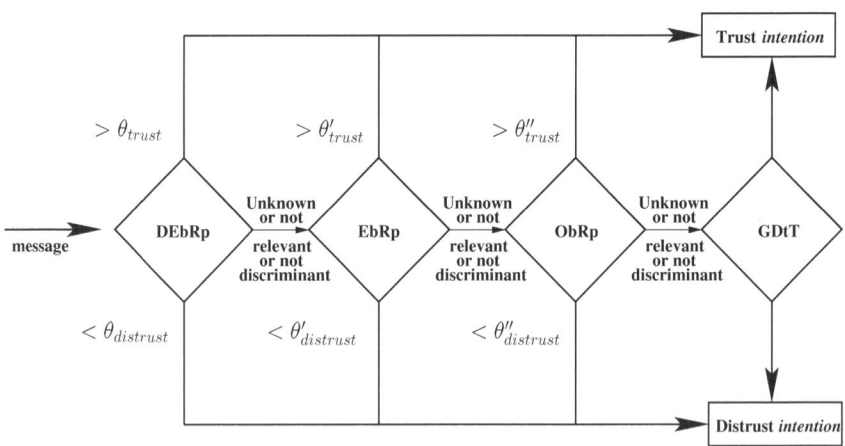

Fig. 7. Using reputation values to decide

should decide whether it trusts or not a target (e.g., anticipating if the target will fulfill or not its commitments, whether it will obey or not a norm...).

Figure 7 shows the decision process. The decision process works as follows: the agent first tries to use the reputation value it considers the most reliable (DEbRp in the figure). This kind of reputation may be sufficient to decide to intend to trust or not a target if it has a high (respectively low) value. This is represented in figure 7 by two thresholds θ_{trust} and $\theta_{distrust}$. If the DEbRp is greater than θ_{trust}, the agent trusts the target and accepts the message it received from it. At the opposite, if the DEbRp is less than $\theta_{distrust}$, the agent distrusts the target and refuses its message. Otherwise, the DEbRp does not permit the agent to decide whether the target should be trusted or not. These other cases consist in specific values of the DEbRp: either the "unknown" value, or a moderate value (between θ_{trust} and $\theta_{distrust}$).

A similar process is then used with the next kind of reputation (ObRp in the figure). The value is compared to two thresholds (θ'_{trust} and $\theta'_{distrust}$ that can be different from the thresholds used for DEbRp) in order to decide whether to trust or not the target. If this value is still not discriminant, EbRp is considered for decision. As a last resort, the agent's GDtT makes the decision.

To simplify the writings the thresholds appear as fixed values, but it is possible to consider various thresholds according to the situation (e.g., to express various levels of risk). Also, Figure 7 shows an ordering of the reputations that we think is common sense and that may be used in a general case: for instance, an agent may consider a reputation computed by another agent less reliable than the reputation that it has itself computed from messages directly observed. However, in some specific cases, it is possible to consider another ordering.

At the end of this decision mechanism, the agent has decided whether to trust or distrust the target. Then, there are two ways to deal with the message received: either the agent took the decision to trust it, in which case the message is accepted, or it took the decision not to trust it, in which case it is rejected. In the latter case the commitment associated with the message is `canceled`.

The main interest of the *trust intention* module is to preserve the agent from being deceived by some undetected lies. There are lies that are not detected by the *lies detection* module. Reputation can then be used not to believe messages sent by agents that have often lied in the past.

At the end of this decision process two undesirable cases may happen: (i) messages that are not lies may be rejected; (ii) undetected lies coming from agents with a high reputation may be accepted. If the former case should be avoided, the receiver does not have to definitely reject the message. It may rather asks some justifications to the target or to other agents. In the latter case, a deception occurs. The lie may be detected *a posteriori* if another message received later leads to an inconsistency with the undetected lie.

5 Conclusion

In this paper we address the problem of detecting dishonest agents, *i.e.* agents that do not respect their commitments. The work of [8] also addresses this same problem, but their approach is centralised, therefore our models differ singularly. In this paper, we consider decentralised and open systems where no agent has complete knowledge of the system and where any agent can enter or leave the system at any time.

Our approach proposes to introduce a trust model for communications in open and decentralised multi-agent systems. First, obligations define what a "good" communicative behaviour for the agents should be. Then, a process that detects lies based on the violation of those obligations is presented. This process marks as violated the commitments that are detected as lies. Reputation values are computed based on the number of positive, neutral or negative experiences, therefore, each time a lie is detected, the reputation value decreases and each time a correct behaviour is detected, the reputation value increases. Also, agents decide whether to accept or not an incoming message based on the reputation they associate to the sender. Consequently, reputation acts as a social sanction for agents that exhibit a prohibited behaviour.

References

1. Definition of non-repudiation, August 2004. http://en.wikipedia.org/wiki/Non-repudiation.
2. J. L. Austin. *How to do things with words*. Oxford University Press, 1962.
3. J. Bentahar, B. Moulin, and B. Chaib-draa. Towards a formal framework for conversational agents. In M.-P. Huget and F. Dignum, editors, *Proceedings of the Agent Communication Languages and Conversation Policies AAMAS 2003 Workshop*, 2003. July 14th 2003, Melbourne, Australia.
4. R. Conte and M. Paolucci. *Reputation in Artificial Societies. Social Beliefs for Social Order*. Kluwer Academic Publishers, 2002.
5. FIPA. Fipa communicative act library specification. Technical Report SC00037J, FIPA: Fundation For Intelligent Phisical Agents, December 2002. Standard Status.
6. N. Fornara and M. Colombetti. Defining interaction protocols using a commitment-based agent communication language. In *Proceedings of the AAMAS'03 Conference*, pages 520–527, 2003.
7. F. Guerin. *Specifying Agent Communication Languages*. PhD thesis, University of London and Imperial College, 2002.
8. J. Heard and R. C. Kremer. Practical issues in detecting broken social commitments. In R. van Eijk, R. Flores, and M.-P. Huget, editors, *Proceedings of the Agent Communication workshop at AAMAS'05*, pages 117–128, Utrecht, The Netherlands, July 2005.
9. Y. Labrou and T. Finin. A semantics approach for kqml - a general purpose communication language for software agents. In *Third International Conference on Information and Knowledge Management*, 1994.
10. D. McKnight and N. Chervany. *Trust in Cyber-societies*, chapter Trust and Distrust Definitions: One Bite at a Time, pages 27–54. Springler-Verlag Berlin Heidelberg, 2001.
11. L. Mui and M. Mohtashemi. Notions of reputation in multi-agent systems: A review. In *AAMAS'2002 and MIT LCS Memorandum*, 2002.
12. G. Muller, L. Vercouter, and O. Boissier. A trust model for inter-agent communication reliability. In *Proceedings of the AAMAS'05 TIAS workshop*, 2005.
13. P. Pasquier, R. A. Flores, and B. Chaib-draa. Modelling flexible social commitments and their enforcement. In *Proceedings of ESAW'04*, 2004.
14. J. Pitt and E. H. Mamdani. A protocol-based semantics for an agent communication language. In *Proceedings of IJCAI'99*, pages 486–491, 1999.
15. J. Sabater and C. Sierra. Social regret, a reputation model based on social relations. *SIGecom Exchanges. ACM*, 3.1:44–56, 2002.

16. M. Schillo and P. Funk. Who can you trust: Dealing with deception. In *In Proceedings of the DTFiAS Workshop, AAMAS'99*, pages 95–106, 1999.
17. J. R. Searle. *Speech Acts: an essay in the philosophy of language.* Cambridge University Press, 1969.
18. M. P. Singh. Agent communication languages: Rethinking the principles. In M.-P. Huget, editor, *Communication in Multiagent Systems*, volume 2650 of *Lecture Notes in Computer Science*, pages 37–50. Springer, 2003.
19. M. Verdicchio and M. Colombetti. A commitment-based communicative act library. In F. Dignum, V. Dignum, S. Koenig, S. Kraus, M. Singh, and M. Wooldridge, editors, *Proceedings of AAMAS'05*, pages 755–761, Utrecht, The Netherlands, July 2005. ACM Press.
20. G. von Wright. Deontic logic. In *Mind*, volume 60, pages 1–15, 1951.

Practical Issues in Detecting Broken Social Commitments

Jason Heard and Rob Kremer

Computer Science Department
University of Calgary
Calgary, Alberta, Canada
{heard, kremer}@cpsc.ucalgary.ca

Abstract. An open system should admit agents from many sources and these agents may have conflicting goals. Therefore, some actions that an agent would like to perform could be detrimental to other agents. Such actions can be either acceptable or unacceptable within a given system. Social norms define what actions are acceptable and unacceptable within a given society. There should be a way to limit the actions of agents to enforce these social norms. One way to begin to accomplish this goal is to have the system observe the actions of agents to model their behaviour. Behaviours that do not conform to specified norms could then be detected, and some action could be taken to prevent agents from performing further actions that violate social norms.

In this paper we discuss the use of social commitments to allow a system to define social norms and detect violations of those norms. Social commitments model an agent's commitments within a society. Some are implied while others are explicitly stated. Our system uses social commitments to define social norms. This paper focusses on the practical requirements that must be met for a system to implement social commitments as a way of defining social norms and detecting violations of those norms. In addition, we give an overview of how our multi-agent system design supports this goal.

1 Introduction

One of the goals of multi-agent systems (MAS) is to achieve synergy between agents. The goal is to accomplish more with a group of agents working together than could be accomplished by all of the agents working individually [1]. In order to do this, agents must be designed so that they can work with other agents. Another goal of multi-agent systems is to admit agents from many sources (or programmers) into the system [2]. These diverse agents may have conflicting goals. It is possible for agents with conflicting goals to work together on portions of their goals (and thereby achieve synergy).

If agents are working on conflicting goals, it may benefit one agent to perform some act that harms another agent. Take, for example, the case of a simple auction. It is generally acceptable to outbid another agent (assuming that you can meet the bid you have given). But it is generally unacceptable for an agent

F. Dignum, R. van Eijk, and R. Flores (Eds.): AC 2005/2006, LNAI 3859, pp. 124–135, 2006.

to state that some resource is worthless, knowing that it is not, so that another agent will bid lower, or not at all on the object. Both actions obviously are detrimental to another agent, but only one would be considered a violation of social norms.

It would be advantageous if the designer of an open system (one that allows agents with conflicting goals to enter it) takes into account these social norms. A system with no checks on norms would not facilitate cooperation, and would not attract many designers or agents to work within it. On the other hand, a system that is too strict would make it difficult to claim that the agents within it are autonomous [3]. The system outlined in this paper does not restrict actions but instead attempts to detect antisocial agents so that they may be avoided as necessary. To create a system with checks on social norms, that system must be able to detect violations. In order to detect norm violations some methodology must be put into place to map social interactions so that norm violations are observable. Social commitments will be used as the criterion to determine if actions conform to social norms within our system. Actions that break social commitments will be considered to be in violation of social norms.

Social commitments model commitments between agents [4,5] at a social level. Social commitments can be used to define societal norms [6], or to formally describe a protocol based on the social commitments implied by that protocol [7]. In order to detect actions that violate social norms as defined above, it is necessary to detect when social commitments are broken. Some work has been done to detect broken commitments [7,8]. Our system differs from previous work in that our system is open and accepts agents that may perform actions the original system designer didn't account for. Once a system detects that an agent has broken a social commitment and has therefore violated a social norm, some actions should be taken to "punish" the responsible agent. These actions (called sanctions) are discussed by Pasquier, Flores, and Chaib-draa [9].

Our system employes the use of a *social commitment observer* agent to detect broken social commitments. The use of special agents to perform monitoring has been done previously with "sentinals" [10]. We propose instead the use of a single agent to perform the monitoring, the use of social commitments as the framework for detecting unacceptable behaviors, and we maintain a focus on detection, leaving corrective activities for future research. In some ways, our system is similar to the systems described in [11] and [12] which employ "governors" and "coordination artifacts" respectively, but these works are primarily focussed on helping the MAS work with external agents, and not necessarily on detecting when those agents violate social norms.

While some work has been done in detecting broken social commitments, it was done under the assumption that the MAS is aware of all major events [8]. These events are given as logical statements. Work has not been done on how a non-logical system would map messages and perceived activities to these logical statements. Here we will attempt to define the requirements that must be met for the system to be aware of all acts that break social commitments. Based on these requirements, we have created a system to detect broken social commitments.

Section 2 outlines the social commitment model that will be used throughout the remainder of this paper. Section 3 breifly describes CASA (Cooperative Agent System Architechture), the basic MAS that was expanded to allow for a social commitment observer. Section 4 details the requirements that must be met in order to detect broken social commitments. Section 5 is a discussion of the details of the implementation of a social commitment observer in CASA. Section 6 offers a conclusion and suggests directions for further research.

2   Social Commitments

Before a system can be designed to detect broken social commitments, social commitments have to be defined and the procedure for creating and disolving commitments must be outlined. We will draw on the model of social commitments outlined in [6] and [8]. This model has been chosen because Alberti and others have already shown that commitments can be detected using various forms of logic. This paper shows how we have implemented the ability to detect broken commitments in CASA.

A commitment is defined as a set including a debtor (x), a creditor (y), a condition (p) and a context (G) [6]. Together, the commitment states that x is committed to y to ensure that p comes about within some social context G. For the remainder of this paper, G will be assumed to be the system outlined in this paper, and is therefore the same in all of our cases. In addition, we informally add to all social commitments a timout (t), which gives the time that a commitment must be fulfilled by. Formally, this is part of the condition, in the form, "p will be fulfilled on or before time t," but for ease of discussion, it will be listed as a separate field in this paper.

Social commitments are formed, modified, and removed using one of the following actions [6]:

create. This action creates a commitment. In our system, this can result from any of the policies, and usually an agent becomes the debtor only when it sends or is sent a message.

discharge. This action occurs when a commitment's condition has been met, and therefore fulfills the commitment. This requires no action by the debtor or creditor other than those actions necessary to bring about the condition. Our system considers this a resolution that meets our social norms (a "good" resolution).

cancel. This action removes a commitment from a debtor, without the consent of the creditor. This is essentially a statement saying that an agent does not intend to fulfill its commitment, and will probably break it. In our system, however, a commitment is not technically broken (and therefore a social norm is not violated) until either an action occurs that makes the condition impossible to fulfill or the timeout is reached without the condition being fulfilled.

release. This action removes a commitment from a debtor with the permission of the creditor. This is considered acceptable within the social norms of our system.

delegate. This action changes the debtor field of the commitment. It requires the permission of the new debtor. Essentially, we are stating that if an agent commits to perform an action that another agent was committed to performing, that agent has passed the responsibility and is no longer required to bring about the condition. However, it could be argued that an agent is still committed, and would be at fault if the other agent did not fulfill the commitment.

assign. This action changes the creditor field of the commitment. It requires the permission of the old creditor.

The social context, G, determines when each of the actions can be performed. We have informally described when these actions are applied in our system, but the details of these *conversation policies* are described in the next section.

It is important to note that although social commitments define acceptable behaviors in our system, agents do not have to be internally aware of social commitments. In other words, when programming an agent, the programmer need not focus on social commitments so long as the agent will, in the end, act in accordance with the policies and the social commitments they create.

2.1 Conversation Policies

Conversation policies are rules that indicate when actions can and should be performed on social commitments. Our system adopts the conversation policies informally described in Table 1. These policies outline acceptable behaviors in and form the basis of our system. The P-propose policy indicates that a certain

Table 1. An informal description of the conversation policies as defined by Flores and Kremer [13]

Policy	Description
P-propose	A proposal commits the proposed agents to reply.
P-counter-offer	A counter-offer is considered a reply, and commits addressees to reply.
P-reply-acc	An acceptance releases proposed agents from the commitment to reply and releases counter-offered agents from the commitment to reply.
P-reply-rej	A rejection releases proposed agents from the commitment to reply and releases counter-offered agents from the commitment to reply.
P-reply-counter	A counter-offer releases proposed agents from the commitment to reply and releases counter-offered agents from the commitment to reply.
P-accept	An acceptance causes the formation of the proposed/counter-offered commitment.
P-release	A release releases the debtor of the given commitment, if sent by the creditor.

Table 2. An informal description of conversation policies based on the fish auction policies described by Venkatraman and Singh [7]

Policy	Description
FA-advertise	An advertisement at some price commits the advertiser to sending fish to the bidder if there is one and only one bid within a given time.
FA-bid	A bid commits the bidder to sending money if it receives fish from the advertiser.
FA-bad	A bad fish message essentially cancels the process, and therefore removes both the advertiser and bidder's commitments in relation to that fish.

degree of politeness is required of agents in the system. The requirements could be amended (politeness does not have to be a requirement) if a system designer desires a more open system.

It is possible for system designers to add new policies to their system. This allows other domain specific policies to be put into place when they would aid in understanding the expectations of agents participating in that system. For example, we have implemented a set of policies that define a fish auction [7]. These are informally described in Table 2. While there are other possible messages in the fish auction, they can all be inferred from these policies. Because the basic set of policies in our system include a way to set up arbitrary commitments (with the P-propose and P-accept policies, among others), new policies do not necessarily need to be created to use other protocols with this system.

3 CASA (Cooperative Agent System Architecture)

The work described in this paper expands upon CASA, a communication-based multi-agent system written in Java. A few of CASA's unique features are used to aid in the development, but any flexible MAS could be used as a basis for this work, with some modifications.

Figure 1 shows a typical run-time configuration of CASA. Every machine running CASA agents runs a special agent called the *local area coordinator* (LAC). The LAC is responsible for resolving agent addresses, keeping track of how to start up agents, and starting agents on behalf of other agents (that may be running on other machines). The CASA framework demands very little of agents running within it, but agents are expected to register with the LAC on start up, and may register information about how they can be re-started (if they want to offer services to other agents on demand). The message contents are standardized to a superset of the FIPA message standard [14].[1] Once registered, CASA agents are free to communicate with one another using the CASA message format over TCP/IP ports. CASA agents may also communicate through a special kind of agent called a cooperation domain, the subject of the next subsection.

---

[1] The actual messages can be in either XML [15] or a KQML-like [16] format.

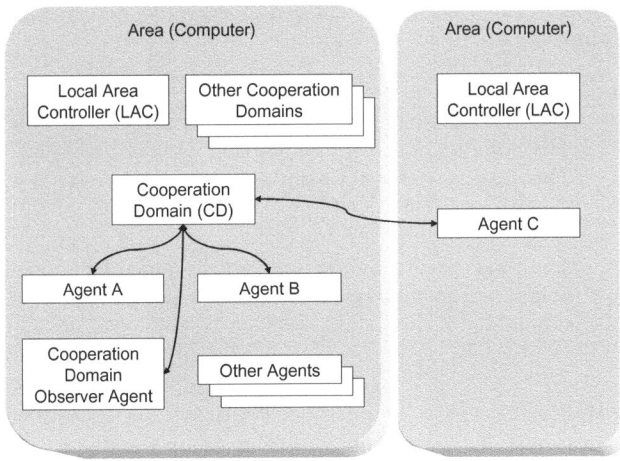

Fig. 1. A typical CASA run-time configuration

3.1 Cooperation Domains in CASA

A *cooperation domain* (CD) is an agent designed to aid agents in communicating in large groups. The CD allows agents to communicate with one another without knowing about every other agent. Agents register with the CD, and as a result they receive all non-private communications that are sent to the CD (including those *they* send). In this paper, a "cooperation domain" refers to either an agent itself or to a virtual location within which all agents (registered to that CD) operate. Figure 1 shows four agents participating in a conversation through a cooperation domain, depicted by the double-headed arrows.[2]

CASA agents are free to communicate directly (not through the CD) but they lose the power of the services potentially offered through the CD. Another advantage of the CD is that it gives the creators of the CD the ability to monitor the communications between its members. Figure 1 shows one such agent, the "Cooperation Domain Observer Agent," performing a special role within an agent conversation. This type of privileged agent can "eavesdrop" on all messages going through the cooperation domain, and is necessary when implementing a social commitment observer (see Sect. 5).

4 Detection Conditions

In order for the social commitment observer agent (or just *observer*) to detect broken social commitments, certain requirements must be met. The detection of broken social commitments is inferred from the observer's observations, the

---

[2] Messages sent in this way may be directed to all the participants (*broadcast*), to a specific subset of the participants (*multi-cast*), to a single agent (*directed*), or to all participants who have a particular *role* in the conversation (*role-cast*).

Table 3. Requirements for a social commitment observer to detect that a social commitment was formed

Requirement	Description
R1-understand	The observer understands social commitments and their structure.
R1-form	The observer observed the act that formed the social commitment. This may be either R1-form-accept or R1-form-policy.
R1-form-accept	The observer observed the acceptance of the social commitment (P-accept).
R1-form-policy	The observer observed an act that, because of a known conversation policy, automatically forms a social commitment (P-propose, for example).

way Sherlock Holmes solves a crime by decoding clues. This means that the observer does not rely on complaints or other error messages to determine if commitments are broken. The observer must infer that a social commitment is broken by observing the communications within the system and using any other means of apprehension it may possess (such as the ability to perceive some environment).

To detect the formation of a social commitment, the following conditions must be met. The observer must understand social commitments (both the concept and their structure). The observer must also observe the action that causes the formation of the commitment. This can happen in two ways. First, a social commitment is formed when an explicit request to form a social commitment was accepted by another agent, as defined by P-accept (see Table 1). A social commitment can also be formed through a conversation policy which results from some communication between agents. This can happen because of P-propose, P-counter-offer, P-inform, or any other policy that forms a commitment. This last requirement does not specify a particular set of policies because further policies can be added to a system by its developer (as mentioned in Sect. 2.1). Table 3 summarizes the conditions outlined above.

Once the observer agent has detected a social commitment it must store this commitment, as the commitment may be formed long before it is broken. The observer must then understand the condition portion of the social commitment.

Table 4. Requirements for a social commitment observer to detect that a social commitment was broken

Requirement	Description
R2-form	The observer detected that a commitment was formed.
R2-store	The observer has stored the commitment that was detected in R2-form.
R2-condition	The observer understands the condition part of the commitment.
R2-no-release	The observer has not observed an action that releases the debtor from the commitment.
R2-break	The observer observes an action that implies that the condition portion of the social commitment can never be satisfied.

This requirement is non-trivial, as our version of an open system includes the possibility of agents not understanding all other commitments. In the case where a commitment has been dissolved properly through one of the conversation policies (described in Sect. 2.1), nothing further will be required of the debtor. Therefore, the observer must detect a commitment that has not been properly dissolved. This implies that the observer is observing all activity of the agent, so that it isn't possible that the observer has missed the proper dissolution of the commitment. Finally, some action must happen that implies that the condition portion of the social commitment can never be satisfied. This action must be observed by the observer. Table 4 summarizes the conditions outlined above.

5   Implementation

In CASA, we implemented an agent that can detect broken social commitments (our *social commitment observer*). In doing so, we attempted to meet all of the requirements outlined in Sect. 4. In the following subsections we discuss how and to what degree we were able to meet each of the requirements.

5.1   Understanding Social Commitments (R1-understand)

The observer's understanding of social commitments begins with the understanding of the debtor and creditor fields of a social commitment. The FIPA standards define a *sender* and *receiver* field within every message. The *sender* field is always the agent that is currently sending the message while the *receiver* field is always the agent currently receiving the message. In CASA, when a cooperation domain is used to forward messages, the *sender* field is always the sending CD (to meet FIPA standards). Since the CD isn't (usually) the agent originally sending the message, it was necessary to add another field to messages within CASA (which is acceptable by FIPA standards). This is the *from* field. It is defined as the original sender of the message. Therefore, within CASA the *from* and *receiver* fields determine the debtor and the creditor of a given commitment. The *from* and *receiver* fields of the message are always *URLDescriptors*, which are used within CASA to both uniquely define an agent and define how to communicate with it (locally or across a network).

5.2   Observing Formation of Social Commitments (R1-form)

To observe the creation of all social commitments, the observer ties into a cooperation domain as a cooperation domain observer (Section 3.1 briefly describes this functionality). This allows the observer to meet the R1-form requirement as described below.

Once each message is received by the social commitment observer, it is processed to determine which conversation policies apply and therefore which commitments must be added to the set of current commitments. This is done by applying each known policy, in turn to the given message. The policies are parsed in no particular order, and the successful operation of one policy does not imply that the other policies will not apply to the message. The addition of a new policy into the system requires only the creation of a new ConversationPolicy subclass.

5.3   Storing Social Commitments (R2-store)

CommitmentEngine objects store social commitments in a map from (debtor× creditor) to a set of conditions. In other words, given a debtor and a creditor, the agent can retrieve a set that defines the conditions that the debtor is committed to bringing about for the creditor. The conditions need not be understood at the point of storage, and may be stored in some general format, such as a string or a bit vector.

5.4   Understanding Conditions (R2-condition)

For any agent, there is a condition that is not understood. This is because our system does not put a restriction on the language used in describing the required condition of a social commitment. Therefore, any finite system will not be able to understand all social commitments. With this difficulty in mind, we have decided to implement the observer such that it only understands the commitments described explicitly by one or more conversation policies. It can still parse that an agent has formed a social commitment because of P-accept, but it may not be able to parse the condition portion of that commitment. In this case, the observer cannot detect when that commitment has been broken. As described below in Sect. 5.5, the observer is still able to detect when a debtor and creditor agree that the debtor should be released from its commitment (with the P-release policy). Future work will focus on this restriction (see Sect. 6).

5.5   Observing the Release from Social Commitments (R2-no-release)

The conversation policies used in Sect. 5.2 are responsible for creating commitments as they are observed. In addition, these policies are responsible for removing commitments from the set of all commitments when they are properly dissolved. This is the case with the P-ack, P-reply, and P-release policies.

Because agents are free to communicate outside of a cooperation domain, it is possible for the following scenario to take place. A message is sent by an agent, Alice, within a cooperation domain that forms a social commitment, and that commitment is detected and stored by the social commitment observer. Then, Alice (or another agent) sends a message that should release Alice from that commitment, but the message is sent outside of the cooperation domain. In this case, the commitment may be marked as broken at some time, even though it was actually properly dissolved. Our system requires that if an agent performs an action that creates a social commitment within a cooperation domain, any message properly dissolving that commitment must also be sent within the cooperation domain. This requirement is not enforceable within CASA. If the requirement is not met, the system may detect that the agent has broken a social commitment, and act as if the agent has broken a social commitment.

5.6 Observing Broken Social Commitments (R2-break)

Like the formation and proper dissolution of commitments, the social commitment observer only detects broken social commitments if the message (or messages) that breaks the commitment is transmitted through the cooperation domain. The main problem with this requirement is not the difficulty of observing the action that breaks a commitment, but the fact that for some commitments, there is no such action. For example, let us assume that an agent, Alice, has a social commitment to another agent, Bob, to send him a message. If we assume that Alice and Bob are computer programs, and will therefore last as long as they are needed, and that we don't care about events beyond the end of the universe (if the universe does end), then Alice will always be able to send Bob a message at some time in the future, and no action would prevent this from occurring.

Because some commitments are not breakable, we have added another field to social commitments: a timeout value. This follows naturally from the fact that there is a *timeout* field in every CASA message. This still fits within our formal definition, because it can be thought of as an addition to the condition portion of the commitment similar to, "This condition will be brought about before *timeout*." The timeout value can be set so that the social commitment never times out (if the designer wishes), but as long as it does, the commitment will eventually be either fulfilled or broken. With a timeout value, we can modify the above example so that Alice has a social commitment to Bob to send him a message before August 1, 2005. This commitment will obviously be broken if Alice has not sent a message to Bob by the specified date. The P-inform and P-request conversation policies outlined in Sect. 2 both have timeouts in the CASA system, and so are easily monitored for breakage. The timeouts of all commitments are checked within the commitment engine every time the *expireCommitments()* function is called. Any commitments broken by the passage of time are treated as if a policy had determined that the commitment has been broken.

5.7 Initial Results

With the above requirements generally fulfilled, our social commitment observer is able to detect agents that fail to reply to requests, don't acknowledge messages when requested, and those that fail to complete correctly the fish auction as defined in [7].

6 Conclusion / Future Work

In this paper we have presented an implementation of a working social commitment observer in an open system. Towards this end, we have outlined the requirements for an observer to detect that a social commitment was formed, and the requirements for an observer to detect that a social commitment was broken. Finally, we gave a detailed description of how we met each of the requirements for detecting broken social commitments. While we feel that we have made good progress in this area, there are several directions for future research.

It would be advantageous to be able to dynamically add policies and known conditions to the set that the social commitment observer understands. This would allow agents to define new requirements for their domains, while maintaining a central authority on commitments within a given cooperation domain. It may be possible to use the act and performative lattices built into CASA to store commitment information to aid the social commitment observer. This is because these lattices can be expanded as needed for each agent, and can then be passed from one agent to another with a standardized request.

It may also be beneficial to add a standard way for agents to "complain" about other agents that have broken social commitments. Because the social commitment observer presented here can detect that any type of commitment has been formed, the observer could confirm that indeed there was a commitment formed between the two agents. There would then have to be a way to determine when complaints are legitimate. This would probably require both the agent that registers the complaint and the agent that is complained about to be aware of the complaint verification process. Any agent unaware of this process would be unfairly judged, because it couldn't aid in the verification process. A comparative analysis of the transparent observation system and a complaint system is a future direction for investigation.

Finally, the social commitment observer can detect when a commitment is broken, but currently only displays a message to the user or writes an entry in a log file. In a system that may involve many communications at any time of day, some form of automated "punishment" to be meted out to agents that have broken social commitments may be necessary. The simplest punishment would probably be the ejection of agents that have broken a specified number of social commitments (or a certain number of commitments per time period). This ejection could be temporary or permanant. An alternative to the ejection of undesirable agents is to provide a service similar to the Better Business Bureau found in many cities. This service would give the number and/or type of commitments broken by some agent at another agent's request.

References

1. Denzinger, J.: Knowledge-based distributed search using teamwork. In: Proceedings of the First International Conference on Multi-Agent Systems, San Francisco, CA, USA (1995) 81–88
2. Hewitt, C.E.: The challenge of open systems. Byte **10** (1985) 223–242
3. Jennings, N.R., Campos, J.R.: Towards a social level characterisation of socially responsible agents. IEEE Proceedings on Software Engineering **144** (1997) 11–25
4. Castelfranchi, C.: Commitments: From individual intentions to groups and organizations. In: Proceedings of the First International Conference on Multi-Agent Systems, San Francisco, CA, USA (1995) 41–48

5. Singh, M.: Social and psychological commitments in multiagent systems. In: AAAI Fall Symposium on Knowledge and Action at Social and Organizational Levels, Monterey, California (1991)

6. Singh, M.P.: An ontology for commitments in multiagent systems: Toward a unification of normative concepts. Artificial Intelligence and Law **7** (1999) 97–113

7. Venkatraman, M., Singh, M.P.: Verifying compliance with commitment protocols. Autonomous Agents and Multi-Agent Systems **2** (1999) 217–236

8. Alberti, M., Gavanelli, M., Lamma, E., Mello, P., Torroni, P.: Specification and verification of agent interaction using social integrity constraints. In: Proceedings of the First International Workshop on Logic and Communication in Multi-Agent Systems (LCMAS 2003). (2003)

9. Pasquier, P., Flores, R., Chaib-draa, B.: Modelling flexible social commitments and their enforcement. In: Proceedings of the Fifth International Workshop on Engineering Societies in the Agents World (ESAW04). (2004)

10. Klein, M., Dellarocas, C.: Domain-independent exception handling services that increase robustness in open multi-agent systems. Working Paper ASES-WP-2000-02, Center for Coordination Science, Massachusetts Institute of Technology, Cambridge, MA, USA (2000) http://ccs.mit.edu/ases.

11. Esteva, M., Padget, J.A., Sierra, C.: Formalizing a language for institutions and norms. In: ATAL '01: Revised Papers from the 8th International Workshop on Intelligent Agents VIII, Springer-Verlag (2002) 348–366

12. Omicini, A., Ricci, A., Viroli, M., Castelfranchi, C., Tummolini, L.: Coordination artifacts: Environment-based coordination for intelligent agents. In: Third International Joint Conference on Autonomous Agents and Multiagent Systems (AAMAS04). Volume 1. (2004) 286–293

13. Flores, R., Kremer, R.: To commit or not to commit: Modelling agent conversations for action. Computational Intelligence **18** (2003) 120–173

14. Foundation for Intelligent Physical Agents (FIPA): FIPA ACL message structure specification. document number SC00061G, FIPA TC communication. (2003) http://www.fipa.org/specs/fipa00061/SC00061G.html.

15. World Wide Web Consortium (W3C): Extensible markup language (XML) (2004) http://www.w3.org/XML/.

16. Finin, T., Labrou, Y., Mayfield, J.: KQML as an agent communication language. In Bradshaw, J., ed.: Software Agents, MIT Press (1997) 291–316

Introducing Preferences into Commitment Protocols[*]

Ashok U. Mallya and Munindar P. Singh

Department of Computer Science
North Carolina State University
Raleigh, NC 27695-7535, USA
{aumallya, singh}@ncsu.edu

Abstract. Commitment protocols enable flexibility in agent interactions by utilizing the semantics of commitments to develop succinct declarative specifications for protocols that allow a large number of executions. As a consequence, commitment protocols enable agents to accommodate varying local policies and respond to exceptions. A consequent weakness of such protocols is that commitment protocols thus fail to distinguish between possible executions that are normal and those that may be allowed but are not ideal. This paper develops an approach for specifying *preferences* among executions that are allowed by a protocol. It captures sets of executions via a simple language and gives them a denotational characterization based on branching-time models. It shows how to incorporate the specifications into rulesets, thereby giving the specifications a natural operational characterization. The rulesets embed into a recent practical framework for protocols called OWL-P. The paper shows that the operational and denotational characterizations coincide.

1   Introduction

Agents can engage in a rich variety of interactions, and need appropriately rich models to support their autonomy and heterogeneity. Commitment protocols, which capture the essence of the desired interactions in high-level terms, are such a model. Protocols regulate the externally observable, social behavior of agents, distinguishing what is allowed from what is not. Current approaches, however, do not make any finer distinctions about what is *normal* and what is not.

This paper is about the main consequences of taking a knowledge engineering stance toward commitment protocols.

- To accommodate the openness of the given system, protocols must apply in a wide range of contexts. That is, they must generally allow multiple execution paths. For example, a purchase protocol should allow the possibility that the goods may be lost and a reminder sent for them.
- To accommodate agent autonomy, protocols must enable the participating agents to choose their actions and responses to the above kinds of conditions as they see fit. For example, a purchase protocol should allow the possibilities that negotiations

---

[*] We thank Amit Chopra, Nirmit Desai, and the anonymous referees for valuable comments. This research was supported partly by the NSF under grant DST-0139037 and partly by a DARPA project.

F. Dignum, R. van Eijk, and R. Flores (Eds.): AC 2005/2006, LNAI 3859, pp. 136–149, 2006.

may fail, that the payment may be made via a third party, that an agent awaiting missing goods may send a reminder for them.

- To be realistic, the protocols themselves must be based on a study of different usage scenarios, wherein not all possible executions are considered equal. For example, as a practical matter, we would all recognize that it is more normal for a purchase protocol to lead to an exchange of goods and money than for a refund to be issued or for the goods to be repossessed by the merchant because of lack of payment.

In other words, protocols should be flexible enough to accommodate exceptions, but should still be described in such a manner that the exceptions are distinguished from the normal executions. Moreover, there is a hierarchy of exceptions, some being more acute than others.

Protocol Preferences and Agent Policies. To capture the above motivations, we propose that protocol specifications be enhanced with modular, pluggable descriptions of the *preferences* among executions of the protocol. These preferences are the protocol designer's view of what are the most normal or most desired executions. In this sense, they have a normative force. Individual agents would have their own *policies* for how they participate in a given protocol. The policies should generally be in line with the protocol preferences. (Verifying compliance with protocol preferences, however, is nontrivial—we return to this point in Section 5.)

Protocols can be refined to yield protocols that serve the same goal but impose additional requirements. For example, payment by cash is a refinement of payment (in general). Agents contemplating interacting can negotiate about the refinement of the protocol that they will enact. For example, if a merchant accepts only cash, payment by check or charge card is ruled out and payment by cash is the only kind of payment that will work.

More interestingly, agents who are participating in a protocol may negotiate about the specific actions that each would take (from among those that are allowed by the given protocol). For example, given that two parties agree to participate as seller and buyer in a purchase protocol, they might then negotiate about whether buyer can have a third party pay on his behalf. Protocol preferences thus provide a basis for argumentation among the parties.

Approach. As explained in greater detail below, in our framework, protocols are denotationally characterized using sets of runs (i.e., computations), and are operationalized via translation into executable rulesets. With the above background, the approach of this paper proceeds as follows to enable augmenting protocol specifications with preferences.

- We augment an existing protocol specification language with an ability to specify preferences among different executions of protocols. For simplicity of specification, we use regular expressions over protocol states to capture executions that are of interest.
- We show how preferences can be operationalized into executable rulesets.
- We show how the above preferences are mapped into a lattice whose points are sets of runs, and characterized via branching time models.
- We show that the model-theoretic and the operational characterizations coincide.

Contributions. Our main contribution is in developing a new methodology for designing commitment protocols. Our methodology can be used for the following

Modeling exceptions. In traditional process models, exceptions are modeled in an ad hoc manner, when the designer demarcates blocks of the process and assigns exception handlers to those blocks. In our approach, exceptions can be defined separately from the specification of the process or the protocol. As a result, different exception conditions can be assigned to the same protocol based on the context of the protocol execution. This is akin to aspect oriented software.

Selecting protocols. When multiple protocols are available for an agent to realize a certain interaction, that agent can negotiate with the other parties involved in the protocol and, based on its preferences, find out if an execution of that protocol with those participants would be acceptable to it. For example, a customer agent that does not wish to enact a hotel booking protocol in which the hotel can cancel the room and award a refund can choose which hotel to interact with if its preferences are made clear before enactment and if the hotel and the customer try and negotiate the protocol to enact based on their preferences.

Organization. The rest of this paper is organized as follows. Section 2 first describes our running example, the purchase protocol. It then describes the background concept of commitments (Section 2.1) and commitment operations (Section 2.1), before introducing our proposed preference specification language (Section 2.3). Section 3 describes two denotational aspects of preferences, the lattice structure (Section 3.1) and the general preferences based on commitments and their operations (Section 3.2). Section 4 relates these to OWL-P rules by first giving a brief description of rules in OWL-P (Section 4.1) and then the translation from preference specifications to OWL-P rules (Section 4.2). Section 5 summarizes the contributions of the paper and discusses related research and directions for further investigation.

2   Proposed Language

Commitment protocols have been in development for some years now. Recently, Desai *et al.*proposed OWL-P as a practical framework and associated language for specifying and enacting commitment protocols [1]. An OWL-P specification identifies roles that participate in the protocol, the messages that are exchanged (with the meanings of the messages in terms of commitments that are created), and a set of rules that constrain the set of runs of the protocol by defining ordering, data flow, and other constraints. The present paper augments the OWL-P language to enable specification of preferences among executions as generated by a protocol.

We formalize protocols as transition systems similar in spirit to commitment machines [9]. Commitment machines generate computations or *runs*, which are sequences of *states* that a valid protocol execution goes through. Each state is a snapshot of the evolving state of the system (as the given agents interact), and is labeled by *propositions* that hold true. Propositions represent facts about the universe of discourse of the protocol such as the actions that the protocol participants have taken, commitments that have been created and operated upon, and messages that have been sent. State changes are caused by *messages* that the participants send to each other. For compatibility with this model, we propose a language based on regular expressions over propositions to specify sets of runs of a protocol over which preferences can be expressed. This section introduces the language, and describes it in detail with the help of a running example that is used throughout the paper.

Running Example: Purchase. In typical executions, the customer requests a price quote from the merchant for a certain item. The merchant quotes a price. The customer accepts the quote. The merchant then ships the item and the customer pays for it. In principle, each party decides whether and how to execute each step.

Let's summarize the key features of the OWL-P framework.

- An OWL-P specification includes the roles, the meanings of messages, and the rules that dictate valid executions.
- An OWL-P specification assigns meanings to messages by specifying how messages assert and retract various propositions and how they create and manipulate commitments.
- In the OWL-P framework, skeletons are derived for each role. A programmer can specify the policies for each agent that plays a given role to determine whether and how to act in enacting the given protocol. Desai *et al.*discuss this aspect at length [1].

In Table 1, the *policy(x,y)* term checks if x wishes to send the message y, and *start* is a special term indicating the start state. For the sake of brevity, this table does not indicate that domain propositions are asserted when the corresponding messages are sent, for example, the proposition $rfq(c, m, x)$ is asserted when the message $rfq(c, m, x)$ is sent. Figure 1 shows some possible executions of the purchase protocol, as per the OWL-P specification. The thick circles denote states at which the protocol can be ended. The figure shows that the protocol can be initiated by any of three messages: the $rfq(c, m, x)$ (request for quote), $quote(m, c, x, p)$ (advertisement from the merchant) and $acceptQ(c, m, x, ?p)$ (customer's willingness to pay any price for x) as a result of rules 1, 2, and 5 in Table 1. The flexibility of commitment protocols arises because they use commitments and other propositions to assign meanings to states and thus capture the essence of an interaction. Treating commitments explicitly enables further kinds of sophisticated reasoning, such as involving delegation and other kinds of manipulation of commitments. For example, a customer can delegate a payment commitment to a third party, such as a bank. We briefly introduce the semantics of commitments to lay the groundwork for preference specification.

2.1 Commitments

A commitment $C(x, y, p)$ denotes that the agent x is responsible to the agent y for bringing about the condition p. Here x is called the *debtor*, y the *creditor*, and p the *condition* of the commitment. The condition is expressed in a suitable formal language. Commitments can also be *conditional*, denoted by $CC(x, y, q, p)$, meaning that x is committed to y to bring about p if q holds. For example, the commitment $CC(m, c, pay(c, m, p)$, $send(m, c, x))$ denotes the commitment by the merchant to the customer to send the item if the customer pays for it.

Table 1. A snippet of the OWL-P specification of the purchase protocol

Role 1: Customer, c
Role 2: Merchant, m

Rule 1: $policy(c, rfq(c, ?m, ?x)) \land start \Rightarrow sendMsg(rfq(c, ?m, ?x))$
Rule 2: $policy(m, quote(m, ?c, ?x, ?p)) \land start \Rightarrow sendMsg(quote(m, ?c, ?x, ?p))$
Rule 3: $policy(m, quote(m, ?c, ?x, ?p)) \land rfq(?c, m, ?x) \Rightarrow sendMsg(quote(m, ?c, ?x, ?p)))$
Rule 4: $policy(c, ?acptRjct(?m, ?x, ?p)) \land quote(?m, c, ?x, ?p) \Rightarrow$
$\qquad sendMsg(?acptRjct(c, ?m, ?x, ?p))$
Rule 5: $policy(c, accept(c, ?m, ?x, ?p)) \land start \Rightarrow sendMsg(accept(c, ?m, ?x, ?p))$
Rule 6: $send(m, c, x) \land \neg pay(c, m, p) \land return(c, m, x) \Rightarrow cancel(\mathsf{C}(c, m, pay(c, m, p))$
...

Message 1: $rfq(c, m, x)$
Meaning: c asks m for the price of a certain item x.
Message 2: $quote(m, c, x, p)$
Meaning: m informs c that the x is available at a price p.
m commits to delivering x to c if c pays for it.
Creates $\mathsf{CC}(m, c, pay(c, m, p), send(m, c, x))$; asserts corresponding proposition.
Message 3: $acceptQ(c, m, x, p)$
c accepts the price p for the item x, as quoted by the merchant m.
c commits to pay an amount p to m if the item x is delivered to it.
Creates $\mathsf{C}(c, m, send(m, c, x), pay(c, m, p))$; asserts corresponding proposition.
Message 4: $rejectQ(c, m, x, p)$
Meaning: c rejects the quote p for the item x as quoted by m.
Message 5: $send(m, c, x)$
Meaning: m delivers the item x to c
Message 6: $pay(c, m, p)$
Meaning: c pays an amount p to m
Message 7: $return(c, m, x)$
Meaning: c returns the item x to m
This message is analogous to $send(c, m, x)$.
Message 8: $refund(m, c, p)$
Meaning: m refunds the amount p to c
This message is analogous to $pay(m, c, p)$.
...

2.2 Commitment Operations

Commitments are created, satisfied, and transformed in certain ways. The following operations are conventionally defined for commitments.

1. CREATE(x, C) establishes the commitment C. This can only be performed by C's debtor x.
2. CANCEL(x, C) cancels the commitment C. This can only be performed by C's debtor x. Generally, cancellation is compensated by making another commitment.
3. RELEASE(y, C) releases C's debtor x from commitment C. This only can be performed by the creditor y.
4. ASSIGN(y, z, C) replaces y with z as C's creditor.

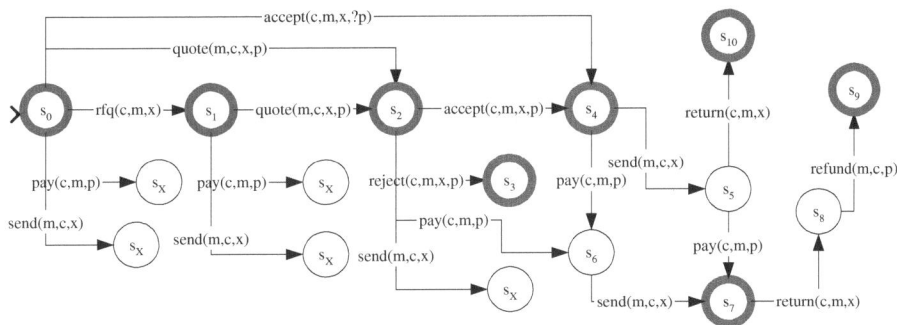

Fig. 1. Purchase Protocol. Thick circles are terminating states, and s_X denotes an error state. Note that this figure does not show the entire state machine.

5. DELEGATE(x, z, C) replaces x with z as the C's debtor.
6. DISCHARGE(x, C) C's debtor x fulfils the commitment.

A commitment is said to be *active* if it has been created, but not yet been operated upon by a *discharge, delegate, assign, cancel*, or *release*. A commitment is *satisfied* when its condition becomes true.

A conditional commitment such as $CC(c, m, send(m, c, x), pay(c, m, p),)$ becomes an unconditional commitment $C(c, m, pay(c, m, p))$ when its condition $send(m, c, x)$ holds. A commitment is *breached* when it is not possible that the commitment will be satisfied. Realistic settings assign deadlines to commitments to detect their breach or satisfaction [5]. Conditional commitments can also be satisfied without a transformation into an unconditional commitment. For example, $CC(c, m, send(m, c, x), pay(c, m, p))$ is satisfied when $pay(c, m, p)$ is true, regardless of the truth value of $send(m, c, x)$.

2.3 Preference Syntax

As we described earlier, we base our proposal on state-based, declaratively specified models of commitment protocols, as in OWL-P. Given this model, we wish to devise a way of specifying preferences among the runs allowed by a protocols. To do this, we need a representation for runs. Instead of writing out entire runs, we adopt a concise specification and a corresponding representation scheme for runs. Our developments are based on Singh's temporal logic for specifying dependencies among events [7].

Consider a protocol P, whose universe of discourse is the set of propositions $\mathbb{P}$. A run r is a sequence of states $\langle s_0 \ldots s_{|r|} \rangle$, for which $[r]^0$ represents the first state s_0. We consider only nonempty runs, i.e., a run must contain an initial state. Likewise, $[r]^\top$ represents the last state of a run, defined only for finite runs. The operator $\prec_r$ orders states temporally with respect to a run r, so that $s_i \prec_r s_j$ implies that s_i occurs before s_j in the run r. For a state s, $[s]$ denotes the set of propositions that label s.

1. $X \cdot Y$ matches any run that has a state s_m whose label contains Y and another state s_n which occurs before s_m with X in its label.
2. $\_$ matches the appropriate parameter of a message or a commitment operation. For example, $rfq(\_, m, x)$ matches all rfq messages sent to m for the item x.

To give a concrete syntax for the above language, and to precisely specify the semantics of such a language in terms of the set of runs that each expression denotes, we use the linear temporal logic-based event ordering language proposed by Singh [7] to specify preferences between sets of executions in that transition system. We use expressions over events in this language to specify sets of runs of a protocol over which preferences can be expressed.

- Although Singh's language is given semantics based on linear models, the models are related in an incremental manner to other possibilities: thus the spirit of it is arguably branching.
- Although we use an event based semantics, the application to state-based models such as OWL-P is straightforward, given that state labels capture that state's history.

We repeat here the syntax and semantics of $\mathcal{I}$ from [7]. I is the start symbol of the BNF for the language of $\mathcal{I}$. In this BNF, *slant* indicates nonterminals, $\longrightarrow$ and $\mid$ are meta-symbols of the BNF, /* and */ begin and end comments respectively, and all other symbols are terminals.

$L_1.\ I \longrightarrow dep \mid dep \wedge I$ /*conjunction: interleaving*/
$L_2.\ dep \longrightarrow seq \mid seq \vee dep$ /* disjunction: choice*/
$L_3.\ seq \longrightarrow bool \mid event \mid event \cdot seq$ /* before: ordering*/
$L_4.\ bool \longrightarrow 0 \mid \top$

Dependency. A dependency is an expression generated by I. It specifies constraints on the occurrence and ordering of events.

Event Literal Set. $\Gamma \neq \{\}$ is the set of event literals used in I. Γ_D is the set of literals mentioned in a dependency D and their complements, for example, $\Gamma_e = \{e, \bar{e}\}$. For a set of dependencies $\mathbb{D}$, we define $\Gamma_{\mathbb{D}}$ as $\Gamma_{\mathbb{D}} = \bigcup_{D \in \mathbb{D}} \Gamma_D$.

The formal semantics of I is based on runs, i.e., sequences of events. Legal runs satisfy the following requirements:

1. Event instances and their complements are mutually exclusive.
2. An event instance occurs at most once in a computation.

These requirements can be satisfied in a system by qualifying the events using time-stamps or analogous schemes for giving them unique IDs. Such qualification of events is done in a separate conceptual layer which is at a lower level of abstraction than the logic layer that we deal with here.

Universe of Runs. $\mathbb{U}_{\mathcal{I}}$ is the universe of runs; it contains all legal runs involving event instances from Γ.

2.4   Preference Semantics

For a run $\tau \in \mathbb{U}_{\mathcal{I}}$ and $I \in \mathcal{I}$, $\tau \models I$ means that I is satisfied over the run τ. This notion can be formalized as follows. Here, τ_i refers to the ith item in τ and $\tau_{[i,j]}$ refers to the subrun of τ consisting of its elements from index i to index j, both inclusive. $|\tau|$ is the last index of τ and may be ω for an infinite run. We use the following conventions in the specification of semantics below: $e, f, \bar{e}, \bar{f}$, etc. are literals; D, E, etc. are dependencies; i, j, k, etc. are temporal indices; and τ, etc. are runs. The semantics of I is

$M_1. \tau \models e$ iff $(\exists i : \tau_i = e)$
$M_2. \tau \models I_1 \vee I_2$ iff $\tau \models I_1$ or $\tau \models I_2$
$M_3. \tau \models I_1 \wedge I_2$ iff $\tau \models I_1$ and $\tau \models I_2$
$M_4. \tau \models I_1 \cdot I_2$ iff $(\exists i : \tau_{[0,i]} \models I_1$ and $\tau_{[i+1,|\tau|]} I_2)$

Denotation. The denotation $[\![D]\!]$ of a dependency D is the set of runs that satisfy D, i.e., $[\![D]\!] = \{\tau : \tau \models D\}$.

Next, we describe how preferences among runs are specified using these expressions. The specification language I supports dependencies to succinctly specify sets of runs. To induce a preference structure over such sets, i.e., to specify if one set is preferred over another, we introduce the *preference relation*.

Preference Relation. Let $\mathbb{R} : 2^{\mathbb{U}_\mathcal{I}} \mapsto 2^{\mathbb{U}_\mathcal{I}}$ be the preference relation between sets of runs. $\mathbb{R}$ is irreflexive, transitive, and anti-symmetric. $(D_i, D_j) \in \mathbb{R}$ means that any run that satisfies the constraints in D_i is preferred over any run that satisfies the constraints in D_j, i.e., $\forall \tau_i, \tau_j : \tau_i \in [\![D_i]\!]$ and $\tau_j \in [\![D_j]\!]$, τ_i is preferred over τ_j.

Commitment protocols can be expressed as a set of dependencies. For a protocol P specified in terms of a set of dependencies D_P, the denotation of the protocol is the set of runs that the protocol allows, and is given by $[\![P]\!] = \bigcup_{D \in D_P} [\![D]\!]$.

Preference Lattice. A preference lattice specifies preferences among a set of dependencies. Each dependency labels one node of the lattice, and a preference relation specifies preferences among these dependencies, and consequently among the nodes they label. A preference lattice $L = \langle D_x, R \rangle$ specifies preferences among the elements of the set of dependencies D_x using the partial order induced by R over D_x. For the above L, we define its event literal set to be the set of all events that are mentioned in the dependencies in D_x, and their negations. $\Gamma_L = \bigcup_{D \in D_x} \Gamma_D$.

As an example, consider the purchase protocol described before. The following preferences can be assigned to sets of runs of this protocol.

- $A = send(m, c, x) \cdot pay(c, m, p)$, i.e., runs in which the item is delivered and subsequently paid for.
- $B = send(m, c, x) \cdot return(c, m, x) \wedge \overline{pay(c, m, p)}$, i.e., runs in which the item is delivered and subsequently returned (without payment).
- $C = send(m, c, x) \cdot pay(c, m, p) \cdot return(c, m, x) \cdot refund(m, c, x)$, i.e., the runs in which the item is first delivered, then paid for, returned and the money refunded.
- A is preferred over B; B is preferred over C, i.e., $(A, B) \in R$ and $(B, C) \in R$.

We envision that designers of protocols will specify such preference structures to tailor existing protocols in ways that best satisfy the interests of the participants of the protocol. In our purchase protocol example, the protocol itself does not dictate any relative ordering between the delivery of goods and the payment. The above preferences, then are used for a particular context in which it is desirable to pay after the goods have been delivered. Preferences can also be used to negotiate particular protocol executions. For example, a merchant might not wish to employ the above preference structure on the purchase protocol since the delivery of the item sold has to be done before payment is received. Such a merchant would have to negotiate with customers about the relative ordering of the payment and the item delivery.

3 Denotational Description of Preferences

This section describes how preferences are modeled using a lattice structure and how this lattice can be used to modularly specify a hierarchy of exceptions.

Preference Node Denotation. The denotation of a preference node N_D labeled by D, with respect to a protocol P and a lattice $L = \langle D_P, R \rangle$, where $D \in D_P$, is the set of runs allowed by the protocol that are also allowed by D, but not by nodes in L that are preferred over N_D. The motivation for the above is that each run can occur in at most one node in the lattice. Thus if a given run is allowed by two sets of runs, one preferred over the other, the less set would not "get credit" for this run. On each path from the top to the bottom of the lattice, a given run can occur at most once. Formally, $[\![N_D]\!] = [\![P]\!] \cap ([\![D]\!] - \bigcup_{(D_i, D) \in R} [\![D_i]\!])$.

Based on the above, we derive the following denotational representation

- $[\![A]\!] = [\![send(m, c, x) \cdot pay(c, m, p)]\!]$. That is, all runs in which the goods are sent and a payment is made, and in that order.
- $[\![B]\!] = [\![send(m, c, x) \cdot return(c, m, x) \wedge \overline{pay(c, m, p)}]\!]$. That is, all runs in which goods are sent and subsequently returned, without a payment being done.
- $[\![C]\!] = [\![send(m, c, x) \cdot pay(c, m, p)return(c, m, x) \cdot refund(m, c, p)]\!]$. That is, all runs in which goods are sent, payment is made, goods are returned, and a refund is given, in that order.

We also calculate a set of "leftover" runs $[\![U]\!]$ that contains all runs that are valid in the protocol but not covered by any of the other preference nodes, $[\![U]\!] = [\![P]\!] \cap (\mathbb{U}_\mathcal{I} - \bigcup_{(D_i, D) \notin R} [\![D_i]\!])$. With respect to Figure 1,

- $[\![A]\!]$ contains runs $\langle s_0 \ldots s_4 s_5 s_7 \ldots \rangle$
- $[\![B]\!]$ contains runs $\langle s_0 \ldots s_4 s_5 s_{10} \rangle$
- $[\![C]\!]$ contains runs $\langle s_0 \ldots s_4 s_5 s_7 s_8 s_9 \rangle$
- Set $[\![U]\!]$ contains all other runs.

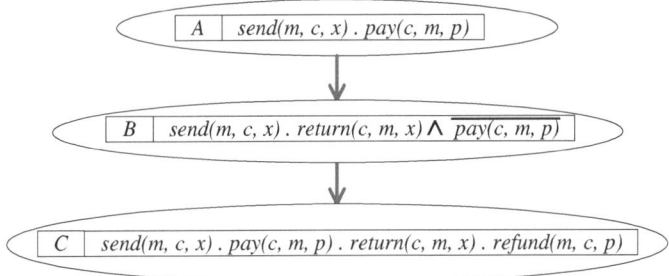

Fig. 2. A preference lattice $L_p = \langle \{A, B, C\}, \{(A, B), (B, C), (A, C)\} \rangle$ induced over the runs of the purchase protocol. Here, $A = send(m, c, x) \cdot pay(c, m, p)$, $B = send(m, c, x) \cdot return(c, m, x) \wedge \overline{pay(c, m, p)}$, and $C = send(m, c, x) \cdot pay(c, m, p) \cdot return(c, m, x) \cdot refund(m, c, x)$.

3.1 Characterization for a Protocol

Figure 2 shows a lattice where each node represents a set of runs, and directed edges point to nodes that are less preferred. Such a preference lattice could be used to specify exception in protocols. For example, all runs in the denotation of U can be marked as runs that cause exceptions. This manner of identifying exceptions is fundamentally different from traditional process-based concepts of exception modeling. In traditional approaches, sub-sequences of the protocol would be identified as scopes of exceptions. The benefit of using our approach is that exceptions are identified in the hierarchy of runs of the protocol, thus a notion of *severity* of an exception can be incorporated into the protocol model. Nodes further down the hierarchy denote more severe exceptions compared to the nodes higher up in the hierarchy. Moreover, the specification of exceptions is independent of both the protocol and the preference structure. In the above example, the same preference structure can be used but with a new specification that the set of runs $[\![C]\!]$ is a set of exception runs. As a consequence of the preference lattice, the set $[\![U]\!]$ is also inferred to be a set of exception runs that are mode severe than the runs in $[\![C]\!]$.

3.2 General Preferences for Commitment Actions

The semantics of commitment operations is the reason for flexibility in enactment of commitment protocols. For example, the customer in the purchase protocol can delegate its commitment to pay (the merchant) to a bank, achieving third party payment. In previous work [4], we have shown how such reasoning can be enabled in agent interaction protocols. Here, we describe how commitment operations can be used to specify preferences between protocol runs.

Consider the purchase protocol. In some cases, the designer might want to prevent cancellation of a an unconditional commitment, i.e., prevention of the cancellation of the customer's commitment to pay after the goods have been delivered or the merchant's commitment to ship the goods after the payment has been made. The preferences for this can be encoded as follows

- $P_1 = send(m, c, x) \cdot pay(c, m, p)$
- $P_2 = pay(c, m, p) \cdot send(m, c, x)$
- $P_3 = send(m, c, x) \cdot return(c, m, x)$
- $P_4 = pay(c, m, x) \cdot refund(m, c, p)$
- $P_5 = pay(c, m, p) \cdot cancel(m, C(m, c, send(m, c, x))) \wedge \overline{send(m, c, x)}$
- $P_6 = send(m, c, x) \cdot cancel(c, C(c, m, pay(c, m, p))) \wedge \overline{pay(c, m, p)}$
- P_1 and P_2 are each preferred over each of P_3, P_4, P_5, and P_6
- P_3 and P_4 are each preferred over P_5 and P_6

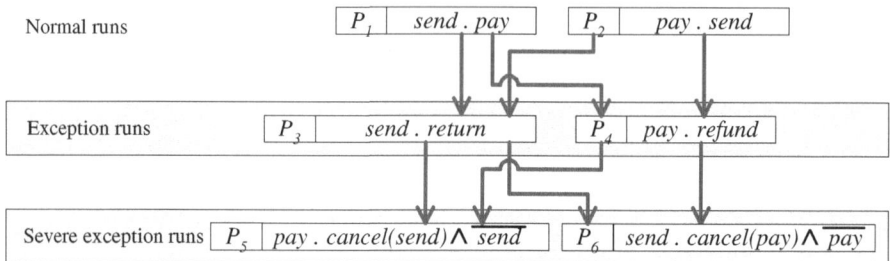

Fig. 3. A lattice for the purchase protocol disallowing cancellation of (unconditional) commitments. Message parameters are omitted for clarity.

Th above preference lattice is shown in Figure 3. There is no preference between P_1 and P_2, no preference between P_3 and P_4, and no preference between P_5 and P_6. This preference structure restricts the runs of the purchase protocol by disallowing cancellation of unconditional commitments. Based on our interpretation of the denotation of the lattice nodes, we obtain the following sets of runs (omitting parameters for clarity):

- $\llbracket P_1 \rrbracket = \llbracket send \cdot pay \rrbracket$. All runs in which the merchant sends the item and the customer pays afterwards.
- $\llbracket P_2 \rrbracket = \llbracket pay \cdot send \rrbracket$. All runs in which the customer pays, after which the merchant sends the item.
- $\llbracket P_3 \rrbracket = \llbracket send \cdot return \wedge \overline{pay} \rrbracket$. All runs in which the customer returns the item and never pays. This run cancels an unconditional commitment, hence it valid, although undesirable.
- $\llbracket P_4 \rrbracket = \llbracket pay \cdot refund \wedge \overline{send} \rrbracket$. All runs in which the merchant refunds the customer's payment and never sends the item. This run cancels an unconditional commitment, hence it is valid, although undesirable.
- $\llbracket P_5 \rrbracket = \llbracket ((pay \cdot cancel(send) \wedge \overline{refund}) \vee (refund \cdot pay \cdot cancel(send))) \wedge \overline{send} \rrbracket$. All runs in which the merchant cancels its commitment to send the item after the customer has paid, never sends the item, and never sends a refund of the customer's payment either.
- $\llbracket P_6 \rrbracket = \llbracket ((send \cdot cancel(pay) \wedge \overline{return}) \vee (return \cdot send \cdot cancel(pay))) \wedge \overline{pay} \rrbracket$. This is similar to $\llbracket P_5 \rrbracket$.

4   Operational Characterization of Preferences

We have seen how preferences among runs can be mapped to a lattice structure where each node represent a set of runs. This, however, is only part of the framework for using preferences in commitment protocols. Since OWL-P is the enactment framework that we use for protocols, operationalization of run preferences requires that these preferences are expressed in a form that is compatible with OWL-P. This section describes how rules are represented in OWL-P, and how a preference lattice can be converted into such rules.

4.1   OWL-P Enactment

Rules in OWL-P can be cast as Event-Condition-Action rules, i.e., on a certain event, if certain conditions hold, then perform a certain action. Consider Table 1, which shows a part of the OWL-P specification of the purchase protocol. Rule 4 states that when an *rfq* message is received (event), if the local policy can determine a binding for the values given (condition), then send an accept or a reject message (action), based on the policy binding. Rule 6 states that when goods are returned (event), if they were delivered by the merchant and the payment was not done (condition, then cancel the customers commitment to pay (action). OWL-P thus allows room for agents to enforce their local policies so they can make best use of the latitude in execution that the protocol allows. In addition to these rules, rules encoding commitment operations are incorporated into every commitment protocol. Given this rule specification in OWL-P, we next present a mapping from the denotational run preference specification to OWL-P-style rules.

4.2   Incorporating Preferences into OWL-P Rules

In OWL-P [1], protocols are specified as rules. During enactment, these rules are augmented by policies local to an agent, thus binding data values and logic for deciding between multiple allowed actions in a protocol to create an executable process. The format of a rule with a policy is

$$\text{On} \quad e$$
$$\text{if } localPolicy(e, x)$$
$$\text{then do} \quad a(x)$$

where e is an event and $a(\cdot)$ is an action (with a corresponding event e_a), which depends on the local policy for its parameters.

Consider the purchase protocol, which requires that the receiver of a $rfq(c, m, itemID)$ message (which is a request for a price quote for an item)–the merchant m–respond the the sender–the customer c–with a $quote(m, c, itemID, price)$ message (which is a price quote). The rule for this requirement will be

$$\text{On} \quad rfq(c, m, itemID)$$
$$\text{if } localPolicy(rfq(c, m, itemID), price)$$
$$\text{then do} \quad quote(m, c, itemID, price)$$

Where multiple choices of action are afforded by the protocol on the same triggering event, there will be one rule for each action, with the same event and condition. In such a case, the local policy decides which rule to enable and which to disable. In case the policy enables multiple rules, the preference specification of the protocol is used to decide which action to take.

5 Discussion

Protocols are intended to help us capture agent interactions in a perspicuous manner. Protocols can be combined to generate richer protocols that correspond to complex processes. Commitment protocols capture the semantic content of the desired interactions thereby enabling flexible agent behavior, as needed in the face of exceptions and opportunities. The approach of this paper is a practical approach that enables us to specify preferences among the executions that can be generated from protocols. Preferences serve as a rough and ready means to capture design goals wherein the normal executions are preferred, yet abnormal executions arising from exceptions or unexpected actions by some of the agents are allowed. The paper developed a declarative representation of preferences and tied it to an operational characterization of protocols.

Related Literature. One of the first operationalization of commitments for agent interaction was done by Yolum and Singh [10]. In their work, protocols were specified by listing legal states in terms of the commitments and domain propositions that hold at that state, and using an event calculus planner to generate the set of runs that were allowed. Winikoff *et al.* [9] have advanced this line of research. Fornara and Colombetti have also proposed a commitment-based interaction protocol framework [2]. However, none of the above approaches specify or operationalize a notion of preferences among the various execution sequences allowed by a protocol. Our work, therefore, is a significant step in this direction. Grosof *et al.* [3] have implemented rule based agent interaction systems where rules are prioritized. Grosof and colleagues propose what are known as *courteous Logic Programs*, or CLPs. In a CLP, when there is ambiguity regarding which rule to fire, i.e., a conflict arising because multiple rules can be fired at a particular state of the world, the priorities assigned to the rules are used to resolve the conflict. Our work is similar to CLPs in this respect, but different in that we propose a scheme in which preferences among *runs* are specified, independent of a protocol specification. Further, we also present a methodology for translating these preferences into rules that can be embedded into the (rule-based) protocol specification.

Our work is based on the concept of social interaction among agents, which gives importance only to the publicly observable behavior of agents. We describe how preferences among runs can exist. However, we do not study how agents can reason about the benefits of using one set of protocol runs over another. Pasquier and Chaib-Draa [6] introduce the cognitive dissonance theory into multiagent communication by incorporating the theory and dialogue game protocols into agent interactions. Their theory explores ways in which agents can decide when to start dialogues with other agents and what kind of dialogues to initiate, among other things. This line of research is complementary to and would strengthen the interaction framework we have presented here. Preferences among the available runs of a protocol have also been studied from the game theoretic point of view by Otterloo *et al.* [8]. They describe a logic that can be used for reasoning about a strategy to adopt in a game when the preferences of other agents in the game are known. The work differs from ours because of the use of games instead of commitment protocols. Also, preferences of agents are assumed to be known by other agents, which does not always apply in real-world applications such as the business interaction we have outlined in this paper. We plan to incorporate such reasoning among agents into our framework.

This paper opens up some additional challenges. Among these are the specification of preferences in richer formal languages so that more subtle distinctions among possible executions can be captured.

References

1. Nirmit Desai, Ashok U. Mallya, Amit K. Chopra, and Munindar P. Singh. Interaction protocols as design abstractions for business processes. *IEEE Transactions on Software Engineering*, 2006. To appear.
2. Nicoletta Fornara and Marco Colombetti. Defining interaction protocols using a commitment-based agent communication language. In *Proceedings of the 2nd International Joint Conference on Autonomous Agents and Multiagent Systems (AAMAS)*, pages 520–527. ACM Press, July 2003.
3. Benjamin N. Grosof and Terrence C. Poon. SweetDeal: Representing agent contracts with exceptions using XML rules, ontologies, and process descriptions. In *Proceedings 12th International Conference on the World Wide Web*, pages 340–349, 2003.
4. Ashok U. Mallya and Munindar P. Singh. A semantic approach for designing commitment protocols. In Rogier Van Eijk, editor, *Developments in Agent Communication*, volume 3396 of *Lecture Notes in Artificial Intelligence*, pages 37–51. Springer, Berlin, 2005.
5. Ashok U. Mallya, Pınar Yolum, and Munindar P. Singh. Resolving commitments among autonomous agents. In Frank Dignum, editor, *Advances in Agent Communication*, volume 2922 of *Lecture Notes in Artificial Intelligence*, pages 166–182, Berlin, 2003. Springer.
6. Philippe Pasquier and Brahim Chaib-Draa. The cognitive coherence approach for agent communication pragmatics. In *Proceedings of the 2nd International Joint Conference on Autonomous Agents and MultiAgent Systems (AAMAS)*, pages 544–551. ACM Press, july 2003.
7. Munindar P. Singh. Distributed enactment of multiagent workflows: Temporal logic for web service composition. In *Proceedings of the 2nd International Joint Conference on Autonomous Agents and MultiAgent Systems (AAMAS)*, 2003.
8. Sieuwert van Otterloo, Wiebe van der Hoek, and Michael Wooldridge. Preferences in game logics. In *Proceedings of the 3rd International Joint Conference on Autonomous Agents and MultiAgent Systems (AAMAS)*, pages 152–159, 2004.
9. Michael Winikoff, Wei Liu, and James Harland. Enhancing commitment machines. In *Proceedings of the AAMAS-04 Workshop on Declarative Agent Languages and Technologies*, 2004.
10. Pınar Yolum and Munindar P. Singh. Flexible protocol specification and execution: Applying event calculus planning using commitments. In *Proceedings of the 1st International Joint Conference on Autonomous Agents and MultiAgent Systems (AAMAS)*, pages 527–534. ACM Press, July 2002.

On the Study of Negotiation Strategies

Leila Amgoud[1] and Souhila Kaci[2]

[1] Institut de Recherche en Informatique de Toulouse (I.R.I.T.)–C.N.R.S.
Université Paul Sabatier, 118 route de Narbonne,
31062 Toulouse Cedex 4, France
[2] Centre de Recherche en Informatique de Lens (C.R.I.L.)–C.N.R.S.
Rue de l'Université SP 16
62307 Lens Cedex, France

Abstract. The basic idea behind a negotiation is that the agents make offers that they judge "good" and respond to the offers made to them until a compromise is reached. The choice of the offer to propose at a given step in a negotiation dialogue is a *strategic* matter. In most works on negotiation dialogues, the agents are supposed to be *rational*, and thus propose and accept only the offers which satisfy all their goals. This strategy is very restrictive since in everyday life, it is difficult to find an offer which satisfies all the agent's goals.

The aim of this paper is to propose less restrictive strategies than the one used in the literature. Those strategies are based not only on the *goals* and beliefs of the agents but also on their *rejections*. A three-layered setting is proposed. The properties of each strategy are given as well as a comparative study between these strategies.

1   Introduction

Autonomous agents evolve in a community and because of the interdependences which may exist between them, the agents need to interact in order to exchange information, ask for services, etc. Negotiation is the most predominant mechanism for communicating and also for making deals. The basic idea behind a negotiation is that the agents make offers that they judge "good" and respond to the offers made to them until a compromise is reached. Since the agents' interests are generally conflicting, an offer which is acceptable for one agent is not necessarily acceptable for another agent.

As argued in [9,10,12,11], the choice of the offer to propose at a given step in a negotiation dialogue is a *strategic* matter. Indeed, the acceptability of an offer depends broadly on the *agent profile* and its *mental states*.

There are very few works on negotiation strategies in general if we except the work done by Maudet et al. in [9,10], and the work done in [1] in the case of argument selection. Concerning the choice of offers, in most works on negotiation dialogues, the agents are supposed to be *rational*, and thus propose and accept only the offers which satisfy all their goals. This strategy is too restrictive since in everyday life, it is difficult to find an offer which satisfies all the agent's goals.

Moreover, recent cognitive psychology studies [6,5,3,13] claim that agents may express and reason on two components: *goals* and *rejections*. Goals describe what the agent would like to realize, and the rejections describe what is not acceptable for that

F. Dignum, R. van Eijk, and R. Flores (Eds.): AC 2005/2006, LNAI 3859, pp. 150–163, 2006.

agent. When both goals and rejections are provided we say that we are in a *bipolar* framework. Beware that *bipolarity* is not *duality* i.e., goals are not simply the complement of rejections. Note however that rejections and goals are related by a coherence condition asserting that what is pursued should not be rejected. A formalization of goals and rejections in a logical setting and reasoning about them have been developed in [2].

We claim that taking into account what an agent rejects, in addition to its goals, in the offer selection enables a more refined selection, and allows to discard rejected offers. Let's suppose, for instance, an agent who has two possible offers x_1 and x_2 to propose at a given step. Suppose also that both offers satisfy all the goals of the agent. In this case, one may say that x_1 is as preferred as x_2 and the agent can propose any of them. However, if x_1 satisfies one of the rejections of that agent, then x_1 will be discarded and the only possible offer is x_2.

The aim of this paper is to propose different strategies allowing agents to select the offers to suggest, and to decide when to accept the offers made to them. These strategies are based on both the goals and the rejections of the agents. We will show that these strategies are less restrictive than the one used in the literature.

This paper is organized as follows: Section 2 presents the different mental states of an agent as well as their role in selecting offers. In fact, the beliefs will delimit the *feasible* offers, the goals will delimit the *satisfactory* ones and finally, the rejections will delimit the *acceptable* offers. In section 3 a general setting for defining strategies is given. In fact, the definition of a strategy consists of fixing three parameters: an ordering, between the goals of and the rejections, which depends on agent's profile, a criterion for defining the acceptability of an offer, and a criterion for defining the satisfaisability of an offer. Section 4 presents different agent profiles, and the way in which the selected offers (called candidate offers) are computed in each case. Section 5 presents a criterion of acceptability, whereas section 6 provides three criteria of satisfaisability. Some strategies are then studied in section 7, and some properties are given in section 8. Section 9 is devoted to some concluding remarks and some perspectives

2   Mental States of the Agents

2.1   Logical Definition

In what follows, $\mathcal{L}$ will denote a first order propositional language. Each negotiating agent has got a set $\mathcal{B}$ of *beliefs*, a set $\mathcal{G}$ of *goals*, and finally a set $\mathcal{R}$ of *rejections*. Beliefs are *informational attitudes* and concern the real world. Goals are *motivational attitudes* and intrinsic to the agent. They represent what an agent wants to achieve or to get. Like goals, rejections are also *motivational attitudes* and intrinsic to the agent. However, they represent what the agent rejects and considers as *unacceptable*.

Beliefs are pervaded with uncertainty i.e., they are more or less certain while rejections and goals may not have equal priority. More formally, we have:

Definition 1 (Mental states of an agent). *Each agent is equipped with three bases: $\mathcal{B}$, $\mathcal{R}$ and $\mathcal{G}$ such that:*

- $\mathcal{B} = \{(b_i, \alpha_i), i = 1, \ldots, n\}$, *where b_i is a formula of the language $\mathcal{L}$, and α_i is an element of the interval $(0, 1]$. The pair (b_i, α_i) means that the certainty degree of* the belief b_i is at least equal to α_i. When α_i is equal to 1 this means that b_i is an integrity constraint which should be fulfilled.

– $\mathcal{R} = \{(r_j, \beta_j), j = 1, \ldots, m\}$, where r_j is a formula of the language $\mathcal{L}$ and β_j is an element of the interval $(0, 1]$. The pair (r_j, β_j) means that the priority degree of the rejection r_j is at least equal to β_j.

– $\mathcal{G} = \{(g_k, \lambda_k), k = 1, \ldots, p\}$ where g_k is a formula of the language $\mathcal{L}$ and λ_k is in the interval $(0, 1]$. The pair (g_k, λ_k) means that the priority degree of the goal g_k is at least equal to λ_k.

Note that for the sake of simplicity, we use numerical numbers to model the priority/uncertainty degrees. However, a simple ordering on formulas holds as well.

Hypothesis 1. *Throughout the paper, the sets of beliefs and rejections are supposed to be* consistent. *For the sake of simplicity, we suppose that all beliefs are completely certain i.e.,* $\alpha_i = 1$ *for* $i = 1, \cdots, n$. *However this work can be easily generalized to the case where beliefs are more or less certain.*

Since we deal with first order formulas, the satisfaction of formulas is different from the one of classical logic. Suppose that we have a set of some facts $\mathcal{F}$ giving an instantiation of first order formulas. Let x be an offer and $\mathcal{H}_x^{\mathcal{F}}$ be the result of instantiating the set $\mathcal{H}$ by x. Then, x satisfies $\mathcal{H}$ if and only if each formula in $\mathcal{H}_x^{\mathcal{F}}$ is true in the set of facts $\mathcal{F}$.

Example 1. Let $\mathcal{F} = \{\neg promotion(AF), stopover(AF), \neg flexible(BA)\}$ and $\mathcal{H} = \{stopover(x), \neg promotion(x) \vee \neg flexible(x)\}$.

Then $\mathcal{H}_{AF}^{\mathcal{F}} = \{stopover(AF), \neg promotion(AF) \vee \neg flexible(AF)\}$. Each formula in $\mathcal{H}_{AF}^{\mathcal{F}}$ is true w.r.t. $\mathcal{F}$ then AF satisfies $\mathcal{H}$.

Now we have $\mathcal{H}_{BA}^{\mathcal{F}} = \{stopover(BA), \neg promotion(BA) \vee \neg flexible(BA)\}$. Then BA doesn't satisfy $\mathcal{H}$ since $stopover(BA)$ is not true in $\mathcal{F}$.

2.2 Role of Beliefs, Rejections and Goals

Although the three sets are involved in the selection of offers, they should be distinguished since they do not necessarily behave in the same way.

Beliefs play a key role in delimiting the set of *feasible* offers.

Definition 2 (Feasible offers). *Let* $x \in X$. *An offer* x *is* feasible *if it satisfies the set of beliefs.*

Let's take the following example about airline companies.

Example 2 (Airline companies). Suppose that the object of the negotiation is an "airline company". Let

– $X = \{AF, AirLib, BA, KLM\}$,
– $\mathcal{B} = \{(\neg promotion(x) \vee \neg flexible(x), 1)\}$,
– $\mathcal{R} = \{(\neg stopover(x), .9), (dayflight(x) \wedge \neg smoking(x), .4), (\neg flexible(x), .1)\}$,
– $\mathcal{G} = \{(promotion(x), .8), (stopover(x), .5),$
  $(dayflight(x), .5)\}$.

Table 1. Some facts

	AF	$AirLib$	BA	KLM
$stopover(x)$	yes	yes	yes	yes
$dayflight(x)$	no	no	yes	yes
$promotion(x)$	no	yes	no	yes
$smoking(x)$			yes	no
$flexible(x)$	yes	no	yes	no

Table 1 gives some facts. For example, we have $stopover(AF)$, $\neg promotion(AF)$, etc. Feasible offers are those which satisfy the set $\mathcal{B}$, namely $\mathbb{F}=\{AF, AirLib, BA, KLM\}$.

Each rejection (r_j, β_j), which should not be satisfied, induces by complementation an integrity constraint $(\neg r_j, \beta_j)$ which should be respected. In what follows, $\mathcal{R}'$ will denote the set of induced integrity constraints from the base $\mathcal{R}$. Such integrity constraints are *intrinsic* to an agent and not "imposed" by the environment. That's why they are not considered as beliefs in $\mathcal{B}$.

The offers which respect the induced integrity constraints will be *acceptable* for the agent.

Definition 3 (Acceptable offers). *Let $x \in X$. An offer x is* acceptable *iff $\mathcal{R}' \Vdash_{c_a} x$. This means that it satisfies the integrity constraints w.r.t. a criterion c_a.*

In the above definition, the acceptability of an offer depends on a criterion c_a. Indeed, one may, for instance, accept an offer which respects all the integrity constrains. Another criterion consists of accepting the offers which respect the most important integrity constraints. In section 5, we will give a criterion for the acceptability of an offer.

Regarding goals, they will delimit the set of *satisfactory* offers. Indeed, the offers which satisfy the goals of an agent according to some criterion will be satisfactory for that agent. The satisfaisability of an offer depends also on the chosen criterion. One may accept the offers which satisfy all its goals. However, it may be the case also that an agent accepts the offers which satisfy at least its most important goals. In section 6, different criteria for the satisfaisability of an offer will be proposed.

Definition 4 (Satisfactory offers). *Let $x \in X$. An offer x is* satisfactory *iff $\mathcal{G} \Vdash_{c_s} x$. This means that the offer x satisfies the goals of the agent w.r.t. a criterion c_s.*

Notations 1

- $\mathcal{R}'_{>\beta} = \{\neg r_j \mid (r_j, \beta_j) \in \mathcal{R} \text{ and } \beta_j > \beta\}$.
- $\mathcal{G}_{>\lambda} = \{g_k \mid (g_k, \lambda_k) \in \mathcal{G} \text{ and } \lambda_k > \lambda\}$.
  $\mathcal{G}_{>\lambda}$ *(resp. $\mathcal{R}_{>\beta}$) corresponds to the conjunction of goals (resp. of constraints induced by rejections) having a weight greater than λ (resp. β).*

- $\mathcal{G}_{=\lambda} = \{g_k \mid (g_k, \lambda_k) \in \mathcal{G} \text{ and } \lambda_k = \lambda\}$. $\mathcal{G}_{=\lambda}$ *corresponds to the conjunction of goals having a priority degree equal to λ.*
- $\bigvee(\mathcal{G}_{=\lambda}) = \bigvee\{g_k \mid (g_k, \lambda_k) \in \mathcal{G} \text{ and } \lambda_k = \lambda\}$. *This corresponds to the disjunction of all the goals with priority degree equal to λ.*

– Let $\succeq$ be a pre-order between sets. The notation $\mathcal{H} \succeq \mathcal{H}'$ means that the $\mathcal{H}$ is at least as preferred as $\mathcal{H}'$. Let $\succ$ be the strict ordering associated with $\succeq$. The symbol $\approx$ stands for the "equality", i.e. when $\mathcal{H}$ and $\mathcal{H}'$ are equally preferred by the agent.

3   General Setting for Offer Selection

Selecting offers is an important decision in a negotiation process since it influences the outcome of the negotiation. This decision follows a three step process:

1. defining a relation $\succeq$ between $\mathcal{B}$, $\mathcal{R}$ and $\mathcal{G}$. The ordering on $\mathcal{B}$, $\mathcal{R}$ and $\mathcal{G}$ is a determining point in the selection of offers. In the next section, we will show that one may not have the same set of candidate offers when $\mathcal{G} \succeq \mathcal{R}$ or $\mathcal{R} \succeq \mathcal{G}$.
   In [4,14], it has been argued that beliefs should take precedence over goals in order to avoid any *wishful thinking*. Regarding rejections, beliefs should also take precedence over them since rejections have the same nature as goals. Moreover, the feasibility of an offer is more important than its acceptability. Thus, the following orderings hold: $\mathcal{B} \succ \mathcal{R}$ and $\mathcal{B} \succ \mathcal{G}$. The ordering between $\mathcal{G}$ and $\mathcal{R}$ is not easy to guess and depends broadly on agents' profiles. Different agents' profiles can then be defined according to the precise ordering between $\mathcal{G}$ and $\mathcal{R}$.
2. defining *criteria* for selecting acceptable offers.
3. defining *criteria* for selecting satisfactory offers.

Definition 5 (Strategy). *Let $\mathcal{B}$, $\mathcal{R}$ and $\mathcal{G}$ be the agent's bases and X the set of offers. A strategy is a triple $<\succeq, \Vdash_{c_a}, \Vdash_{c_s}>$. This system will return a set $\underline{S} \subseteq X$ of candidate offers.*

In the above definition, we speak about a *set of candidate offers*. The reason is that it may be the case that several offers will have the same preference for the agent.

4   Different Agent Profiles

The ordering between beliefs and the other two sets is in some sense imposed by the nature of the different mental states. However, things seem different for fixing the ordering between $\mathcal{R}$ and $\mathcal{G}$. This ordering depends on the agent's profile. Indeed, there are three possibilities for comparing the two sets:

1. the case where both sets have the same preference ($\mathcal{R} \approx \mathcal{G}$).
2. the case where $\mathcal{R}$ is preferred to $\mathcal{G}$ ($\mathcal{R} \succ \mathcal{G}$).
3. the case where $\mathcal{G}$ is preferred to $\mathcal{R}$ ($\mathcal{G} \succ \mathcal{R}$).

Each of the three possibilities corresponds to a specific agent profile. Formally:

Definition 6 (Consensual agent). *Let $\{\mathcal{B}, \mathcal{R}, \mathcal{G}\}$ be the bases of an agent A. A is consensual iff $\mathcal{R} \approx \mathcal{G}$.*

A consensual agent computes separately the acceptable offers and the satisfactory offers among feasible ones w.r.t. some criteria. The candidate offers are those which are both acceptable and satisfactory.

Definition 7. *Let A be a consensual agent. The set of* candidate *offers* $\underline{S} = S_1 \cap S_2$ *such that:*

1. *$S_1, S_2 \subseteq X$, and*
2. *$\forall x \in S_1$, x is feasible and acceptable, and*
3. *$\forall x \in S_2$, x is feasible and satisfactory.*

This approach is too requiring since it may lead to an empty set of *candidate* offers.

Definition 8 (Cautious agent). *Let $\{\mathcal{B}, \mathcal{R}, \mathcal{G}\}$ be the bases of an agent A. A is* cautious *iff $\mathcal{R} \succ \mathcal{G}$.*

A cautious agent starts by selecting the acceptable offers among the feasible ones. The candidate offers are the satisfactory (w.r.t. some criteria) offers among the acceptable ones. Formally:

Definition 9. *Let A be a cautious agent. The set of* candidate *offers is $\underline{S} = \{x \in S'$ such that x is satisfactory\}, where*

1. *$S' = \{x \in X$ such that x is feasible and acceptable\}.*
2. *S' is maximal for $(\subseteq)$ among the sets satisfying the first condition.*

This approach is cautious since the agent prefers to select acceptable offers, among feasible ones, even if none of them satisfies any goal.

Definition 10 (Adventurous agent). *Let $\{\mathcal{B}, \mathcal{R}, \mathcal{G}\}$ be the bases of an agent A. A is* adventurous *iff $\mathcal{G} \succ \mathcal{R}$.*

An adventurous agent selects first satisfactory offers among feasible ones, then among the offers it gets, it will choose those which are acceptable w.r.t. some criteria.

Definition 11. *Let A be an adventurous agent. The set of* candidate *offers is $\underline{S} = \{x \in S'$ such that x is acceptable\}, where*

1. *$S' = \{x \in X$ such that x is feasible and satisfactory\}.*
2. *S' is maximal for $(\subseteq)$ among the sets satisfying the first condition.*

This approach is too adventurous since it may lead the agent to select offers which are not acceptable at all.

5   Acceptability of Offers

An offer is acceptable if it respects the integrity constraints induced by rejections. In some situations, one cannot find an offer which satisfies all the constraints, and the set of candidate offers is empty. To relax this criterion, an agent may accept the offers which respects the constraints at a certain level, called *acceptability level*. Indeed, the acceptability level is the complement to 1 of the degree of the less important constraint that should be respected by offers. Formally:

Definition 12 (Acceptability level). *Let $x \in X$. The* acceptability level *of an offer x, denoted $Level_A(x) = 1 - min\{\beta$ such that x satisfies $\mathcal{R}'_{>\beta}\}$.*
If x falsifies $\mathcal{R}'_{>\beta}$ for all β then $Level_A(x) = 0$.

This criterion has already been used in possibilistic logic and belief revision [7,15]. The acceptable offers are the ones with a greater acceptability level. Indeed, such offers satisfy more important integrity constraints.

Definition 13 (Acceptability criterion). *Let $x \in X$ and $\mathcal{R}$ be the set of rejections. The offer x is acceptable, denoted*

$$\mathcal{R}' \Vdash_{Level} x, if f Level(x)_A \geq Level_A(x'), \forall x' \in X.$$

Example 3. In example 2, $\mathcal{R}' \Vdash_{Level} AF, BA$. Indeed, $Level_A(AF)=Level_A(BA)=1$ since both AF and BA satisfy $\mathcal{R}'_{>0} = stopover(x) \wedge (\neg day flight(x) \vee smoking(x)) \wedge flexible(x)$, while $Level_A(AirLib) = .9$ and $Level_A(KLM) = .6$.

6   Satisfiability of Offers

It is natural that an agent aims to satisfy all its goals. When this is not possible, it may try to satisfy as much as possible prioritized goals. A *cardinality*-based selection mode seems appropriate in this case. Before defining this criterion, let's first introduce some notations.

Let $\beta_1, \cdots, \beta_m$ be the weights appearing in $\mathcal{G}$ s.t. $1 \geq \beta_1 > \cdots > \beta_m > 0$. Let $\mathcal{G}' = \mathcal{G}_1 \cup \ldots \cup \mathcal{G}_m$ be the representation of $\mathcal{G}$ in its well ordered partition. Each $\mathcal{G}_j$, called *layer*, contains formulas of $\mathcal{G}$ having the weight β_j. Let x be an offer and $\mathcal{S}_x = \mathcal{S}_x^1 \cup \ldots \cup \mathcal{S}_x^m$ where $\mathcal{S}_x^j$ is a subset of $\mathcal{G}_j$ containing the goals of $\mathcal{G}_j$ satisfied by x.

Definition 14 (Cardinality-based criterion). *Let $x \in X$. x is satisfactory, denoted*

$$\mathcal{G} \Vdash_{Card} x, iff \forall x' \in X:$$

- $\exists k$ s.t. $\forall j = 1, \ldots, k - 1; |\mathcal{S}_x^j| = |\mathcal{S}_{x'}^j|$ and $|\mathcal{S}_x^k| > |\mathcal{S}_{x'}^k|$, or
- $|\mathcal{S}_x^j| = |\mathcal{S}_{x'}^j|$ for $j = 1, \cdots, m$,

where $|\mathcal{S}_x^j|$ is the number of formulas in $\mathcal{S}_x^j$.

Let's illustrate this criterion on the following example:

Example 4. Recall that $\mathbb{F} = \{AF, AirLib, BA, KLM\}$.
Let's first put $\mathcal{G}$ under its well ordered partition: $\mathcal{G}' = \mathcal{G}_1 \cup \mathcal{G}_2$, where $\mathcal{G}_1 = \{promotion(x)\}$ and $\mathcal{G}_2 = \{stopover(x), day flight(x)\}$. Then,
$\mathcal{S}_{AF} = \{\} \cup \{stopover(x)\}$,
$\mathcal{S}_{AirLib} = \{promotion(x)\} \cup \{stopover(x)\}$,
$\mathcal{S}_{BA} = \{\} \cup \{stopover(x), day flight(x)\}$ and
$\mathcal{S}_{KLM} = \{promotion(x)\} \cup \{stopover(x), day flight(x)\}$.
$\mathcal{G} \Vdash_{Card} KLM$ because it is the only offer which satisfies the maximum of prioritized goals.

The cardinality-based criterion gives priority to the offers which satisfy a maximum of prioritized goals. A weaker version of this criterion consists of choosing the offers which satisfy at least one prioritized goal. Formally:

Definition 15 (Disjunctive satisfaction level). *Let $x \in X$. The disjunctive satisfaction level of an offer x is $Level_{DS}(x) = max\{\lambda$ such that x satisfies $\bigvee(\mathcal{G}_{=\lambda})\}$.*
If x falsifies all formulas of $\mathcal{G}$ then $Level_{DS}(x) = 0$.

Indeed satisfactory offers are those which satisfy at least one prioritized goal. We define now the disjunctive-based criterion:

Definition 16 (Disjunctive-based criterion). *Let $x \in X$. $\mathcal{G} \Vvdash_{Disj} x$, iff $Level_{DS} \geq Level_{DS}(x'), \forall x' \in X$.*

Example 5. As shown in the previous example, the use of a cardinality-based criterion, only one offer (KLM) is satisfactory for the agent. However, using the disjunctive criterion, we can get more satisfactory offers. Indeed, $Level_{DS}(KLM) = Level_{DS}(Airlib)$ $= .8$ with $\bigvee \mathcal{G}_{=.8} = \{promotion(x)\}$. Consequently, $\mathcal{G} \Vvdash_{Disj} AirLib, KLM$.

Another refinement of the cardinality-based criterion can be defined. The idea here is similar to the one behind the acceptability criterion. A satisfactory offer is the one which satisfies as much prioritized goals as possible. A satisfaction level is defined as follows:

Definition 17 (Conjunctive satisfaction level). *Let $x \in X$. The satisfaction level of an offer x is $Level_{CS}(x) = 1 - min\{\lambda$ such that x satisfies $\mathcal{G}_{>\lambda}\}$.*
If x falsifies $\mathcal{G}_{>\lambda}$ for all λ then $Level_{CS}(x) = 0$.

Satisfactory offers are then the ones which have a small satisfaction level, since the smaller this level is, the more important the number of satisfied prioritized goals is. Formally:

Definition 18 (Conjunctive-based selection). *Let $x \in X$. $\mathcal{G} \Vvdash_{Conj} x$ iff $Level_{CS} \geq Level_{CS}(x'), \forall x' \in X$.*

Example 6. We have $Level_{CS}(KLM) = 1$ while $Level_{CS}(AF) = Level_{CS}(BA) = 0$ and $Level_{CS}(AirLib) = .5$. Then $\mathcal{G} \Vvdash_{Conj} KLM$.
   Note that we get the same result as the one obtained by using the cardinality-based criterion because KLM satisfies all agent's goals but this is not always the case

We can show that if an offer is satisfactory w.r.t the cardinality criterion, it is also satisfactory w.r.t the conjunctive criterion. Similarly, each offer which is satisfactory w.r.t the conjunctive criterion is also satisfactory w.r.t the disjunctive criterion. Formally:

Proposition 1. *Let $\mathcal{B}$, $\mathcal{R}$, $\mathcal{G}$ be three bases of an agent and $x \in X$.*

$$(\mathcal{G} \Vvdash_{Card} x) \Rightarrow (\mathcal{G} \Vvdash_{Conj} x) \Rightarrow (\mathcal{G} \Vvdash_{Disj} x).$$

7 Particular Strategies

A strategy for selecting the offers to propose during a negotiation dialogue has three parameters: an ordering between $\mathcal{R}$ and $\mathcal{G}$, an acceptability criterion and finally a satisfaisability criterion. Different systems can then be defined using the criteria suggested in the previous sections. Table 2 summarizes these systems (strategies). This section aims at presenting some of these strategies as well as their properties.

Table 2. Different strategies

	$\Vert\vdash_{Level}$, $\Vert\vdash_{Conj}$	$\Vert\vdash_{Level}$, $\Vert\vdash_{Disj}$	$\Vert\vdash_{Level}$, $\Vert\vdash_{Card}$
Consensual $(\mathcal{R} \approx \mathcal{G})$	- drastic - pessimistic	optimistic	$\times$
Cautious $(\mathcal{R} \succ \mathcal{G})$	$\times$	relaxed	requiring
Adventurous $(\mathcal{G} \succ \mathcal{R})$	$\times$	$\times$	$\times$

Definition 19 (Drastic strategy). *Let* $\mathcal{B}$, $\mathcal{R}$ *and* $\mathcal{G}$ *be the agent's bases and* X *the set of offers. A* drastic system *is a triple* $<\succeq, \Vert\vdash_{Level}, \Vert\vdash_{Conj}>$, *such that*

- $\mathcal{R} \approx \mathcal{G}$, *and*
- $Level_A(x) = Level_{CS}(x) = 1$ *for candidate offers.*

In such a system, an agent computes separately acceptable and satisfactory offers. Acceptable offers are those which falsify *all rejections* while satisfactory offers are those which satisfy *all goals*. Candidate offers are then those which are both acceptable and satisfactory. However the drawback of this approach is that it is too restrictive and may lead to an empty set of candidate offers.

Example 7. Since $Level_A(x)$ should be equal to 1, acceptable offers are feasible ones which satisfy all constraints in $\mathcal{R}'$, i.e. they falsify **all rejections**. They satisfy $stopover(x) \wedge (\neg dayflight(x) \vee smoking(x)) \wedge flexible(x)$. Then the set of acceptable offers is $\mathcal{A} = \{AF, BA\}$.

Satisfactory offers are feasible ones which satisfy **all goals** since $Level_{CS} = 1$. They satisfy $stopover(x) \wedge dayflight(x) \wedge promotion(x)$. Then the set of satisfactory offers is $\mathcal{S} = \{KLM\}$.

Now candidate offers are those which are both acceptable and satisfactory however this set is empty.

Note that if we only consider goals in this example then the candidate offer is KLM which is not acceptable (i.e., rejected) by the agent following the chosen acceptability criterion.

Definition 20 (Optimistic strategy). *Let* $\mathcal{B}$, $\mathcal{R}$ *and* $\mathcal{G}$ *be the agent's bases and* X *the set of offers. An* optimistic system *is a triple* $<\succeq, \Vert\vdash_{Level}, \Vert\vdash_{Disj}>$, *where* $\mathcal{R} \approx \mathcal{G}$.

With an optimistic strategy, one looks for offers which falsify as most as possible prioritized rejections and satisfy as at least one prioritized goal [8]. Formally these offers satisfy

$$\mathcal{R}'_{>\beta} \wedge (\bigvee \mathcal{G}_{=\lambda})$$

s.t. β is as low as possible and λ is as high as possible.

Let $\{\beta_1, \cdots, \beta_n\}$ and $\{\lambda_1, \cdots, \lambda_m\}$ be the degrees appearing in $\mathcal{R}$ and $\mathcal{G}$ respectively. Note that following definition 12, more β_i is close to 1, more offers satisfying the associated rejection are unacceptable. Also following definition 15, more λ_j is close to 1, more offers satisfying the associated goals are satisfactory.

We first put $\beta = 0$ and $\lambda = \lambda_1$. This means that preferred offers are those which satisfy all the constraints induced by rejections (i.e., falsify all rejections) and satisfy at least one goal from the prioritized ones, if possible. If the intersection of the corresponding acceptable and satisfactory offers is not empty then we declare offers belonging to the intersection as the candidate ones otherwise we either increase β or decrease λ. To ensure that we choose β as low as possible and λ as high as possible, we fix the values of β and λ in the following way:

$$\begin{cases} \beta = 0 \text{ and } \lambda = \lambda_2 & \text{if } 1 - \beta_n < \lambda_2 \\ \beta = \beta_n \text{ and } \lambda = \lambda_1 & \text{if } 1 - \beta_n > \lambda_2 \\ \beta = \beta_n \text{ and } \lambda = \lambda_2 & \text{otherwise.} \end{cases} \qquad (1)$$

The idea behind the optimistic strategy is to select offers which maximize acceptability or satisfaction. First note that if some offer falsifies all rejections having a weight strictly greater than β but satisfies at least one rejection with a weight equal to β then it is unacceptable to a degree β. Indeed it is acceptable to a degree equal to $1 - \beta$ following definition 12.

Following equation (1), we give up rejections with weight β_n if $1 - \beta_n$ (which represents the acceptability degree of offers satisfying at least one of these rejections following definition 12) is higher than λ_2 which represents the satisfaction degree of offers satisfying one of its corresponding goals following definition 15.

Once the values β and λ are fixed, if there are offers satisfying $\mathcal{R}'_{>\beta} \wedge (\bigvee \mathcal{G}_{=\lambda})$ then we stop otherwise we either increase β or decrease λ, and so on.

Example 8. First we put $\beta = 0$ and $\lambda = .8$. We have $\mathcal{R}'_{>0} = stopover(x) \wedge (\neg dayflight(x) \vee smoking(x)) \wedge flexible(x)$ and $\bigvee \mathcal{G}_{=.8} = promotion(x)$.

Then acceptable offers are feasible ones which satisfy $\mathcal{R}'_{>0}$. They are AF and BA.

Satisfactory offers are feasible ones which satisfy $\bigvee \mathcal{G}_{=.8}$, they are $AirLib$ and KLM. Indeed the intersection of the two sets is empty.

Now we put $\beta = .1$ and $\lambda = .8$ since offers satisfying the rejection $(\neg flexible(x), .1)$ are acceptable to a degree equal to .9 while those satisfying $(promotion(x), .8)$ are satisfactory to a degree equal to .8. The acceptability degree is greater than the satisfaction degree.

Now acceptable offers satisfy $stopover(x) \wedge (\neg dayflight(x) \vee smoking(x))$. They are AF, $AirLib$ and BA.

Satisfactory offers satisfy $promotion(x)$. They are $AirLib$ and KLM. Indeed there is only one candidate offer which is $AirLib$.

In the case where we only consider goals, candidate offers are $AirLib$ and KLM however KLM is rejected.

Definition 21 (Pessimistic strategy). *Let $\mathcal{B}$, $\mathcal{R}$ and $\mathcal{G}$ be the agent's bases and X the set of offers. A pessimistic strategy is a triple $<\succeq, \Vdash_{Level}, \Vdash_{Conj}>$, where $\mathcal{R} \approx \mathcal{G}$.*

With a pessimistic strategy, one selects offers which satisfy as much as prioritized integrity constraints and goals. Formally these offers should satisfy

$$\mathcal{R}'_{>\beta} \wedge \mathcal{G}_{>\lambda},$$

with α and β are as low as possible. We follow the same reasoning as in the optimistic strategy to ensure that α and β are as low as possible.

Example 9. Following the drastic strategy, there is no offer which satisfies all constraints induced by rejections and all goals.

Now we put $\beta = .1$ and $\lambda = 0$. Then acceptable offers are those which satisfy $\mathcal{R}'_{>.1}$. They are AF, $AirLib$ and BA.

Satisfactory offers satisfy $promotion(x) \wedge stopover(x) \wedge dayflight(x)$. There is only one satisfactory offer which is KLM. Again, the set of candidate offers is empty.

Let us now put $\beta = .4$ and $\lambda = 0$. Then acceptable offers satisfy $stopover(x)$. They are AF, $AirLib$, BA and KLM. Indeed there is a candidate offer which is KLM.

Note that we obtain the same result as the case where we only consider goals. However this is not always the case.

Definition 22 (Requiring strategy). *Let $\mathcal{B}$, $\mathcal{R}$ and $\mathcal{G}$ be the agent's bases and X the set of offers. A requiring strategy is a triple* $<\succeq, \Vdash_{Level}, \Vdash_{Card}>$, *where* $\mathcal{R} \succ \mathcal{G}$.

Among feasible offers, the agent selects first acceptable offers which falsify as much as prioritized rejections and among acceptable offers, it selects those which satisfy as much as possible goals.

Let $\mathbb{F}$ be the set of feasible offers. According to definition 13, the set of acceptable offers are defined as follows:
$\mathcal{A} = \{x : x \in \mathbb{F} \text{ and } \mathcal{R} \Vdash_{Level} x\}$.

The candidate offers are: $\underline{\mathcal{S}} = \{x : x \in \mathcal{A} \text{ and } \mathcal{G} \Vdash_{Card} x\}$. Note that if all acceptable offers falsify all goals then they are equal w.r.t. cardinality-based criterion and then selected as candidate offers.

Example 10. The minimal weight in $\mathcal{R}$ s.t. the set of acceptable offers is not empty is equal to 0. Offers satisfying $\mathcal{R}'_{>0}$ are BA and AF i.e., $\mathcal{A} = \{BA, AF\}$.

BA is preferred to AF following cardinality-based criterion, then there is only one candidate offer which is BA.

Note that if we only consider goals then there is one candidate offer KLM which is not acceptable for the agent w.r.t. the chosen acceptability criterion.

Definition 23 (Relaxed strategy). *Let $\mathcal{B}$, $\mathcal{R}$ and $\mathcal{G}$ be the agent's bases and X the set of offers. A relaxed strategy is a triple* $<\succeq, \Vdash_{Level}, \Vdash_{Disj}>$, *where* $\mathcal{R} \succ \mathcal{G}$.

Among feasible offers, the agent selects first those which falsify as most as prioritized rejections and among acceptable offers, it selects those which satisfy at least one prioritized goal as far as possible.

Acceptable offers are computed in the same way as for the requiring criterion. Candidate offers x are now acceptable ones which satisfy $\mathcal{G} \Vdash_{Disj} x$

Example 11. The set of acceptable offers is the same as in the requiring criterion namely $\mathcal{A} = \{AF, BA\}$.

There is no acceptable offer which satisfies the prioritized goal "promotion(x)" then we look for those which satisfy "stopover(x)" or "dayflight(x)". The candidate offers are AF and BA.

Here also, if we only consider goals then candidate offers are $AirLib$ and KLM which are not acceptable for the agent following the chosen acceptability criterion.

8   Properties of the Different Strategies

We defined in the previous section a three-layered setting where different strategies have been proposed for offers selection. As shown on the running example, these strategies give different results however some of them are related.

Proposition 2. *Let* $\underline{S}_1, \underline{S}_2$ *and* $\underline{S}_3$ *be the sets of candidate offers returned respectively by the drastic, requiring and the relaxed strategies. Then,*

$$\underline{S}_1 \subseteq \underline{S}_2 \subseteq \underline{S}_3.$$

This result means that requiring strategy is a weakening of drastic strategy and it is weakened by relaxed strategy. In other words, more we weaken the strategy more there are offers to propose. This is an important point in a negotiation dialogue since the more an agents has a large choice, the more the negotiation has better chance to success (to reach an agreement).

The following proposition states that using requiring and relaxed strategies, the set of candidate offers is not empty as soon as the set of acceptable offers is not empty.

Proposition 3. *Let* $\mathcal{A}$ *be the set of acceptable offers computed in the requiring (resp. relaxed) strategy. If* $\mathcal{A}$ *is not empty then the set of candidate offers is not empty in these strategies.*

In contrast to requiring and relaxed criteria, drastic criterion may lead to an empty set of candidate offers even if the set of acceptable offers is not empty. This is shown in example 7. Indeed in negotiation framework, the use of such criteria may lead negotiation to a failure.

As we said in the introduction, existing works on negotiation only consider goals in offers selection. Considering both rejections and goals in this selection enriches the selection process by providing various and different strategies as given in the previous section. Let us consider now the proposed strategies and apply them to a unipolar framework where only goals are considered. Then we have:

Proposition 4. *When we only consider goals, the optimistic and the relaxed strategies are equivalent.*

Readers may wonder whether is it really necessary to distinguish between rejections and goals and not simply use a single set where constraints induced by rejections are prioritized over goals. However this is not possible since we use here first order formulas and in the computation of acceptable offers, we do not look for the consistency of $\mathcal{R}$ (in fact it is supposed to be consistent) but for the *existence* of offers satisfying constraints induced by rejections. Let us consider again our example and put both constraints induced by rejections and goals in the same set. We get $\{(stopover(x), \beta_1), (\neg dayflight(x) \lor smoking(x), \beta_2), (flexible(x), \beta_3), (promotion(x), \lambda_1), (stopover(x), \lambda_2), (dayflight(x), \lambda_2)\}$, with $\beta_1 > \beta_2 > \beta_3 > \lambda_1 > \lambda_2$ however this doesn't make sense for all criteria except the drastic one since candidate offers should satisfy all elements of this set.

9   Conclusion

This paper studies the notion of strategy for selecting offers during a negotiation dialogue. In fact, the choice of the offer to propose at a given step is very important in a negotiation dialogue since this influences the outcome of the dialogue. For example, a too restrictive strategy may lead to an empty set of candidate offers and then the negotiation fails. The more the strategy gives a large choice of offers, the more the negotiation has a better chance to success, and consequently that the agent reach an agreement.

We have proposed a general setting for defining a strategy, which consists of fixing three parameters: the agent's profile, a criterion for defining acceptable offers and finally another criterion for defining satisfactory offers. The three parameters are defined on the basis of three mental states of an agent: its beliefs, its goals and its rejections. The agent's profile consists of determining whether rejections and goals are equally preferred or not.

We have proposed different agent's profiles and different criteria for the notions of acceptability and satisfiability of offers. A combination of an agent's profile, a criterion for selecting acceptable offers and a criterion for selecting the satisfactory ones gives birth to different strategies which are more or less restrictive. We have studied some of these strategies.

At the best of our knowledge, very few works have addressed the problem of offer selection. Moreover all existing works only consider goals in this process. We claim that rejections play also a key role in this problem since they allow to discard rejected offers.

An extension of this work would be to study more deeply the remaining strategies summarized in Table 2, and to compare them to the others. Another interesting work to do consists of integrating these strategies in a more general architecture of a negotiation dialogue. The idea is to study the outcome of the dialogue in the case where all the negotiating agents use the same strategy, and also in the case where they use different strategies.

References

1. L. Amgoud and N. Maudet. Strategical considerations for argumentative agents. In *Proc. of the 10th International Workshop on Non-Monotonic Reasoning, session "Argument, Dialogue, Decision", NMR'2002*, 2002.
2. S. Benferhat, D. Dubois, S. Kaci, and H. Prade. Bipolar representation and fusion of preferences in the possibilistic logic framework. In *8th International Confenrence on Principle of Knowledge Representation and Reasoning (KR'02)*, pages 421–432, 2002.
3. J.C. Borod. The neuropsychology of emotion. Oxford University Press,, 2000.
4. J. Broersen, M. Dastani, and L. van der Torre. Realistic desires. *Journal of Applied Non-Classical Logics*, 12(2):287–308, 2002.
5. J.T. Cacioppo and G.G. Bernston. The affect system: Architecture and operating characteristics. *Current Directions in Psychological Science*, 8, 5:133–137, 1999.
6. J.T. Cacioppo, W.L. Gardner, and G.G. Bernston. Beyond bipolar conceptualizations and measures: The case of attitudes and evaluative space. *Personality and Social Psychology Review*, 1, 1:3–25, 1997.

7. D. Dubois, J. Lang, and H. Prade. Possibilistic logic. *In Handbook of Logic in Artificial Intelligence and Logic Programming*, D. Gabbay et al., eds, 3, Oxford University Press:pages 439–513, 1994.
8. D. Dubois, D. LeBerre, H. Prade, and R. Sabbadin. Logical representation and computation of optimal decisions in a qualitative setting. In *AAAI-98*, pages 588–593, 1998.
9. A. Kakas, N. Maudet, and P. Moraitis. Flexible agent dialogue strategies and societal communication protocols. In *Proc. 3rd International Joint Conference on Autonomous Agents and Multi-Agent Systems (AAMAS'04)*, 2004.
10. A. Kakas, N. Maudet, and P. Moraitis. Layered strategies and protocols for argumentation based agent interaction. In *Proc. AAMAS'04 1st International Workshop on Argumentation in Multi-Agent Systems, (ArgMAS'04)*, 2004.
11. S. Kraus, K. Sycara, and A. Evenchik. *Reaching agreements through argumentation: a logical model and implementation*, volume 104. Journal of Artificial Intelligence, 1998.
12. I. Rahwan, S. D. Ramchurn, N. R. Jennings, P. McBurney, S. Parsons, and L. Sonenberg. Argumentation-based negotiation. *Knowledge engineering review*, 2004.
13. E.T. Rolls. Precis of "brain and emotion". *Behavioral and Brain Sciences*, 23(2):177–234, 2000.
14. R.H. Thomason. Desires and defaults: A framework for planning with inferred goals. In *Proceedings of the seventh International Confenrence on Principle of Knowledge Representation and Reasoning (KR'00)*, pages 702–713, 2000.
15. M.A. Williams. Transmutations of Knowledge Systems. In J. Doyle and al. Eds, editors, *International Conference on principles of Knowledge Representation and reasoning (KR'94)*, pages 619–629. Morgan Kaufmann, 1994.

Strategies for Ontology Negotiation: Finding the Right Level of Generality

Jurriaan van Diggelen, Edwin D. de Jong, and Marco A. Wiering

Institute of Information and Computing Sciences
Utrecht University, the Netherlands
{jurriaan, dejong, marco}@cs.uu.nl

Abstract. In heterogeneous multi agent systems, communication is hampered by the lack of shared ontologies. Ontology negotiation is a technique that enables pairs of agents to overcome these difficulties by exchanging parts of their ontologies. As a result of these micro level solutions, a communication vocabulary emerges on a macro level. The goal of this paper is to ensure that this communication vocabulary contains words of the right level of generality, i.e. not overspecific and not over-generalized. We will propose a number of communication strategies that enable the agents to achieve these goals. Using experimental results, we will compare their performance.

1 Introduction

A fundamental communication problem in open multi agent systems (MAS's) is caused by the heterogeneity of the agent's knowledge sources, or more specifically of the underlying *ontologies*. Although ontologies are often advocated as a complete solution for knowledge sharing between agents, this is only true when all agents have knowledge about each others' ontology. The most straightforward way to establish this would be to develop one common ontology which is used by all agents [6]. However, this scenario would be very unlikely in open multi agent systems, as those on the internet, because it would require all involved system developers to reach consensus on which ontology to use. Moreover, a common ontology forces an agent to abandon its own world view and adopt one that is not specifically designed for its task [3]. This may result in a suboptimal situation.

Ontology negotiation [2] has been proposed as a technique that enables agents to preserve their local ontologies, and solve communication problems at agent-interaction time. Communication problems between heterogeneous agents are solved by establishing a shared communication vocabulary (or CV). Communication proceeds by translating from the speaker's local ontology to the communication vocabulary, which the hearer translates back to its own local ontology. When two agents start communicating, they first try to cope with the situation as is. When the speaker uses a word that the hearer does not understand, it solves the problem at hand by teaching the meaning of this word to the hearer. This enables two agents that regularly communicate with each other to build towards a solution for their semantic integration problem on an as-need basis.

F. Dignum, R. van Eijk, and R. Flores (Eds.): AC 2005/2006, LNAI 3859, pp. 164–180, 2006.

Whereas an ontology negotiation protocol provides a nice solution to incrementally establish a communication vocabulary between a *pair* of heterogeneous agents, it is not straightforward how this solution scales to *whole* multi agent systems. A decentralized approach such as ontology negotiation may give rise to a proliferation of different CV's between different agent pairs in the system. This would be disadvantageous for the agents, as agents would have to use different words with different agents, which would make communication unnecessarily complicated. Furthermore, agents would have to spend much effort on building CV's, as the CV that has been built up with one agent may not be useful for communication with another agent. Therefore, when two agents participate in ontology negotiation to resolve their mutual misunderstandings, they should also pursue the goal of establishing a uniform and effective CV for the benefit of the whole community.

In this paper we will describe communication strategies for ontology negotiation protocols that take this global goal into account. These strategies prescribe which words and meanings the agents should teach each other during ontology negotiation. Regarding the words, we aim for a situation where every agent uses the same unique word for the same meaning. This is to be established by the agent's *word selection strategy* which we have studied in earlier work [13]. Regarding the meanings, we aim for a communication vocabulary which enables the agents to communicate at the right level of generality. Agents with different areas of expertise should not communicate at an *overspecific* level, as not everything that is of interest to one agent is also of interest to another agent. To prevent the CV from becoming bulky and difficult to learn, the CV should not contain such overspecific meanings. However, the meanings in the CV should not be *overgeneralized* either to enable the agents to convey sufficient information. Finding the right balance between specificity and generality of words is to be established by the *meaning selection strategy*. In this paper, we will show how a well designed meaning selection strategy contributes to faster semantic integration in the group of agents.

In the next section, we review related work. In Section 3, we describe the framework and explain how the communication protocols and strategies fit in. Section 4 presents the model that is used for the experiments. According to that model, some integration measures are proposed that measure the degree of semantic integration. Section 5 gives a precise description of the meaning selection strategy. In Section 6 the results of the experiments are presented, and the different meaning selection strategies are compared. We conclude in Section 7.

2 Related Work

Most solutions that have been proposed for semantic integration problems are not flexible enough to be suitable for large open MAS's. Approaches such as ontology alignment [8] require ontologies to be aligned before the agents start interacting. In open MAS's it is not known beforehand which agents will interact with each other, and therefore, one can not tell in advance which ontologies must be aligned.

Ontology agents [1,9] have been proposed as central services that reconcile heterogeneous ontologies at agent-interaction time by translating between ontologies. Such services have access to a library of concept-mappings between every ontology in the system. In large open MAS's, such a library would become too complex to be reliably maintainable.

Therefore, for large open systems, a *decentralized* technique is needed that allows agents to solve ontology problems among themselves at the time they arise. W. Truszkowski and S. Bailin have coined the term *Ontology Negotiation* to refer to such approaches [2]. Other approaches for ontology negotiation are [17,16,15].

Because the field of ontology negotiation is relatively new, and it is a very ambitious approach to achieve semantic integration [12], there are still many open problems. One of these problems is how a uniform CV that is shared among the whole *group of agents* may result from conversations that have taken place between *pairs of agents*. The question how a global language system arises from the interactions between individual agents is well studied in the language evolution community [11,4]. Most of these approaches serve an explanatory goal, i.e. understanding how a communication system may evolve in a group of heterogeneous agents. Our goals, however, are purely constructive, i.e. we aim at designing communication strategies that can be used during ontology negotiation in order to establish a communication vocabulary of a certain quality. In particular we aim for an *optimal distributed communication vocabulary* [14], meaning that the CV is minimal in size and sufficiently expressive. One of the ways to make the CV minimal in size, is to ensure that the agents communicate at the right level of generality, which is the topic of this paper.

3   Framework

3.1   Ontologies and Vocabularies

Figure 1 shows an example of two agents in our framework. The dashed rectangle shows the meaning space in the system, i.e. the meanings that are assumed to exist in the environment of the agents. In the example, the meanings that constitute the meaning space are $m1$ to $m8$.

The agent's ontology assigns names to meanings in the meaning space. For example, the ontology of Ag1 specifies that $m1$ is called "substance" and that $m2$ is called "food". A meaning with its corresponding name will be called a *concept*. An arrow from concept c to concept d represents that concept c is more general than concept d, and conversely that concept d is more specific than concept c.

Not every agent assigns the same names to the meanings in the meaning space. For example, Ag1 calls $m1$ "substance" and $m2$ "food", whereas Ag2 calls $m1$ "matter" and $m2$ "nutrition". To avoid naming-conflicts (two agents assigning the same name to different meanings), we assume that every agent uses a unique set of names in its ontology. This can be easily achieved by prefixing the names in the ontology with namespaces.

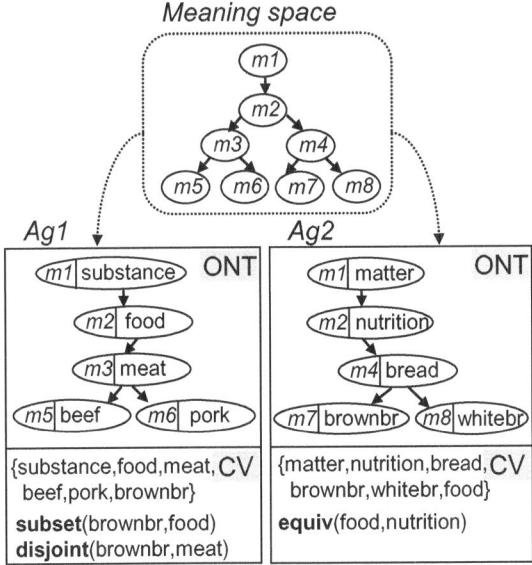

Fig. 1. Example ontologies

The property that every agent in the system uses distinct names to represent meanings is one source of the heterogeneity of the ontologies. Another source is that the ontologies of the agents contain concepts that correspond to different meanings. For example, the meanings $m4$, $m7$ and $m8$ are present in the ontology of Ag2, but are not present in the ontology of Ag1. This is a typical characteristic of heterogeneous multi agent systems, where every agent uses an ontology that is tailored to its own specific task. For example, Ag1 can be thought of as being a butcher as its ontology reflects expertise on meat. Ag2 can be thought of as being a baker as its ontology reflects expertise on bread.

Whereas the agents use the concepts in their ontology (ONT) for local knowledge representation and reasoning, for communication they use their communication vocabulary (CV). Note that the words in the communication vocabulary are not necessarily shared with the other agents. The CV contains the words that an agent may use to communicate something, regardless whether this word will actually be understood by the listener or not. Initially, the CV of an agent contains only the names of the concepts in its local ontology, as these are the only words that it knows for the meanings in its ontology. Because these words are unique, none of the other agents will understand them. When an agent is not understood by another agent, it explains the meaning of the uncomprehended word, after which the listener adds the word to its communication vocabulary. For example, the word "food" in the communication vocabulary of Ag2 is the result of a conversation in which Ag1 used "food", Ag2 did not understand it, after which Ag1 taught the meaning of "food" to Ag2. This teaching process enabled Ag2 to formulate a definition of the word "food" in terms of its ontology, namely "**equiv**(food,nutrition)". This states that the word "food" is equivalent

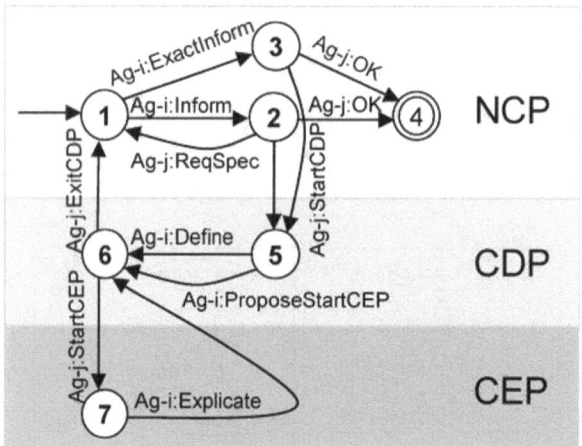

Fig. 2. Message protocol

in meaning with the "nutrition" concept in its ontology. A definition may also state that a word in the CV means something more specific than a concept in the ontology. For example, "**subset**(brownbr,food)" in the CV of Ag1.

3.2   Communication Protocol

Figure 2 shows an ontology negotiation protocol that is used in ANEMONE [15]. Using this protocol, agents like Ag1 and Ag2 may successfully communicate if this is enabled by their communication vocabularies. Otherwise the agents extend their communication vocabularies to make communication possible. Three layers can be distinguished in this protocol. The upper layer is the Normal Communication Protocol (NCP), which deals with information exchange between the agents. If this is not possible, the agents switch to the Concept Definition Protocol (CDP), where the agents give a definition of a word in terms of other words. If this is not possible (when the listener does not understand the definition), the agents switch to the Concept Explication Protocol (CEP), where the agents convey the meaning of a word by pointing to examples.

We will explain the protocol in further depth below. Communication starts in state 1 where Ag-i wishes to communicate a meaning from its ontology to Ag-j. For example, suppose that Ag2 wishes to communicate the meaning $m8$ (corresponding to the concept "whitebr") to Ag1. In state 1, Ag2 must select an appropriate word in the communication vocabulary to communicate $m8$. There are different possibilities for this. The first possibility is to select a word in the CV that is equivalent in meaning with $m8$ (such as the word "whitebr"), and send a message "ExactInform(whitebr)" after which it ends up in state 3. If the CV of Ag1 would have contained the word "whitebr", Ag1 would have translated this word to its own ontology, and responded "OK". As Ag1 does not know the meaning of "whitebr", it responds with "StartCDP" to incite Ag2 to convey the meaning of "whitebr" in the Concept Definition Protocol. Another possibility for Ag2 to convey the meaning $m8$ is to choose a word in the CV that means something more general than $m8$ (such as the words "bread", "nutrition", "food" or "matter"), and send a message with "inform" after which it ends up in state 2. When Ag1 does not know the word used in the message, it responds "StartCDP" to start the Concept Definition Protocol. If Ag1 knows the meaning of the word, it checks whether the message is not overgeneralized. If it believes the message might be overgeneralized, it responds "ReqSpec" (Request specification) to incite Ag2 to use a more specific word. If Ag1 assesses that the message is not overgeneralized, it translates the message to its ontology and responds "OK". The method for recognizing overgeneralized messages we use here is a simplified version of the one used in the ANEMONE protocol. If the receiver's ontology contains no concepts that mean something more specific than the word in the message, the receiver assesses that the message is not overgeneralized. In this case, the receiver regards requesting for a more specific word useless, because its ontology is not fine grained enough to process any extra information. If the receiver's ontology contains concepts that are more specific than the meaning of the word, the receiver believes that the message might be overgeneralized and responds "ReqSpec".

The agents enter the Concept Definition Protocol in state 5, where Ag-i defines the meaning of the word in terms of other words in the communication vocabulary. Suppose that Ag2 wishes to define "nutrition", it sends a message "Define(equiv(nutrition, food))" to Ag-1, which enables Ag1 to derive the definition of "nutrition" after which Ag1 answers "ExitCDP". If the receiver of the "Define" message does not understand the definition of a message, it responds "StartCEP" to start the Concept Explication Protocol which incites the sender to explicate the meaning of the word by pointing to examples. If the sender of the definition is not able to give a definition (for example, Ag2 does not know any other word for "whitebr"), it sends the message "ProposeStartCEP".

In the Concept Explication Protocol (state 7), the agent conveys the meaning of the word by giving a set of positive and negative examples. More information on this type of concept learning can be found in [5].

3.3   Communication Strategies

Having described the ontology negotiation protocol, we will now describe how the communication strategy fits in.

Word Selection Strategy
Suppose that Ag2 has the intention to convey the meaning $m2$. It has two words in its communication vocabulary that correspond to this meaning, namely "nutrition" and "food". The *word selection strategy* selects one of these word. In previous work [13], we have shown that the most effective word selection strategy is to choose the word that has most frequently been used by other agents. In this paper, we will use this word selection strategy, and focus on the other communication strategy: the meaning selection strategy.

Meaning Selection Strategy

Consider again the situation in state 1 of the protocol where Ag2 intends to convey the meaning $m8$ ("whitebr"). As has been argued in the previous section, Ag2 may convey this meaning by choosing a word that means $m8$ or a word that means something more general than $m8$, i.e. a word that means $m4$, $m2$ or $m1$. The meaning selection strategy prescribes which meaning Ag2 should choose. A good meaning selection strategy selects a meaning that is not overgeneralized in order not to provoke the response "ReqSpec". However, the meaning selection strategy should not select a meaning that is too specific either, to prevent the communication vocabulary from becoming large and filled with words that are unnecessarily specific. Examples of overgeneralized concepts are $m1$ and $m2$, as from a god's eye perspective we can predict that this will provoke a "ReqSpec" answer from Ag1. An example of an overspecific concept is $m8$, because from a god's eye perspective we can determine that this word contains superfluous information for Ag1. $m4$ is at the right level of generality. It is not overspecific as it is more general than $m8$ and thereby more widely applicable. Furthermore, from a god's eye perspective, we can assess that it is not overgeneralized as it will not provoke a "ReqSpec" answer.

Of course, the agents do not have access to this god's eye perspective. They therefore do not know which words are overgeneralized and which are overspecific. The difficulty of the meaning selection strategy lies in the making of an *educated guess* which word is at the right level of specificity. Before we describe how this can be done, we will present the model in which we can test different strategies.

4   Model

The experiments are performed using a set of agents $MAS = \{Ag_1..Ag_n\}$. The ontologies of the agents are randomly created and, like the ontologies in Figure 1, may cover different parts of the meaning space. The formal counterpart of the meaning space in Figure 1 is defined using graph theory [7]. A meaning space M is defined as a rooted tree (V, E), where V is a set of vertices, E is a set of directed edges, and a particular vertex in V is designated as the root. A vertex v_j is a child of vertex v_i iff $\langle v_i, v_j \rangle \in E$. A vertex with no children is called a *leaf*; a vertex that is not a leaf is called *internal*. A vertex v_j is a *descendant* of vertex v_i (and conversely v_i is an *ancestor* of v_j) iff there is a directed path from v_i to v_j. If T is a rooted tree with root v_0, then $ln(v_i)$ denotes the *level number* of v_i which equals the length of the unique directed path from v_0 to v_i. The depth of a tree is the largest level number achieved by a vertex in that tree. The following definition is useful to characterize the shape of a meaning space.

Definition 1. *A meaning space $M = (V, E)$ is defined according to $B = (b_0, .., b_d)$ if:*

- *d is the depth of the tree M*
- *for each $v_i \in V$, v_i has $b_{ln(v_i)}$ children*

For example, the meaning space in Figure 1 is defined according to $(1,2,2,0)$, because $m1$ (at level number 0) has 1 child; $m2$ (at level number 1) has 2 children; $m3$ and $m4$ (at level number 2) have 2 children; $m5$, $m6$, $m7$ and $m8$ (at level number 3) have 0 children.

An ontology ONT is defined as a tuple $\langle \mathcal{C}, M, \mathcal{I} \rangle$, where $\mathcal{C}$ is a set of concept names, $M = (V, E)$ is a meaning space and $\mathcal{I}$ is a bijective mapping from $\mathcal{C}$ to V. To be able to characterize the ontologies in the system, we use the following definition

Definition 2. *Given an ontology ONT $= \langle \mathcal{C}, M, \mathcal{I} \rangle$, where $M = (V, E)$. ONT is defined according to B and B_g if*

- *M is defined according to B, and*
- $V \subseteq V'$, $E \subseteq E'$, *where*
  - $M' = (V', E')$ *is a meaning space defined according to B_g.*

For example, the ontologies of Ag1 and Ag2 in Figure 1 are defined according to $B = (1, 1, 2, 0)$ and $B_g = (1, 2, 2, 0)$.

4.1 Integration Measures

In this section, we will define some measures which indicate how well the agents can understand each other. Suppose that Ag_i wishes to communicate a meaning m to Ag_j. If Ag_i can do this in only the NCP layer (the upper layer in the protocol of Figure 2), the understandings rate between Ag_i and Ag_j with respect to meaning m is 1; if the agents have to visit the CDP or CEP layer, the understandings rate is 0.

Definition 3. *MPUR: Meaning and Pair dependent Understandings Rate. $MPUR(m, \langle Ag_i, Ag_j \rangle)$ is*

- *1 if the conversation to communicate m from Ag_i to Ag_j finishes without visiting the CDP and CEP layer*
- *else 0.*

The following measure indicates how well an agent Ag_i can communicate an average concept to Ag_j (ONT_i is defined as a tuple $\langle \mathcal{C}, \langle V, E \rangle, \mathcal{I} \rangle$, according to definition 2):

Definition 4. *PUR: Pair dependent understandings rate $PUR(\langle Ag_i, Ag_j \rangle) = \frac{1}{\#V_i} \sum_{m \in V_i} MPUR(m, \langle Ag_i, Ag_j \rangle)$*

The following measure indicates how well an average agent can communicate an average meaning to an average other agent.

Definition 5. *UR: Understandings rate $UR = \frac{1}{n^2} \sum_{Ag_i, Ag_j \in MAS} PUR(\langle Ag_i, Ag_j \rangle)$*

If the understandings rate is 1, every agent can communicate everything to every other agent.

5   Finding the Right Level of Generality

Using the different integration measures introduced in the previous section, we can characterize overgeneralized and overspecific concepts in further depth.

5.1   From a God's Eye View

Property 1. Teaching overgeneralized concepts does not increase $MPUR$ (definition 3).

We will illustrate this property using the example where Ag2 intends to communicate $m8$ (the meaning of "whitebr") to Ag1. Suppose Ag2's meaning selection strategy selects the overgeneralized meaning $m1$ (the meaning of "matter"). Before Ag2 sends this message, $MPUR(m8, \langle Ag2, Ag1 \rangle) = 0$ (because Ag1 does not understand the word "matter"). After Ag2 has taught the concept "matter" to Ag1, $MPUR(m8, \langle Ag2, Ag1 \rangle)$ still equals 0 (because "matter" invokes a "ReqSpec" response and Ag2's second attempt to convey $m8$ fails). Now suppose that Ag2's meaning selection strategy selects the meaning $m4$ (corresponding to the word "bread"). This meaning is not overgeneralized, because $MPUR(m8, \langle Ag2, Ag1 \rangle)$ becomes 1 after the concept "bread" has been taught to Ag1 (because "bread" invokes an "OK" response).

Property 2. Teaching overspecific concepts gives rise to little increase in PUR (definition 4).

Consider again the situation where Ag2 intends to communicate $m8$ ("whitebr") to Ag1. Suppose that the CV's of Ag1 and Ag2 are still in their initial configuration, i.e. they only contain the names of the concepts in their ontologies. Suppose that Ag2's meaning selection strategy selects the meaning $m8$ (corresponding to the word "whitebr"). Before Ag2 sends this message, $PUR(\langle Ag2, Ag1 \rangle) = 0$ (Ag2 can not communicate anything to Ag1). After Ag2 has taught the word "whitebr" to Ag1, $PUR(\langle Ag2, Ag1 \rangle) = \frac{1}{5} \cdot MPUR(m8, \langle Ag2, Ag1 \rangle) = \frac{1}{5}$. Now, suppose that Ag2's meaning selection strategy would have selected "bread". After Ag2 has taught the word "bread" to Ag1, $PUR(\langle Ag2, Ag1 \rangle) = \frac{1}{5} \cdot (MPUR(m8, \langle Ag2, Ag1 \rangle) + \frac{1}{5} \cdot MPUR(m7, \langle Ag2, Ag1 \rangle) + \frac{1}{5} \cdot MPUR(m4, \langle Ag2, Ag1 \rangle)) = \frac{3}{5}$. Note that, compared to the word "bread", the teaching of the word "whitebr" gives rise to little increase in understandings rate between the pair (and therefore also in understandings rate in general). This is why "whitebr" is overspecific, and "bread" is not.

5.2   From an Agent View

Property 1 and 2 characterize overgeneralized and overspecific words by describing how their teaching influences the integration measures. However, this characterization can not be immediately used by an agent to find the right level of generality. Because one agent does not have access to the other agent's ontology, it can not compute how the teaching of a word influences the understandings rate. Therefore the agents follow the *expected increase in understandings rate*.

We use the notation $Exp(c, MPUR(m, \langle Ag_i, Ag_j \rangle))$ to refer to the expected value of $MPUR(m, \langle Ag_i, Ag_j \rangle)$, after the concept c has been taught. Given that the current $MPUR(m, \langle Ag_i, Ag_j \rangle)$ is 0, the expected value after c is taught can be calculated as follows (M_i is the meaning space in Ag_i's ontology, and M_j the meaning space in Ag_j's ontology)

- if $\mathcal{I}(c) = m$ then $Exp(c, MPUR(m, \langle Ag_i, Ag_j \rangle)) = 1$
- if m is a descendant of $\mathcal{I}(c)$ in M_i then
  $Exp(c, MPUR(m, \langle Ag_i, Ag_j \rangle)) = \Pr(\mathcal{I}(c)$ is not internal in $M_j)$
- if the first two conditions do not hold then
  $Exp(c, MPUR(m, \langle Ag_i, Ag_j \rangle)) = 0$

The first condition states that if c exactly means m, then the agent is certain that teaching the word c enables communication of the meaning m. The second condition states that, if c means something more general than m, the expected $MPUR$ equals the probability that the other agent does not consider the word c overgeneralized. In our case this boils down to the probability that the meaning of c is a leaf in M_i, i.e. the ontology of Ag_j does not contain more specific concepts than c. The last condition states that, if c is not equal or more general than m, c can not be used to communicate m, and therefore the teaching of c will not increase the $MPUR$ w.r.t. m.

The expected PUR (corresponding to definition 4) after c is taught can be calculated by averaging over the expected $MPUR$'s:

- $Exp(c, PUR(\langle Ag_i, Ag_j \rangle)) =$
  $\frac{1}{\#V_i} \sum_{m \in V_i} Exp(c, MPUR(m, \langle Ag_i, Ag_j \rangle))$

Because the agents must base their decision which meaning to select on *expectations*, the agents can not be certain that they find the right level of generality. Therefore, they must decide whether to attach more value to expected $MPUR$, or to expected PUR. This decision is set down in the parameters θ_1 and θ_2 which indicate the importance of respectively $MPUR$, and PUR. Using these parameters, the meaning that the meaning selection strategy selects is given by:

Definition 6. *Given that Ag_i intends to communicate a meaning m. The meaning selection strategy is described by:*
$argmax_{c \in \mathcal{C}_i}(\theta_1 \cdot Exp(c, MPUR(m, \langle Ag_i, Ag_j \rangle)) +$
$\theta_2 \cdot Exp(c, PUR(\langle Ag_i, Ag_j \rangle))$, *where:*

- θ_1 *is the importance factor for MPUR*
- θ_2 *is the importance factor for PUR*

In the next section we will investigate the effects of different importance factors for $MPUR$ and PUR.

6   Experiments

For our experiments, we adopt a group of 15 agents. An agent's ontology is randomly created according to $B_g = (3, 3, 3, 3, 3, 0)$ and $B = (2, 2, 2, 2, 1, 0)$, and contains 46 concepts. An experiment consists of t steps, where at each step a random speaker and hearer is selected from the group of agents, and a random concept from the speaker's ontology. We have prevented the same hearer-speaker-concept pair to be selected twice in the same experiment. The speaker communicates the concept to the hearer using a dialogue that conforms to the ANEMONE communication protocol (Figure 2) and a word selection strategy that selects the most frequently used word [13]. The speaker follows a meaning selection strategy that conforms to definition 6. After each step, we measure the following:

1. UR: the understandings rate, calculated according to definition 5.
2. Avg. Dialogue length : The average length of a dialogue of a randomly selected speaker-hearer-concept.
3. Avg. Nr. CDP : The average number of times that a concept is taught in (only) the CDP layer, in a dialogue of a randomly selected speaker-hearer-concept.
4. Avg. Nr. CEP : The average number of times that a concept is taught in the CEP layer, in a dialogue of a randomly selected speaker-hearer-concept.

In the next sections we will describe the results of six different experiments that were performed using different meaning selection strategies. To obtain statistical significance, we have performed every experiment 10 times of which we will present the mean outcomes. For all results, the standard deviation was less than 5 percent of the mean.

6.1   Agents That Know the Ontology Model

In the previous section, we have argued that the speaker can determine the expected MPUR after teaching a concept by using the probability that the hearer's ontology contains no subconcepts of that concept. In this section, we assume that the agents know the ontology model, i.e. they know that $B = (2, 2, 2, 2, 1, 0)$ and $B_g = (3, 3, 3, 3, 3, 0)$. With this knowledge, an agent Ag_i can compute the probability that a meaning m is considered (non-) overgeneralized by an agent Ag_j as follows:

– if $ln(m) <$ *the depth of M* then $\Pr(m$ is internal in $M_j) = \prod_{i=0}^{ln(m)} \frac{b_i}{b_i^g}$
– if $ln(m) =$ *the depth of M* then $\Pr(m$ is internal in $M_j) = 0$
– $\Pr(m$ is not internal in $M_j) = 1 - \Pr(m$ is internal in $M_j)$

In these formulae, $b_0, .., b_d$ are typical elements of vector B, and $b_0^g, .., b_d^g$ are typical elements of B_g.

   For example, in our experiments, the probability that a meaning at layer number 0 is internal is $\frac{2}{3}$. The probability that a meaning at layer number 4 is internal is $\frac{2}{3} \cdot \frac{2}{3} \cdot \frac{2}{3} \cdot \frac{2}{3} \cdot \frac{1}{3}$. The probability that a meaning at layer number 5 is internal is 0.

   A common pattern of dialogues in ANEMONE is that the speaker speaks a relatively general concept c, after which the hearer requests for specification, after which the speaker applies its meaning selection strategy a second time and speaks a more specific concept d. When the speaker applies the meaning selection strategy for the second time, it can use extra knowledge to compute the probability that d is considered overgeneralized by the hearer, namely that concept c *is* considered overgeneralized. We incorporate this idea in the meaning selection strategy using a conditional probability. An agent Ag_i that knows that a meaning n is overgeneralized for the hearer Ag_j computes the probability that a (more specific) meaning m is considered overgeneralized as follows:

$Pr(e1|e2) = \frac{Pr(e1)}{Pr(e2)}$, where

- $e1$ is the event that m is internal in M_j
- $e2$ is the event that n is internal in M_j, where n is an ancestor of m.

This can be proven as follows. According to Bayes theorem [10], $Pr(e1|e2) = \frac{Pr(e2|e1) \cdot Pr(e1)}{Pr(e2)}$. Note that $Pr(e2|e1)$ is 1, because $e2$ is implied by $e1$. Hence, $Pr(e1|e2) = \frac{Pr(e1)}{Pr(e2)}$.

Experiment 1
In the first experiment, we used parameters $\theta_1 = 1$ and $\theta_2 = 0$. In other words the agents only take the expected *MPUR* into account in their meaning selection strategy. Because they are only interested in the expected increase in MPUR concerning the meaning that they *currently* want to convey, we call this strategy a *short term strategy* (STS). The results of applying a short term strategy for 10000 steps is shown in Figure 3. The situations at 0 steps can be explained as follows. Because the agents have not taught any concepts to each other, no agent understands any other agent, hence UR is 0. This means that in every dialogue, the agents have to visit the CDP or CEP layer of the protocol. Because the agents do not share any words that they can use for giving concept

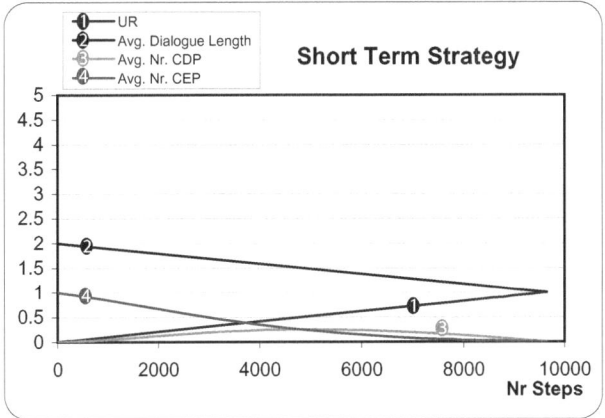

Fig. 3. Results experiment 1

definitions, all teaching of new words is done using CEP (where the meaning of a word is conveyed by pointing to shared instances). Hence Avg.Nr.CEP is 1 and Avg.Nr.CDP is 0. Because the agents visit the CEP layer every dialogue, the average dialogue length is 2.

As the number of steps increase, the agents teach concepts to each other, and the UR slowly increases. Also, the Avg.Nr.CDP increases because giving definitions becomes a viable option to teach new concepts, once a substantial amount of concepts is shared. As a result of this, there is less need for CEP, and the Avg. Nr CEP slowly decreases. Hence, the Avg. dialogue length also decreases.

Experiment 2
In experiment 2, we used parameters $\theta_1 = 0$ and $\theta_2 = 1$. In other words, the agents only take the expected PUR into account in their meaning selection strategy. Because they are interested in the expected increase in MPUR concerning any concept in their ontology, regardless whether they currently intend to convey it or not, we call this a *long term strategy* (LTS). The results of applying the long term strategy for 10000 steps is shown in Figure 4.

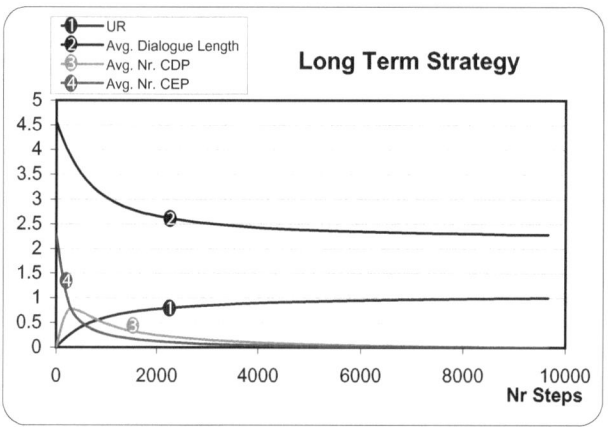

Fig. 4. Results experiment 2

Using the long term strategy, the Avg.Nr.CEP is relatively high in the beginning. This is because the speaker may end up teaching three or four general concepts to the hearer, before it teaches the concept that is specific enough for the hearer to accept. As a result of this, the Avg. dialogue length is also relatively high. We can also observe that the strategy that aims at increasing the PUR, indeed gives rise to a fast increase in UR. Therefore, the Avg.Nr.CEP and Avg. Dialogue length decrease quickly in the beginning.

One of the reasons that experiment 2 exhibits a faster increase of UR than experiment 1 is that the Avg.Nr.CEP is higher in experiment 2 than in experiment 1. Another reason is that the concepts that are taught in experiment 1 are overspecific and therefore only increase UR a little (property 2). To support this claim we included Figure 6 where the strategies in experiments 1 and 2 (and 3) are compared in a graph with the total number of CEP on the x-axis. Furthermore, this figure reveals that the total number of CEP that is required to reach an UR of 1 is around 1300 using LTS, and around 5000 using STS. Therefore, the communication vocabulary that is produced by LTS is also much smaller than the CV that is produced by STS.

The following table compares the short term strategy (experiment 1) with the long term strategy (experiment 2).

	STS	LTS
Increase in UR	-	+
Initial Avg.Nr.CEP.	+	-
Avg. Dialogue Length	+	-

With respect to a fast increase in UR, the LTS performs better than the STS. However, the dialogues in the LTS are longer, and the Avg.Nr.CEP is high in the beginning. In the following experiment, we aim at achieving the best of both worlds.

Experiment 3
In experiment 3, we used parameters $\theta_1 = 1$ and $\theta_2 = 5$, such that the agents take the expected *MPUR* and *PUR* into account. Because it is a mixture of the short term strategy and the long term strategy, we call this the *medium term strategy* (MTS). The results are shown in Figure 5. As this Figure reveals, the MTS gives rise to a faster increase of UR than the STS (experiment 1), and it gives rise to shorter dialogues and initial Avg.Nr.CEP than the LTS.

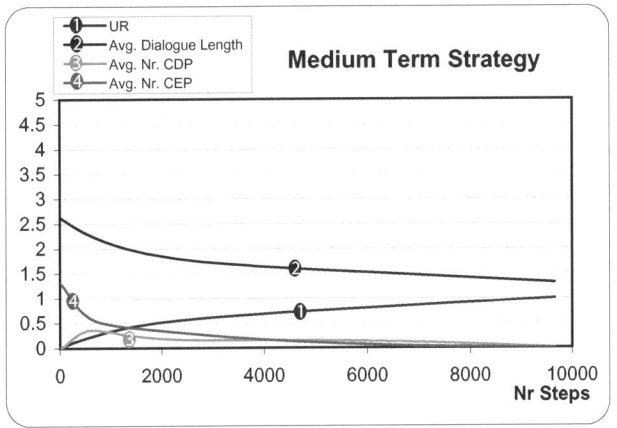

Fig. 5. Results experiment 3

6.2 Agents That Learn the Ontology Model

The three experiments described in the previous section build on the assumption that the agents know the ontology model. In this section, we do not make this

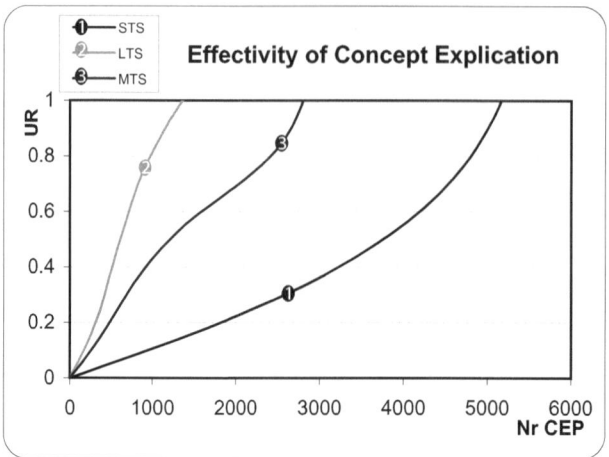

Fig. 6. Comparison of experiments 1,2 and 3

assumption, and make the agents learn the ontology model during their conversations. This is done as follows. For every meaning in its ontology, an agent keeps track of:

- N_1 the number of agents that regarded the meaning overgeneralized. These agents have responded "ReqSpec" to Inform-messages containing this meaning.
- N_2 the number of agents that did not regard the meaning overgeneralized. These agents have responded "OK" to inform-messages containing this meaning.

N_1 and N_2 are both initialized to 1. Using these values for meaning m, agent Ag_i can approximate the probability that m is internal in a meaning space M_j as follows:

- $\Pr(m$ is internal in $M_j) = \frac{N1}{N1+N2}$

Experiment 4,5,6

Experiments 4,5 and 6 were performed using STS, LTS and MTS respectively, with agents that learn the ontology model as they participate in conversations. Figure 7 shows the results of experiments 4,5 and 6 in a similar fashion as Figure 6. This figure reveals that STS in experiment 4 gives rise to very similar results as STS in experiment 1. This is because STS incites agents to select the most specific meaning. The inaccurate approximation of the ontology model in experiment 4, does change this strategy, as the agents will continue to select the most specific meaning anyway. The LTS incites the agents to select the most general meaning. Therefore, the LTS in experiment 5 gives rise to the same results as the LTS in experiment 2. The situation is different with the MTS, which incites agents to select a meaning that is a right balance between specificity and

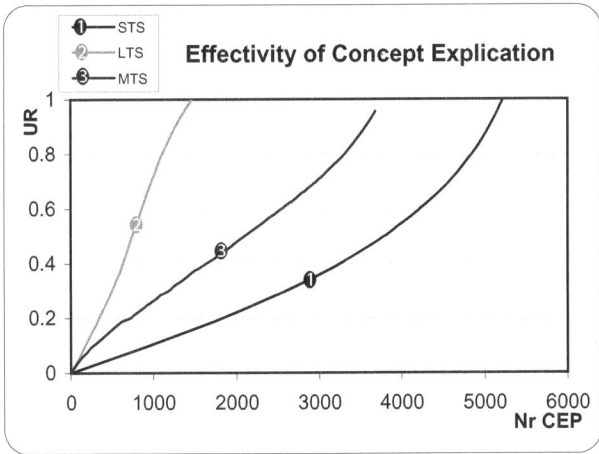

Fig. 7. Comparison of experiments 4,5 and 6

generality. An inaccurate approximation of the ontology model, does influence the results of the MTS, as can be seen when the results of experiment 3 are compared with experiment 6 in Figure 6 and 7.

7   Conclusion

In this paper, we have argued that finding the right level of generality is important for ontology negotiation. We have experimentally supported this claim by comparing different communication strategies that incite the agents to convey their information at different levels of generality. An agent that conveys information using a very specific word, runs the risk that the other agent does not know the word. An agent that conveys information using a very general word, runs the risk of being too vague which would result in a lengthy dialogue.

We have also shown that the agents can reliably assess the right level of generality themselves. They may do this by recording how many other agents do and do not consider a meaning overgeneralized. As an agent participates in conversations, it builds up a model of the other agents' ontologies, which enables it to find the right level of generality.

We believe that the communication strategies discussed in this paper are useful for agents in heterogeneous systems, as they prescribe which individual actions the agents must undertake in order to achieve the global goal of establishing an effective communication vocabulary. We intend to continue this line of research by incorporating tasks in the model. In such a model, the criteria of overgeneralization and overspecification become dependent on the tasks that the agents are discussing. Furthermore, we intend to enrich the ontologies of the agents with additional constructs such as attributes and part-of relations.

References

1. FIPA Ontology Service Specification. http://www.fipa.org/specs/fipa00086/.
2. S. Bailin and W. Truszkowski. Ontology negotiation between intelligent informa-tion agents. *Knowledge Engineering Review*, 17(1):7–19, 2002.
3. T. Bylander and B. Chandrasekaran. Generic tasks for knowledge-based reasoning: the right level of abstraction for knowledge acquisition. *Int. J. Man-Mach. Stud.*, 26(2):231–243, 1987.
4. E. D. de Jong and L. Steels. A distributed learning algorithm for communication development. *Complex Systems*, 14(4), 2003.
5. S. A. Goldman and M. J. Kearns. On the complexity of teaching. *Journal of Computer and System Sciences*, 50(1):20–31, Feb. 1995.
6. T. Gruber. A translation approach to portable ontology specifications. *Knowledge Acquisition*, 5(2):199–220, 1993.
7. D. Malik and M. Sen. *Discrete Mathematical Structures: Theory and Applications*. Blackwell, 2004.
8. N. F. Noy and M. A. Musen. Prompt: Algorithm and tool for automated ontology merging and alignment. *In Proceedings of the National Conference on Artificial Intelligence (AAAI)*, 2000.
9. A. D. Preece, K. ying Hui, W. A. Gray, P. Marti, T. J. M. Bench-Capon, D. M. Jones, and Z. Cui. The KRAFT architecture for knowledge fusion and transfor-mation. *Knowledge Based Systems*, 13(2-3):113–120, 2000.
10. J. Rice. *Mathematical Statictics and Data Analysis*. Duxbury Press, 1995.
11. L. Steels. Language as a complex adaptive system. In M. Schoenauer, editor, *Proceedings of PPSN VI*, Lecture Notes in Computer Science. Springer-Verlag, Berlin, Germany, September 2000.
12. M. Uschold and M. Gruninger. Creating semantically integrated communities on the world wide web. *Semantic Web Workshop Co-located with WWW 2002 Hon-olulu*, 2002.
13. J. van Diggelen, R. Beun, F. Dignum, R. van Eijk, and J.-J. Meyer. A decentralized approach for establishing a shared communication vocabulary. *Proceedings of the International Workshop on Agent Mediated Knowledge Management (AMKM'05)*.
14. J. van Diggelen, R. Beun, F. Dignum, R. van Eijk, and J.-J. Meyer. Optimal communication vocabularies and heterogeneous ontologies. In *Developments in Agent Communication*, LNAI 3396. Springer Verlag, 2004.
15. J. van Diggelen, R. Beun, F. Dignum, R. van Eijk, and J.-J. Meyer. ANEMONE: An effective minimal ontology negotiation environment. *Proceedings of the Fifth Conference on Autonomous Agents and Multi-agent Systems (AAMAS)*, 2006.
16. J. Wang and L. Gasser. Mutual online ontology alignment. *Proceedings of the Workshop on Ontologies in Agent Systems, held with AAMAS 2002*.
17. A. Williams. Learning to share meaning in a multi-agent system. *Autonomous Agents and Multi-Agent Systems*, 8(2):165–193, 2004.

Combining Normal Communication with Ontology Alignment

Jurriaan van Diggelen, Robbert Jan Beun, Frank Dignum, Rogier M. van Eijk, and John-Jules Meyer

Institute of Information and Computing Sciences
Utrecht University, the Netherlands
{jurriaan, rj, dignum, rogier, jj}@cs.uu.nl

Abstract. This paper considers the combination of agent communication and ontology alignment within a group of heterogeneous agents. The agents align their ontologies by constructing a shared communication vocabulary. Because ontology alignment is not a goal in itself, the agents refrain from it unless they believe it to be inevitable. We discuss three protocols that all implement lazy ontology alignment, although they give rise to different communication vocabularies.

1 Introduction

Most protocols which are studied in the agent communication community build on the assumption that the agents share a common ontology (we refer to these as *normal* communication protocols). However, normal communication protocols are difficult to apply in open multi agent systems, as those on the internet, in which common ontologies are typically *not* available. In these systems, it is difficult to realize consensus between all involved system developers on which ontology to use. Moreover, a common ontology is disadvantageous for the problem solving capacities of the agents as different tasks typically require different ontologies [2].

Over the last decade, much research has been conducted on the alignment of heterogeneous ontologies. Most approaches that deal with these issues require some form of human intervention. Prompt [9] and Chimaera [7] are examples of tools that assist humans in merging and aligning ontologies. However, in open multi agent systems, ontologies have to be aligned on such a large scale, that human involvement in this task is no longer feasible. Recently, a few approaches have been proposed that address the problem of heterogeneous ontologies in a fully automatic way [10,12,14]. The primary focus of these approaches is on concept learning: making the meaning of a concept clear to another agent. These techniques might seem to make normal communication protocols applicable in systems with heterogeneous ontologies: before the agents start cooperating, they teach the concepts in their ontologies to each other. This way, each agent would know every other agent's ontology, which would solve their incomprehension. However, such an approach is highly unpractical in an open multi agent system as it requires an agent to learn a vast amount of foreign concepts before it is

F. Dignum, R. van Eijk, and R. Flores (Eds.): AC 2005/2006, LNAI 3859, pp. 181–195, 2006.

able to communicate even the smallest piece of information. To make matters worse, this must be done not only once, but continuously as new agents enter and leave the system all the time.

In this paper, we explore ways to *efficiently* combine ontology alignment techniques with normal agent communication protocols. To make our results as generally applicable as possible, we deal with these issues in a highly abstract and formal way. Our approach allows the agents to preserve their private ontologies for knowledge representation and reasoning. To communicate, the agents build an intermediate ontology (or interlingua [13]). This ontology is shared among all agents and indirectly aligns their ontologies. Because the intermediate ontology is only used for communication purposes, we refer to it as *communication vocabulary* (or cv). Initially, the communication vocabulary is empty. The agents enable themselves to communicate by adding concepts to the cv. This way, the agents gradually extend the cv whenever they consider this necessary. Hence, the ontology alignment technique boils down to adding concepts to the cv at the proper moments. Normal communication proceeds by translating a concept from the speaker's private ontology to the communication vocabulary which the hearer translates back again to its own private ontology.

The communication protocols we propose all implement a combination of normal communication and ontology alignment. We evaluate these protocols according to the following criteria:

- Does the combination give rise to a small, yet sufficiently expressive communication vocabulary?
- Does the combination implement lazy ontology alignment?

The first question is of particular importance as the communication vocabulary should not simply become the union of every agent's private ontology, as often occurs in practice. This way, every agent would have to learn every other agent's ontology. Not only is this very resource-consuming, the situation only gets worse as more agents enter the system. In an open system, it would give rise to a forever growing communication vocabulary rendering itself useless in the long run. As is shown in [3], a *minimal* communication vocabulary may already fully align the agents ontologies.

The second question is of particular importance because the agents should be able to communicate even if their ontologies are not fully aligned. Otherwise the agents would have to learn a large number of concepts to align their complete ontologies, before they can start communicating the matter at hand. Usually, a limited number of shared concepts suffices for the successful communication of a particular matter. Therefore, the ontology alignment protocol should be *lazy*, providing local solutions for communication problems as they arise.

Section 2 describes the conceptual framework which provides the formal underpinning to study the different ontologies in a MAS. Using these notions, we define what qualifies as successful communication. Section 3 describes the operational framework dealing with the implementation of ontologies. Section 4 concerns communication. We briefly describe a formal abstraction of a concept learning technique. On the operational level, we describe three protocols which combine ontology alignment with normal communication. They all implement lazy ontology alignment, but differ in quality w.r.t. minimal cv construction.

2   Conceptual Framework

We assume that the agents have access to the same elements in the universe of discourse (Δ), and use the same symbols to refer to these individuals (given by the set IND). We will focus on the 1-ary relations between these individuals, namely sets of individuals. A conceptualization is defined as a set of 1-ary relations; it is thus a subset of 2^{Δ}. In our framework, the agents may conceptualize their world differently and are therefore allowed to adopt different conceptualizations. Note that, at this level, the elements in the conceptualization are not yet named. This is done by the ontology, which *specifies* the conceptualization [5]. The ontology introduces a set of symbols $\mathcal{C}$ which, when interpreted under their intended interpretation, refer to the elements in the conceptualization (conforming to the treatment by Genesereth and Nilsson in [4]). We will refer to the intended interpretation function with $\mathcal{I}^{INT}$.

Because we are mainly interested in the relations between concepts, an ontology is defined as a preorder $\mathcal{O} = \langle \mathcal{C}, \leq \rangle$ where $\leq \subseteq \mathcal{C} \times \mathcal{C}$ is a relation for which $\forall x, y \in \mathcal{C}.x \leq y \Leftrightarrow \mathcal{I}^{INT}(x) \subseteq \mathcal{I}^{INT}(y)$. This states that an ontology specifies a conceptualization as a preorder which is conforming to the subset ordering on the intended interpretations of the concepts. We will write $x \equiv y$ as a shorthand for $x \leq y \wedge y \leq x$, and $x < y$ as a shorthand for $x \leq y \wedge \neg(y \leq x)$.
Given a subset X of $\mathcal{C}$, we define the following:

- an element $x \in X$ is minimal iff $\neg\exists y \in X.y < x$
- an element $x \in X$ is maximal iff $\neg\exists y \in X.x < y$

Let us now consider a simple multi agent system consisting of 2 agents α_1 and α_2. We use 1 or 2 in subscript notation whenever we need to stress that something belongs to α_1 or α_2. In the system, the following ontologies are important ($i \in \{1, 2\}$):

- $\mathcal{O}_i = \langle \mathcal{C}_i, \leq_i \rangle$: the private ontology of α_i.
- $\mathcal{O}_{cv} = \langle \mathcal{C}_{cv}, \leq_{cv} \rangle$: the communication vocabulary.
- $\mathcal{O}_{i \cdot cv} = \langle \mathcal{C}_{i \cdot cv}, \leq_{i \cdot cv} \rangle$, where $\mathcal{C}_{i \cdot cv} = \mathcal{C}_i \cup \mathcal{C}_{cv}$: the private ontology of α_i, the cv and their interrelations.
- $\mathcal{O}_{1 \cdot 2} = \langle \mathcal{C}_{1 \cdot 2}, \leq_{1 \cdot 2} \rangle$, where $\mathcal{C}_{1 \cdot 2} = \mathcal{C}_1 \cup \mathcal{C}_2$: a God's eye view of the private ontologies of α_1 and α_2.
- $\mathcal{O}_{1 \cdot 2 \cdot cv} = \langle \mathcal{C}_{1 \cdot 2 \cdot cv}, \leq_{1 \cdot 2 \cdot cv} \rangle$, where $\mathcal{C}_{1 \cdot 2 \cdot cv} = \mathcal{C}_{1 \cdot 2} \cup \mathcal{C}_{cv}$: a God's eye view of all ontologies in the MAS.

Example: Consider a travel-agent α_1 and an internet travel service α_2 (conforming to the scenario envisioned in [6]). Figure 1 graphically represents the ontologies in the system using Euler diagrams. $\mathcal{O}_1$ and $\mathcal{O}_2$ are the agent's private ontologies; when combined, these ontologies form $\mathcal{O}_{1 \cdot 2}$.

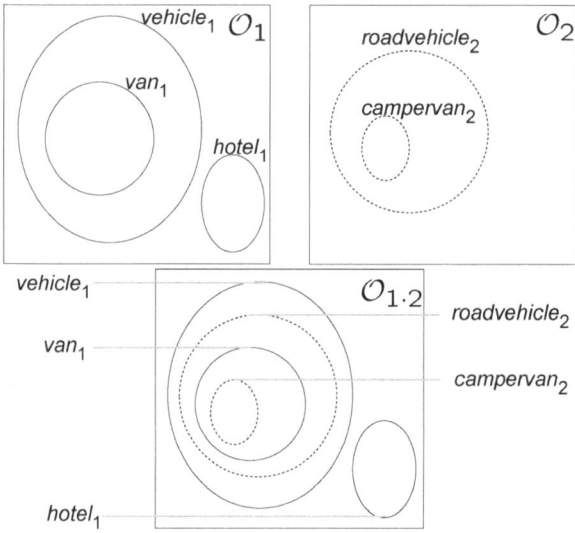

Fig. 1. Example ontologies

2.1 Knowledge Distribution

Not every ontology is known by the agents. For example, $\mathcal{O}_2$ is unknown to α_1 (the agents can not "look inside each others head"). $\mathcal{O}_{cv}$ on the other hand, is known by every agent, whereas $\mathcal{O}_{1.2.cv}$ is only partially known by the agents. We distinguish between local knowledge, common knowledge and implicit knowledge [8]. Local knowledge refers to the knowledge of an individual agent which is not accessible to other agents. Something is common knowledge if it is known by every agent and every agent knows that every agent knows it, which is again known by every agent etc. Something is implicit knowledge within a group, if someone in the group knows it, or the knowledge is distributed over the members of the group. By means of communication, the agents can only acquire knowledge which was already implicit in the group.

Assumption 1

- $\mathcal{O}_i$ is local knowledge of α_i.
- $\mathcal{O}_{cv}$ is common knowledge of the group.
- $\mathcal{O}_{i.cv}$ is local knowledge of α_i.
- $\mathcal{O}_{1.2}$ is implicit knowledge of the group.

Note that this assumption implies that also $\mathcal{O}_{1.2.cv}$ is implicit knowledge within the group. In section 3 it is shown how these characteristics are implemented in the system.

2.2   Communication

Consider communication between agent α_i (the speaker) and α_j (the hearer). α_i translates its private concept $\in \mathcal{C}_i$ to a concept in the communication vocabulary $\in \mathcal{C}_{cv}$, which α_j translates back again to a concept $\in \mathcal{C}_j$. We refer to these concepts as follows:

- The transferendum ($\in \mathcal{C}_i$): what is to be conveyed. α_i (the speaker) intends to convey the meaning of this concept to α_j.
- The transferens ($\in \mathcal{C}_{cv}$): what conveyes. This concept functions as a vehicle to convey the meaning of the transferendum to α_j.
- The translatum ($\in \mathcal{C}_j$): what has been conveyed. α_j (the hearer) interprets the received message as this concept.

Using these three concepts, we define the requirements of successful communication. The first requirement deals with the *quality* of information exchange, i.e. soundness. The definition of soundness states that the interpretation of the message by the hearer (the translatum) must follow from what the speaker intended to convey in the message (the transferendum).

Definition 1. *Sound Communication*
Let C_i be the transferendum, and C_j be the translatum. Communication is sound iff $C_i \leq C_j$.

It is not difficult to satisfy only the soundness requirement of communication. In the extreme case, the translatum is the top concept to which all individuals in Δ belong. This is guaranteed to be sound as this concept is a superset of all other concepts. However, an assertion stating that an individual belongs to the top concept, does not contain any information about the individual; it is a trivial fact. For this reason, a second requirement is needed which also takes the *quantity* of information exchange into account.

   The lossless requirement states that the translatum should not only be a consequence of the transferendum, but should also be the strongest consequence. This ensures that as much information as possible is preserved in the communication process.

Definition 2. *Lossless communication*
Let C_i be the transferendum and C_j the translatum. Communication is lossless iff C_j is minimal among the set $\{C_j'|C_i \leq C_j'\}$.

Note that in definition 1 and 2 no mention is made of the transferens. This is because the concepts in the communication vocabulary only serve as vehicles to convey the speaker's information to the hearer. To enable sound and lossless communication, there must be sufficient vehicles available.

3   Operational Framework

This section discusses the data-structures and actions that can be used to implement the conceptual framework. Note that this is only one of many possible implementations. The properties of the components describe the circumstances under which the requirements of assumption 1 are met.

We first discuss how $\mathcal{O}_i$ can be implemented as local knowledge of α_i. As standard in description logic knowledge bases, the agent's knowledge is represented by a tuple $\langle \mathcal{T}_i, \mathcal{A}_i \rangle$, containing a TBox and an ABox [1]. The TBox $\mathcal{T}_i$ contains a set of terminological axioms which specify the inclusion relations between the concepts; it represents the agent's ontology. The ABox $\mathcal{A}_i$ contains a set of membership statements which specify which individuals belong to which concepts; it represents the agent's operational knowledge. $\mathcal{T}_i$ and $\mathcal{A}_i$ are further explained below.

The set of concepts $\mathcal{C}_i$ is defined conforming to the description logic $\mathcal{ALC}$ without roles. Given a set of atomic concepts $\mathcal{C}_i^a$ with typical elements c_i, d_i, the set $\mathcal{C}_i$ with typical elements C_i, D_i, is defined by the BNF:
$C_i ::= c_i |\bot| \top |\neg C_i| C_i \sqcap D_i | C_i \sqcup D_i$.

The semantics of the elements in $\mathcal{C}_i$ is defined using an interpretation function $\mathcal{I}$ which maps concepts to sets of individuals. $\mathcal{I}$ is such that $\mathcal{I}(\top) = \Delta$, $\mathcal{I}(\bot) = \emptyset$, $\mathcal{I}(\neg C) = \Delta \backslash \mathcal{I}(C)$, $\mathcal{I}(C \sqcap D) = \mathcal{I}(C) \cap \mathcal{I}(D)$ and $\mathcal{I}(C \sqcup D) = \mathcal{I}(C) \cup \mathcal{I}(D)$. A terminological axiom is a statement of the form $C \sqsubseteq D$. A TBox $\mathcal{T}$ is a set of terminological axioms. An interpretation $\mathcal{I}$ satisfies a terminological axiom $C \sqsubseteq D$, written $\models_\mathcal{I} C \sqsubseteq D$ iff $\mathcal{I}(C) \subseteq \mathcal{I}(D)$. For a set of statements Γ, we write that $\models_\mathcal{I} \Gamma$ iff for every $\gamma \in \Gamma$, it holds that $\models_\mathcal{I} \gamma$. We write that $\Gamma \models \Gamma'$ iff for all $\mathcal{I}$: $\models_\mathcal{I} \Gamma$ implies $\models_\mathcal{I} \Gamma'$. We assume that enough terminological axioms are contained in $\mathcal{T}_i$, s.t. it fully implements the local knowledge of agent α_i over $\leq_i$, i.e.

Property 1. For $i \in \{1, 2\}$: $\mathcal{T}_i \models C_i \sqsubseteq D_i$ iff $C_i \leq D_i$.

Given a TBox, the relation $\sqsubseteq$ can be computed efficiently using standard DL reasoning techniques.

A membership statement is defined as a statement of the form $C(a)$, where C is a concept and a an individual name ($\in$ IND). IND refers to the set of individual names; we assume that the part of $\mathcal{I}$ which maps elements of IND to elements of Δ is common knowledge. An interpretation function $\mathcal{I}$ satisfies a membership statement $C(a)$ iff $\mathcal{I}(a) \in \mathcal{I}(C)$. The ABox $\mathcal{A}$ is a set of membership statements. We assume that the ABox is sound w.r.t. to the intended representation, i.e. $\models_{\mathcal{I}^{INT}} \mathcal{A}$. Note that we do not assume that the ABox *completely* specifies the intended interpretation. This would make communication unnecessary as the agents would already know everything. The assumption of a complete ABox is, nevertheless, unrealistic. Typically, the domain of discourse will be of such size that it is unfeasible to enumerate all membership statements.

Let us now focus on $\mathcal{O}_{cv}$. For the purposes of this paper, it suffices to define the set $\mathcal{C}_{cv}$ as a simpler language than $\mathcal{C}_i$; in particular, we leave out the $\sqcup$ and $\sqcap$ constructors. Given a set of atomic concepts $\mathcal{C}_{cv}^a$, the elements in $\mathcal{C}_{cv}$ are defined as $C_{cv} ::= c_{cv} |\bot| \top |\neg C_{cv}$. The omission of the $\sqcup$ and $\sqcap$ constructors makes it easier for an agent to achieve local knowledge of $\mathcal{O}_{i \cdot cv}$; an extension of the framework to deal with a cv that includes these constructors is straightforward. The agents store their knowledge about $\leq_{cv}$ in a TBox, $\mathcal{T}_{i \cdot cv}$. The protocols described in 4 are such that every agent knows the ordering between the concepts in $\mathcal{C}_{cv}$:

Property 2. For $i \in \{1,2\}$: $\mathcal{T}_{i \cdot cv} \models C_{cv} \sqsubseteq D_{cv}$ iff $C_{cv} \leq_{cv} D_{cv}$.

Our next focus is $\mathcal{O}_{i \cdot cv}$. Because the local knowledge of $\mathcal{O}_i$, and the common knowledge of $\mathcal{O}_{cv}$ has already been discussed above, we only need to focus on the relations between the concepts in $\mathcal{C}_i$ and those in $\mathcal{C}_{cv}$. This knowledge of agent α_i is stored using terminological axioms of the form $C_i \sqsubseteq C_{cv}$ or $C_{cv} \sqsubseteq C_i$. These terminological axioms are added to the TBox $\mathcal{T}_{i \cdot cv}$. The communication protocols implement local knowledge of $\mathcal{O}_{i \cdot cv}$ by giving rise to $\mathcal{T}_{i \cdot cv}$ with the property:

Property 3. For $i \in \{1,2\}$:

- $\mathcal{T}_{i \cdot cv} \models C_{cv} \sqsubseteq C_i$ iff $C_{cv} \leq_{i \cdot cv} C_i$
- $\mathcal{T}_{i \cdot cv} \models C_i \sqsubseteq C_{cv}$ iff $C_i \leq_{i \cdot cv} C_{cv}$

Until now, we have described how the first three items of assumption 1 are implemented using common techniques available from description logic research. The fourth item of the assumption is not yet met. The data structures as described until now do not give rise to implicit knowledge of the relations between two different agent's private concepts. This is a necessary condition for any system where the agents must learn to share meaning. Two agents can not learn something from each other which was not already implicitly present beforehand. To solve this, we build on the assumption that an agent not only knows the ordering between its private concepts, but also has access to the intended interpretation of its private concepts. This is done using the action `Classify`.

Action `Classify(C,a)`
Output specification:
if $a \in \mathcal{I}^{INT}(C)$ **then** add $C(a)$ to $\mathcal{A}$
else add $\neg C(a)$ to $\mathcal{A}$

For example, `Classify` can be thought of as a subsystem of a robot which recognizes and classifies objects in the real world. This underlies Luc Steels' approach to language creation [11]. In a scenario where the domain of discourse consists of text corpora, the action `Classify` can be implemented using a text classification technique like those used in spam filters.

4   Communication

The communicative abilities of the agents are specified as actions. During the execution of actions, messages are sent through the instruction send(α_j, $\langle$topic, $p_1, .., p_n \rangle$), where α_j is the addressee of the message, the topic specifies what the message is about, and $p_1..p_n$ are parameters of the message. The effect of this instruction is that α_j is able to perform a `Receive`(α_i, $\langle$topic, $x_1, .., x_n \rangle$) action, where α_i is the sender of the message and $x_1..x_n$ are instantiated to $p_1..p_n$. For clarity reasons, we will omit `Receive` actions from the protocols. In the specification of actions and protocols we will adopt α_i as the sender and α_j as the receiver of messages.

We first describe how concept learning is established in our framework. Then, we describe how this concept learning technique can be used in combination with normal communication to establish lazy ontology alignment.

4.1 Concept Learning

The agents extend the communication vocabulary using the action AddConcept. We first describe the changes in ontologies from the conceptual level. In describing these changes we use the notion of projection:

Definition 3. *Let $\mathcal{O} = \langle \mathcal{C}, \leq \rangle$ be an ontology. For $\mathcal{C}' \subseteq \mathcal{C}$, we define $\mathcal{O} \upharpoonright \mathcal{C}'$ to be $\langle \mathcal{C}', \{\langle x, y \rangle | \langle x, y \rangle \in \leq \wedge x, y \in \mathcal{C}'\} \rangle$*

Suppose α_i performs the action $\text{AddConcept}(\alpha_j, C_i, c_{cv})$. As a result, the knowledge in the system changes. Let $\mathcal{O}$ be the ontology before the action, and $\mathcal{O}^+$ be the ontology after the action. The change in ontologies is described as follows ($i \in \{1, 2\}$):

1. $\mathcal{O}^+_{1 \cdot 2 \cdot cv} = \langle \mathcal{C}^+_{1 \cdot 2 \cdot cv}, \leq^+_{1 \cdot 2 \cdot cv} \rangle$, where $\mathcal{C}^+_{1 \cdot 2 \cdot cv} = \mathcal{C}_{1 \cdot 2 \cdot cv} \cup \{c_{cv}\}$ and $\leq^+_{1 \cdot 2 \cdot cv}$ is the reflexive, transitive closure of $\leq_{1 \cdot 2 \cdot cv} \cup \{\langle C_i, c_{cv} \rangle, \langle c_{cv}, C_i \rangle\}$.
2. $\mathcal{O}^+_{cv} = \mathcal{O}^+_{1 \cdot 2 \cdot cv} \upharpoonright (\mathcal{C}_{cv} \cup \{c_{cv}\})$
3. $\mathcal{O}^+_{i \cdot cv} = \mathcal{O}^+_{1 \cdot 2 \cdot cv} \upharpoonright (\mathcal{C}_{i \cdot cv} \cup \{c_{cv}\})$
4. $\mathcal{O}^+_{j \cdot cv} = \mathcal{O}^+_{1 \cdot 2 \cdot cv} \upharpoonright (\mathcal{C}_{j \cdot cv} \cup \{c_{cv}\})$

We now describe the changes in ontologies from the operational level. In doing so, it suffices to regard only items two, three and four, as the first item follows from these.

The second item ($\mathcal{O}^+_{cv}$) concerns common knowledge. Because α_i knows the exact meaning of c_{cv}, it knows $\mathcal{O}^+_{cv}$. To make it common knowledge, α_i sends the information ($\leq^+_{cv} \setminus \leq_{cv}$) to α_j. This is done in the message with the "boundaries" topic (specified below). The third item ($\mathcal{O}^+_{i \cdot cv}$) follows straightforward from the knowledge of α_i that $c_{cv} \equiv C_i$. The fourth item ($\mathcal{O}^+_{j \cdot cv}$) is the most difficult one to establish. Given that $C_i \equiv c_{cv}$, neither $\mathcal{O}_{i \cdot cv}$, nor $\mathcal{O}_{j \cdot cv}$ gives sufficient information to establish the relations in $\mathcal{O}^+_{j \cdot cv}$. Therefore, α_i conveys this information to α_j by sending an *ostensive definition* [15], consisting of a set of positive and negative examples of concept c_{cv}. Upon receiving these examples, α_j uses inductive inference to derive the relations of c_{cv} with the concepts in its private ontology. This is done in the message with the "explication" topic.

The action AddConcept is specified as follows. Remember that the agents have access to the intended interpretation of concepts using the Classify action described earlier.

Action $\text{AddConcept}(\alpha_j, c_{cv}, C_i)$

- add $\langle c_{cv}, \langle C_i, C_i \rangle \rangle$ to $\mathcal{T}_{i \cdot cv}$
- send $(\alpha_j, \langle \text{boundaries}, c_{cv}, \{D_{cv} | c_{cv} \leq D_{cv}\}, \{E_{cv} | E_{cv} \leq c_{cv}\} \rangle)$
- send $(\alpha_j, \langle \text{explication}, c_{cv}, \{p | \mathcal{I}(p) \in \mathcal{I}^{INT}(C_i)\}, \{n | \mathcal{I}(n) \notin \mathcal{I}^{INT}(C_i)\} \rangle)$

Action Receive($\langle$boundaries,c_{cv},Sup,Sub $\rangle$)

- *for every $C'_{cv} \in$ Sup: add $c_{cv} \sqsubseteq C'_{cv}$ to $\mathcal{T}_{j \cdot cv}$*
- *for every $C'_{cv} \in$ Sub: add $C'_{cv} \sqsubseteq c_{cv}$ to $\mathcal{T}_{j \cdot cv}$*

The "boundaries" message ensures that the ordering on $\mathcal{C}_{cv}$ is common knowledge between α_i and α_j, thereby satisfying property 2.

Action Receive($\langle$explication,c_{cv},P,N $\rangle$)

- add $c_{cv} \sqsubseteq C_j$ to $\mathcal{T}_{j \cdot cv}$, where C_j is minimal among the set $\{C'_j | \forall p \in P.\mathcal{I}(p) \in \mathcal{I}^{INT}(C'_j)\}$
- add $D_j \sqsubseteq c_{cv}$ to $\mathcal{T}_{j \cdot cv}$, where D_j is maximal among the set $\{D'_j | \forall n \in N.\mathcal{I}(n) \notin \mathcal{I}^{INT}(D'_j)\}$

We assume that the number of examples in the sets P and N are sufficiently large, such that all information about the concept C_i is conveyed to α_j. Under this assumption, property 3 holds.

4.2 Protocols for Lazy Ontology Alignment

Building a communication vocabulary is not the primary goal of the agents, but only a means to achieve successful communication. Therefore, the agents should only resort to ontology alignment when their communication vocabulary falls short of successful communication, i.e. the ontology alignment protocol should be lazy. This requires the agents to know when their communication qualifies as successful. In section 2.2 we defined successful communication as being sound and lossless. Whereas these properties are defined using a God's eye view over the agents ontologies, the agents can only use their local knowledge to assess these properties. This plays a central role in our discussions on lazy ontology alignment. Three different protocols are discussed below.

Protocol 1. In protocol 1, only messages are sent which are guaranteed to result in lossless communication. This requires the sender of a message to know whether its message will result in lossless communication or not. The sender knows that the receiver's knowledge about a transferens is as *accurate* as possible (property 3). Therefore, the sender knows that whenever it uses a transferens which corresponds *exactly* to the transferendum, lossless communication will be established. This idea is captured in the precondition of the InformExact action. If this speech act cannot be performed, the agent is forced to add the term to the communication vocabulary.

Action InformExact($\alpha_j, C_i(a)$)
if $\exists C_{cv}.C_{cv} \equiv C_i$ **then** send($\alpha_j, \langle$InformExact$, C_{cv}(a)\rangle$)
else fail

Action Receive($\langle$ InformExact$,C_{cv}(a)\rangle$)
Add $C_j(a)$ to $\mathcal{A}_j$, where C_j is minimal among the set $\{C'_j | C_{cv} \leq C'_j\}$

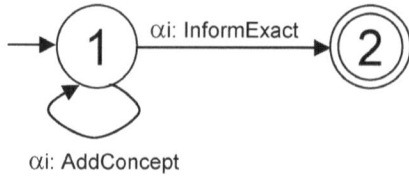

Fig. 2. Protocol P1

It is not difficult to prove that in protocol 1, communication proceeds in a loss-less fashion as defined in definition 2. The event that is triggered upon receiving an InformExact message, produces a translatum C_j which is minimal among the set $\{C_j'|C_{cv} \leq C'\}$. Because the action that produces an InformExact message requires the transferendum C_i to be equivalent to C_{cv}, it follows that C_j is also minimal among the set $\{C_j'|C_i \leq C'\}$, thereby meeting the lossless requirement.

Example: Consider the ontologies in figure 1. Initially $\mathcal{C}_{cv} = \{\top, \bot\}$. Suppose that α_1 intends to convey the assertion $van_1(a)$. Below, the actions are described which are performed by the agents. We describe some of the instructions that are executed *within* an action; these are preceded with ⌊.

α_1 : AddConcept$(\alpha_2, van_{cv}, van_1)$
α_1 : InformExact$(\alpha_2, van_1(a))$
⌊α_1 : send$(\alpha_2, \langle \text{InformExact}, van_{cv}(a)\rangle)$
α_2 : receive$(\alpha_1, \langle \text{InformExact}, van_{cv}(a)\rangle)$
⌊α_2 :add $roadvehicle_2(a)$ to $\mathcal{A}$

Now, suppose that α_2 intends to convey the message $campervan_2(a)$, and that $\mathcal{C}_{cv}^a = \{van_{cv}\}$. Here, and in the following examples, the meaning of concepts in $\mathcal{C}_{cv}^a$ is as expected, e.g. $van_{cv} \equiv van_1$. The agents perform the following actions:

α_2 : AddConcept$(\alpha_1, campervan_{cv}, campervan_2)$
α_2 : InformExact$(\alpha_1, campervan_2(a))$
⌊α_2 : send$(\alpha_1, \langle \text{InformExact}, campervan_{cv}(a)\rangle)$
. . .

Although P1 always allows lossless communication, it does not give rise to a minimal cv. The condition maintained by the sender is a *sufficient* condition for lossless communication, but it is not a *necessary* condition. In the second dialogue of the example, it was not necessary to add a new concept to the cv, as lossless communication was already enabled by the concept van_{cv}. Some-times, the sender adds concepts to the cv that do not contribute to successful communication. After the agents have exchanged a number of messages, the communication vocabulary will simply consist of every transferendum that was conveyed by one of those messages. The following protocol attempts to overcome the problem of redundantly adding concepts to the cv.

Protocol 2. In protocol 2, the sender uses an InformExact speech act when allowed. When this is not allowed, i.e. the sender is not able to express itself *exactly* in shared concepts, it does not immediately add the concept to the communication vocabulary. Instead, it conveys the message *as accurately as possible* using a more general concept. It is upon the receiver to decide whether this approximation is accurate enough to meet the lossless criterion.

Because the receiver does not know the transferendum, it cannot directly check definition 2 for lossless communication. However, the receiver knows two things about the transferendum, which enables it, in some cases, to check the lossless condition nonetheless. Firstly, it knows that the transferendum is more specific than the transferens. Secondly, it knows that the transferens is the most accurate translation of the transferendum to the communication vocabulary. Therefore, any concept in $\mathcal{C}_{cv}$ which is more specific than the transferens is *not* more general than the transferendum. These ideas underly the action OK.

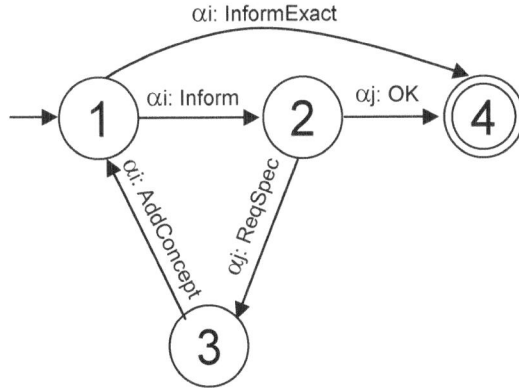

Fig. 3. Protocol P2

Action $\texttt{Inform}(\alpha_j, C_i(a))$
$\text{send}(\alpha_j, \langle \text{Inform}, C_{cv}(a) \rangle)$ *where C_{cv} is minimal among the set* $\{C_{cv}|C_i \leq C_{cv}\}$

The event that is triggered when an inform message is received is equal to the event that is triggered when an InformExact message is received. The OK action fails if the receiver cannot assess that communication was lossless; otherwise it responds with OK.

Action $\texttt{OK}(\alpha_i)$
Responding to $\langle \text{inform}, (C_{cv}(a)) \rangle$
if $\neg \exists C_j$ *for which*

1. $C_j < D_j$, *where D_j is minimal among the set* $\{C'_j|C_{cv} \leq C'_j\}$ *(D_j is the translatum)*
2. $\neg \exists C'_{cv}.C'_{cv} < C_{cv} \wedge C_j \leq C'_{cv}$

then $\text{send}(\alpha_i, \langle \text{OK} \rangle)$
else fail

If the receiver cannot respond with OK, it requests for specification (ReqSpec). After this, the sender adds a concept to the communication vocabulary.

Theorem 1. *If the receiver responds* OK *then communication was lossless.*

Proof: Suppose C_i is the transferendum, C_{cv} the transferens and C_j the translatum. We prove the theorem by showing that the situation where the receiver responds OK while communication was *not* lossless leads to a contradiction. The conditions for sending and receiving an inform speech act ensure that $C_i \leq C_{cv} \leq C_j$, and therefore $C_i \leq C_j$. Non-lossless communication means that C_j is *not* minimal among the set $\{C'_j | C_i \leq C'_j\}$. Therefore $\exists C'_j . C_i \leq C'_j < C_j$. This C'_j meets the first condition in the if-statement of OK; therefore, the second condition must be false, i.e. $\exists C'_{cv} . C'_{cv} < C_{cv} \land C'_j \leq C'_{cv}$. Therefore, $C_i \leq C'_{cv} \land C'_{cv} < C_{cv}$. This is in contradiction with the condition of Inform which states that C_{cv} should be minimal among the set $\{C'_{cv} | C_i \leq C'_{cv}\}$. □

Example: Consider the ontologies in figure 1. Suppose that α_2 wishes to communicate $campervan_2(a)$, and that $\mathcal{C}^a_{cv} = \{van_{cv}\}$. The dialogue proceeds as follows:

α_2 : Inform$(\alpha_1, campervan_2(a))$
$\llcorner \alpha_2$: send$(\alpha_1, \langle$Inform, $campervan_{cv}(a)\rangle)$
α_1 : Receive $(\alpha_2, \langle$Inform, $campervan_{cv}(a)\rangle)$
$\llcorner \alpha_1$: add $van_1(a)$ to $\mathcal{A}_1$
α_1 : OK

In this example, α_1 responded with OK, because in $\mathcal{O}_1$ the information provided by van_1 is as accurate as possible.

Now, suppose that α_2 wishes to communicate $campervan_2(a)$, $\mathcal{C}^a_{cv} = \{vehicle_{cv}\}$.
α_2 : Inform$(\alpha_1, campervan_2)$
$\llcorner \alpha_2$: send$(\alpha_1, \langle$Inform, $vehicle_{cv}(a)\rangle)$
α_1 : Reqspec
α_2 : AddConcept$(\alpha_1, campervan_{cv}, campervan_2)$
α_2 : InformExact$(\alpha_1, campervan_2(a))$
$\dots$

In this example α_1 did not respond OK at first, because van_1 caused the action the fail. Hereby, α_1 correctly recognized non-lossless communication.

Now, suppose that α_2 wishes to communicate $roadvehicle_2(a)$, and $\mathcal{C}^a_{cv} = \{vehicle_{cv}, van_{cv}, (vehicle \sqcap \neg van)_{cv}\}$ (in the extended framework, $(vehicle \sqcap \neg van)_{cv}$ can be compositionally defined in $\mathcal{C}_{cv}$, instead of atomic)
α_2 : Inform$(\alpha_1, roadvehicle_2(a))$
$\llcorner \alpha_2$: send$(\alpha_1, \langle$Inform, $vehicle_{cv}(a)\rangle)$
α_1 : Receive $(\alpha_2, \langle$Inform, $vehicle_{cv}(a)\rangle)$
$\llcorner \alpha_1$: add $vehicle_1(a)$ to $\mathcal{A}_1$
α_1 : OK

In this example, α_1 responded OK, because it knew that if α_2 had more information available about individual a, e.g. van_1, it would have used a more specific term, e.g. van_{cv}. Hereby, α_1 correctly recognized lossless communication.

Protocol P2 enables the agents to communicate without having to share all their private concepts. However, the protocol may still give rise to a communication vocabulary which is unnecessary large. Protocol 3 allows the agents to remove superfluous concepts from their communication vocabulary.

Protocol 3. Concepts can be removed from the vocabulary if they are *redundant*. Redundant concepts have the property that their removal does not affect the expressiveness of the cv. We measure the expressiveness of the communication vocabulary, as the number of private concepts that can be losslessly communicated, without having to extend the cv.

Definition 4. *If c_{cv} is redundant in $\mathcal{C}_{cv}^a$, then $\mathcal{C}_{cv}^a \backslash \{c_{cv}\}$ allows for lossless communication of the same concepts as $\mathcal{C}_{cv}^a$.*

Whereas this definition can be verified from a God's eye view perspective, an agent can only indirectly check its validity. Agent α_i knows which transferendum C_i uses which transferens C_{cv} (it knows how to send an inform message). It also knows which transferens C_{cv}, is translated into which translatum C_i (it knows how to receive an inform message). This enables α_i to know that a concept C_{cv} is redundant if the following holds for c_{cv}:

- no transferendum $\in C_i$ requires transferens c_{cv}. This means that α_i would never use c_{cv} in its messages.
- there is another transferens $C_{cv}' \in \mathcal{C}_{cv} \backslash \{c_{cv}\}$, which yields the same translatum as c_{cv}, and is more general than c_{cv}. This means that, as far as α_i is concerned, α_j might as well use C_{cv}' instead of c_{cv}, when α_j informs α_i about something.

An agent performs a RemoveConcept action on a concept c_{cv}, when it considers it redundant using the criteria described above. Concepts may become redundant after a new term is added to the communication vocabulary. Therefore, P3 allows the RemoveConcept action *after* AddConcept. Because both agents have different perspectives on the redundancy of terms, both agents get a chance to perform RemoveConcept. Due to space limitations, we will confine ourselves to this informal treatment of RemoveConcept.

Example: Consider the ontologies in figure 1. Suppose that α_1 wishes to communicate $vehicle_1(a)$, $\mathcal{C}_{cv}^a = \{van_{cv}, roadvehicle_{cv}\}$.
$\alpha_1 : \text{Inform}(\alpha_2, vehicle_1(a))$
$\llcorner \alpha_1 : \text{send}(\alpha_2, \langle \text{Inform}, \top(a) \rangle)$
$\alpha_2 : \text{Reqspec}$
$\alpha_1 : \text{AddConcept}(\alpha_2, vehicle_{cv}, vehicle_1)$
$\alpha_1 : \text{RemoveConcept}(\alpha_1, roadvehicle_{cv})$
$\alpha_1 : \text{Exit}$
$\alpha_2 : \text{Exit}$
$\alpha_1 : \text{InformExact}(\alpha_2, vehicle_1(a))$
$\cdots$

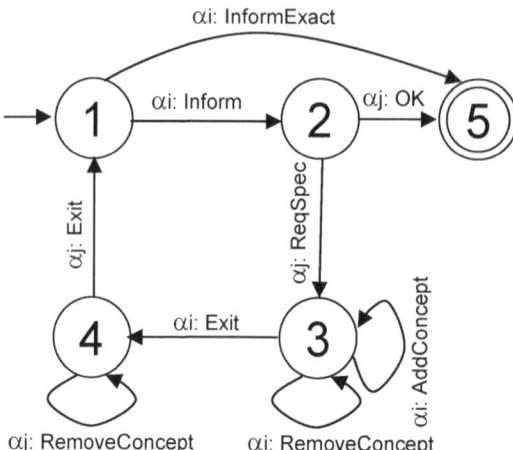

Fig. 4. Protocol P3

In this example α_1 considers the concept *roadvehicle*$_{cv}$ redundant after it has added *vehicle*$_{cv}$. As a sender, α_1 would never use *roadvehicle*$_{cv}$, and as a receiver α_1 finds *vehicle*$_{cv}$ equally accurate as *roadvehicle*$_{cv}$.

5   Conclusion

In this paper we have proposed some extensions to normal communication protocols that allow agents with heterogeneous ontologies to communicate. We have focussed on *lazy* ontology alignment and *minimal* cv construction. By lazy ontology alignment, we mean that the agents seek *local* solutions for communication problems *when they arise*. By minimal cv construction, we mean that the agents come up with a simple solution, i.e. the number of concepts in the communication vocabulary remains relatively *small*.

The protocols described in this paper all implement lazy ontology alignment. With respect to minimal ontology development, P3 performs best, followed by P2, followed by P1. We will continue this line of research by considering situations with more than two agents. Furthermore, we will test the framework in some real-life scenarios of collaborating personal assistants.

References

1. F. Baader, D.L. McGuinnes, and P.F. Patel-Schneider. *The description logic handbook: Theory, implementation and applications.* Cambridge University Press, 2003.
2. T. Bylander and B. Chandrasekaran. Generic tasks for knowledge-based reasoning: the right level of abstraction for knowledge acquisition. *Int. J. Man-Mach. Stud.*, 26(2):231–243, 1987.

3. J. van Diggelen, R.J. Beun, F. Dignum, R.M. van Eijk, and J.-J.Ch. Meyer. Optimal communication vocabularies and heterogeneous ontologies. In R.M. van Eijk, M.-P. Huget, and F. Dignum, editors, *Developments in Agent Communication*, LNAI 3396. Springer Verlag, 2004.

4. Michael R. Genesereth and Nils J. Nilsson. *Logical foundations of artificial intelligence*. Morgan Kaufmann Publishers Inc., 1987.

5. T.R. Gruber. A translation approach to portable ontology specifications. *Knowledge Acquisition*, 5(2):199–220, 1993.

6. M. Luck, P. McBurney, and C. Preist. Agent technology: Enabling next generation computing. *Agent link community*, 2003.

7. D. L. McGuinness, R. Fikes, J. Rice, and S. Wilder. The chimaera ontology environment. In *Proceedings of the Seventeenth National Conference on Artificial Intelligence (AAAI 2000)*.

8. J-J. Ch. Meyer and W. Van Der Hoek. *Epistemic Logic for AI and Computer Science*. Cambridge University Press, 1995.

9. N. F. Noy and M. A. Musen. Prompt: Algorithm and tool for automated ontology merging and alignment. *In Proceedings of the National Conference on Artificial Intelligence (AAAI)*, 2000.

10. M. Obitko and V. Marik. Mapping between ontologies in agent communication. In *Proceedings of the CEEMAS 2003, Prague, Czech Republic*, Lecture Notes on Artificial Intelligence 2691, pages 191–203. Springer-Verlag, 2003.

11. L. Steels. *Synthesising the Origins of Language and Meaning Using Co-evolution, Self-organisation and Level formation*. Edinburgh University Press, 1998.

12. Y. Tzitzikas and C. Meghini. Ostensive automatic schema mapping for taxonomy-based peer-to-peer systems. In *Proceedings of the 7th International Workshop on Cooperative Information Agents*, Helsinki, Finland, 2003.

13. M. Uschold and M. Gruninger. Creating semantically integrated communities on the world wide web. *Semantic Web Workshop Co-located with WWW 2002 Honolulu*, 2002.

14. A.B. Williams. Learning to share meaning in a multi-agent system. *Autonomous Agents and Multi-Agent Systems*, 8(2):165–193, 2004.

15. L. Wittgenstein. *Philosophische untersuchungen - Philosophical investigations*. Basil Blackwell, Oxford, german-english edition, 1953.

Towards Design Tools for Protocol Development[*]

Pınar Yolum

Department of Computer Engineering
Boğaziçi University
TR-34342 Bebek, Istanbul, Turkey
pinar.yolum@boun.edu.tr

Abstract. Interaction protocols enable agents to communicate with each other effectively. Whereas several approaches exist to specify interaction protocols, none of them has design tools that can help protocol designers catch semantical protocol errors at design time. As research in networking protocols has shown, flawed specifications of protocols can have disastrous consequences. Hence, it is crucial to systematically analyze protocols in time to ensure correct specification. This paper studies and formalizes important generic properties of commitment protocols that can ease their correct development significantly. Since these properties are formal, they can easily be incorporated in a software tool to (semi-) automate the design and specification of commitment protocols. Where appropriate we provide algorithms that can directly be used to check these properties in such a design tool.

1   Introduction

Multiagent systems consist of autonomous, interacting agents. For the agents to interact effectively, their interactions should be regulated. Multiagent interaction protocols provide a formal ground for realizing this regulation. However, developing effective protocols that will be carried out by autonomous agents is challenging [2,3].

Similar to the protocols in traditional systems, multiagent protocols need to be specified rigorously so that the agents can interact successfully. Some important properties of network protocols have been studied before, where a protocol was represented as a finite state machine (FSM) [4,5]. However, FSMs are not well-suited for dynamic environments of multiagent systems [6,7,8]. Contrary to the protocols in static systems, multiagent protocols need to be specified flexibly so that the agents can exercise their autonomy by making choices or by dealing with exceptions as best suits them.

Recently, social constructs are being used to specify agent interactions. These approaches advocate declarative representations of protocols and give semantics to protocol messages in terms of social (and thus observable) concepts. Alberti *et al.* specify interaction protocols using social integrity constraints and reason about the expectations of agents [9]. Fornara and Colombetti base the semantics of agent communication on commitments, such that the meanings of messages are denoted by commitments

---

[*] This paper also appears as [1]. This research has been supported by Boğaziçi University Research Fund under grant BAP05A104.

F. Dignum, R. van Eijk, and R. Flores (Eds.): AC 2005/2006, LNAI 3859, pp. 196–210, 2006.

[10]. Yolum and Singh develop a methodology for specifying protocols wherein protocols capture the possible interactions of the agents in terms of the commitments to one another [8,11].

In addition to providing flexibility, these approaches make it possible to verify compliance of agents to a given protocol. Put broadly, commitments of the agents can be stored publicly and agents that do not fulfill their commitments at the end of the protocol can be identified as non-compliant. In order for these approaches to make use of all these advantages, the protocols should be designed rigorously. For example, the protocol should guarantee that, if an agent does not fulfill its commitment, it is not because the protocol does not specify how the fulfillment can be carried out. The aforementioned approaches all start with a manually designed, correct protocol. However, designing a correct protocol in the first place requires important correctness properties to be established and applied to the protocol. A correct protocol should define the necessary actions (or transitions) to lead a computation to its desired state. Following a protocol should imply that progress is being made towards realizing desired end conditions of the protocol. The followed actions should not yield conflicting information and lead the protocol to unrecoverable errors. That is, the protocol should at least allow a safe execution.

This paper develops and formalizes design requirements for developing correct and consistent *commitment protocols* [12,8]. However, the underlying ideas are generic and can be applied to other social approaches as well. These requirements detect inconsistencies as well as errors during design time. These requirements can easily be automated in a design tool to help protocol designers to develop protocols.

The rest of the paper is organized as follows. Section 2 gives a technical background on event calculus and commitments. Section 3 reviews commitment protocols. Sections 4 and 5 develop correctness and consistency requirements, respectively. Section 6 shows how these requirements can be implemented in a design tool. Section 7 discusses the recent literature in relation to our work.

2   Technical Background

We first give a brief overview of event calculus, which we use to formalize the design requirements. Next, we summarize Yolum and Singh's formalization of commitments and their operations.

2.1   Event Calculus

The event calculus (EC) is a formalism based on many-sorted first order logic [13]. The three sorts of event calculus are *time points* (T), *events* (E) and *fluents* (F). Fluents are properties whose truth values can change over time. Fluents are manipulated by initiation and termination of events. Table 1 supplies a list of predicates to help reason about the events in an easier form. Below, events are shown with $a, b, \ldots$; fluents are shown with $f, g, \ldots$; and time points are shown with t, t_1, and t_2.

We introduce the subset of the EC axioms that are used here; the rest can be found elsewhere [14]. The variables that are not explicitly quantified are assumed to be universally quantified. The standard operators apply (i.e., $\leftarrow$ denotes implication and $\wedge$

Table 1. Event calculus predicates

$Initiates(a, f, t)$	f holds after event a at time t.
$Terminates(a, f, t)$	f does not hold after event a at time t.
$Initially_P(f)$	f holds at time 0.
$Initially_N(f)$	f does not hold at time 0.
$Happens(a, t_1, t_2)$	event a starts at time t_1 and ends at t_2.
$Happens(a, t)$	event a starts and ends at time t.
$HoldsAt(f, t)$	f holds at time t.
$Clipped(t_1, f, t_2)$	f is terminated between t_1 and t_2.
$Declipped(t_1, f, t_2)$	f is initiated between t_1 and t_2.

denotes conjunction). The time points are ordered by the $<$ relation, which is defined to be transitive and asymmetric.

1. $HoldsAt(f, t_3) \leftarrow Happens(a, t_1, t_2) \wedge Initiates(a, f, t_1) \wedge (t_2 < t_3) \wedge \neg Clipped(t_1, f, t_3)$
2. $Clipped(t_1, f, t_4) \leftrightarrow \exists a, t_2, t_3 \ [Happens(a, t_2, t_3) \wedge (t_1 < t_2) \wedge (t_3 < t_4) \wedge Terminates(a, f, t_2)]$
3. $\neg HoldsAt(f, t) \leftarrow Initially_N(f) \wedge \neg Declipped(0, f, t)$
4. $\neg HoldsAt(f, t_3) \leftarrow Happens(a, t_1, t_2) \wedge Terminates(a, f, t_1) \wedge (t_2 < t_3) \wedge \neg Declipped(t_1, f, t_3)$

2.2 Commitments

Commitments are obligations from one party to another to bring about a certain condition [15]. A base-level commitment $C(x, y, p)$ binds a debtor x to a creditor y to bring about a condition p [16]. When a base-level commitment is created, x becomes responsible to y for satisfying p, i.e., p should hold sometime in the future. The condition p does not involve other conditions or commitments.

A conditional commitment $CC(x, y, p, q)$ denotes that if the condition p is satisfied, x will be committed to bring about condition q. Conditional commitments are useful when a party wants to commit only if a certain condition holds or only if the other party is also willing to make a commitment. It is easy to see that a base-level commitment is a special case of a conditional commitment, where the condition is set to true. That is, $C(x, y, p)$ is an abbreviation for $CC(x, y, true, p)$. Commitments are represented as fluents in the event calculus. Hence, the creation and the manipulation of the commitments are shown with the *Initiates* and *Terminates* predicates.

Compared to the traditional definitions of obligations, commitments can be carried out more flexibly [16]. By performing operations on an existing commitment, a commitment can be manipulated (e.g., delegated to a third-party). We summarize the operations to create and manipulate commitments [16,8]. In the following discussion, x, y, z denote agents, c, c' denote commitments, and e denotes an event.

1. *Create(e, x, $C(x, y, p)$):* When x performs the event e, the commitment c is created. $\{Happens(e, t) \wedge Initiates(e, C(x, y, p), t)\}$

2. *Discharge(e, x,* C(x, y, p))*:* When x performs the event e, the commitment c is re-solved.
   {*Happens(e, t)* $\wedge$ *Initiates(e, p, t)*}
3. *Cancel(e, x,* C(x, y, p))*:* When x performs the event e, the commitment c is can-celed. Usually, the cancellation of a commitment is followed by the creation of another commitment to compensate for the former one.
   {*Happens(e, t)* $\wedge$ *Terminates(e,* C$(x, y, p), t)$}
4. *Release(e, y,* C(x, y, p))*:* When y performs the event e, x no longer need to carry out the commitment c.
   {*Happens(e, t)* $\wedge$ *Terminates(e,* C$(x, y, p), t)$}
5. *Assign(e, y, z,* C(x, y, p))*:* When y performs the event e, commitment c is elimi-nated, and a new commitment c' is created where z is appointed as the new creditor.
   {*Happens(e, t)* $\wedge$ *Terminates(e,* C$(x, y, p), t)$ $\wedge$
   Initiates(e, C$(x, z, p), t)$}
6. *Delegate(e, x, z,* C(x, y, p))*:* When x performs the event e, commitment c is elimi-nated but a new commitment c' is created where z is the new debtor.
   {*Happens(e, t)* $\wedge$ *Terminates(e,* C$(x, y, p), t)$ $\wedge$
   Initiates(e, C$(z, y, p), t)$}

The following rules operationalize the commitments. Axiom 1 states that a commitment is no longer in force if the condition committed to holds. In Axiom 1, when the event e occurs at time t, it initiates the fluent p, thereby discharging the commitment C(x, y, p).

Commitment Axiom 1. *Discharge(e, x,* C(x, y, p)) $\leftarrow$ *HoldsAt(*C$(x, y, p), t)$ $\wedge$ *Happens(e, t)* $\wedge$ *Initiates(e, p, t)*

The following axiom captures how a conditional commitment is resolved based on the temporal ordering of the commitments it refers to. When the conditional commitment CC(x, y, p, q) holds, if p becomes true, then the original commitment is terminated but a new commitment is created, since the debtor x is now committed to bring about q.

Commitment Axiom 2. *Initiates(e,* C$(x, y, q), t)$ $\wedge$ *Terminates(e,* CC$(x, y, p, q), t)$ $\leftarrow$ *HoldsAt(*CC$(x, y, p, q), t)$ $\wedge$ *Happens(e, t)* $\wedge$ *Initiates(e, p, t)*

3   Commitment Protocols

A commitment protocol is a set of actions such that each action is either an operation on commitments or brings about a proposition. Agents create and manipulate commitments they are involved in through the protocol they follow. An agent can start a protocol by performing any of the actions that is allowed by the role it is playing. The transitions of the protocol are computed by applying the effect of the action on the current state. In most cases this correspond to the application of commitment operations. Figure 1 gives an overview of the possible transitions. Given a protocol specification, actions of the protocol can be executed from an arbitrary initial state to a desired final state. A protocol run can be viewed as a series of actions; each action happening at a distinct time point.

Example 1. We consider the Contract Net Protocol (CNP) as our running example [17]. CNP starts with a manager requesting proposals for a particular task. Each participant either sends a proposal or a reject message. The manager accepts one proposal among the submitted proposals and (explicitly) rejects the rest. The participant with the accepted proposal informs the manager with the proposal result or the failure of the proposal.

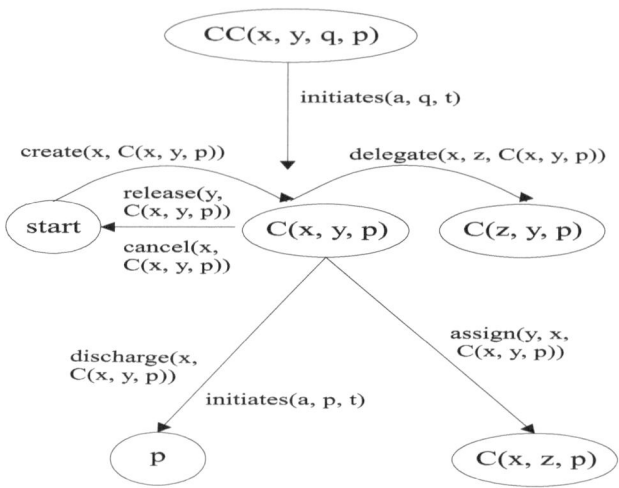

Fig. 1. Commitment transitions

Example 2. By sending a proposal to the manager, a participant creates a conditional commitment such that if the manager accepts the proposal, then the participant will deliver the result of the proposal (e.g., CC(participant, manager, accepted, result). If the manager then sends an accept message, this conditional commitment will cease to exist but the following base-level commitment will hold: C(participant, manager, result). Since the commitments can be easily manipulated, the participant can manipulate its commitment in the following ways: (1) it can discharge its commitment by sending the result as in the original CNP (discharge), (2) it can delegate its commitment to another participant, who carries out the proposal (delegate), or (3) it can send a failure notice as in the original protocol (cancel). Meanwhile, if for some reason, the manager no longer has a need for the proposed task, (1) it can let go of the participant (release) or (2) let another agent benefit from the proposal (assign).

4   Protocol Correctness

Analysis of commitment protocols poses two major challenges. One, the states of a commitment protocol are not given *a priori* as is the case with FSMs. Two, the transitions are computed at run time to enable flexible execution. To study a commitment protocol, we study the possible protocol runs that can result. A protocol run specifies the actions that happen at certain time points. We base the definition of a protocol state on these time points. More specifically, a state of the protocol corresponds to the set of propositions and commitments that hold at a particular time point in a particular run.

To ease the explanation, we introduce the following notation. Let F be the set of fluents in the protocol. F is $CS \cup CCS \cup PS$ such that CS is the set of base-level commitments, CCS is the set of conditional commitments and PS is the set of propositions in the protocol. Let c be a commitment such that $c \in CS$ then $O(c)$ is the set of operations allowed on the commitment c in the protocol and $O = \{O(c) : c \in CS\}$. Since a commitment cannot be part of a protocol if it cannot be created, we omit the create operation from the set. Hence, $O(c)$ can contain five types of operations in Section 2.2, namely, discharge, cancel, release, delegate, and assign. We assume that all the propositions referred by the commitments in CS and CCS are in PS.

Definition 1. A *protocol state* $s(t)$ captures the *content* of the protocol with respect to a particular time point t. A protocol state $s(t)$ is a conjunction of $HoldsAt(f, t)$ predicates with a fixed t but possibly varying f. Formally, $s(t) \equiv \bigwedge_{f \in F'} HoldsAt(f, t)$ such that $F' \subseteq F$.

Two states are equivalent if the same fluents hold in both states. Although the two states are equivalent, they are not strictly the same state since they can come about at different time points.

Definition 2. The $\equiv$ operator defines an equivalence relation between two states $s(t)$ and $s(t')$ such that $s(t) \equiv s(t')$ if and only if $\forall f \in F : (HoldsAt(f, t) \iff HoldsAt(f, t'))$.

Protocol execution captures a series of operations for making and fulfilling of commitments. Intuitively, if the protocol executes successfully, then there should not be any open base-level commitments; i.e., no participant should still have commitments to others. This motivates the following definition of an end-state.

Definition 3. A protocol state $s(t)$ is a *proper* end-state if no base-level commitments exist. Formally, $\forall f \in F : HoldsAt(f, t) \Rightarrow f \notin CS$.

Generally, if the protocol ends in an unexpected state, i.e., not a proper end-state, one of the participants is not conforming to the protocol. However, to claim this, the protocol has to ensure that participants have the choice to execute actions that will terminate their commitments. The following analysis derives the requirements for correct commitment protocols.

Holzmann labels states of a protocol in terms of their capability of allowing progress [4]. Broadly put, a protocol state can be labeled as a progressing state if it is possible to move to another state. For a protocol to function correctly, all states excluding the proper end-states should be progressing states. Otherwise, the protocol can move to a state where no actions are possible, and hence the protocol will not progress and immaturely end.

Definition 4. A protocol state $s(t)$ is progressing if both of the following hold:

- $s(t)$ is not a proper end-state (e.g., $s(t) \Rightarrow$
  $\exists f \in CS : HoldsAt(f, t))$.

– there exists an action that if executed creates a transition to a different state. (e.g., $s(t) \Rightarrow \exists t' : t < t' \wedge s(t) \not\equiv s(t'))$ ∎

At every state in the protocol, either the execution should have successfully completed (i.e., proper end-state) or should be moving to a different state (i.e., progressing state).

Definition 5. A protocol $\mathcal{P}$ is *progressive* if and only if each possible state in the protocol is either a proper end-state or a progressing state.

This follows intuitively from the explanation of making progress. Lemma 1 formalizes a sufficient condition for ensuring that a commitment protocol is progressive,

Lemma 1. Let $\mathcal{P}$ be a commitment protocol and c be a base-level commitment. If $\forall c \in CS : O(c) \neq \emptyset$, then $\mathcal{P}$ is progressive.

Proof. By Definition 5, every state in $\mathcal{P}$ should be a proper end-state or a progressing state. If a state does not contain open commitments then it is a proper end-state (Definition 3). If the state does contain a base-level commitment, then since at least one operation exists to manipulate it, the protocol will allow a transition to a new state. Thus, the state is a progressing state (Definition 4).

Ensuring a progressing protocol is the first step in ensuring correctness. If a protocol is not progressing, then the participants can get stuck in an unexpected state and not transition to another state. However, progress by itself does not guarantee that the interactions will always lead to a proper end-state. This is similar in principle to livelocks in network protocols, where the protocol can transition between states but never reach a final state [4, p.120].

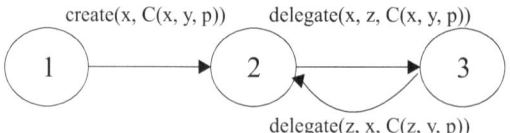

create(x, C(x, y, p))   delegate(x, z, C(x, y, p))

1   2   3

delegate(z, x, C(z, y, p))

Fig. 2. Infinitely delegating a commitment

Example 3. Consider a participant x whose proposal has been accepted (hence, C(x, manager, result). Next, the participant delegates its commitment to another participant z (hence, C(z, manager, result)). Next, participant z delegates the commitment back to participant x and thus the protocol moves back to the previous state (C(x, manager, result)). Participants x and z delegate the commitment back and forth infinitely.

Obviously, the situation explained in Example 3 is is not desirable. It is necessary to ensure progress but this is not sufficient to conclude that the protocol is making *effective* progress.

Definition 6. A cycle in a protocol refers to a non-empty sequence of states that start and end at equivalent states. A cycle can be formalized by the content of the beginning and ending states. That is, an execution sequence is a cycle if: $\exists t, t', t'' \in T : (s(t) \equiv s(t')) \wedge (t < t'' < t') \wedge (s(t) \not\equiv s(t''))$.

Definition 7. An infinitely repeating cycle is a cycle with progressing states such that if the protocol gets on to one of the states then the only possible next transition is to move to a state in the cycle [4].

In Example 3, the two delegate actions form an infinitely repeating cycle. Once the protocol gets into either state 2 or state 3, it will always remain in one of these two states.

Lemma 2. An infinitely repeating cycle does not contain any proper end-states.

Proof. By Definition 7 an infinitely repeating cycle only contains progressing states and by Definition 4, a progressing state cannot be an end-state.

Given a cycle, it is easy to check if it is infinitely repeating. Informally, for each state in the cycle, we need to check if there is a possible transition that can cause a state outside the cycle. This can be achieved by applying all allowed operations (by the proposition) to the commitments that exist in that state. As soon as applying a commitment operation to a state in the cycle yields a state not included in the cycle, the procedure stops, concluding that the cycle is not infinitely repeating.

Lemma 3. Let l be a cycle. Let $c \in CS$ be a commitment that holds at a state $s(t)$ on this cycle at any time t. If discharge, cancel or release $\in O(c)$ then cycle l is not infinitely repeating.

Proof. A cycle is not infinitely repeating if there is a path from a state in the cycle to a state outside the cycle. Discharging, canceling, or releasing a commitment will lead the protocol to go to a proper end-state. Since no proper end-state is on an infinitely repeating cycle, the cycle will not repeat (Lemma 2).

Example 4. In Example 3, if either participant could discharge the commitment or could have been released from the commitment, then there need not have been an infinitely repeating cycle.

Definition 8. A protocol $\mathcal{P}$ is *effectively progressive* if and only if and only if (1) $\mathcal{P}$ is progressive and (2) $\mathcal{P}$ does not have infinitely repeating cycles.

Theorem 1. $\mathcal{P}$ is an effectively progressive protocol if for any commitment $c \in CS$ either (1) discharge $\in O(c)$ or cancel $\in O(c)$ or release $\in O(c)$ or (2) by applying finite number of operations a commitment c' is reached for which discharge $\in O(c')$ or cancel $\in O(c')$ or release $\in O(c')$.

Proof. In both cases, for all commitments in $\mathcal{P}$, there is at least one operation defined. Hence, by Lemma 1, $\mathcal{P}$ is progressive. Assume that $\mathcal{P}$ has an infinite cycle. By Lemma 3, there has to be a commitment c'' holding in some state on the cycle for which none of the operations lead to a state with discharge, cancel, or release operators. Since $\mathcal{P}$ does not allow such a state, $\mathcal{P}$ does not contain an infinitely repeating cycles.

Example 5. The protocol P contains three actions: accept a proposal (create (acceptProposal, participant, C(participant, manager, proposal))), authorize a subcontractor to carry out the proposal (delegate(authorize, participant, subcontractor, C(participant, manager, proposal))), and carry out the proposal (discharge(carryOut, subcontractor, C(subcontractor, manager, proposal))).

The protocol in Example 5 is effectively progressive since the commitment C(participant, manager, proposal) can be delegated to someone who can apply one of the discharge, cancel, or release operations. An algorithm that checks for an effectively progressive protocol is given in Section 6.

5   Protocol Consistency

In Section 4 we have defined the requirements to guarantee that a protocol can effectively progress. However, in addition to effective progress, a protocol should always preserve a consistent computation. In other words, a protocol that functions correctly does not allow creation of conflicting information. Following the CNP example, a participant cannot both refuse to send a proposal and send a proposal at the same time. That is, the available information that is created by the protocol should be consistent at every time point of the protocol. To explain the consistency requirements for a commitment protocol, we again start with studying individual states. Since each state is defined in terms of holding commitments and propositions, we start by defining when the commitments and propositions are inconsistent.

Definition 9. Let p and r be two propositions such that $p, r \in PS$. If p entails the negation of r, that is, false$\leftarrow HoldsAt(p, t) \wedge HoldsAt(r, t)$ then p and r are *conflicting*. A protocol state $s(t)$ is *consistent* if $s(t) \not\equiv$ false.

Obviously, the protocol should never enter an inconsistent state. The set of operations defined for a commitment should ensure that only consistent states are realized. Notice that we allow two base-level commitments to exist together even if the propositions that need to be brought out by these commitments are conflicting. That is, a state could contain two commitments $C(x, y, p)$ and $C(x, y, r)$ such that p and r are conflicting. Obviously, both commitments cannot be satisfied simultaneously. Hence, discharging one commitment restricts the discharging of the second commitment.

Definition 10. A protocol $\mathcal{P}$ is *consistent* if and only if $\mathcal{P}$ is progressive and each possible state in the protocol is consistent.

Lemma 4. Let $\mathcal{P}$ be a commitment protocol and c and c' be two base-level commitments in CS such that c and c' have conflicting propositions. If $O(c) = O(c') = \{$discharge$\}$, then $\mathcal{P}$ is not consistent.

Proof. Let $C(x, y, p)$ and $C(x, y, r)$ be any two commitments in CS with conflicting propositions. If either of them is not discharged, then the protocol state will contain a base-level commitment. By Definition 3, it will not be a proper end-state. If both of them discharge, the protocol will move to the false state. Thus, by Definition 10, it will not be consistent.

Theorem 2. Let $\mathcal{P}$ be an effectively progressive commitment protocol, and c and c' be two base-level commitments in CS with conflicting propositions. If either release$\in O(c')$ or cancel$\in O(c')$ then $\mathcal{P}$ is consistent.

Proof. If discharge $\notin O(c)$, then $\mathcal{P}$ can never move into the false state and hence will be consistent. If discharge $\in O(c)$, by Lemma 4, c' needs to define an operation other that discharge to avoid the false state. By Theorem 1, commitment c' should define at least one of discharge, release, or cancel. Since discharge is eliminated by Lemma 4, at least release, or cancel should be defined.

Example 6. Assume that a participant commits to send a proposal and at the same time refuses to send a proposal (commits not to send a proposal). Then the participant will not be able to discharge both of its commitments. On the other hand, if the participant can cancel one of its commitment or if the manager releases the participant from one of them, then the protocol can continue consistently.

6 Algorithms

The results of the previous sections can be implemented in a design tool. This section provides algorithms to compute the derived correctness and consistency requirements of Theorems 1 and 2.

A commitment graph $G = (V, E)$ consists of a set of nodes V and a set of edges E. Each node denotes a single possible base-level commitment in a given protocol. A directed edge between node u to v denotes an operation applied on the commitment at node u, yielding node v. A commitment graph contains two designated nodes, namely RC and D. These nodes do not contain any commitments. RC is used as a sink node for all commitments for which a release or a cancel operation is defined. In other words, if a node u is connected to node RC then the operation on edge (u, RC) could only be a release or a cancel operation (since these operations resolve the commitment, and do not create other commitments). Similarly, node D is a sink node for commitments for which discharge is defined. If a node u is connected to node D then the operation on edge (u, D) could only be a discharge. If there is an edge (u, v) such that v is not the RC or the D node, then the operation associated with the edge is either a delegate or an assign.

Algorithm 1 takes as input the base-level commitment set CS and operations set O and builds a commitment graph. The algorithm starts by creating the RC and the D nodes. Then, the algorithm iterates over the set of possible commitments that can be created by the protocols ($possible - commitments$) and adds a new node for each commitment. After adding a node for a commitment, it goes through the operations set of the commitment and adds an edge between the node and the RC state for cancel and release operations and an edge between the node and the D state for discharge operation. If there is an assign or a delegate operation, the algorithm applies the operation on the commitment and creates a new node with the resulting commitment. The resulting commitment corresponds to the initiated commitment as explained in Section 2.2. The new commitment is added to the set of possible commitments.

We assume that the graph contains a standard adjacency matrix that can determine if a node has an edge to another node. In the commitment graph, this shows whether applying a single action can transform the commitment either to another commitment or lead it to one of the discharge, cancel, or release states. The $adjacentTo$ method serves this purpose. If a commitment node has at least one outgoing edge, then the commitment is said to have a neighbor (i.e., $hasNeighbors()$ method is true).

Algorithm 1. Build-commitment-graph(CS: Set of base-level commitments; O: Set of operations on base-level commitments)

```
 1:  Create a new node RC {RC stands for a sink node for release and cancel}
 2:  Create a new node D {D stands for a sink node for discharge}
 3:  possible-commitments = CS
 4:  while (possible-commitments ! = ∅) do
 5:     Remove a commitment c
 6:     Add a new node c to V
 7:     for i = 1 to |O(c)| do
 8:        if (O(c)[i] == delegate) then
 9:           Add a new node c.delegate to V
10:           Add (c, c.delegate) to E
11:           Add c.delegate to possible-commitments
12:        else if (O(c)[i] == assign) then
13:           Add a new node c.assign to V
14:           Add (c, c.assign) to E
15:           Add c.assign to possible-commitments
16:        else if (O(c)[i] == release) || (O(c)[i] == cancel) then
17:           Add (c, RC) to E
18:        else if (O(c)[i] == discharge) then
19:           Add (c, D) to E
20:        end if
21:     end for
22:  end while
```

Algorithm 2. Color-graph(G:Commitment Graph)

```
 1:  visited = ∅
 2:  whiteList = ∅
 3:  blackList = ∅
 4:  for i = 1 to |V| do
 5:     if (V(i) ∉ visited) then
 6:        visit(V(i))
 7:     end if
 8:  end for
```

Algorithm 2 checks if all the commitments in the commitment graph can be resolved. To do this, it functions like a search algorithm. Algorithm 2 takes as input a commitment graph and visits each node (with Algorithm 3) to color each node. If a node satisfies the properties in Theorem 1, then it is colored white, if not black. The algorithm terminates when all nodes are colored.

Algorithm 3 takes as input the node u that will be visited, goes through the nodes as in depth first search (DFS), and assigns a color. White nodes are stored in the $whiteList$ and the black nodes are stored in the $blackList$. All visited nodes are stored in the $visited$ set. Initially, nodes do not have any color. The node u is first added to the $visited$ set.

If u does not have any outgoing edges, then it is a singleton in the graph and is not connected to the rest of the graph. Hence, the commitment has no operations defined

---

Algorithm 3. visit(u: node)

1: Add u to $visited$
2: **if** (u.adjacentTo(D OR CR)) **then**
3:     Add u to $whiteList$
4: **else if** (u.hasNeighbors()) **then**
5:     **while** ($u \notin whiteList$) AND ($\exists E(u,v)$: $v \notin visited$) **do**
6:         **if** ($v \notin$ visited) **then**
7:             visit(v)
8:         **end if**
9:         **if** ($v \in whitelist$) **then**
10:            Add u to $whiteList$
11:        **else**
12:            Add u to $blackList$
13:        **end if**
14:    **end while**
15: **else**
16:    Add u to $blackList$
17: **end if**

---

and thus cannot be resolved. Such nodes are labeled as black and put into $blackList$. If the commitment at node u has one of the discharge, cancel, or release operations defined (there is an edge between u and RC or u and D), then the color of the node u becomes white. This means that the protocol allows commitment node u to be resolved.

Otherwise, the neighbors of the node u are analyzed. If any one neighbor node v is already white, then u is also labeled as white. The intuition is that if the commitment at v can be resolved and if the commitment at u can be transformed (by delegate or assign) to v, then v can be resolved, too. If no neighbor node is already white, then the algorithm visits neighbor nodes that are not already visited. The aim is to find a directed path from the current node to a white node. When a white node is found, then all nodes on the path become white and are inserted into $whiteList$. If a white node cannot be reached by a directed path, then all nodes on the path become black and are added to the $blackList$. Algorithms 2 and 3 are a variant of DFS and thus computes the set of unresolvable commitments in $O(|E|)$ [18]. The protocol designer can modify the protocol until the $blackList$ computed by this algorithm is empty.

Algorithm 4. Check-consistency(G: Commitment Graph)

1: $inconsistentList=\emptyset$
2: **for** $i = 1$ to $|V|$-1 **do**
3:     **for** $j = i + 1$ to $|V|$ **do**
4:         Determine if $V(i)$ and $V(j)$ are conflicting
5:         **if** conflicting($V(i)$ and $V(j)$) **then**
6:             **if** ($\nexists E(V(i), RC)$) AND ($\nexists E(V(j), RC)$) **then**
7:                 Add $V(i)$ and $V(j)$ to $inconsistentList$
8:             **end if**
9:         **end if**
10:    **end for**
11: **end for**

Algorithm 4 checks the protocol consistency (Theorem 2). The algorithm compares all commitments to each other to see if they have conflicting propositions. If so, the algorithm checks if either of the commitments can be released or canceled.

The $inconsistentList$ keeps the pairs of commitments that fail the test. Algorithm 4 computes the set of inconsistent commitments in $O(|V|^2)$. After this set is computed, a protocol designer can modify the protocol until the set of inconsistent commitments is empty.

7   Discussion

This work derives some design-time requirements for commitment protocols. These requirements are concerned with allowing sufficient actions for agents to carry out their actions. However note that we are not concerned about the choices of the agents in terms of which actions to take. Looking back at Example 3, assume that agent x could also execute an action that could discharge its commitment (to carry out the proposal), but choose instead to delegate it to agent z. The protocol then would still loop infinitely. However, our purpose here is to make sure that agent x has the choice of discharging. The protocol should allow an agent to terminate its commitment by providing at least one appropriate action. It is then up to the agent to either terminate it or delegate it as

The algorithms given in Section 6 can be implemented in a design tool. The design tool should be fed with a description of the protocol, which contains the actions and the commitment operation each action corresponds to as specified in Section 3. The commitment and operation set of the protocol can then be easily formed and fed into Algorithm 1 for creating a commitment graph. Once, there is a commitment graph both Algorithms 2 and 4 can be applied to check correctness and consistency, respectively.

We review the recent literature with respect to our work. Fornara and Colombetti develop a method for agent communication, where the meanings of messages denote commitments [10]. In addition to base-level and conditional commitments, Fornara and Colombetti use precommitments to represent a request for a commitment from a second party. They model the life cycle of commitments in the system through update rules. However, they do not provide design requirements on correctness or consistency as we have done here. The requirements and algorithms developed here can easily be applied to their framework.

Artikis *et al.* develop a framework to specify and animate computational societies [19]. The specification of a society defines the social constraints, social roles, and social states. Social constraints define types of actions and the enforcement policies for these actions. A social state denotes the global state of a society based on the state of the environment, observable states of the involved agents, and states of the institutions. Our definition of a protocol state is similar to the global state of Artikis *et al.*. The framework of Artikis *et al.* does not specify any design rules to establish the correctness of the executed societies. It would be interesting to apply the design ideas here to their setting where in addition there are social constraints.

Dignum *et al.* formalize interaction protocols within an organization through contracts [20]. They develop a language for specifying contracts that can capture various contracts and their deadlines. They use the interaction protocols to realize the objectives of the organization that the agents are situated in. However, they do not provide a methodology for analyzing contracts defined in that language as we have done here.

Alberti *et al.* specify interaction protocols using social integrity constraints [9]. Given a partial set of events that have happened, each agent computes a set of expectations based on the social integrity constraints; e.g., events that are expected to happen based on the given constraints. If an agent executes an event that does not respect an expectation, then it is assumed to have violated one of the social integrity constraints. We have studied the violating of commitments in richer time structure elsewhere [21]. Alberti *et al.* does not provide any design rules to ensure the correctness of their interaction protocols. Since the commitments and their operations are more flexible than the expectations defined by Alberti *et al.*, our requirements can also be applied to their framework.

Endriss *et al.* study protocol conformance for interaction protocols that are defined as deterministic finite automaton (DFA) [22]. The set of transitions of a DFA are known *a priori*. If an agent always follows the transitions of the protocol, then it is compliant to the given protocol. Hence, the compliance checking can be viewed as verifying that the transitions of the protocol are followed correctly.

McBurney and Parsons propose posit spaces protocol to handle e-commerce transactions of agents [6]. The protocol consists of five locutions: propose, accept, delete, suggest_revoke, and ratify_revoke. The usage of propose and accept locution resembles the conditional commitments in commitment protocols. The delete locution corresponds to the release, or discharge operation. Suggest_revoke and ratify_revoke enable canceling of posits. McBurney and Parsons do not provide any design rules to develop posit space protocols as we have done here. The analysis constructed in this paper may be applied in the posit space framework.

In our future work, we plan to work on other design criteria for commitment protocols, such as requirements for avoiding possible deadlocks as well as requirements for conditional commitments.

References

1. Yolum, P.: Towards design tools for protocol development. In: Proceedings of the 4th International Joint Conference on Autonomous Agents and MultiAgent Systems (AAMAS), ACM Press (2005) 99–105
2. Huget, M.P., Koning, J.L.: Requirement analysis for interaction protocols. In: Proceedings of the Central and Eastern European Conference on Multiagent Systems (CEEMAS). Volume LNAI 2691., Springer-Verlag (2003) 404–412
3. Jennings, N.R.: On agent-based software engineering. Artificial Intelligence **177** (2000) 277–296
4. Holzmann, G.J.: Design and Validation of Computer Protocols. Prentice-Hall, New Jersey (1991)
5. Gouda, M.G.: Protocol verification made simple: a tutorial. Computer Networks and ISDN Systems **25** (1993) 969–980
6. McBurney, P., Parsons, S.: Posit spaces: A performative model of e-commerce. In: Proceedings of the 2nd International Joint Conference on Autonomous Agents and MultiAgent Systems (AAMAS), ACM Press (2003) 624–631

7. Bentahar, J., Moulin, B., Meyer, J.J.C., Chaib-draa, B.: A logical model for commitment and argument network for agent communication. In: Proceedings of the 3rd International Joint Conference on Autonomous Agents and MultiAgent Systems (AAMAS), ACM Press (2004) 792–799

8. Yolum, P., Singh, M.P.: Flexible protocol specification and execution: Applying event calculus planning using commitments. In: Proceedings of the 1st International Joint Conference on Autonomous Agents and MultiAgent Systems (AAMAS), ACM Press (2002) 527–534

9. Alberti, M., Daolio, D., Torroni, P.: Specification and verification of agent interaction protocols in a logic-based system. In: Proceedings of the ACM Symposium on Applied Computing (SAC), ACM Press (2004) 72–78

10. Fornara, N., Colombetti, M.: Operational specification of a commitment-based agent communication language. In: Proceedings of the 1st International Joint Conference on Autonomous Agents and MultiAgent Systems (AAMAS), ACM Press (2002) 535–542

11. Yolum, P., Singh, M.P.: Reasoning about commitments in the event calculus: An approach for specifying and executing protocols. Annals of Mathematics and Artificial Intelligence **42** (2004) 227–253

12. Venkatraman, M., Singh, M.P.: Verifying compliance with commitment protocols: Enabling open Web-based multiagent systems. Autonomous Agents and Multi-Agent Systems **2** (1999) 217–236

13. Kowalski, R., Sergot, M.J.: A logic-based calculus of events. New Generation Computing **4** (1986) 67–95

14. Shanahan, M.: Solving the Frame Problem: A Mathematical Investigation of the Common Sense Law of Inertia. MIT Press, Cambridge (1997)

15. Castelfranchi, C.: Commitments: From individual intentions to groups and organizations. In: Proceedings of the International Conference on Multiagent Systems. (1995) 41–48

16. Singh, M.P.: An ontology for commitments in multiagent systems: Toward a unification of normative concepts. Artificial Intelligence and Law **7** (1999) 97–113

17. for Intelligent Physical Agents (FIPA), F.: Contract net interaction protocol specification (2002) Number 00029.

18. Cormen, T.H., Leiserson, C.E., Rivest, R.: Design and Analysis of Algorithms. MIT Press (1990)

19. Artikis, A., Pitt, J., Sergot, M.: Animated specifications of computational societies. In: Proceedings of the 1st International Joint Conference on Autonomous Agents and MultiAgent Systems (AAMAS), ACM Press (2002) 1053–1061

20. Dignum, V., Meyer, J.J., Dignum, F., HansWeigand: Formal specification of interaction in agent societies. In: 2nd Goddard Workshop on Formal Approaches to Agent-Based Systems (FAABS), Maryland (2002)

21. Mallya, A.U., Yolum, P., Singh, M.P.: Resolving commitments among autonomous agents. In Huget, M.P., Dignum, F., eds.: Proceedings of the AAMAS Workshop on Agent Communication Languages and Conversation Policies, LNAI 2922, Springer Verlag (2003) 166–182

22. Endriss, U., Maudet, N., Sadri, F., Toni, F.: Protocol conformance for logic-based agents. In: Proceedings of the International Joint Conference on Artificial Intelligence (IJCAI), Morgan Kaufmann Publishers (2003) 679–684

Adaptiveness in Agent Communication: Application and Adaptation of Conversation Patterns

Felix Fischer[1,3], Michael Rovatsos[2], and Gerhard Weiss[3]

[1] Department of Informatics, University of Munich, 80538 Munich, Germany
fischerf@tcs.ifi.lmu.de
[2] School of Informatics, University of Edinburgh, Edinburgh EH8 9LE, UK
mrovatso@inf.ed.ac.uk
[3] Department of Informatics, Technical University of Munich, 85748 Garching, Germany
weissg@in.tum.de

Abstract. Communication in multi-agent systems (MASs) is usually governed by agent communication languages (ACLs) and communication protocols carrying a clear cut semantics. With an increasing degree of *openness*, however, the need arises for more flexible models of communication that can handle the uncertainty associated with the fact that adherence to a supposedly agreed specification of possible conversations cannot be ensured on the side of other agents.

In this paper, we argue for *adaptiveness* in agent communication. We present a particular approach that combines *conversation patterns* as a generic way of describing the available means of communication in a MAS with a decision-theoretic framework and various different machine learning techniques for *applying* these patterns in and *adapting* them from actual conversations.

1   Introduction

Traditional approaches to agent communication, with their roots in speech act theory [1], do not respect the *autonomy* of individual agents in that they suppose effects of communication on agent's mental states [25,3] or a normative quality of publicly visible commitments [7,26]. In environments involving some degree of *openness* like, for example, design heterogeneity or dynamically changing populations, such a "normative" attitude is put into question by the fact that adherence to supposedly agreed modes of communication cannot be ensured on the side of other agents. While this can be seen as a witness of a fundamental conflict between agent autonomy and the need for cooperation (and communication) with other agents toward a joint goal, there is also a more practical side to this problem.

Compared to the long-established areas of interaction protocol and agent communication language (ACL) research (see, e.g., [12,9]), the development of agent architectures suitable for dealing with provided communication mechanisms in practical terms has received fairly little attention. As yet, there exists no uniform framework for defining the interface between the inter-agent communication layer and intra-agent reasoning, i.e. how specifications of interaction protocols and communication semantics influence agent rationality or, in turn, are influenced themselves by agents' rational decision-making processes. Moreover, there is a growing concern that most specification methods for ACLs and interaction protocols do not provide sufficient guidance as

F. Dignum, R. van Eijk, and R. Flores (Eds.): AC 2005/2006, LNAI 3859, pp. 211–226, 2006.

to which part of the semantics of communication should be specified at a supra-agent level and which part of them is only a result of agents' mental processing and cannot be captured without knowledge of their internal design. Clearly, concentrating on one of these two sides may either overly constrain agent autonomy (i.e., agents would merely "execute" centralised communication procedures that modify their internal states) or lead to uncertainty about the consequences of communication (e.g. in terms of adherence to previously created commitments) and loss of social structure altogether. This poses two central questions:

1. If strict adherence to communication languages and protocols cannot be taken for granted, how can meaningful and coherent communication be ensured?
2. Observing the course of conversations that take place in a MAS, how can agents effectively organise this kind of knowledge and relate it to existing specifications, so that they can actually benefit from it?

An obvious answer to these questions would be to devise a *probabilistic* model of agent conversation, and update it in order to maximise communicative success. There are two problems, though. Firstly, generic "purely" probabilistic models are not very well suited to describe intelligent agents (including symbolic agent communication), since their behaviour is not at all "random". Instead, one would rather like to identify patterns and relational properties of communication (like communication protocols containing variables, for example). The resulting view resembles decision-theoretic learning and reasoning, where the classical paradigm of direct control exerted on an uncertain environment is replaced by a more indirect influence via communication between (and hence via the allegedly rational reasoning processes of) intelligent agents. Secondly, agent communication cannot exist on its own, but is only a means to the end of coordinating or cooperating with respect to some "physical" actions (i.e., communication works as a kind of mediator between actions). Hence, success (or optimality) in communication will somehow have to be defined in terms of the actions it entails.

This view is in line with *empirical communication semantics* [21], where the meaning of an utterance (or sequence thereof) is defined solely in terms of its expected consequences as given by past experience (to say it in terms of speech act theory [1], the meaning of illocutions is defined solely in terms of their expected perlocutions). Currently two different "flavours" of empirical communication semantics exist, borrowing from two different sociological schools of thought. Interaction frames [23] view empirical semantics from the perspective of symbolic interactionism (particularly [8]), thus focusing on how an individual deals with the communication mechanisms available in a given social system, while expectation networks [14] take the (more global) point of view of social systems theory (see, e.g., [13]) to develop methods to analyse the evolving semantics of communication across an entire society of agents.

In this paper, we focus on a particular instance of the interaction frame approach, which is formally defined in section 2. In section 3, we introduce a formal framework for decision-theoretic reasoning about communication, using interaction frames to represent different classes of conversation and thus to structure the reasoning process hierarchically. In section 4, we further use methods from the fields of case-based reasoning, inductive logic programming and cluster analysis to devise a formal scheme for the adaptation of interaction frames from the actual conversations conducted in a MAS, enabling agents to autonomously (i.e., independent of users and system designers) create and maintain a concise model of the different classes of conversation on the basis of an initial set of ACL and protocol specifications. To our knowledge, the work described in this paper constitutes the first approach to adaptive communication management for deliberative, knowledge-based agents, which is an important prerequisite for building agents that communicate and act in full appreciation of the autonomy of their respective peer.

2 Conversation Patterns

The greatest common denominator of the multitude of different methods for specifying ACL semantics and interaction protocols (see, e.g., [15,27] for examples in this volume) is that they describe the *surface structure* of possible dialogues and logical *constraints* for the applicability of these. The former corresponds to a set of admissible message sequences, the latter may include statements about environmental conditions, mental states of the participating agents, the state of commitment stores, etc. In the most simplistic case, these structure/constraint pairs can be represented as a set of *conversation patterns*, i.e. combinations of a conversation trace and a set of conditions. For example,

$$\langle \texttt{request}(\texttt{a},\texttt{b},\texttt{pay}(\$100)) \rightarrow \texttt{do}(\texttt{b},\texttt{pay}(\$100)), \{can(\texttt{b},\texttt{pay}(\$100))\} \rangle$$

expresses that a request of agent a is followed by an action if the requestee b is able to execute the action, i.e. pay a an amount of \$100. The question serving as a point of departure for the research presented in this paper is how we can build agents that are capable of processing a set of such (conditioned) conversation patterns in a goal-oriented and adaptive fashion, given that the reliability of these specification is contingent on others' (and the agent's own) adherence to their prescriptive content.

Before turning to practical reasoning with and adaptation of conversation patterns, though, we introduce interactions frames as a slightly more complex form of conversation pattern, quoting [4] for a formal definition of a particular instance of the interaction frame data structure. This definition uses a language $\mathcal{M}$ of speech-act [1] like message and action patterns of the form $\texttt{perf}(A,B,X)$ or $\texttt{do}(A,Ac)$. In the case of messages (i.e., exchanged textual signals), $\texttt{perf}$ is a performative symbol (e.g. $\texttt{request}$, $\texttt{inform}$), A and B are agent identifiers or agent variables and X is the content of the message taken from a first-order language $\mathcal{L}$. In the case of physical actions (i.e., actions that manipulate the physical environment) with the pseudo-performative $\texttt{do}$, Ac is the action executed by A (a physical action has no recipient as it is assumed to be observable by any agent in the system). Both X and Ac may contain non-logical substitution variables used for generalisation purposes (as opposed to logical "content" variables used by agents to indicate quantification or to ask for a valid binding). We further use $\mathcal{M}_c \subset \mathcal{M}$ to denote the language of "concrete" messages that agents use in communication (and that do not contain variables other than content variables). Frames are then defined as follows:

Definition 1 (Interaction frame). *An* interaction frame *is a tuple* $F = (T, \Theta, C, h_T, h_\Theta)$, *where*

- $T = \langle p_1, p_2, \ldots, p_n \rangle$ *is a sequence of message and action patterns* $p_i \in \mathcal{M}$, *the* trajectory,
- $\Theta = \langle \vartheta_1, \ldots, \vartheta_m \rangle$ *is an ordered list of* variable substitutions,
- $C = \langle c_1, \ldots, c_m \rangle$ *is an ordered list of* condition sets, *such that* $c_j \in 2^L$ *is the condition set relevant under substitution* ϑ_j,
- $h_T \in \mathbb{N}^{|T|}$ *is a* trajectory occurrence counter *list counting the occurrence of each prefix of the trajectory* T *in previous conversations, and*
- $h_\Theta \in \mathbb{N}^{|\Theta|}$ *is a* substitution occurrence counter *list counting the occurrence of each member of the substitution list* Θ *in previous conversations.*

While the trajectory $T(F)$ models the surface structure of message sequences that are admissible according to frame F, each element of $\Theta(F)$ resembles a past binding of the variables in $T(F)$, and the corresponding element of $C(F)$ lists the conditions required for or precipitated by the execution of F in this particular case. $h_T(F)$ finally indicates how often F has been executed completely or just in part, $h_\Theta(F)$ is used to avoid duplicates in $\Theta(F)$ and $C(F)$. What hence distinguishes interaction frames from the methods commonly used for the specification of ACL and protocol semantics is that they allow for an explicit representation of *experience* regarding their practical use.

The semantics of frames has been defined accordingly as a probability distribution over the possible continuations of an interaction that has started with $w \in \mathcal{M}_c$ and is computed by summing up over a set $\mathcal{F}$ of known frames:

$$P(w'|w) = \sum_{\substack{F \in \mathcal{F} \\ ww' = T(F)\vartheta}} P(\vartheta|F, w)P(F|w) \qquad (1)$$

This equation views $\mathcal{F}$ as a compact yet concise representation of the interactions that have taken place so far and projects past regularities into the future. This global view, however, will hardly be computationally feasible in realistic domains, and it also contradicts the way conversation patterns are used in practice. One would rather expect different protocols for different purposes, and not all of them need to be reasoned over at the same time while engaging in a particular kind of interaction.

In the following section, we will instead introduce a framework for conducting decision-theoretic reasoning about frame selection, as well as action selection within a single frame. For this hierarchical approach to be reasonable as well as successful, it is required that the different frames concisely capture the different classes of conversations that can take place. This requirement has to hold as well for frames used by external observers to model, analyse or describe the interactions in a MAS. Particular emphasis will hence have to be put on the acquisition and adaptation of communication patterns from the actual interactions in a MAS, such that the resulting set of patterns corresponds to the different classes of interactions as perceived by the agent or external observer. Methods for the adaptation of interaction frames will be explored in section 4.

3   Reasoning with Conversation Patterns

The distinguishing feature of interaction frames as compared to (the methods commonly used for the specification of) interaction protocols is their ability to capture instance information, i.e. information about how particular conversation patterns have been used in the past according to the agent's experience. This additional information provides agents with a facility to reason about the semantics of communication in an adaptive fashion. In accordance with the empirical semantics view that considers the meaning of communication as a function of its consequences as experienced through the eyes of a subjective observer, agents can adapt existing frame conceptions with new observations of encounters and project past regularities into the future. In *open systems*, in which agents may or may not obey a set of pre-defined conversation patterns, this can be expected to improve agents' communication abilities significantly, particularly with respect to a strategic use of communication.

3.1 Frame Semantics

To gain deeper insight into adaptive agent communication in general and reasoning about communication patterns in particular, we will now take a procedural view on the probabilistic semantics of interaction frames defined by equation 1.

The semantics of a set $\mathcal{F} = \{F_1, \ldots, F_n\}$ of frames is as follows: Given an *encounter prefix* $w \in \mathcal{M}_c^*$, i.e. a sequence of messages already uttered in the current encounter (possibly the empty sequence) and a *knowledge base* $KB \in 2^L$ of beliefs currently held by the reasoning agent[1], $\mathcal{F}$ defines a set of possible *continuations* $w' \in \mathcal{M}_c^*$, which can be computed as follows:

1. Filter out those frames whose trajectories do not prefix-match w.
2. For each remaining frame F, consider the possible postfixes of $T(F)$ for prefix w, each of them corresponding to a particular variable substitution (where w has already committed certain variables to concrete values).
3. Only consider those substitutions for which at least one of the context conditions in $C(F)$ is satisfied under KB.

For each of these possible continuations, we can then compute a *continuation probability* by virtue of similarity, frequency and relevance considerations. The resulting probability distribution over continuations w' is the *semantics* of w under $\mathcal{F}$.

Definition 2. *Let* $\vartheta_f(F, w) = unifier(w, T(F)[1{:}|w|])$ *be the most general unifier of w and the corresponding trajectory prefix* $T(F)[1{:}|w|]$ *of F. Then, the* set of possible substitutions *under frame F, beliefs KB, and conversation prefix w is defined as*

$$\Theta_{poss}(F, KB, w) = \left\{ \vartheta \,\middle|\, \exists \vartheta'.\vartheta = \vartheta_f(F, w)\vartheta' \wedge \exists i.KB \models C[i]\vartheta \right\}.$$

In this definition, *unifier*(v, w) denotes the most general unifier of two message pattern sequences v and w, $S\vartheta$ denotes application of substitution ϑ to a (set or list of) logical formula(e) or message(s) S (depending on the context). In other words, Θ_{poss} is the set of substitutions that are extensions of ϑ_f for which at least one condition in $C(F)$ is satisfied. Accordingly, the continuations w' of w that should be expected to occur with

---

[1] In equation 1, the agent's knowledge is implicit in the terms $P(\vartheta|F, w)$ and $P(F|w)$. More precisely, we could have written $P(\vartheta|F, w, KB)$ and $P(F|w, KB)$. For notational convenience, we further assume that knowledge bases use the same logical language as is used in the content language of messages.

non-zero probability (according to F and under KB) are exactly those that result from the application of a substitution in Θ_{poss} to the postfix of $T(F)$.

In order to conduct (quantitative) decision-theoretic reasoning about frames, however, the exact quantities of the probabilities $P(\vartheta|F,w)$ have to be determined. In order to obtain well-defined probabilities even for substitutions ϑ that have never occurred before in actual interactions, we avail ourselves of a method commonly used in the area of *case-based reasoning* [11]. Starting from a *similarity measure* σ defined on message pattern sequences, we compute the similarity of any possible substitution to a frame by taking into account the frequencies of previous cases and the relevance of their corresponding condition sets in a single frame.

Definition 3. *Let* $\sigma : \mathcal{M}^* \times \mathcal{M}^* \to [0,1]$ *be a similarity measure on message pattern sequences. Let* $c_i(F,\vartheta,KB)$ *denote the relevance of the ith condition of F under* ϑ *and KB. Then, the similarity of substitution* ϑ *to frame F is defined as*

$$\sigma(\vartheta,F) = \sum_{i=1}^{|\Theta(F)|} \left(\overbrace{\sigma(T(F)\vartheta, T(F)\Theta(F)[i])}^{similarity} \cdot \overbrace{h_\Theta(F)[i]}^{frequency} \cdot \overbrace{c_i(F,\vartheta,KB)}^{relevance} \right)$$

In other words, $\sigma(\vartheta,F)$ assesses to which extent ϑ is "applicable" to F. Definition 4 in section 4.1 will introduce a distance metric d_* on the set $\mathcal{M}_c^*$ of finite-length message sequences, such that $d_*(v,w)$ is the distance between message sequences v and w. Using this metric, we can define $\sigma(v,w) = 1 - d_*(v,w)$. A possible way to define c_i would be to let $c_i(F,\vartheta,KB) = 1$ if $KB \models C(F)[i]\vartheta$ and 0 otherwise, such that only those substitutions of F contribute to the similarity whose corresponding conditions are satisfied under ϑ and under current belief KB.

The conditional probability $P(\vartheta|F,w)$ in equation 1 can be computed by assigning a probability

$$P(\vartheta|F,w) \propto \sigma(\vartheta,F) \qquad (2)$$

to all $\vartheta \in \Theta_{poss}(F,KB,w)$ and a probability of zero to any other substitution. $P(F|w)$ simply corresponds to the number $h_T(F)[|h_T(F)|]$ of successful completions of F normalised over all frames that prefix-match w.

3.2   Decision Making with Frames

In the introductory section, we have argued for the integration of agent communication with decision-theoretic reasoning, by which agents strive for long-term maximisation of expected utility. We hence assume that agents are equipped with a *utility function* $u : \mathcal{M}_c^* \times 2^L \to \mathbb{R}$, such that $u(w,KB)$ denotes the utility associated with executing a message (and action) sequence w in belief state KB. As we have pointed out, substantial positive or negative utility can only be assigned to physical actions in the environment (though messages may be given a small negative utility to express the communication cost incurred by them).

In principle, such a utility function could be combined directly with the continuation probabilities of equation 1 to derive utility-maximising decisions in communication. However, it will hardly be feasible to compute the continuation probabilities directly, and this approach would also contradict the role usually played by conversation patterns. As we have said, we will instead use a hierarchical approach based on selecting the appropriate frame for a given situation and then optimising behaviour within this frame. The former activity is referred to as *framing* and will be described in the following section. The latter is standard expected utility maximisation using frames and can be described by the following abstract decision-making procedure:

1. If no encounter is running, consider starting one. If a message m is received, update the encounter prefix: $w \leftarrow wm$.
2. If no frame F has been selected, go to 10.
3. *Validity check:* If $|T(F)| = w$, go to 9; if $unifier(T(F)[1:|w|], w) = \bot$, go to 10.
4. *Adequacy check:* If $\Theta_{poss}(F, w, KB) = \emptyset$, go to 10
5. Compute the expected utility for each *own substitution* ϑ_s:

$$E[u(\vartheta_s, F, w, KB)] = \sum_{\vartheta_p} \left(u\big(postfix(T(F), w)\vartheta_s\vartheta_p, KB\big) \cdot P\big(\vartheta_p | \vartheta_s, F, w\big) \right)$$

6. Determine the optimal substitution $\vartheta^* = \arg\max_{\vartheta_s} E[u(\vartheta_s, F, w, KB)]$.
7. *Desirability check:* If $u(postfix(T(F), w)\vartheta^*\vartheta_p, KB) < b$, go to 10.
8. Perform $m^* = T(F)[|w| + 1]\vartheta^*$; update the encounter prefix: $w \leftarrow wm^*$
9. If no message arrives until deadline, terminate the encounter; go to 1.
10. *Framing:* Select F, go to 3.

The actual (framing) reasoning cycle is bracketed by steps 1 and 9 which cater for initiating encounters and ending them if no more messages are received (i.e., if the other agent does not reply when expected to, and to make sure we heed additional messages sent by the other party after we considered the encounter completed). We assume encounter initiation on the side of the agent to be spawned by some sub-social reasoning layer, e.g. a BDI [19] engine, which determines whether and about what to converse with whom, depending on the possibility of furthering some private goal through interaction.

Steps 3, 4 and 7 are used to evaluate the usefulness of the currently active frame F. The former two cases are straightforward: If the frame has been completed, if it does not match the encounter prefix w, or if $\Theta_{poss}(F, w, KB)$ is empty, F cannot be used any longer. For the latter case, we have to assess the expected utility $E[u(\vartheta_s, F, w, KB)]$ of any "own" substitution ϑ_s. To this end, we have to conduct an adversarial search over substitutions jointly determined by the agent and her peer, as each of the two agents commits certain variables to concrete values in their turn-taking moves. Using definition 3 and equation 2, the probability for an opponent's substitution ϑ_p in the remaining steps of $T(F)$ can be computed as

$$P(\vartheta_p | \vartheta_s, F, w) = \frac{P(\vartheta_p \wedge \vartheta_s | F, w)}{P(\vartheta_s | F, w)} = \frac{\sigma(\vartheta_f(F, w)\vartheta_s\vartheta_p, F)}{\sum_{\vartheta} \sigma(\vartheta_f(F, w)\vartheta_s\vartheta, F)},$$

where $\vartheta_p \wedge \vartheta_s$ denotes the event of the peer choosing ϑ_p and the reasoning agent choosing ϑ_p after having committed to the fixed substitution $\vartheta_f(F, w)$, so that the final "joint" substitution will be $\vartheta_f(F, w)\vartheta_s\vartheta_p$.

With this, u can be used to compute the utility of the postfix of $T(F)$ for prefix w (corresponding to application of $\vartheta_f(F,w)$), with ϑ_p and ϑ_s applied to obtain a ground message (and action) sequence still to be executed along $T(F)$. If the utility of the post-fix under the optimal substitution ϑ^* is below some threshold b, the frame is discarded. Otherwise, the next step m^* along the trajectory of F is performed.

So far, we have said nothing about the process of updating the frame repository $\mathcal{F}$ upon encounter termination (whether after successful completion or failure of selecting an appropriate frame). This will be done in detail in section 4. What now remains to be specified is a search strategy to decide between different candidate frames in step 10. Effectively, it is this search strategy that determines the degree of complexity reduction achieved by restricting the search space to a single active frame while looking for the optimal next message or action.

3.3 Framing

Given that the frames in $\mathcal{F}$ concisely capture the different classes of conversations that can take place in a MAS, *hierarchical reinforcement learning* (HRL) techniques [2] can be used learn an optimal strategy for frame selection. In HRL, actions available in a "generic" Markov Decision Process (MDP) are combined into macro-operators that can be applied over an extended number of decision steps, the general idea being that compound time-extended policies, which (hopefully) optimally solve sub-problems of the original MDP, help to reduce the overall size of the state space. Using such macro-actions, an agent can use S(emi-)MDP (i.e., state history dependent) variants of learning methods such as Q-learning [28] to optimise its long-term "meta"-strategy over these macro-policies.

An intuitive HRL approach that lends itself to an application to interaction frames particularly well is the options framework [17]. In this framework, an *option* is a triple $o = (I, \pi, \beta)$ consisting of an input set $I \subseteq S$ of MDP states, a (stationary, stochastic) policy $\pi : S \times \mathcal{A} \to [0, 1]$ over primitive actions $\mathcal{A}$ and states S, and a stochastic termination condition $\beta : S \to [0, 1]$. Option o is admissible in a state s iff $s \in I$. If invoked, o will behave according to π until it terminates stochastically according to β. This definition can be used to re-interpret interaction frames as options, where π is the (deterministic) strategy defined by determining m^*, and I and β are defined by the validity, adequacy and desirability checks performed during the reasoning process of the previous section.

Let $s : \mathcal{M}_c^* \times 2^L \to S$ be some state abstraction function[2] that returns a state for each pair (w, KB) of perceived encounter prefix w and belief KB. If we regard each frame $F \in \mathcal{F}$ as an option in the above sense, we can apply the SMDP Q-learning update rule

$$Q(s,F) \leftarrow (1-\alpha)Q(s,F) + \alpha \left[\hat{R}(s,F) + \gamma^\tau \max_{F' \in \mathcal{F}} Q(s',F') \right],$$

where $s = s(w, KB)$ and $s' = s(ww', KB')$ are the states resulting from the encounter sequences w and ww' and the corresponding knowledge base contents KB and KB' as perceived between two re-framing decisions, α is an appropriately decreasing learning

---

[2] It is unrealistic to assume that $\mathcal{M}_c^* \times 2^L$ itself could be used as state space due to its unmanageable size.

rate and τ is the number of steps during which F was the active frame (i.e., $\tau = |w'|$). Further, $\hat{R}(s,F)$ is the discounted reward accumulated in steps $t+1, \ldots t + (\tau - 1)$.

Using the long-term utility estimates represented by Q, we can determine the optimal frame to select as

$$F^*(w, KB) = \arg\max_{F \in \mathcal{F}} Q(s(w, KB), F),$$

while applying a "greedy in the limit" infinite exploration strategy to avoid running into local minima. It should be noted that this way of learning a frame selection strategy allows for optimising framing decisions *within* encounters as well as *between* subsequent encounters, at least if there is some utility-relevant connection between them.

4   Adaptation of Conversation Patterns

As we have already said, the need for its acquisition and adaptation from actual interactions is an inherent property of empirical semantics. Using a set of interaction frames for representation, we have further argued that these frames need to model different classes of interactions within a MAS. In particular, this feature is critical with respect to the reasoning framework described in the previous section.

In this section, we will present a method for the adaptation and acquisition of models of empirical semantics using the formalisation of interaction frames given in section 2. For this, we will introduce a metric on the space $\mathcal{M}_c^*$ of finite-length message sequences and then extend it to a metric between frames. This allows us to interpret a frame repository (i.e., a set of known frames) as a (possibly fuzzy) clustering in the "conversation space", and hence to measure the quality of a frame acquisition and adaptation method in terms of the quality of the clustering it produces (referred to as "cluster validity" in [10]). According to this interpretation, adaptation from a new conversation either introduces a new cluster (viz frame) or it adds to an existing one with or without modifying the trajectory of the respective frame. The different alternatives can be judged heuristically in terms of the corresponding cluster validities, which we will use to devise an algorithm for the adaptation of frame repositories. To perform the necessary frame modifications in any of the above cases, we will also present a generic algorithm for merging two frames into one.

Due to lack of space, proofs and examples have largely been omitted from this description. The interested reader is referred to [6] for a more detailed description.

4.1   A Distance Metric on Message Sequences

As a basis of our interpretation of interaction frames as clusters, we will start by introducing a distance metric on the set of possible messages and then extend it to finite-length message sequences. Since messages as defined above are essentially first-order objects, we could simply use a general purpose first-order distance like the one proposed in [24]. In [6], we have instead introduced a family of mappings on messages that are parametrised on two functions d_s and D_s and allow us to add a "semantic" flavour in the form of domain-specific knowledge. The most basic (and domain-independent) instance of this family is in fact a metric on messages (in particular, it satisfies the triangle inequality), and can easily be extended to message sequences.

Definition 4 (Distance between message sequences). *Let* $d : \mathcal{M}_c \times \mathcal{M}_c \rightarrow [0,1]$ *be a mapping on messages with*

$$d(m,n) = \begin{cases} \frac{1}{|m|+1} \sum_{i=1}^{|m|} d(m_i,n_i) & \text{if } \underline{m} = \underline{n} \\ 1 & \text{otherwise.} \end{cases}$$

Further, let $|v|$ *and* v_i *denote the length and ith element of sequence* v. *We define*

$$d_*(v,w) = \begin{cases} \frac{1}{|v|} \sum_{i=1}^{|v|} d(v_i,w_i) & \text{if } |v| = |w| \\ 1 & \text{otherwise.} \end{cases}$$

As we haven shown in [6], d_* is indeed a metric on the set $\mathcal{M}_c^*$ of finite-length message sequences.

4.2 A Metric on Frames

Having defined a metric d_* on the set of finite-length message sequences, we will now extend this metric (a metric on *points*, so to speak) to a metric on frames by interpreting these as sets of the message sequences they represent (i.e., point *sets*).

[18] proposes a general formalism to define a distance metric between finite sets of points in a metric space. The distance between two sets A and B is computed as the weight of the maximal flow minimal weight flow through a special distance network $N[X,d,M,W,A,B]$ between the elements of the two sets.

Definition 5 (Netflow distance). *Let* X *be a set with metric* d *and weighting function* W, M *a constant. Then for all* $A,B \in 2^X$, *the* netflow distance *between* A *and* B *in* X, *denoted* $d_{X,d,M,W}^N(A,B)$, *is defined as the weight of the maximal flow minimal weight flow from s to t in* $N[X,d,M,W,A,B]$.

As further shown in [18], $d_{X,d,M,W}^N(A,B)$ is a metric on 2^X and can be computed in polynomial time (in $size_W(A)$ and $size_W(B)$ and in the time needed to compute the distance between two points) if all weights are integers. Also, this metric is claimed to be much better suited for applications where there is likely a point with a high distance to any other point than, for example, the Hausdorff metric (which only regards the maximum distance of any point in one set to the closest point in the other set).

Additionally, one can assign weights to the elements of A and B in order to alleviate the difference in cardinalities between the two sets. Interpreting (integer) weights as element counts yields a metric on *multisets*, which is ideally suited to measure the distance between interaction frames in which multiple instances of a particular message sequence have been stored (corresponding to a substitution count larger than one). Mapping each frame to the set of messages it represents and weighting each element with the respective substitution count, we directly obtain a metric d_f on frames.

Definition 6 (Distance between frames). *Let*

$$m_f(F) = \{m \in \mathcal{M}_c^* | \exists \vartheta \in \Theta(F). \, m = T(F)\vartheta\}$$

be the set of message sequences stored in frame F. *Let*

$$W(m_f(F))(m) = h_\Theta(F)[i] \text{ iff } m = T(F)\Theta(F)[i]$$

be a weighting function for elements of $m_f(F)$. Then, the distance between two frames *F and G, denoted $d_f(F,G)$, is defined as the maximal flow minimal weight flow from s to t in the transport network $N[\mathcal{M}_c^*, d_*, 1, W, m_f(F), m_f(G)]$.*

As shown in [6], d_f is a metric on the set of frames, and $d_f(F,G)$ can be computed in polynomial time in $\sum_{i<|\Theta(F)|} h_\Theta(F)[i]$, $\sum_{i<|\Theta(G)|} h_\Theta(G)[i]$ and the time required to compute d_*.

4.3 Validity of Frame Modifications

Based on the metrics defined in the previous sections, we can interpret interaction frames as clusters of points in the space of message sequences, which in particular allows us to define the quality of a set of frames as a model for actual interactions in terms of the quality of the corresponding clustering.

[10] refers to this quality as *cluster validity* and defines the validity of a particular cluster as the ratio between its compactness, i.e. average distance between points within this cluster, and its isolation, i.e. minimum distance to any other cluster. Accordingly, we define the compactness and isolation of a frame using the metrics d_* and d_f on message sequences and frames, respectively.

Definition 7 (Frame compactness and isolation). *Let $\mathcal{F}$ be a set of frames, $F \in \mathcal{F}$ a single frame. The* compactness *of F is then defined as the (normalised) average distance between the individual messages stored in it, weighed by their respective occurrence counts:*

$$c(F) = \left(\sum_{i=1}^{|\Theta(F)|} \sum_{j=i+1}^{|\Theta(F)|} h_i \cdot h_j \right)^{-1} \cdot \sum_{i=1}^{|\Theta(F)|} \sum_{j=i+1}^{|\Theta(F)|} h_i \cdot h_j \cdot d_* \big(T(F)\vartheta_i, T(F)\vartheta_j \big)$$

where $\vartheta_i = \Theta(F)[i]$ and $h_i = h_\Theta[i]$ denote the ith substitution of F and the corresponding count. The isolation *of F in $\mathcal{F}$ is defined as the minimal distance to any other frame in $\mathcal{F}$:*

$$i(F, \mathcal{F}) = \min_{G \in \mathcal{F} \setminus \{F\}} d_f(F, G)$$

Since $c(F)$ uses d_* for distances within a single frame F only, there exists a more efficient way of computing it. If we write $w(v,m)$ to denote the *weight* of a variable v in a message pattern m (i.e., the sum of coefficients of $d(v, \cdot)$ in $d_*(m, m\vartheta)$ for some substitution ϑ), then we can precompute $w(v, T(F))$ for any variable v in the trajectory of F, and rewrite $c(F)$ to

$$c(F) \propto \sum_{i=1}^{|\Theta(F)|} \sum_{j=i+1}^{|\Theta(F)|} h_i \cdot h_j \cdot \sum_v w\big(v, T(F)\big) \cdot d_*\big(v\vartheta_i, v\vartheta_j\big)$$

According to definition 7, $c(F)$ is zero for frames with only one distinct substitution, so defining overall validity as the sum or product of individual validities $i(F, \mathcal{F})/c(F)$ is not a good idea. Instead, we define the validity of a frame repository $\mathcal{F}$ as the ratio between average isolation and average compactness for all the frames in $\mathcal{F}$, taking special care of situations where only frames with a single substitution exist.

Definition 8 (Frame validity). *Let $\mathcal{F}$ be a set of frames. The* validity *of $\mathcal{F}$ is defined as*

$$v(\mathcal{F}) = \begin{cases} \frac{\sum_{F \in \mathcal{F}} i(F, \mathcal{F})}{\sum_{F \in \mathcal{F}} c(F)} & \textit{if } \exists F \in \mathcal{F} . \, |\Theta(F)| > 1 \\ \frac{1}{|\mathcal{F}|} \sum_{F \in \mathcal{F}} i(F, \mathcal{F}) & \textit{otherwise} \end{cases}$$

In analogy to cluster analysis we conjecture that the higher the validity $v(\mathcal{F})$ of a frame repository $\mathcal{F}$ built from a particular set of concrete interactions, the better it models the different classes of conversation in a MAS. Facing different alternatives for the incorporation of an interaction that has just been perceived, each of them corresponding to a specific modification of $\mathcal{F}$, we can judge their quality simply by measuring $v(\mathcal{F})$ before and after this modification and hence devise an algorithm that tries to maintain a frame repository with the highest possible validity.

4.4 Frame Abstraction and Merging

Before we can apply the results of the previous section to an algorithm for the acquisition and adaptation of interaction frames from actual interactions, we will first have to make explicit the actual modifications that can be performed on interaction frames and sets thereof in order to adapt them to newly observed interactions. We do so by providing a general algorithm for merging two interaction frames into one. This algorithm can then be used to simply add a new message to an existing frame (by interpreting the message as a "singular" frame with ground trajectory and only the empty substitution) or to reorganise a whole repository. In order to distinguish these two activities, and according to the point in time they are performed relative to the actual interactions, we might refer to them as online and offline merging.

Starting with frame trajectories and following Occam's Razor, the trajectory of the frame obtained by merging F and G should be the least abstract message pattern sequence that can be unified with both trajectories $T(F)$ and $T(G)$ using standard first-order unification, i.e. the *least general generalisation* (lgg) [16] of the two, denoted $lgg(T(F), T(G))$. The following inductive definition of least general generalisation for message sequences can be turned into a simple algorithm for its computation.

Definition 9 (Least general generalisation). *The least general generalisation (lgg) of two terms is given by*

$$lgg(f(s_1, \ldots, s_k), g(t_1, \ldots, t_l)) = \begin{cases} f(lgg(s_1, t_1), \ldots, lgg(s_k, t_k)) & \textit{if } f = g \textit{ and } k = l \\ x & \textit{otherwise,} \end{cases}$$

where x is a new variable (i.e., one that does not occur in any s_i or t_i) such that $lgg(s, t)$ is unique for any subterms s and t throughout the lgg (i.e., equal terms are replaced with the same variable). The lgg of two messages with the same performative is given by $lgg(p(a, b, x), p(c, d, y)) = p(lgg(a, c), lgg(b, d), lgg(x, y))$. It is undefined if the performatives differ. The lgg of two message sequences of equal length is given by $lgg((m_1, \ldots, m_k), (n_1, \ldots, n_k)) = (lgg(m_1, n_1), \ldots, lgg(m_k, n_k))$. As before, it has to be ensured that $lgg(s, t)$ is unique throughout the lgg for any two subterms s and t.

In an algorithm, uniqueness of the lgg is usually achieved by means of a table that holds the lggs computed so far for any pair of arguments.

Along with the lgg, definition 9 also yields two substitutions, namely the most general unifier (mgu) of the lgg with each of its arguments, and we use the abbreviation $\vartheta_m(m,n) = mgu(m, lgg(m,n))$. To obtain the substitutions and conditions of the merged frame, the ϑ_m have to be applied to the substitutions and conditions of the respective frame. For this, let F be one of the frames to merge, let t denote the trajectory of the resulting frame and c_j and ϑ_j the condition and substitution of the resulting frame that correspond to $C(F)[j]$ and $\Theta(F)[j]$. If the new frame is to hold all the conversations of F, then $t\vartheta_i = T(F)\Theta(F)[i]$ has to hold for $1 \leq i \leq |\Theta(F)|$. The definition of ϑ_m implies that $T(F) = t\vartheta_m(T(F), \cdot)$ and thus $t\vartheta_m(T(F), \cdot)\Theta(F)[i] = t\vartheta_i$.

If accordingly ϑ_i is computed as $\vartheta_i = \vartheta_m(T(F), \cdot)\Theta(F)[i]$, however, information might be lost about correlations between multiple conversations originating from the same frame. To retain this kind of information, substitutions should be concatenated rather than applied unless the right side of $\vartheta_m(T(F), \cdot)$ is a variable (which is quite common, as it results from the introduction of a new variable for a variable in the course of computing the lgg). The following definition formalises this concept of selective application of a substitution.

Definition 10. *Let* $\vartheta = [v_1/t_1, \ldots, v_n/t_n]$ *be a single variable substitution and* $\Theta = \langle s_1, \ldots, s_m \rangle$ *a list of substitutions. Then,* $\vartheta \bowtie \Theta$ *denotes the list of substitutions that results from selectively prepending* ϑ *to each element of* Θ *and is given by* $\vartheta \bowtie \Theta = \langle r_1, \ldots, r_m \rangle$ *where* $r_i = [v_1/r_{i1}, \ldots, v_n/r_{in}] \cdot s_i$ *and*

$$r_{ij} = \begin{cases} t_j s_i & \text{if } t_j \text{ is a variable} \\ t_j & \text{otherwise} \end{cases}$$

As for the conditions of the merged frame, $c_i\vartheta_i = C(F)\Theta(F)[i]$ has to hold analogously. Replacing ϑ_i with the above result yields $c_i\vartheta_m\Theta(F)[i] = C(F)\Theta(F)[i]$ and thus $c_i\vartheta_m = C(F)$. Writing ϑ^{-1} for the "inverse" of a substitution ϑ (replacing terms by variables), c_i can hence be defined as $c_i = C(F)\vartheta_m^{-1}$. This finally leads us to the following definition of a merging operation on frames:

Definition 11 (frame merging). *Let F and G be two interaction frames with* $|T(F)| = |T(G)|$. *Then, the result of* merging F and G, *denoted by* $M(F,G)$, *is given by*

$$
\begin{aligned}
M(F,G) = \langle & lgg\big(T(F), T(G)\big), \\
& C(F)\vartheta_m\big(T(F), T(G)\big)^{-1} \cdot C(G)\vartheta_m\big(T(G), T(F)\big)^{-1}, \\
& \vartheta_m\big(T(F), T(G)\big) \bowtie \Theta(F) \cdot \vartheta_m\big(T(G), T(F)\big) \bowtie \Theta(G), \\
& hmax(F,G), \\
& h_\Theta(F) \cdot h_\Theta(G) \rangle,
\end{aligned}
$$

where $hmax(F,G) = \langle h_1, h_2, \ldots \rangle$ *with*

$$h_i = \begin{cases} max\{h_T(F)[i], h_T(G)[i], \sum_k h_\Theta(M(F,G))[k]\} & \text{if } i = |T(F)| \\ max\{h_T(F)[i], h_T(G)[i], h_{i+1}\} & \text{if } i < |T(F)|. \end{cases}$$

The rather complex definition of the step counter values for the merged frame stems from the fact that it is impossible to determine the value $h_T(merge(F,G))$ would have taken if $merge(F,G)$ had been in the repository during all the conversations stored in F and G just from the information provided by F and G. On the other hand, it is also impossible to determine which additional conversations would have been stored in $merge(F,G)$ if this had been the case, so it seems fair to approximate h_T based on the following observations: Obviously, $\max(h_T(F), h_T(G))$ is a lower bound for $h_T(merge(F,G))$. In addition to that, the sum of the values of h_Θ is a lower bound for the value of $h_T[\|T\|]$, since it resembles the exact number of past conversations stored in the frame. Finally, for each i, $h_T[i]$ is a lower bound for $h_T[j]$ with $j < i$. Hence, as we cannot infer any upper bounds from the counter values alone, we simply choose the values of $h_T(merge(F,G))$ such that the bounds are tight. If only online merging is used, this approximation always yields accurate values for h_T.

4.5   An Algorithm for Learning Frames

Based on the formal notion of validity of a set of frames presented in section 4.3, which extends cluster validity to the space of multi-agent conversations, and on the frame merging procedure given in section 4.4, the following simple algorithm computes the best way to incorporate a newly observed message sequence m into a frame repository $\mathcal{F}$:

function $flea(\mathcal{F},m)$ **returns** a frame repository
inputs: frame repository $\mathcal{F}$, message sequence m
  /* compute the singular frame F for m */
  $F := \big(m, C_m, \{\}, \langle 1, \ldots, 1\rangle, \langle 1\rangle\big)$
  /* compute the set $\mathbb{F}$ of alternatives for inclusion of m */
  $\mathbb{F} := \big\{\mathcal{F} \cup \{F\}\big\} \cup \bigcup_{F' \in \mathcal{F}}\big\{\mathcal{F} \setminus \{F'\} \cup M(F', F)\big\}$
  /* return the most valid frame repository */
  return $\arg\max_{\mathcal{F}' \in \mathbb{F}} v(\mathcal{F}')$

While the surface structure of a particular message sequence equals the message sequence itself, identification of a set C_m of logical conditions that held during a conversation (according to the observer's world model) and that were *relevant* or *crucial* is clearly a nontrivial task. If frames exist, however, the execution of which was hindered due to reasons of context (especially if pre-specified "protocol" frames are used), these can be used to identify conditions other than those (physically) required for the execution of the individual messages.

Since the above algorithm only considers a single frame at a time for inclusion into the repository, it is unable to detect structures in the space of interactions that develop over time. This corresponds to a more general problem of *order dependence* in incremental unsupervised learning and might in practice result in several frames actually modelling the same class of interactions. This problem can be handled, though, by supplementing the above online merging algorithm with one that periodically checks if two frames in the repository can be merged to increase its overall validity.

5 Conclusion

In this paper, we have presented a novel approach to *adaptive agent communication*. Agents in open environments that communicate according to high-level pre-specified conversational patterns can use the approach to augment these patterns with empirical observation of actual conversations, and conduct decision-theoretic reasoning about them in the framework of empirical semantics. Interaction frames have been used as the central data structure, allowing for the integration with our previous work on interaction frames [4,5,20]. The basic principles of the approach, however, could also be applied to other, possibly more complex, forms of representation.

Our current work focuses on an experimental exploration of the benefits and limitations of our approach in real-world "communication learning" tasks. An experimental evaluation in the context of proposal-based and argumentation-based negotiation can be found in [22]. Further applications include performance measurement of a MAS or of individual agents with respect to communication or the design of new interaction protocols. An open issue that will have to be dealt with in future work to allow for the acquisition of conversation patterns from scratch is the discovery of conditions that were relevant or crucial for a particular class of conversation. While inductive logic programming techniques may again be the appropriate means to attack this problem, the transition to relative least general generalisation (which might be required to handle background knowledge already available for a particular class of conversation) would make this one disproportionately harder to solve.

References

1. J. L. Austin. *How to do things with Words*. Clarendon Press, 1962.
2. A. G. Barto and S. Mahadevan. Recent advances in hierarchical reinforcement learning. *Discrete Event Dynamic Systems*, 13(4):41–77, 2003.
3. P. R. Cohen and H. J. Levesque. Communicative actions for artificial agents. In *Proceedings of the First International Conference on Multi-Agent Systems (ICMAS)*, pages 65–72, 1995.
4. F. Fischer and M. Rovatsos. An empirical semantics approach to reasoning about communication. *Engineering Applications of Artificial Intelligence, Special Section on Best Papers of CIA 2004*, 18(7):809–823, 2005.
5. F. Fischer, M. Rovatsos, and G. Weiss. Hierarchical reinforcement learning in communication-mediated multiagent coordination. In *Proceedings of the 3rd International Joint Conference on Autonomous Agents and Multiagent Systems (AAMAS)*, pages 1334–1335. ACM Press, 2004.
6. F. Fischer, M. Rovatsos, and G. Weiss. Acquiring and adapting probabilistic models of agent conversation. In *Proceedings of the 4th International Joint Conference on Autonomous Agents and Multiagent Systems (AAMAS)*, pages 106–113. ACM Press, 2005.
7. N. Fornara and M. Colombetti. Operational specification of a commitment-based agent communication language. In *Proceedings of the 1st International Joint Conference on Autonomous Agents and Multiagent Systems (AAMAS)*, pages 536–542. ACM Press, 2002.
8. E. Goffman. *Frame Analysis: An Essay on the Organisation of Experience*. Harper and Row, New York, NY, 1974. Reprinted 1990 by Northeastern University Press.
9. M.-P. Huget, editor. *Communication in Multiagent Systems*, volume 2650 of *Lecture Notes in Artificial Intelligence*. Springer-Verlag, Berlin, Germany, 2003.

10. A. K. Jain and R. C. Dubes. *Algorithms for clustering data.* Prentice Hall, Upper Saddle River, NJ, 1988.

11. J. L. Kolodner. *Case-Based Reasoning.* Morgan Kaufmann, San Francisco, CA, 1993.

12. M. T. Kone, A. Shimazu, and T. Nakajima. The state of the art in agent communication languages. *Knowledge and Information Systems*, 2:259–284, 2000.

13. N. Luhmann. *Social Systems.* Stanford University Press, Palo Alto, CA, 1995.

14. M. Nickles, M. Rovatsos, and G. Weiss. Empirical-rational semantics of agent communication. In *Proceedings of the Third International Joint Conference on Autonomous Agents and Multiagent Systems (AAMAS)*, 2004.

15. S. Paurobally, J. Cunningham, and N. Jennings. A formal framework for agent interaction semantics. In this volume.

16. G. Plotkin. A note on inductive generalization. *Machine Intelligence*, 5:153–163, 1971.

17. D. Precup. *Temporal Abstraction in Reinforcement Learning.* PhD thesis, Department of Computer Science, University of Massachusetts, Amherst, 2000.

18. J. Ramon and M. Bruynooghe. A polynomial time computable metric between point sets. *Acta Informatica*, 37(10):765–780, 2001.

19. A. S. Rao and M. P. Georgeff. An abstract architecture for rational agents. In *Proceedings of Knowledge Representation and Reasoning (KR&R)*, pages 439–449, 1992.

20. M. Rovatsos, F. Fischer, and G. Weiss. Hierarchical reinforcement learning for communicating agents. In *Proceedings of the 2nd European Workshop on Multiagent Systems (EUMAS)*, pages 593–604, 2004.

21. M. Rovatsos, M. Nickles, and G. Weiss. Interaction is meaning: A new model for communication in open systems. In *Proceedings of the 2nd International Joint Conference on Autonomous Agents and Multiagent Systems (AAMAS)*, 2003.

22. M. Rovatsos, I. Rahwan, F. Fischer, and G. Weiss. Adaptive strategies for practical argument-based negotiation. In *Proceedings of the 2nd International Workshop on Argumentation in Multi-Agent Systems (ArgMAS)*, 2005.

23. M. Rovatsos, G. Weiss, and M. Wolf. An Approach to the Analysis and Design of Multi-agent Systems based on Interaction Frames. In *Proceedings of the 1st International Joint Conference on Autonomous Agents and Multiagent Systems (AAMAS)*. ACM Press, 2002.

24. M. Sebag. Distance induction in first order logic. In *Proceedings of the 7th International Workshop on Inductive Logic Programming*, 1997.

25. M. P. Singh. A semantics for speech acts. *Annals of Mathematics and Artificial Intelligence*, 8(1–2):47–71, 1993.

26. M. P. Singh. A social semantics for agent communication languages. In *Proceedings of the IJCAI Workshop on Agent Communication Languages*, 2000.

27. M. Verdicchio and M. Colombetti. A commitment-based communicative act library. In this volume.

28. C. Watkins and P. Dayan. Q-learning. *Machine Learning*, 8:279–292, 1992.

Can I Please Drop It?
Dialogues About Belief Contraction

Henk-Jan Lebbink[1,2], Cilia Witteman[2], and John-Jules Meyer[1]

[1] Computer Science, Utrecht University, the Netherlands
henkjan@cs.uu.nl
[2] Social Science, Radboud University Nijmegen, the Netherlands

Abstract. This paper presents a dialogue game in which agents in a multiagent system try to contract beliefs in agreement with other agents. The dialogue game defines the semantics of the communicative act of asking support to contract beliefs. In addition, a decision game is presented that defines when agents are allowed to contract propositions from their private belief states. These games if combined allow agents to contract beliefs in a distributed fashion.

1 Introduction

Of general interest in the domain of multiagent systems (MAS) is the situation in which agents disagree about what to believe. Different approaches can be taken to tackle such disagreements. In Lebbink et al. [1], agents try to resolve disagreements by requesting other agents to accept propositions such that the dispute is resolved. An agent could also try to convince other agents to accept to retract certain propositions. Yet another approach is taken in this article, in which agents propose to contract their own beliefs. This paper deals with dialogue games that enable agents to ask other agents whether they support the speaker's belief contraction.

Dialogue games have recently received more attention in the field of computer science, and, especially, in the community of MAS [2,3]. In MAS, autonomous software agents communicate and cooperate to reach private and collective goals. Issues related to cooperation and plans are not addressed, our focus will be primarily on the agent's motivation to communicate proposals and their answers. A dialogue typology by Walton and Krabbe [4] identifies four different categories of dialogues by distinguishing the agents' initial situations and goals. The categories are: Persuasion dialogues, in which agents seek to convince other agents to believe propositions [5,6]; Negotiation dialogues, in which participants seek to agree on how to divide a resource [7,8]; Deliberation dialogues, in which participants make plans by discussing which actions to perform in which situations [9]; Informati on seeking dialogues, in which agents seek to find truth-values of propositions by asking other agents [10,11,12]. The current work contributes to the category of persuasion dialogues: asking others to agree *not* to believe propositions.

F. Dignum, R. van Eijk, and R. Flores (Eds.): AC 2005/2006, LNAI 3859, pp. 227–242, 2006.

Beun [11] and Lebbink et al. [1] describe communicative acts and communication rules that form dialogue games that agents play to balance their desire
and belief states. Such dialogue games consist of preconditions for uttering communicative acts, and post-conditions that state the agents' cognitive states after
incoming and outgoing information has been processed. To describe the motivation to request and ask for support of belief contractions, agents have desires
not to believe propositions.

Under the assumption that agents benefit from coordinating their decisions,
agents may need to seek approval for dropping their beliefs, especially when they
are engaged in plans that require agreement about beliefs. Agents may need to
seek approval for dropping beliefs if they are, for example, engaged in cooperative plans that require agreements about beliefs. To effect such coordination,
we set the objective to define dialogue games in which belief contractions are
coordinated between agents in a distributed fashion. In an example dialogue,
medical expert Sarah asks Fred whether he supports her belief contraction that
a patient is diagnosed with a certain disease. To agree on this, Fred needs to contract other beliefs that are preconditions (i.e. symptoms) that made him agree
with the diagnosis. To coordinate this contraction, he starts a sub-dialogue to
contract these preconditions.

We start by discussing related and—however inspiring—unrelated work. Section 4 describes the agent's motivation to confer with others to contract beliefs;
the agent's cognitive state is presented and an example dialogue is given. Section 5 deals with the agent's decision games for fixing beliefs. We then turn to a
dialogue game with questions whether other agents support belief contractions
(Section 6). We conclude in Section 7.

2   Representing Inconsistent Information

A paraconsistent logic is a non-trivial logic that allows both a statement and
its negation to be asserted without absurdity following [13,14]. A proposition in
these logics is a statement that is true or false, or *both*. In classical, modal logic
and most other standard logics, anything can be proven from a contradiction
(ex contradictione quodlibet). In a paraconsistent logic the logical principle that
anything follows from absurdity is dropped, thus allowing absurdity without
being proverbially called 'explosive'.

Different approaches can be taken to represent inconsistent propositions from
classical logic in a consistent manner; these representations are called paraconsistent propositions. In Lebbink et al. [12,1], a multi-valued logic is defined in
which propositions have truth-values taken from a bilattice structure [15,16].
This logic does not have a Kripke style possible world semantics [17] such as
adopted in modal logic [18], nor a Tarskian deflationist semantics (redundancy
semantics) [19] that most classical logics adopt, but a Wittgensteinian semantics
based on use [20]. Roughly, in a semantics based on use, a community of agents
agrees about the criteria to determine a proposition's truth-value, including
the truth-value associated with inconsistency. In a paraconsistent logic with a

use-semantics, agents can assign interpretations to propositions that are inconsistent in the classical sense. For our current purpose of defining dialogue games, we will use belief sets that allow paraconsistent propositions; we will however not define paraconsistent propositions, but we will assume these propositions can be represented in belief sets consistently.

3   Related Work

Belief revision is taken to be the changing of one's beliefs after acquiring new information [21,14]. In general, agents often have a bounded capacity to check whether new information is consistent with their current beliefs. These agents could be justified to believe that new information is consistent with their current beliefs, and only later conclude that the information is not. In such situations, agents have to contract beliefs to regain a consistent belief state. If agents are *a priori* justified to accept new beliefs, and they conclude later that the new beliefs do introduce contradictions, then the agents' behaviour does not adhere to the postulates of belief revision [22]. However, if an agent corrects her faulty behaviour by contracting sufficient information, her belief state may become consistent again and her overall behaviour could adhere to the postulates of belief revision. The analysis whether our agent's behaviour obey s the AGM postulates is beyond the scope of this article. This is because the current focus is on the rules to coordinate belief contractions that results in a distributed contraction process.

Most philosophers and logicians embrace epistemic commitment as a goal of logic; it is this epistemic commitment agents may said to have towards their beliefs. While most logics—such as dynamic deontic logic [23]—regard commitments as actions to do something, in our approach beliefs are regarded as commitments to assert "to believe" something. Under a semantics based on use, according the community that agreed on the criteria for an agent to correctly predicate "to believe" a proposition, an agent may predicate "to believe" the proposition, if the criteria to do so have been met [20]. That is to say that if criteria have been met, the agent commits herself to believe the consequences of these criteria.

The current approach defines the semantics of communicative acts with pre-conditions and post-conditions in a similar fashion as the *de facto* standard on ACLs from FIPA [24]. These ACL's provide a mentalist semantics of communicative acts, but leave unspecified what agents may believe about other agents after receiving and uttering communicative acts. What is also lacking is a treatment of questions for belief contractions. Recently however, in [25] an extension of FIPA ACLs has been proposed in which communicative acts are defined with argumentation-theoretic preconditions. One of these acts implements the semantics for contracting propositions to undercut arguments. In our approach, unbalanced cognitive states will motivate agents to communicate [26,11]. Our communicative acts are not focussed on arguments why certain beliefs have to be discarded, but whether—or not—agents balance their desire and belief states.

In general, our agents' desires to believe certain propositions can originate from collaborative or competitive plans, or from exogenous sources such as users.

4   An Agent's Motivation and Her Cognitive State

Next the agent's cognitive state will be presented and her motivation to confer with other agents when to contract beliefs. To aid the presentation of dialogue games, two key players are given a name: Sarah will be denoted by variable s and she is the speaker in the dialogue; John will be denoted by variable j and he listens to what Sarah has to say. Our dialogue game can handle n participants; other agents have names drawn from the set of agent names $\mathcal{A}$.

4.1   Motivation to Confer with Other Agents on Belief Contractions

An agent can be said to be motivated to ask other agents for permission to contract her beliefs if she is not certain that her other beliefs are indirectly justified by the beliefs she is about to contract. Consider the following situation. If Sarah believes a certain proposition p and she believes that John believes that she believes p, John could have used Sarah's beliefs to justify his own beliefs, say to believe proposition q. If Sarah were to contract her belief p then John's belief q could become unjustified; Sarah however does not need to be aware of the existence of such specific and potentially unjustified proposition q, but she can know that if she were to contract p without conferring with John, unjustified propositions can in principle exists.

A selfish agent need not be bothered whether other agents believe propositions that are unjustified because of the selfish agent's unwillingness to confer with others. However, even a selfish agent may be justified and motivated to check with others if she has justified (private) beliefs based on testimony of other agents' beliefs. These latter beliefs may become unjustified due to imprudent contraction, possibly also rendering beliefs of the careless agent unjustified. This situation could have been avoided if careless agent Sarah had conferred with John that she is about to contract her believe in p. John could have protested to the proposed contraction by revealing dependencies between their beliefs. This communication regarding a proposed contraction will be formally modelled.

We assume that an agent is not allowed to have conflicting desires, such as the desire to believe p and at the same time the desire to be ignorant about p. However, agents can have mutually conflicting desires. For example, Sarah may desire to believe p and John may desire that Sarah does *not* believe p. Agents will give precedence to private desires and are assumed to behave cooperatively unless they have mutually conflicting desires.

4.2   The Agent's Cognitive State

An agent's cognitive state is assumed to consist of a finite number of mental states, which are taken to be theories of multi-valued logic (MVL) [12,1]. A belief state based on a theory of MVL allows an agent to have a lack of belief, partial belief, and even inconsistent belief in a consistent manner. However, without loss of generality, a mental state will be a set of atomic propositions.

We will not present a full repertoire of all possible mental states agents may have regarding themselves and others; only those are identified that are used in the present paper. Sarah's private belief state is denoted B_s; $\psi \in B_s$ states that she believes proposition ψ. John's private desire $D_j I_j$ is the set of propositions that John desires to be ignorant about, i.e. those propositions that John desires *not* to believe; $\psi \in D_j I_j$ states his desires not to believe ψ. Mental state $B_s B_j$ is the set of manifested beliefs of John that Sarah is aware of; $\psi \in B_s B_j$ states that Sarah believes that John believes ψ. An agent can be aware of other agents' desires; $\psi \in B_s D_j I_j$ states that Sarah is aware that John desires not to believe ψ. Manifested ignorance state $B_s I_j$ is the set of propositions that Sarah is aware that John does not believe; $\psi \in B_s I_j$ states that Sarah is aware that John does not believe ψ. Other mental states such as higher-order manifested mental states are defined likewise; all mental states have a formal semantics based on theories of MVL.

Mental states are part of structure CS which represents the agent's cognitive state: $CS_s \models \Pi$ states that the set of criteria Π hold for Sarah's cognitive state. To put that Sarah does not believe that John believes ψ, and, at the same time, that she does desire John to be ignorant about ψ, is denoted by $CS_s \models \{(\psi \notin B_s B_j), (\psi \in D_s I_j)\}$. Sarah may not believe that John believes ψ, while at the same time, she may not believe that John does not believe ψ, this is denoted by $CS_s \models \{(\psi \notin B_s B_j), (\psi \notin B_s I_j)\}$. If Π is a singleton set, we write $CS_s \models \psi \in B_s$ instead of $CS_s \models \{\psi \in B_s\}$. We write $\{CS_s, CS_j\} \models \Pi$ instead of $\forall \pi \in \Pi \ (CS_s \models \pi \ 'or' \ CS_j \models \pi)$.

Because mental states are sets of propositions, addition and contraction of propositions is equal to set-theoretic inclusion and exclusion respectively. The action of contracting belief $\psi \in B_s$ from Sarah's cognitive state is denoted $cont(CS_s, \psi, B_s)$ yielding CS_s', after which $CS_s' \models \psi \notin B_s$. An *inference rule* is introduced as a special proposition, $\phi \longmapsto \psi$; it will be given a semantics with an agent's decision rule in Section 5.2.

4.3   Example Dialogue

For the example dialogue, assume the following situation in which three medical experts Sarah, John and Fred consult each other about their patient's situation. A few weeks ago Sarah told John and Fred that she believes proposition ψ that "the patient is suffering from disease X". However, new lab results indicate that this diagnosis should be refuted. Because Sarah believes that John and Fred believe that she believes ψ, she first has to contract her previous diagnosis before she can make a new one.

In Figure 1.1, Sarah rings Fred and John asking whether they agree that she contracts her belief in proposition ψ. The communicative act $qbc_1(\psi)$ is a question with the reading: "is it ok if I drop my belief that the patient is suffering from disease X". In subsequent sections, the communicative act will be given a formal semantics. If a contraction of ψ is possible for John, he may grant Sarah's request (Figure 1.2). Fred however cannot accept Sarah to contract her belief in ψ, because, in the example, he believes proposition ϕ that "the patient shows symptom Y", and this symptom is a sufficient criterion to determine disease X. Fred can only accept not to believe that the patient has disease X if he also accepts not to believe that the patient has symptom Y. Fred asks Sarah and John whether he may drop his belief ϕ in a counter-question $qbc_3(\phi)$. In Figure 1.3, both Sarah and John resp ond that Fred may drop his belief ϕ. In the last figure, Fred responds to Sarah that it is okay with him that she drops her belief in ψ.

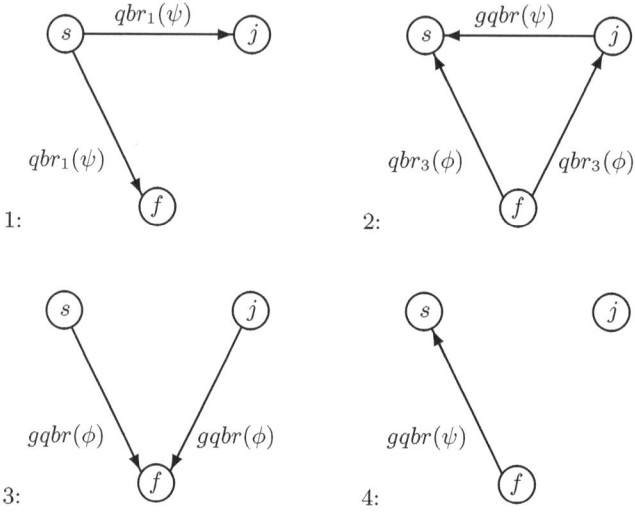

Fig. 1. Dialogues about belief contraction with a sub dialogue

The dialogue started by Sarah resulted in a sub dialogue started by Fred to drop those propositions to positively answer the first dialogue. In subsequent sections, dialogue and decision rules will be presented to formalize similar patterns of communication and decision-making.

Example 1 (Agent's initial cognitive states). The agents from the example dialogue are equated with the following cognitive states. All agents believe that ϕ is a sufficient criterion to determine ψ, denoted $\phi \rightarrowtail \psi$.

- $CS_s \models \{(\psi, \phi \rightarrowtail \psi \in B_s, B_s B_j, B_s B_f, B_s B_j B_s, B_s B_f B_s), (\psi \in D_s I_s)\}$;
- $CS_j \models \{(\psi, \phi \rightarrowtail \psi \in B_j, B_j B_s, B_j B_f, B_j B_s B_j, B_j B_f B_j)\}$;
- $CS_f \models \{(\phi, \psi, \phi \rightarrowtail \psi \in B_f, B_f B_s, B_f B_j, B_f B_s B_f, B_f B_j B_f)\}$.

5   Decision Games for Fixing Beliefs

A generic definition of decision games will be provided First, which will be instantiated in Section 5.2 with a game to decide to believe. This game provides intuition what it means for a proposition to be cognitively entrenched (Section 5.3), which will be needed in the definition of the game to decide to be ignorant (Section 5.4).

5.1   Decision Games

A decision game is a finite set of decision rules that define in which situations agents are allowed to make decisions. A decision rule itself is defined by the preconditions and post-conditions of a decision. A generic decision rule for a decision $\delta \in \mathcal{L}_D$ is defined as a template which can be instantiated with a concrete decision. The decision language is denoted $\mathcal{L}_D$. A decision δ is *allowed* for Sarah if the set of preconditions of δ hold in Sarah's cognitive state, i.e. $CS_s \models pre(\delta)$. After the decision is made, Sarah's cognitive state is updated, resulting in a new cognitive state in which the post-conditions of δ hold, i.e. $CS'_s \models post(\delta)$.

$$CS_s \models pre(\delta) \quad \Longrightarrow \quad CS'_s \models post(\delta)$$

In sections 5.2 and 5.4, decision δ will be instantiated with decision $d2a(s, \psi, B_s) \in \mathcal{L}_D$, which states that Sarah decides to *add* proposition ψ to her belief state, and decision $d2c(s, \psi, B_s) \in \mathcal{L}_D$, which states that Sarah decides to *contract* ψ from her belief state.

5.2   A Decision Game to Decide to Believe

Different cognitive processes can be distinguished that describe (or prescribe) an agent's ability to come to believe propositions. A distinction can be made between (i) the agent's process of deciding to believe a proposition based on her private beliefs and private inference rules, and (ii) the agent's decision process based on manifested beliefs of others. The two decisions are distinguished with an index 1 and 2.

An agent may derive a new belief ϕ from an inference rule $\psi \rightarrowtail \phi$ and its antecedent ψ. For reasons of efficiency, this decision rule may only be applied if the agent does not already believe the consequent ϕ. Sarah is allowed to decide to believe proposition ϕ if the following three criteria hold, i.e. if the three criteria are part of the preconditions of the decision $d2a_1(s, \phi, B_s)$.

$$(\psi \in B_s), \ (\psi \rightarrowtail \phi \in B_s), \ (\phi \notin B_s) \ \in \ pre(d2a_1(s, \phi, B_s)) \tag{1}$$

Next we consider another decision describing the agent's ability to obtain new beliefs by conforming to other agents' beliefs. We restrict the agents' ability to decide to believe propositions that balance an unbalanced desire and belief state. An agent's cognitive state is said to have an unbalanced state if the agent desires to believe a proposition but does not believe it. These unbalanced states are the motivation to perform decisions, and, as we will see later, to utter communicative acts.

Sarah is allowed to decide to believe a proposition if the following criteria hold. She believes that John believes proposition ψ, she does not herself believe ψ, and she desires to believe ψ.

$$(\psi \in B_s B_j), \ (\psi \notin B_s), \ (\psi \in D_s B_s) \ \in \ pre(d2a_2(s, \psi, B_s)) \qquad (2)$$

The post-conditions are straightforward. After Sarah has decided to believe ψ, she does in fact believe ψ, i.e. $(\psi \in B_s) \in post(d2a(s, \psi, B_s))$.

5.3   Cognitive Preconditions and Cognitive Entrenchment

Set Π_1 is a cognitive precondition on set Π_2 if Π_1 is a set of conditions on a cognitive state, and if Π_1 holds in the cognitive state and the cognitive state is closed under decision-making, then Π_2 will hold in that cognitive state. A cognitive precondition will be used in this chapter to define purposeful decision-making, and in subsequent chapters to define purposeful communication.

A set of conditions on a cognitive state Π_1 is a *direct* cognitive precondition for a set of conditions on the same cognitive state Π_2 if the following condition holds. If and only if a decision $\delta \in \mathcal{L}_D$ exists for which Π_1 is part of the preconditions of δ, and Π_2 is part of the post-conditions of δ.

Definition 1 (Direct cognitive preconditions). *Given sets Π_1, Π_2 and decision $\delta \in \mathcal{L}_D$, set Π_1 is a partial cognitive precondition for Π_2, denoted $dpc(\Pi_1, \delta, \Pi_2)$, if holds:*

$$dpc(\Pi_1, \delta, \Pi_2) \quad if \quad \Pi_1 = pre(\delta) \quad and \quad \Pi_2 \subseteq post(\delta) \qquad (3)$$

A cognitive precondition is the transitive closure of direct cognitive precondition over a finite sequence of decisions $\langle \delta_1, \ldots, \delta_{n-1} \rangle$. Due to decision δ_1, set Π_1 is a direct cognitive precondition for some set Π_2 which, due to decision δ_2, is a direct cognitive precondition for set Π_3, etc. Set Π_n is part of the post-conditions of the last decision δ_{n-1}.

Definition 2 (Cognitive preconditions). *Given sets Π_1, Π_n and a sequence of decision $\langle \delta_1, \ldots, \delta_{n-1} \rangle$ with $n \leq 2$ and $\delta_1, \ldots, \delta_{n-1} \in \mathcal{L}_D$, set Π_1 is a cognitive precondition for Π_n, denoted $cp(\Pi_1, \langle \delta_1, \ldots, \delta_{n-1} \rangle, \Pi_n)$, if holds:*

$$\begin{aligned} cp(\Pi_1, \langle \delta_1, \delta_2, \ldots, \delta_{n-1} \rangle, \Pi_n) \quad &\equiv \quad \exists \Pi_2 \cdots \Pi_{n-1} \\ (dpc(\Pi_1, \delta_1, \Pi_2) \wedge dpc(\Pi_2', \delta_2, \Pi_3) \wedge (\Pi_2 \subseteq \Pi_2') \wedge \cdots \wedge \\ dpc(\Pi_{n-2}', \delta_{n-2}, \Pi_{n-1}) \wedge dpc(\Pi_{n-1}', \delta_{n-1}, \Pi_n) \wedge (\Pi_{n-1} \subseteq \Pi_{n-1}') \end{aligned} \qquad (4)$$

An agent $s \in \mathcal{A}$ will have at her disposal a set of decisions $\Delta_s \subseteq \mathcal{L}_D$. The set Π_1 is a cognitive precondition for Π_n if s has a finite sequence of decisions $\langle \delta_1, \ldots, \delta_{n-1} \rangle$ with $\delta_1, \ldots, \delta_{n-1} \in \Delta_s$ such that Equation 4 holds. Furthermore, we define the following abbreviations, and if Π_1 or Π_n is a singleton set, we leave out the set and write its element.

$$\Delta_s \models \Pi_1 // \Pi_n \equiv \exists \delta_1 \cdots \delta_{n-1} \in \Delta_s \ cp(\Pi_1, \langle \delta_1, \ldots, \delta_{n-1} \rangle, \Pi_n) \qquad (5)$$

$$\Delta_s \models \Pi_1 / \Pi_n \equiv (\Delta_s \models \Pi_1' // \Pi_n) \wedge (\Pi_1 \subseteq \Pi_1') \qquad (6)$$

Cognitive precondition describe relations between different states of an agent's cognitive state. The presence of decisions form a relation that describes which properties of a cognitive state hold as a result of decisions and other cognitive state properties if the cognitive state is closed under decision-making. This relation between a cognitive state and the same cognitive state closed under decision-making will be used especially to purposefully adopt and discard beliefs with the aim of satisfying desires.

A condition on a cognitive state is cognitively entrenched in the cognitive state if after making the condition invalid, it will become valid again after closing the cognitive state under decision-making. Stated differently, if a condition holds in an agent's cognitive state, then if the agent makes a decision after which the condition is not valid anymore, the agents is allowed to make a decision such that the condition is valid again.

Cognitive entrenchment can be defined for any mental state. For our current needs, it suffices to define entrenchment for beliefs only. A proposition ψ is *cognitively entrenched* in an agent's belief state if the agent has a sequence of decision at her disposal that would become applicable if proposition ψ were removed from her belief state. Removing proposition ψ would trigger decision which would result in the agent adopting belief ψ again. This is denoted by $\psi \Subset B_s$.

$$CS_s, \Delta_s \models \psi \Subset B_s \quad \text{iff} \quad \Delta_s \models \Pi // \psi \in B_s \quad \text{and} \quad cont(CS_s, \psi, B_s) \models \Pi \quad (7)$$

5.4   A Decision Game to Decide to Be Ignorant

The motivation to decide to be ignorant is defined in a similar fashion as the motivation to decide to believe a proposition based on manifested beliefs; both motivations are defined as an unbalanced desire and belief state. Two semantically different decisions are distinguished with index 1 and 2.

Sarah is allowed to contract ψ from her belief state if the following criteria hold. She desires not to believe ψ, she believes ψ, ψ is not cognitively entrenched in her belief state, and she is not motivated to confer with other agents (Section 4.1).

$$\begin{array}{c} (\psi \in D_s I_s), \ (\psi \in B_s), \ (\psi \notin B_s), \\ \{\psi \notin B_s B_a B_s \mid a \in \mathcal{A} \setminus s\} \end{array} \in \ pre(d2r_1(s, \psi, B_s)) \quad (8)$$

The second situation in which Sarah is allowed to contract ψ is if the following criteria hold. She believes that John desires to be ignorant about ψ, she believes ψ, ψ is not cognitively entrenched in her belief state, and she is not motivated to confer with other agents.

$$\begin{array}{c} (\psi \in B_s D_j I_j), \ (\psi \in B_s), \ (\psi \notin B_s), \\ \{\psi \notin B_s B_a B_s \mid a \in \mathcal{A} \setminus s\} \end{array} \in \ pre(d2r_2(s, \psi, B_s)) \quad (9)$$

The post-conditions are straightforward. After Sarah has decided not to believe ψ, she is in fact ignorant about ψ, i.e. $(\psi \notin B_s) \in post(d2r(s, \psi, B_s))$.

Example 2 (Sarah contracts ψ but not ϕ). In the example dialogue, the new lab results indicate that proposition ϕ "the patient shows symptom Y" is not valid anymore. Sarah desires not to believe ψ because she wanted to diagnose a different disease; although ψ is not entrenched in her belief state anymore, and she desires not to believe the proposition, she may not contract ψ because she believes that the others believe that she still believes ψ. $CS_s \models \psi \in B_s B_j B_s \cap B_s B_f B_s$. Consequently, she is not allowed to contract her belief ψ.

6   Dialogue Game with Questions for Belief Contraction

The following chapter will present communicative acts that allow agents to exchange information. These communicative acts will be given a meaning in what we will call dialogue games, which are sets of rules on the usage of communicative acts. The moves of a dialogue game are the utterances in a dialogue between agents. Stated differently, the exchange of information is the result of a game in which agents take turns to make moves that reflect the utterance of communicative acts. With language games, the later Wittgenstein described that the meaning of words and sentences are determined by criteria for their correct usage [20]. In a similar fashion will we describe that the meaning of communicative acts is determined by the criteria for their correct usage. A dialogue game defines the meaning of communicative acts with rules on how use the acts correctly.

6.1   Dialogue Games

The abstract communicative act $\lambda(s, j, \psi)$ states that speaker Sarah utters a λ act with contents proposition ψ to listener John. A generic dialogue rule for $\lambda(s, j, \psi)$ states that if all criteria part of the set of preconditions hold in Sarah's cognitive state, then, after the utterance of the act, the post-conditions hold for Sarah *or* John. Confusion for which agent the post-condition hold is unlikely because (as we see later) mental states unambiguously refer to either the speaker or listener.

$$CS_s \models pre(\lambda(s, j, \psi)) \quad \Longrightarrow \quad \{CS'_s, CS'_j\} \models post(\lambda(s, j, \psi))$$

In this section, communicative act λ will be instantiated with acts to express questions for belief contractions and their possible answers.

6.2   Questions for Belief Contraction Approval

Sarah is in the state of being *motivated* to ask approval to be ignorant about a proposition ψ if the following two criteria hold. Sarah believes ψ, and she has the desire to be ignorant about ψ. Stated differently, if she believes ψ, and she desires to be ignorant about ψ, then she has a motive to ask John whether she may be ignorant about ψ. The act reads "may I be ignorant about ψ?"; *qbc* is short for a question for belief contraction. To differentiate between different acts, this *qbc* is indexed 1.

$$(\psi \in D_s I_s), \ (\psi \in B_s) \ \in \ pre(qbc_1(s, j, \psi)) \tag{10}$$

The situation in which Sarah is allowed to utter a qbc can be restricted. Sarah is motivated to ask all other agents for approval to discard beliefs; however, she needs only address this to those agents she believes that are aware that she believes the proposition she desires to discard (cf. Section 4.1)

$$(\psi \in B_s B_j B_s) \in pre(qbc_1(s, j, \psi)) \tag{11}$$

After utterance of $qbc(s, j, \psi)$, John may conclude that Sarah has the desire to be ignorant about ψ, and that she believes ψ. John's cognitive state should change, yielding the following post-conditions.

$$(\psi \in B_j D_s I_s), \ (\psi \in B_j B_s) \in post(qbc_1(s, j, \psi)) \tag{12}$$

After the utterance of the $qbc(s, j, \psi)$, Sarah may conclude that John is aware that she desires to be ignorant about ψ, and, in addition, that John is aware that she believes ψ. Sarah's cognitive state has changed according to the following post-conditions.

$$(\psi \in B_s B_j D_s I_s), \ (\psi \in B_s B_j B_s) \in post(qbc_1(s, j, \psi)) \tag{13}$$

To prevent the situation that Sarah utters the same qbc more than once, the following precondition is added, $(\psi \notin B_s B_j D_s I_s) \in pre(qbc_1(s, j, \psi))$.

Example 3 (Sarah confers with John and Fred about ψ). After Sarah has contracted ϕ (Example 2), ψ is not entrenched anymore, and because she has the desire to not believe ψ she could have contracted her belief ψ had it not been that she still needs to confer with the others. The preconditions of the qbc_1 apply in such situations; Sarah may utter a qbc_1 to both John and Fred.

6.3   Affirmative Answers to Questions

Sarah is motivated to utter an affirmative response to a $qbc(j, s, \psi)$ if she believes that John has the desire to be ignorant about ψ, and she is ignorant about ψ. This act is called granting a qbc, $gqbc$ for short.

$$(\psi \in B_s D_j I_j), \ (\psi \notin B_s) \in pre(gqbc_1(s, j, \psi)) \tag{14}$$

A variation to this communicative act is the act in which Sarah pleases John by responding affirmatively although she does believe ψ. In this situation, Sarah has suggested that she does not believe ψ although she does. As a result, John is incorrectly justified to believe that Sarah does not believe ψ. From Sarah's perspective, it does not matter whether John has an incorrect picture of Sarah's cognitive state because she is not aware of a dependency of her (private) beliefs with John's incorrect belief of her belief. That is, for all Sarah's (other) beliefs ϕ holds that these do not have a cognitive precondition which is Sarah's belief that John believes ψ. Sarah cannot be bothered whether John's beliefs regarding her beliefs are incorrect, because these incorrect beliefs would not make her (private) beliefs unjustified.

$$\begin{matrix} (\psi \in B_s D_j I_j), \ (\psi \in B_s), \\ \{\neg(\psi \in B_s B_j/\phi \in B_s) \mid \phi \in B_s\} \end{matrix} \in \ pre(gqbc_2(s, j, \psi)) \qquad (15)$$

After the utterance of a $gqbc(s, j, \psi)$, listener John may deduce that Sarah is ignorant about ψ. The following post-conditions hold for John's cognitive state.

$$(\psi \in B_j I_s) \in \ post(gqbc(s, j, \psi)) \qquad (16)$$

Similar post-conditions hold for the speaker. Speaker Sarah may conclude that John is aware that she is ignorant about ψ, i.e. $\psi \in B_s B_j I_s$. A weaker post-condition is that Sarah does *not* believe that John believes that she believes ψ, i.e. $\psi \notin B_s B_j B_s$. Although the former condition implies the latter (but not *vice versa*), we will explicitly list it, because we have not given a (formal) relation between the different mental states. Note that this weaker post-condition is used in the precondition to contract a proposition (Section 5.4). The following post-conditions hold for Sarah.

$$(\psi \notin B_s B_j B_s), \ (\psi \in B_s B_j I_s) \in \ post(gqbc(s, j, \psi)) \qquad (17)$$

To prevent Sarah from uttering the same *gqbc* more than once, she should not believe that John already believes that she is ignorant about ψ, i.e. $(\psi \notin B_s B_j I_s) \in pre(gqbc(s, j, \psi))$.

Example 4 (John answers Sarah affirmatively). Assume John never had believed that the patient shows symptoms Y, i.e. ϕ. After the update of Sarah's communicative act $qbc_1(\psi)$ to John (Figure 1.2), John believes that Sarah desires to be ignorant about ψ. Because none of his other beliefs are based on his believe in ψ, he is allowed to respond with a $gqbc_2(\psi)$.

6.4   Auxiliary Questions for Belief Contraction

The act of posing an auxiliary question to approve belief contraction is a question about a proposition which is believed by the agent and which is (part of) the reason why another belief is cognitively entrenched.

Two different auxiliary questions are presented and are indexed 2 and 3. Sarah is motivated to put an auxiliary question (with index 2) regarding ψ if the following four criteria hold. Sarah desires to be ignorant about ϕ, she believes ϕ, ψ is a cognitive precondition for belief ϕ, and she believes ψ.

$$\begin{matrix} (\phi \in D_s I_s), \ (\phi \in B_s), \ (\psi \in B_s), \\ (\psi \in B_s/\phi \in B_s) \end{matrix} \in \ pre(qbc_2(s, j, \psi)) \qquad (18)$$

If the preconditions of a qbc_2 hold for Sarah's cognitive state, at least one cognitive precondition ($\psi \in B_s$) exists if ψ is cognitively entrenched in her belief state. To achieve a non-entrenched state, Sarah needs to contract belief ψ; she asks support for this action by asking the other agents for approval. This sub dialogue may terminate in the situation in which ψ is not entrenched anymore.

Sarah is motivated to put an auxiliary question (with index 3) regarding ψ if the following criteria hold. Sarah believes that John desires to be ignorant about ϕ, she believes ϕ, ψ and ψ is a cognitive precondition for belief ϕ.

$$(\phi \in B_s D_j I_j),\ (\phi \in B_s),\ (\psi \in B_s), \atop (\psi \in B_s/\phi \in B_s)\ \in\ pre(qbc_3(s,j,\psi)) \tag{19}$$

Additional preconditions are equal to those of the qbc_1. Additionally, because the listening agent cannot distinguish an auxiliary question from a regular question, the post-conditions are equal to those of a regular question. Questions may trigger auxiliary questions, which are perceived as regular questions, which may trigger new additional auxiliary questions. In this fashion, new dialogues are initiated resulting in a distributed process of agents considering to contract beliefs.

Example 5 (Fred poses auxiliary questions). In the example, Fred believes that the patient shows symptom Y, i.e. he believes ϕ. Fred also believes ψ due to ϕ, and ψ is entrenched in his belief state. After the update of communicative act $qbc_1(s, f, \psi)$ (Figure 1.1), Fred is aware of Sarah desire to be ignorant about ψ, To 'un-entrench' ψ, he needs to contract ϕ first. With $qba_3(f, s, \phi)$ and $qba_3(f, j, \phi)$ (Figure 1.2), he confers with John and Sarah whether he may.

6.5   Negative Answers to Questions

If Sarah has run out of options (that is, communicative acts) to 'un-entrench' proposition ψ, she is unable to become ignorant about ψ. If in such situations an agent asks her for approval to drop ψ, Sarah cannot comply, because she cannot un-entrench ψ and can therefore only answer negatively. In the current dialogue game, Sarah has run out of (auxiliary) questions if for all cognitive preconditions ϕ for some ψ that needs to be un-entrenched, the post-conditions of the act of a $gqbc$ or $dqbc$ regarding ψ hold for all other agents. This means that all other agents have responded to her qbc's to un-entrench ψ, which seem to have failed. The act is called denial of a qbc, $dqbc$ for short.

$$\{(post(gqbc(a, s, \phi)) \lor post(dqbc(a, s, \phi)))\mid (a \in \mathcal{A} \setminus s) \land (\phi \in B_s/\psi \in B_s)\} \tag{20}$$

Sarah may utter a $dqbc$ in response to a $qbc(j, s, \psi)$ if the following three criteria hold. Sarah believes that John has the desire to be ignorant about ψ, she believes ψ, and she ran out of (auxiliary) questions which, if answered, could have resulted in the situation in which ψ is not cognitively entrenched anymore.

$$(\psi \in B_s D_j I_j),\ (\psi \in B_s),\ (20)\ \in\ pre(dqbc(s, j, \psi)) \tag{21}$$

Addressee John may derive properties of Sarah's cognitive state from the motivations of a $dqbc(s, j, \psi)$. Note that the propositions that could have convinced Sarah to become ignorant are not accessible to John. In a similar fashion, Sarah can derive properties of John's cognitive state.

$$(\psi \in B_j B_s),\ (\psi \in B_s B_j B_s)\ \in\ post(dqbc(s, j, \psi)) \tag{22}$$

To rule out that the *dqbc* is superfluous, the following precondition should hold: $(\psi \notin B_s B_j B_s) \in pre(dqbc(s, j, \psi))$.

7 Discussion and Conclusions

Our goal was to define a dialogue game in which agents can contract beliefs in a coordinated and distributed fashion. An agent is said to be motivated to confer with other agents if it is possible that her current beliefs depend on the beliefs she is about to contract. If these dependencies do not exist, propositions can be contracted safely (as far as the agent can know). Agents are allowed to lie about their beliefs if this would not introduce ungrounded beliefs as far as agents can know from their local perspective; no global guarantees of ungrounded propositions are given.

We succeeded in defining a dialogue game that specifies when agents have to contract beliefs such that contraction is coordinated and distributed. The agents do not use global knowledge about other agent's cognitive state, but instead use only local knowledge to coordinate contractions. The semantics of the different communicative acts allow the agent to initiate new and related sub-dialogues. These sub-dialogues result in the distributed nature of the process of agents contracting beliefs. These sub-dialogues are not about arbitrary propositions, but are confined to the propositions that are related to those propositions agents desire to contract. In multiagent systems, different agents may entertain different believe in ψ, and these beliefs may justify other agent's beliefs. If only one agent desires to contract a belief, it may be necessary that several agents also need to contract beliefs for the first agent to achieve successfully her desire to become ignorant about ψ.

Future research will address problems that result when agents use the rules of the dialogue and decision games with only their local knowledge. An application of these dialogue games is in the definition of agents agreeing to disagree about propositions [26]: Agents have run out of communicative acts, including acts for contracting beliefs, to resolve a disagreement. If such a pervasive disagreement were identified, a dialogue about meaning revision would be justified.

References

1. Lebbink, H.J., Witteman, C., Meyer, J.J.: A dialogue game to offer an agreement to disagree. In: Second International Workshop for Programming Multi-Agent Systems: Language and Tools (ProMAS'04), New York, NY, USA (2004) 103–114 Held with the Third International Joint Conference on Autonomous Agents and Multi-Agent Systems (AAMAS'04).
2. Parsons, S., Wooldridge, M., Amgoud, L.: Properties and complexity of some formal inter-agent dialogues. Journal of Logic and Computation **13** (2003) 347–376
3. Reed, C.A.: Dialogue frames in agent communication. In Demazeau, Y., ed.: Proceedings of the Third International Conference on Multi-Agent Systems (ICMAS 98), Paris, IEEE Press (1998) 246–253

4. Walton, D.N., Krabbe, E.C.W.: Commitment in Dialogue: Basic Concepts of Interpersonal Reasoning. SUNY Press. Albany, NY, USA (1995)

5. McBurney, P., Parsons, S.: Representing Epistemic Uncertainty by means of Dialectical Argumentation. Annals of Mathematics and Artificial Intelligence, Special Issue on Representations of Uncertainty **32** (2001) 125–169

6. Prakken, H.: On Dialogue Systems with Speech Acts, Arguments, and Counterarguments. In Ojeda-Aciego, M., de Guzman, M.I.P., Brewka, G., Pereira, L.M., eds.: Proceedings of the 7th European Workshop on Logic for Artificial Intelligence (JELIA'00), Berlin, Germany, Springer Lecture Notes in AI 1919, Springer Verlag (2000) 224–238

7. McBurney, P., van Eijk, R.M., Parsons, S., Amgoud, L.: A Dialogue game protocol for agent purchase negotiations. Journal of Autonomous Agents and Multi-Agent Systems **7** (2003) 232–273

8. Sadri, F., Toni, F., Torroni, P.: Logic agents, dialogues and negotiation: and abductive approach. In Schroeder, M., Stathis, K., eds.: Proceedings of the Symposium on Information Agents for E-Commerce, Artificial Intelligence and the Simulation of Behaviour Conference (AISB 2001), York, UK, AISB (2001)

9. Hitchcock, D., McBurney, P., Parsons, S.: A framework for deliberation dialogues. In Hansen, H.V., Tindale, C.W., Blair, J.A., Johnson, R.H., eds.: Proceedings of the Fourth Biennial Conference on the Ontario Society of the Study of Argumentation (OSSA 2001), Windsor, Ontario, Canada (2001)

10. Hulstijn, J.: Dialogue Models for Inquiry and Transaction. PhD thesis, Universiteit Twente, Enschede, The Netherlands (2000)

11. Beun, R.J.: On the Generation of Coherent Dialogue: A Computational Approach. Pragmatics & Cognition **9** (2001) 37–68

12. Lebbink, H.J., Witteman, C., Meyer, J.J.: Dialogue Games for Inconsistent and Biased Information. Electronic Lecture Notes of Theoretical Computer Science **85** (2004)

13. Rescher, N., Brandom, R.: The Logic of Inconsistency. A Study in Non-Standard Possible-World Semantics and Ontology. Basil Blackwell, Oxford (1980)

14. Priest, G., Tanaka, K.: Paraconsistent Logic. In Zalta, E.N., ed.: The Stanford Encyclopedia of Philosophy. (Winter 2004)

15. Ginsberg, M.L.: Multivalued Logics: A Uniform Approach to Reasoning in Artificial Intelligence. Computational Intelligence **4** (1988) 265–316

16. Arieli, O., Avron, A.: Bilattices and paraconsistency. In: First World Congress on Paraconsistency (WCP'97), Gent, Belgium (1997)

17. Kripke, S.: Semantical considerations on modal logic. Acta Philosophica Fennica **16** (1963) 83–94

18. Meyer, J.J.C., van der Hoek, W.: Epistemic Logic for AI and Computer Science. Cambridge University Press (1995)

19. Horwich, P.: Meaning. Clarendon Press, Oxford , UK (1998)

20. Ellenbogen, S.: Wittgenstein's Account of Truth. SUNY series in philosophy. State University of New York Press (2003)

21. Koons, R.: Defeasible Reasoning. (Spring 2005)

22. Gärdenfors, P.: Knowledge in Flux: Modeling the Dynamics of Epistemic States. A Bradford book. The MIT Press (1988)

23. Dignum, F., Weigand, H., Verharen, E.: A formal specification of deadlines using dynamic deontic logic. Technical report, CSR 96-09, Eindhoven University of Technology (1996)

24. FIPA: Communicative act library specification. standard sc00037j. Technical report, Foundation for Intelligent Physical Agents (2002)

25. McBurney, P., Parsons, S.: Locutions for argumentation in agent interaction protocols. In: Third International Joint Conference on Autonomous Agents and Mulit-Agent Systems (AAMAS'04), New York, NY, USA (2004) 164–178
26. Lebbink, H.J., Witteman, C., Meyer, J.J.: A dialogue game to offer an agreement to disagree. In: Third international joint conference on Autonomous Agents & Multi-Agent Systems (AAMAS'04), New York, NY, USA (2004) 1238–1239

Commitment-Based Policies in Persuasion Dialogues with Defeasible Beliefs

Ioan Alfred Letia and Raluca Vartic

Technical University of Cluj-Napoca
Department of Computer Science
Baritiu 28, RO-3400 Cluj-Napoca, Romania
{letia, rvartic}@cs-gw.utcluj.ro

Abstract. We advance a model to express the preconditions for engaging in dialogues in terms of the agents' mental attitudes, in a defeasible logic context (beliefs are divided into strict and defeasible ones). Then, we give a protocol for the persuasion dialogue between two agents, which provides the means of identifying both false premises and logical fallacies. Communicative acts are organized in a hierarchy, and relations between speech acts and social commitments are expressed via policies involving operations on social commitments. Including commitments renders an observable behaviour of the communicating agents.

Keywords: agent, argumentation, protocol.

1   Introduction

There are two main trends for designing agent communication. The first is based on the mental attitudes of the agents, where speech acts can be initiated when a set of preconditions hold, and a so called rational effect is produced after they have been uttered. The second approach relies on the notion of commitment, which can be seen as a responsibility to the community of agents taken by the speaker agent. Recent work has considered the benefits and shortcomings of the two trends, and has searched for ways to combine them, in order to exploit the advantages provided by each one [1]. This paper is also an attempt to merge the two approaches, but our focus is on protocols for dialogues.

Agents can engage in different dialogue types (such as information seeking, inquiry, persuasion). Starting a particular kind of dialogue is triggered by a set of preconditions, traditionally expressed in terms of the agents' mental states [2], an approach we preserve throughout the paper, but which we intend to extend by assuming agents practice reasoning mechanisms involving defeasible logic.

Parts of an agent's knowledge may often be uncertain or incomplete, and a system of preferences would be needed to decide between rules with conflicting conclusions. We claim that by introducing defeasibility into the agents' knowledge bases a convenient mechanism for treating such issues, which are quite common in the real world, is provided. We also believe that defeasible logic is

F. Dignum, R. van Eijk, and R. Flores (Eds.): AC 2005/2006, LNAI 3859, pp. 243–257, 2006.

suitable for the dynamics of the dialogue, which may cause agents to add new knowledge or change their existing beliefs.

We propose a refinement of protocols, arguing that they should allow for the verification of both the correctness of the premises and the soundness of the logical argumentation. We illustrate our method by focusing on a protocol for the persuasion dialogue.

Once this protocol is defined, we intend to provide a link to social commitments. We claim this is necessary because an external observer can only notice the messages exchanged by agents, which is usually not enough to deduce what protocol has been employed, and hence there is no way for an external agent to verify the compliance of the agents to protocols. On the other hand, if there is a link between the communication acts and commitments, the observer can infer the compliance of agents to community rules by watching how the social commitments evolve [3].

2   Redefining the Dialogues

The first contribution of this paper is providing the rules that trigger certain dialogues, in a defeasible logic context. We take as a starting point the work in [2], which includes a recent classification of the possible dialogues between communicating agents, and gives the preconditions required to initiate each type of dialogue, in terms of the agents' mental states. We intend to extend that analysis and argue that real argumentation scenarios often require a more complex representation of the agents' knowledge. Their beliefs are not equally strong, and some rules may only be useful in certain situations. Defeasible logic provides the means to capture such a scenario, in terms of strict and defeasible rules, defeaters and a system of preferences which can decide between rules with conflicting conclusions.

2.1   Defeasible Knowledge and Reasoning

Traditional mechanisms for knowledge representation fail to expressively depict the complexity of real environments. We often rely on rules like "People in our country speak our language" when asking a random passer-by for the time, for example. This rule may not fire if the person is a foreign tourist, so it is not a rule that always leads to an indisputable conclusion when its premises are true, but it is useful in most cases. Defeasible logic allows this kind of rules, called defeasible rules, to be stated, and they will hold whenever there is no stronger evidence pointing to the contrary. Superiority relations between defeasible rules with conflicting conclusions state that one rule overrides another.

Of course, it is possible to express such knowledge using classical logic as well, but in defeasible logic it comes handy, while in classical logic it is more difficult and quite unnatural. Dialogues often involve statements that can be reasonable in a certain context, but become useless when the context is changed. Defeasible logic provides a natural manner for expressing such situations. Another thing to be considered is that information previously unknown to agents may be provided during discussions, and such information sometimes causes agents to revise their knowledge. Classical logic is rigid to changes, entire rules would have to be rewritten, while defeasible logic is quite flexible from this point of view, by allowing new rules to be included in the knowledge base, and priority relations to state which rule is preferred. This feature can also be used to introduce exceptions for rules, a common practice in dynamic or unknown environments, where new information may be found at every step.

As computers are integrated into real life scenarios, humans tend to be reluctant with respect to computers making decisions for them. In order for humans to accept results provided by computers in fields where they were the decision makers and experts, like law, medicine, politics or business, computers need to provide their results in a meaningful manner. As defeasible logic resembles human reasoning, arguments expressed in this logic are easy to understand.

Conclusions in defeasible logic with regard to a literal q can be: $+\Delta q$: q is definitely provable (using only strict rules), $-\Delta q$: q is not definitely probable, $+\partial q$: q is defeasibly provable, $-\partial q$: q is not defeasibly provable.

We use defeasible logic for dialogues to divide beliefs (B) into strict (BS) and defeasible (BD) ones. For example, we can say that an agent X has a strict belief that p is true if it can prove $+\Delta p$ (it can prove p using only strict rules). Agent X has a defeasible belief that p holds if it can prove $+\partial p$ and $-\Delta p$ (it cannot prove p using just strict rules but it can prove it, and the proof includes defeasible rules). If agent X either strictly or defeasibly believes p holds, than we can state that X believes p to be true. Similar notations are used for representing that an agent knows whether (W) some p is true or false:

$$BS_Xp \rightarrow B_Xp$$
$$BD_Xp \rightarrow B_Xp$$
$$WS_Xp \rightarrow W_Xp$$
$$WD_Xp \rightarrow W_Xp$$

2.2 Dialogues

The new dialogue preconditions are presented in Table 1, where we use the following notations: A - agreement, C - conflict of opinions, P - persuasion dialogue, IS - information seeking dialogue, I - inquiry dialogue, V - verification dialogue, Q - query-like dialogue.

Table 1. Dialogue preconditions

	B_AB_Bp	$B_ABS_B\neg p$	$B_ABD_B\neg p$	$B_A\neg WS_Bp$	$B_AWD_Bp\wedge$ $\neg B_AB_Bp\wedge$ $\neg B_AB_B\neg p$	$B_AWS_Bp\wedge$ $\neg B_AB_Bp\wedge$ $\neg B_AB_B\neg p$
$BS_Ap\ I_AB_Bp$	A	C	P	P	P	
$BD_Ap\ I_AB_Bp$	A		P	P	P	
$\neg W_Ap\ I_AW_Ap$	IS	IS	IS	I	IS	IS
I_AW_Ap	Q	Q	Q	Q	Q	Q
I_AB_Ap	Q	Q	Q	Q	Q	Q
$I_AB_AB_Bp$	V	V	V	V	V	V

The use of defeasible logic has an impact on the preconditions required for the persuasion dialogue. Agent A has no chance of success when trying to convince an agent B of something that directly contradicts one of agent B's strict beliefs. This makes sense if we are considering one's chances of convincing a political party member that it is better to vote for the competition. We see the first benefit of including defeasible logic in the scene. The table also identifies the situation where agents stand on irreconcilable conflicting positions, both having strict conflicting beliefs, or when they agree with respect to a proposition p.

2.3   A Protocol for Persuasion Dialogues

We begin by defining a protocol we call WhySupport (WS), which would be engaged by an agent X in order to find the reasons behind a certain proposition p (for example after Y has asserted p).

The protocol has been enhanced to allow reasoning about inferences. We argue that for an argument (p) to be accepted by an agent, it is not enough to have all the elements of the support of the argument accepted, but the agent additionally has to accept that the support (S) of the argument will indeed lead to the conclusion $(S \Rightarrow p)$. Therefore, we introduce a new protocol called HowArgument, explained and defined right after this protocol. The WhySupport protocol starts with agent X asking agent Y for the backing of p, and Y will respond with the support for p. Agent X can accept or reject the justification or it can engage the protocol WhySupport for some (possibly all) of the elements of the reply.

WhySupport(X, Y, p)

1. $X: Why(p)$
2. $Y: ReplySupport(p, S)$, where S is the support of an argument for p
3. for each s in S: $\begin{cases} X: Accept(s), & if\ B_X Acceptable(s) \\ X: Reject(s), & if\ BS_X \neg s \\ WhySupport(X, Y, s), otherwise \end{cases}$
4. $\begin{cases} X: Accept(S \Rightarrow p), & if\ B_X Acceptable(S \Rightarrow p) \\ X: Reject(S \Rightarrow p), & if\ BS_X \neg (S \Rightarrow p) \\ HowArgument(X, Y, S \Rightarrow p), otherwise \end{cases}$
5. X: Accept(p) or Reject(p)

We notice that an agent will reject something that contradicts one of its strong (strict) beliefs. When a rejection occurs, the protocol ends. Receiving a rejection on a rule p without being asked for an explanation for p is a sign the communication partner has a strict rule suggesting $\neg p$.

The protocol HowArgument can be applied in the process of accepting an argument p with the support S, when the agent cannot readily accept that if all the elements in S hold, p will also hold $(S \Rightarrow p)$. For example, one might not find readily acceptable the argument p=*perimeter of the triangle is 12*, with the support S=(*triangle is right, leg1 is 3, leg2 is 4, $h^2 = leg1^2 + leg2^2$, perimeter=h+leg1+leg2*), and ask for additional explanations, which could be for example R=(h=5). Now the agent has to accept that all the elements of R are true, and S and R together will lead to p.

HowArgument(X, Y, $S \Rightarrow p$)

> 1. $X: \ How(S \Rightarrow p)$
> 2. $Y: \ ReplyArgument(S \Rightarrow p, R), \ where \ S \cup R \Rightarrow p$
> 3. *for each* r *in* R: $\begin{cases} X: Accept(r), & if \ B_X Acceptable(r) \\ X: Reject(r), & if \ BS_X \neg(r) \\ WhySupport(X, Y, r), \ otherwise \end{cases}$
> 4. $\begin{cases} X: Accept(S \cup R \Rightarrow p), & if \ B_X Acceptable(R \Rightarrow p) \\ X: Reject(S \cup R \Rightarrow p), & if \ BS_X \neg(R \Rightarrow p) \\ HowArgument(X, Y, S \cup R \Rightarrow p), \ otherwise \end{cases}$
> 5. $X: \ Accept(S \Rightarrow p) \ or \ Reject(S \Rightarrow p)$

This protocol allows an agent to reject an argument, even though it believes its support to be true. Agents can reject an argument if they believe there are falsehoods among the premises or logical fallacies (sophisms).

The WhySupport and HowArgument protocols can be used to define protocols for different dialogue types. We take as an example the persuasion dialogue and define the following protocol:

Persuasion(X, Y, p)

> 1. $X: \ Assert(p)$
> 2. $\begin{cases} Y: \ Accept(p), & if \ B_X Acceptable(p) \\ Y: \ Reject(p), & if \ BS_Y \neg p \\ WhySupport(Y, X, p), \ otherwise \end{cases}$
> 3. *if the result of the previous step was a rejection:*
> $Persuasion(Y, X, \neg p), \ if \ I_Y B_X \neg p$

The protocol starts with agent X trying to convince agent Y that a proposition p holds. Y has 4 options: it can accept or reject X's assertion and the protocol ends, it can reject the assertion and try to persuade X that in fact $\neg p$ holds (if it has an intention to influence X to believe $\neg p$), or it can seek for the justification for X's utterance (why? how?) before reaching a conclusion.

An interesting discussion is what happens in case agent Y believes defeasibly that $\neg p$ is the case, and agent X engages agent Y in a persuasion dialogue with the goal of influencing agent Y to believe p. Agent Y cannot readily accept or reject X's statement, so it will engage the WhySupport protocol, in order to obtain more information, which will help it make a better decision.

The main enhancement as against existing persuasion protocols is the possibility to demand an explanation for inferences. Other protocols [2] allow agents to call for justifications for previous utterances, but it is not clear what happens if an agent X is provided with an acceptable (true) support, but X has no proof that the given support will indeed lead to the alleged consequence. If we presume the inference ends up being accepted, the agents could easily be persuaded with arguments like: "You should vote for Y because the Earth is not flat", or less obvious, but not uncommon ones like: "You should get a Ford Taurus because it is the most popular selling car in its class", or "All birds are animals. Lassie is an animal. Hence Lassie is a bird". On the other hand, if unreadily acceptable inferences lead to the whole argument being rejected, agents would be given only one

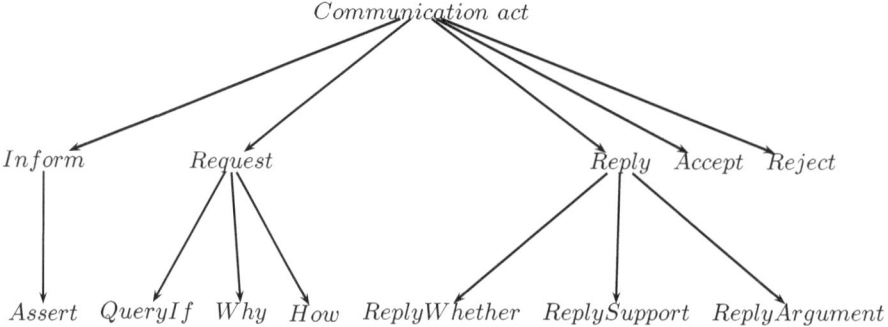

Fig. 1. Taxonomy of communicative acts

chance to provide an argument standing for an inference acceptable to another agent. As agent knowledge is usually not public, this may often be impossible, and valid arguments could end up being rejected, such as the initial argument given for the perimeter of a triangle, stated earlier.

The given examples of logical fallacies show why it is not enough to check for the truth state of the premises. The problem of determining the truth of a statement by means of argumentation is not straightforward. Both formal validity of arguments and material truth have to be verified. Formal validity has been rigorously defined by argumentation corpora. Providing mechanisms for checking the validity requirements for all argument types (categorical, disjunctive, hypothetical) is beyond the scope of this paper. What we do provide is an enhancement to argument validation, by allowing agents to demand and provide a vindication for claimed implications. This increases the persuader's chances of proving its point if it is a valid one, and it decreases the chances for the agent to be persuaded to be fooled. An interesting problem that still stands is how the agents will deal with information that cannot be checked using their knowledge bases. We do not deal with this issue here, but a possible solution is seeking the help of another agent, or asking a human specialist.

3   Commitment-Based Dialogues

Unlike mental attitudes, which are private to the agent, commitments have a public nature. They link the agents to the community they are part of. By observing the evolution of the commitments in a society of agents, one can draw conclusions about the behaviour of the agents. An agent is well behaved if it fulfills its commitments promptly.

A commitment is a relation between two agents (the debtor and the creditor), and it represents the responsibility of the debtor to execute an action $(C(debtor, creditor, action))$.

A subsumption lattice has been used [3] to arrange the FIPA ACL performatives, and social commitments to observe agent behaviour, taking into consideration just the messages passed between agents.

We give our own taxonomy for the set of communicative acts (CAs) likely to occur in agent dialogues in figure 1. We have used non-FIPA communication acts for the sake of expressivity. A mapping to FIPA performatives can be performed. For example, the three subtypes of reply could be expressed by a reply performative, and a part of the content of the message (a flag) would be used to identify the type of reply.

An agent can represent this hierarchy using strict rules (figure 2).

$$r1 : type(M, inform) \rightarrow type(M, communicationAct)$$
$$r2 : type(M, request) \rightarrow type(M, communicationAct)$$
$$r3 : type(M, reply) \rightarrow type(M, communicationAct)$$
$$r4 : type(M, accept) \rightarrow type(M, communicationAct)$$
$$r5 : type(M, reject) \rightarrow type(M, communicationAct)$$
$$r6 : type(M, assert) \rightarrow type(M, inform)$$
$$r7 : type(M, queryIf) \rightarrow type(M, request)$$
$$r8 : type(M, why) \rightarrow type(M, request)$$
$$r9 : type(M, how) \rightarrow type(M, request)$$
$$r10 : type(M, replyW) \rightarrow type(M, reply)$$
$$r11 : type(M, replyS) \rightarrow type(M, reply)$$
$$r12 : type(M, replyA) \rightarrow type(M, reply)$$

Fig. 2. Hierarchy of communication acts

Similar to [3], agent communication is modeled to act upon social commitments. A communication act may add or delete social commitments, and hence an outsider could observe the state of social commitments within a community of agents. Commitments involve one agent performing an action for another agent. In this paper, we restrict actions to speech acts. The messages are translated to commitment operators through a set of policies, expressed as defeasible rules in figure 3.

For instance, a *request* utterance adds an obligation for the receiver to reply on the subject (r14). A *reply* sent by solicited agent on the content of the initial request will remove this obligation (r20). Child nodes (subtypes) inherit the policies of their parent nodes, and may add policies of their own. For example, in case agent X will send a message of type *why* (*Why(p)* for example) to agent Y, we will have to apply two policies (r14 and r16), and so agent Y will have a commitment to reply to agent X, and another commitment to reply with the support for the content of the initial message (*p*). If agent Y replies with the support for *p*, two commitment policies will be applied (r20 and r22), and both commitments will be deleted, because a message of type *replySupport* is also of type *reply* (r11).

In this example, an *inform* message activates a commitment for the informed agent to accept or reject the information provided. This requirement may be too strong for some agent societies, so we must allow for variations of policies in order to fit the specifics of every community of agents.

An external observer can only see the messages exchanged between agents, which is usually not enough to deduce what protocol is being used. Instead, the

$r13 : sent(F, T, M), type(M, inform), firstElem(M, C) \Rightarrow c(T, F, accRej(C))$
$r14 : sent(F, T, M), type(M, request), firstElem(M, C) \Rightarrow c(T, F, reply(C))$
$r15 : sent(F, T, M), type(M, queryIf), firstElem(M, C) \Rightarrow c(T, F, replyW(C))$
$r16 : sent(F, T, M), type(M, why), firstElem(M, C) \Rightarrow c(T, F, replyS(C))$
$r17 : sent(F, T, M), type(M, how), firstElem(M, C) \Rightarrow c(T, F, replyA(C))$
$r18 : sent(F, T, M), type(M, accept), firstElem(M, C) \Rightarrow \neg c(F, T, acceptReject(C))$
$r19 : sent(F, T, M), type(M, reject), firstElem(M, C) \Rightarrow \neg c(F, T, acceptReject(C))$
$r20 : sent(F, T, M), type(M, reply), firstElem(M, C) \Rightarrow \neg c(F, T, reply(C))$
$r21 : sent(F, T, M), type(M, replyW), firstElem(M, C) \Rightarrow \neg c(F, T, replyW(C))$
$r22 : sent(F, T, M), type(M, replyS), firstElem(M, C) \Rightarrow \neg c(F, T, replyS(C))$
$r23 : sent(F, T, M), type(M, replyA), firstElem(M, C) \Rightarrow \neg c(F, T, replyA(C))$

$r18 > r13, \; r19 > r13, \; r20 > r14, \; r21 > r15, \; r22 > r16, \; r23 > r17$

Fig. 3. Commitment policies

observer will be able to infer the state of the social commitments by identifying the speech acts employing social policies.

4 Running Example

As an example we illustrate a possible persuasion dialogue between an adept of Einstein's general relativity theory and someone only familiar with Newton's laws of physics, considering the communicative acts in figure 1, and the policies and commitments expressed as defeasible rules in 3. In this particular discussion, the ignorant Newton fan (N) wants to convince the Einstein adept (E) that time and space are absolute. E disagrees, and makes N acquainted with some elements of general relativity.

Here is the sample dialogue:

N: Time and space are absolute.
E: No, they are not.
N: Why would you say that?
E: Einstein's general relativity laws prove they are not.
N: How?
E: Since the speed of light is constant, time and space are not
   absolute.
N: How could the speed of light be constant?
E: Experiments prove that it is.
N: Apparently they do. I don't really understand how this goes,
   but I guess you have a point.
N: How does this prove time and space are not absolute?
E: If the speed of light is the same for all observers, regardless
   of their motion relative to the source of the light, then clearly
   distances are stretched and shrunk, and hence they are not
   absolute.
N: Oh, I get it now.

We denote by *tsa* the proposition "time and space are absolute", by *el* "Einstein's general relativity laws", by *ccst* the proposition "the speed of light is constant", by *e* the "experiments" and by *tsss* the statement "time and space stretch and shrink".

We will use this sample dialogue to illustrate the effects of the mental states on the communicative acts uttered by agents (table 2), and the effects of these communicative acts on both the mental attitudes of the agents (table 2) and the social commitments (table 3).

Table 2. Trace of mental states in the dialogue

Mental triggers	CAs	Changes in Mental States
$BD_N tsa$ $I_N B_E tsa$ $B_N \neg W S_E tsa$	N: Assert(tsa)	$B_E B_N tsa$
$BS_E \neg tsa$	E: Reject(tsa)	$B_N BS_E \neg tsa$
$BS_E \neg tsa$ $I_E B_N \neg tsa$ $B_E BD_N tsa$	E: Assert(¬tsa)	
$BD_N tsa$	N: Why(¬tsa)	
$BS_E el \rightarrow \neg tsa$ $BS_E el$	E: Reply-support(¬tsa, el)	$B_N B_E el \Rightarrow \neg tsa$ $B_N B_E el$
$B_N Acceptable(el)$	N: Accept(el)	$B_N el$
$\neg B_N el \Rightarrow \neg tsa$	N: How(el ⇒ ¬tsa)	
$BS_E[el, ccst] \rightarrow \neg tsa$ $BS_E ccst$	E: Reply-argument(el ⇒ ¬tsa, ccst)	$B_N B_E[el, ccst] \Rightarrow \neg tsa$ $B_N B_E ccst$
$\neg B_N ccst$	N: Why(ccst)	
$BS_E e \rightarrow ccst$ $BS_E e$	E: Reply-support(ccst, e)	$B_N B_E e \Rightarrow ccst$ $B_N B_E e$
$B_N Acceptable(e)$	N: Accept(e)	$B_N e$
$B_N Acceptable(e \Rightarrow ccst)$	N: Accept(e ⇒ ccst)	$B_N e \Rightarrow ccst$
$B_N Acceptable(ccst)$	N: Accept(ccst)	$B_N ccst$
$\neg B_N[el, ccst] \Rightarrow \neg tsa$ $B_N ccst$ $BD_N tsa$	N: How([el, ccst] ⇒ ¬tsa)	
$BS_E tsss$ $BS_E[ccst, tsss] \rightarrow \neg tsa$	E: Reply-argument(ccst ⇒ ¬tsa, tsss)	$B_N B_E tsss$ $B_N B_E[ccst, tsss] \Rightarrow \neg tsa$
$B_N Acceptable(tsss)$	N: Accept(tsss)	$B_N tsss$
$B_N Acceptable($ $[el, ccst, tsss] \Rightarrow \neg tsa)$	N: Accept([el, ccst, tsss] ⇒ ¬tsa)	$B_N[el, ccst, tsss] \Rightarrow \neg tsa$
$B_N \neg tsa$	N: Accept(¬tsa)	$B_N \neg tsa$

In table 2, the messages sent by the agents appear in the second column. The first column represents the subset of the agent mental states triggering these speech acts, whilst the third column shows the changes regarding the mental attitudes of the agents (like new beliefs) induced by the messages.

For example, in the first row, we assume that the preconditions for agent N to start a persuasion dialogue hold. As a consequence, the protocol will start with agent N sending the first message ($N :\ Assert(tsa)$), stating that time and space are absolute. From this message, agent E can tell that agent N believes *tsa* (second column).

Next, in the second row, we notice agent E strictly believes that the content of the message previously sent by N is not the case, and so it will reject N's statement ($E : Reject(tsa)$). Agent N does not have access to E's beliefs, but the prompt rejection of its assertion signals that E strictly believes that "time and space are absolute" is a false statement. From now on, N knows that it is not worth trying to persuade E on this matter.

We have assumed agent E, on the other hand, intends to influence N to adopt its position on the time and space fabric ($I_E B_N \neg tsa$), and it also believes N's position on the matter is not rigid ($B_E BD_N tsa$), conditions which will trigger the initiation of a persuasion dialogue in the opposite direction and having as subject the negation of the original one. If agent E had a strict belief that tsa was true, there would be no possible reconciliation. But in our example, agent N is willing to debate the truth of its belief ($BD_N tsa$), and step by step is provided with evidence it has to accept.

Before the last row, agent N has two conflicting defeasible rules in its knowledge base:

$$r1 : nl \Rightarrow tsa.$$
$$r2 : el, ccst, tsss \Rightarrow \neg tsa.$$

The first rule (r1) states that when applying Newton's laws of physics, time and space are absolute. The second rule (r2), states that if we are applying Einstein's general relativity theory, because the speed of light is constant and time and space stretch and shrink, one can conclude that time and space are not absolute. The agent will need to establish preferences among these rules, in order to be able to reach a conclusion. We have assumed the agent inferred the superiority relation:

$$r2 > r1$$

This superiority relation allows agent N to conclude that time and space are not absolute (the last row of table 2), when the discussion takes place in the context of Einstein's general relativity laws. And the first rule is still there to be used, in a context where general relativity is not applied, but Newton's laws of physics are.

An agent is rigid to revising its position about a statement if this position employs only strict rules. By contrast, the agent is open to changing its position regarding a defeasible belief ($BD_A b$), if presented with an argument suggesting its contrary ($\neg b$), on the condition that this argument is stronger (from the agent's point of view) than the argument the agent itself can derive in order to defend its belief.

In table 3, we are concerned with the evolution of social commitments as messages are exchanged. In the first column we have the CAs, in the second column the operation corresponding to the CA, and in the third column the active social commitments after the CA in the first column has been uttered.

The message that starts the persuasion protocol (first row: $N : Assert(tsa)$) adds a commitment for the receiving agent to accept or reject the assertion (second column), and thus the commitment $C(E, N, ar(tsa))$ becomes active (third column). We assume that agents have among their goals displaying a good social behaviour, which they can achive by complying to social norms, and in our case by promptly fulfilling their commitments.

Table 3. Trace of commitments in the dialogue

CAs	Commitment operations	Commitments
N: Assert(tsa)	+C(E, N, ar(tsa))	C(E, N, ar(tsa))
E: Reject(tsa)	-C(E,N,ar(tsa))	
E: Assert(¬tsa)	+C(N, E, ar(¬tsa)	C(N, E, ar(¬tsa))
N: Why(¬tsa)	+C(E, N, rs(¬tsa))	C(N, E, ar(¬tsa))
	+C(E, N, r(¬tsa))	C(E, N, rs(¬tsa))
		C(E, N, r(¬tsa))
E: Reply-support(¬tsa, el)	-C(E, N, rs(¬tsa))	C(N, E, ar(¬tsa))
	-C(E, N, r(¬tsa))	
N: Accept(el)		C(N, E, ar(¬tsa))
N: How(el ⇒ ¬tsa)	+C(E, N, ra(el ⇒ ¬tsa))	C(N, E, ar(¬tsa))
	+C(E, N, r(el ⇒ ¬tsa))	C(E, N, ra(el ⇒ ¬tsa))
		C(E, N, r(el ⇒ ¬tsa))
E: Reply-argument(	-C(E, N, ra(el ⇒ ¬tsa))	C(N, E, ar(¬tsa))
el ⇒ ¬tsa, ccst)	-C(E, N, r(el ⇒ ¬tsa))	
N: Why(ccst)	+C(E, N, rs(ccst))	C(N, E, ar(¬tsa))
	+C(E, N, r(ccst))	C(E, N, rs(ccst))
		C(E, N, r(ccst))
E: Reply-support(ccst, e)	-C(E, N, rs(ccst))	C(N, E, ar(¬tsa))
	-C(E, N, r(ccst)	
N: Accept(e)		C(N, E, ar(¬tsa))
N: Accept(e ⇒ ccst)		C(N, E, ar(¬tsa))
N: Accept(ccst)		C(N, E, ar(¬tsa))
N: How([el, ccst] ⇒ ¬tsa)	+C(E, N, ra([el, ccst] ⇒ ¬tsa))	C(N, E, ar(¬tsa))
	+C(E, N, r([el, ccst] ⇒ ¬tsa))	C(E, N, ra([el, ccst] ⇒ ¬tsa))
		C(E, N, r([el, ccst] ⇒ ¬tsa))
E: Reply-argument(	-C(E, N, ra([el, ccst] → ¬tsa))	C(N, E, ar(¬tsa))
[el, ccst] ⇒ ¬tsa, tsss)	-C(E, N, r([el, ccst] ⇒ ¬tsa))	
N: Accept([el, ccst] ⇒ tsss)		C(N, E, ar(¬tsa))
N: Accept(		
[el, ccst, tsss] ⇒ ¬tsa)		
N: Accept(¬tsa)	-C(N, E, ar(¬tsa))	

Agent E will respect its obligation to accept or to reject the absolutness of time and space by sending a message that rejects *tsa* (second row). The effect will be the deletion of the obligation induced by the previous line, and thus the set of active commitments will become empty. The dialogue continues, with new commitments for agents to respond being added and with agents promptly obeying.

We notice that if all agents comply to the protocol, all the commitments induced by the protocol will have been fulfilled at the end. In order to satisfy this requirement, we have to correctly identify the CAs inducing policies on commitments.

We can consider some improvements for the dialogue above. For example, rejecting a statement p, and asserting $¬p$ is superfluous. If a set of rules can express that $Reject(p)$ is subsumed by $Assert(¬p)$, the agent could skip sending the *Reject* message.

Another improvement refers to the intermediary steps taken by an agent in order to find the conclusion with regard to an issue it is committed to accept or reject. If we could restrict the agents to send over only the relevant messages and perform the other operations internally, the number of exchanged messages would be reduced (table 4). For example, in the case of the Why-Support protocol, it is inefficient for the initiating agent to reveal the way it deals with the justification

Table 4. Trace of the improved dialogue

Messages	Internal ops	Commitments
N: Assert(tsa)		C(E, N, ar(tsa))
E: Assert(¬tsa)		C(N, E, ar(¬tsa))
N: Why(¬tsa)		C(N, E, ar(¬tsa)) C(E, N, rs(¬tsa)) C(E, N, r(¬tsa))
E: Reply-support(¬tsa, el)		C(N, E, ar(¬tsa))
	Accept(el)	C(N, E, ar(¬tsa))
N: How(el ⇒ ¬tsa)		C(N, E, ar(¬tsa)) C(E, N, ra(el ⇒ ¬tsa)) C(E, N, r(el ⇒ ¬tsa))
E: Reply-argument(el ⇒ ¬tsa, ccst)		C(N, E, ar(¬tsa))
N: Why(ccst)		C(N, E, ar(¬tsa)) C(E, N, rs(ccst)) C(E, N, r(ccst))
E: Reply-support(ccst, e)		C(N, E, ar(¬tsa))
	N: Accept(e) N: Accept(e ⇒ ccst) N: Accept(ccst)	C(N, E, ar(¬tsa))
N: How([el, ccst] ⇒ ¬tsa)		C(N,E,ar(¬tsa)) C(E,N,ra([el, ccst] ⇒ ¬tsa)) C(E, N, r([el, ccst] ⇒ ¬tsa))
E: Reply-argument(, [el,ccst] ⇒ ¬tsa,tsss)		C(N,E,ar(¬tsa))
	N: Accept(tsss) N: Accept([el,ccst, tsss] ⇒ ¬tsa) N: Infer(r2>r1)	C(N, E, ar(¬tsa))
N: Accept(¬tsa)		

provided by the other agent. Instead, it could just send a message when reaching a conclusion (acceptance or rejection) regarding the initial statement, or when it has to request further clarification. The same stands for the How-Argument protocol.

In table 4, the messages between agents appear in the first column, and the internal operations performed by the agents in the second column. We can see the result is a fairly short dialogue (11 messages) for a relatively complex problem. If we allow more complex statements (for example $[el, e] \rightarrow ccst$ as the support for $\neg tsa$) the dialogue can be simplified even further, most of the effort can focus on the agents' internal reasoning, and communication is minimized.

5   Related Work

Papers [4] and [2] propose definitions of protocols for different types of dialogues, including persuasion. Similar work has been proposed as protocols for dialogue games [5,6]. These protocols assume an agent should be given only one chance to build an argument to be accepted by others. Should an agent not find the argument acceptable because it fails to see the logical connections, these approaches do not give the initiator of the dialogue the chance to defend its argument by providing details regarding its logical implications. The protocol suggested by us includes a more complex method of investigating the issue discussed by the agents, by supplying a mechanism for checking the accuracy of the logical argumentation.

These approaches do not commit to a mechanism for agents pondering on the acceptability of arguments. Including defeasible logic for reasoning upon speech acts and communication protocols is a first, to the best of our knowledge, although this is not the first time defeasibility has been found useful for agent interactions (it has been used to represent business contracts [7], and for declaring negotiation strategies [8]).

An alternative for representing uncertain, incomplete knowledge is the rough sets, where imprecise concepts are represented as a pair of precise concepts, namely the lower and upper approximation. The lower approximation is a set including only the objects that certainly belong to the concept, while the upper approximation contains the objects which have a probability of belonging to the concept. This is somewhat analogous to the situations when a statement is strictly or defeasibly provable. Weakest sufficient condition and strongest necessary condition are used to generate approximate queries [9], and answers to these queries allow classifying the objects into the ones belonging to the concept, the ones not belonging to the concept and the ones for which the membership is unknown. This representation has proven useful to a large range of domains, such as bioinformatics, financing or engineering, and it is a valid alternative for representing agent knowledge. We will look deeper into the advantage rough sets could bring to our work.

Research on communication based on mental attitudes revolves around the specification for an agent communication language proposed by FIPA [10], and reusing the work in this direction is the main argument for preserving this approach. An improved semantics for the FIPA CAs and a layered framework to facilitate protocol verification has also been reported [11].

Commitments attempted to solve the problems conveyed by the mentalistic approach [12] (the contrast between the public character of the conversation and the private nature of the goals and beliefs of the agents, the impossibility to check the compliance of the agents to the ACL semantics and the fact that the sincerity assumption is not appropriate for non-cooperative systems).

The need for messages to reflect changes in the social reality of the multi-agent system, an issue addressed by this paper, has already been tackled [13], within a commitment based semantics for FIPA communication acts, involving a manipulation of commitments and precommitments. This approach takes into consideration commitments regarding the content of the messages, and not the CAs themselves, which is why the solution in [3] fit our needs better.

McGinnis et al propose adaptive protocols, by means of synthesis rules [14], an approach using the LCC (Lightweight Coordination Calculus) language and framework [15], which brings the advantage of dynamic, flexible protocol. This method takes advantage of communication patterns (request-reply), as do we with the help of policies. The example of information seeking dialogue given in [14] does not allow refining the argumentation by challenging inferences, but this feature could be easily added. We have preferred to define a static protocol and use performatives instead of dialogue structures, because our focus was on how specific protocols could be refined, but there is no reason why synthesized protocols should not be used within a community of agents with communication enhanced to support reasoning validation. However, this approach is better suited for domains with highly irregular communication.

6   Conclusions and Future Work

Using defeasible beliefs for stating the preconditions of dialogues induces an increased efficiency of dialogues, by pointing out situations when dialogues should not be initiated, or when dialogues should end, and it introduces a more detailed view of how agents stand in regard to certain statements. Defeasibility also allows agents to discuss and agree on matters which are not rigorously provable, but are very often encountered in real dialogues, and the derived arguments are comprehensible

We claimed that dialogue protocols should allow the verification of both the correctness of the premises and the accuracy of the logical argumentation. We have advanced a persuasion protocol which meets these requirements, and we have discussed its behaviour on an example, but the other types of interactions could also benefit from our approach.

Furthermore, the relations between speech acts and social commitments allow the verification of the compliance of agents to the behaviour desired in a given agent community. The evolution of mental states is important for the evolution of the dialogue, while the evolution of social commitments can be used to reason on the compliance of the agents to the policies of the community.

We will extend our work to cover all types of dialogue involving argumentation, such as inquiry, deliberation, information-seeking, query. We shall also define protocols for other types of interactions, such as political debates, where the main goal is not convincing each other, but persuading the audience. Finally, we want to verify our theoretical studies by building a system of agents that conform to these protocols. Some of the challenges we have identified so far are avoiding the scanning of the entire database in order to check trigger conditions for dialogue types when knowledge changes occur, and handling new, unverifiable information.

Another improvement refers to enhancing the existing protocols to support practical reasoning and verification of the fulfillment of commitments regarding actions which are not communication related. If an agent agrees to execute an action, a commitment regarding that action should become active.

Acknowledgements

We are grateful to the anonymous reviewers for useful comments. Part of this work was supported by the grant 27702-990 from the National Research Council of the Romanian Ministry for Education and Research.

References

1. Boella, G., Hulstijn, J., van der Torre, L.: A synthesis between mental attitudes and social commitments in agent communication languages. In Skowron, A., ed.: Intelligent Agent Technology. (2005) 358–364
2. Cogan, E., Parsons, S., McBurney, P.: What kind of an argument are we going to have today. In: 4th International Joint Conference on Autonomous Agents and Multiagent Systems, Utrecht, Netherlands, ACM Press (2005) 544–551
3. Kremer, R., Flores, R.: Using a performative subsumption lattice to support commitment-based conversations. In: 4th International Joint Conference on Autonomous Agents and Multiagent Systems, Utrecht, Netherlands, ACM Press (2005) 114–121
4. Parsons, S., Wooldridge, M., Amgoud, L.: An analysis of formal inter-agent dialogues. In: 1st International Joint Conference on Autonomous Agents and Multiagent Systems, ACM Press (2002) 394–401
5. McBurney, P., Parsons, S.: Games that agents play: a formal framework for dialogue between autonomous agents. Journal of Logic, Language, and Information —Special issue on logic and games **11**(3) (2002)
6. Amgoud, L., Maudet, N., Parsons, S.: Modelling dialogues using argumentation. In: 4th International Conference on Multi-Agent Systems, IEEE Computer Society (2000) 31–38
7. Governatori, G., Hoang, D.P.: DR-CONTRACT: An architecture for e-contracts in defeasible logic. In: EDOC Workshop on Contract Architecures and Languages. (2005)
8. Skylogiannis, T., Antoniou, G., Skylogiannis, N., Governatori, G.: DR-NEGOTIATE - a system for automated agent negotiation with defeasible logic-based strategies. In: IEEE International Conference on e-Technology, e-Commerce and e-Service. (2005) 44–49
9. Doherty, P., Szałas, A., Łukaszewicz, W.: Approximative query techniques for agents with heterogeneous ontologies and perceptive capabilities. In: 9th International Conference on the Principles of Knowledge Representation and Reasoning, AAAI Press (2004) 459–468
10. FIPA: Fipa communicative act library specification. Technical report, Foundation for Intelligent Physical Agents (2002)
11. Paurobally, S., Cunningham, J., Jennings, N.R.: A formal framework for agent interaction semantics. In: 4th International Joint Conference on Autonomous Agents and Multiagent Systems, Utrecht, Netherlands, ACM Press (2005) 91–98
12. Singh, M.P.: A social semantics for agent communication languages. In: Issues in Agent Communications. LNCS 1916, Springer (2000) 31–45
13. Verdicchio, M., Colombetti, M.: A commitment-based communicative act library. In: 4th International Joint Conference on Autonomous Agents and Multiagent Systems, Utrecht, Netherlands, ACM Press (2005) 755–761
14. McGinnis, J., Robertson, D., Walton, C.: Protocol synthesis with dialogue structure theory. In: 4th International Joint Conference on Autonomous Agents and Multiagent Systems, Utrecht, Netherlands, ACM Press (2005) 1329–1330
15. Robertson, D.: A lightweight coordination calculus for agent systems. In: Declarative Agent Languages and Technologies. LNCS 3476, Springer (2005) 183–197

Reliable Group Communication and Institutional Action in a Multi-agent Trading Scenario

Stephen Cranefield

Department of Information Science
University of Otago
PO Box 56, Dunedin, New Zealand
scranefield@infoscience.otago.ac.nz

Abstract. This paper proposes the use of reliable group communication as a complement to traditional asynchronous messaging in multi-agent systems. In particular, the mechanism of message publication on a virtually synchronous group communication channel is described and an example electronic trading scenario (the game of Pit) is used to illustrate how this form of communication supports the design of interaction protocols in which a shared perception of the order of messages is important. It is also shown that this style of messaging can be used to support the definition of social commitments based on a shared understanding of message order within a conversation.

1 Introduction

One of the most common criteria used in definitions of the term "agent" is a requirement for the entity under consideration to be autonomous [1]. This criterion has led researchers in the field of multi-agent systems to focus on asynchronous modes of communication such as KQML [2] or FIPA ACL [3] messaging, because handling a synchronous message (such as a remote method call in a distributed object-oriented system) requires the recipient to devote some of its computational resources to handling incoming requests at a time dictated by the initiator, and this implies a loss of some of its autonomy.

However, it has also been recognised by the MAS community that in order for agents to form societies in which agents can collaborate or provide services to each other, there must be some standards or agreements within the societies on ontologies, interaction protocols and notions of commitment and trust. Adopting a common ontology and interaction protocol can be seen as a choice made by an agent (or agent designer) to forgo some of its autonomy in order to gain the benefits of being part of a community.

For a similar reason there is a need for communications infrastructure in multi-agent systems to provide a range of communication mechanisms, including those with stronger guarantees than are provided by asynchronous messaging. Providing a range of communication mechanisms will give agents (or protocol and institution designers) a range of options that can be used for specific interactions, just as a human may seek a face-to-face meeting or make a phone call when reaching a rapid consensus is desired, and two parties negotiating a house sale may use a different communication channel than they would for negotiating a choice of film to watch together. In particular,

F. Dignum, R. van Eijk, and R. Flores (Eds.): AC 2005/2006, LNAI 3859, pp. 258–272, 2006.

the available communication mechanisms should include the ability to reliably multi-cast messages to groups of agents, not only for efficient distribution of information to multiple parties, but also to enable commitments made between agents to be publicly observed and therefore more likely to be honoured (e.g. consider the wedding vows exchanged between bride and groom in the presence of witnesses).

This paper focuses on a particular model of reliable group communication: the use of named channels that can be configured to guarantee the property of *virtual synchrony*: all agents connected to the same channel will perceive all message 'publication' and agent joining and leaving events in the same order. We argue that there are many situations, particularly in commerce, where the order of a set of messages sent by various agents is highly significant. In a distributed system with asynchronous communication, interaction protocols for such scenarios must be complicated with interactions to implement transactional behaviour or to detect and recover from invalid states to ensure that the agents involved reach a common understanding of the interaction state. In contrast, implementing virtually synchronous group communication channels within the agent infrastructure and extending interaction protocol notations to include the publication of messages on such channels should allow simpler (and therefore more understandable and maintainable) interaction protocols to be developed for such situations. We illustrate the use of this mechanism within an interaction protocol for an electronic trading scenario: an electronic version of the card game Pit.

There is increasing interest in models of agent communication that are based on social semantics, and in particular the notion of public commitments made between agents is a subject of much research. In this paper we show how publications on a virtually synchronous channel can be defined to count as institutional acts representing the making of commitments that are conditional on a shared understanding of the interaction history. We believe this ability will be useful in developing agent-based e-commerce systems.

The structure of the paper is as follows. Section 2 discusses previous work on group communication in multi-agent systems, gives a brief overview of reliable group communication mechanisms, and presents the notion of virtually sychronous group communication channel used in this paper. Section 3 describes the card game Pit and presents an interaction protocol for a phase of Pit based on such channels. This is followed in Section 4 by an analysis of this scenario using a formal model of commitments and institutional action developed by Verdicchio and Colombetti. A summary of their formalism is presented and it is used to model reliable group communication and the use of publications that 'count as' making a conditional commitment to change to a trading state in the Pit scenario. Finally, some related work is discussed in Section 5, and Section 6 concludes the paper.

2   Reliable Group Communication

In distributed systems it is useful to be able to send the same information to a set of distributed processes with a single command. This is referred to as broadcasting, or, when distinct groups of recipients can be specified, multicasting. When all processes are running on a network that supports a multicast network protocol, such as IP Multicast, there can be sizable performance gains over replicating unicast messages to multiple recipients. However, at the application level, and for agents in particular, there can be benefits from having a multicast communication primitive available, even if the underlying implementation must simulate this by sending multiple unicast messages. Kumar et al. [4] argue that communication addressed to groups is a common feature of human society, and so it is important that agent communication languages and their underlying semantics support group communication. Busetta et al. [5] discuss the use of channeled multicasting for agent communication where messages can be addressed to channels that have a name, a theme (a list of terms from an application-specific taxonomy) and an IP multicast group address. Their architecture allows agents to "tune in" to channels of interest to receive messages that were addressed to channel names or themes, rather than to individually named agents. This architecture then allows specialist agents (when requested) to "overhear" conversations and provide additional information to the participants when appropriate, and it can also be used for monitoring the behaviour of agents.

This paper extends the above work by considering the use of *reliable* group communication channels for agent communication. Researchers into data replication, failure detection and failure recovery in distributed systems have developed protocols that provide applications with multicast primitives having various reliability guarantees [6]. Depending on the application, desirable properties may include *FIFO ordering* (messages are guaranteed to be received in the order that each process sent them), *causal ordering* (if B sends a message after receiving a message from A, all recipients of the two messages see them in this order), *agreed ordering* (all recipients see all messages in the same order), *safety* (agreed ordering with the additional guarantee of atomic delivery: a message is either delivered to all members or, in the case of any members having failed, none) and *virtual synchrony* (all processes observe the same events in the same order, including processes joining or leaving a group)[1]. The JGroups library [8] combines these ideas with a channel-based architecture. Java applications can create a channel that is connected to a named group—all agents having channels connected to a group are automatically members of that group. The channel constructor is passed a symbolic description of the stack of protocols that are to be used in the channel's implementation, and these can be chosen so that particular properties such as safety and virtual synchrony are assured by the underlying protocols.

In this paper we assume that the following operations (which are supported by the Java JGroups library [8]) are available to agents:

Join a named group
   The agent connects to a virtually synchronous channel associated with the group.
Submit a message for *publication* on a group's channel
   The agent submits a message to a channel so that it will be sent to all members of a group (including the sender).
Leave a named group
   The agent leaves a group by disconnecting from the associated channel, or (depending on the channel properties) this event may be considered by other group members to have implicitly occurred if the agent's channel fails to respond to pings—in JGroups these are optionally sent as part of the channel's protocol stack.

---

[1] This list follows the terminology of Dolev and Malki [7].

In addition, whenever an agent joins or leaves a group the agent receives a message from the channel containing an updated "view" of the group membership.

3   Example Scenario: The Pit Game

This section discusses an example scenario where a reliable group communication channel provides an agent with guarantees about another agent's state that would be complex to achieve using forms of communication with weaker guarantees.

Pit [9] is a card game dating from 1904 that simulates commodity trading in the American Corn Exchange of that era. It is notable for the way in which players trade cards publicly in a concurrent and asynchronous manner. As an application involving concurrent activity, competitive behaviour and rules designed to ensure fair play, Pit is a good testbed application for investigating issues of electronic agent communication and institutional rules and actions. It has the flavour of a realistic e-commerce scenario while also having a simple and well defined economy in which the players seek to profit through trade. It is for this reason that we choose Pit as an example application. Pit could be implemented using many implementation technologies. We are interested in a solution that views Pit as an electronic institution [10], with explicit representations of the commitments that agents make to each other. In the type of real e-trading scenarios that Pit is based on, such explicit representations of the social state will be necessary to support reasoning about agent compliance and to justify judgements about trust and the imposition of sanctions.

Previous work has investigated the use of MAS techniques to implement an extended version of Pit designed to be scalable to large numbers of players [11], and the game theory of a simplified version of Pit [12]. This paper is based on the original version of Pit (or, at least, an electronic version that is intended to be as close as possible to the original) and, in particular, investigates one state transition in the game.

In the simplest form of Pit there is a deck of cards, each representing a unit of a tradeable commodity such as barley, with nine identical cards for each commodity. The game proceeds in repeated rounds of card trading until one player wins by reaching a score of 500 points. A round begins with each player being randomly dealt nine cards and ends when a player manages to "corner the market" on a single commodity by possessing all nine cards of that type, and is the first to announce this fact. The score earned for this ranges from 60 to 100 points, depending on the commodity. Once dealing is completed, trading takes place by players concurrently and vocally advertising the number of cards they wish to trade (which must be at least two, and the cards must be of the same commodity). When a trading partner is identified, the trading partners exchange the agreed number of cards, consider their new hand and either announce the achievement of a "corner" or select some new cards to trade and then return to the advertising phase. At all times, a player can only see the face of his or her own cards—the other players' cards can not be distinguished from each other as their backs have a uniform appearance.

In the physical game, players advertise the number of cards they wish to trade by holding those cards up in the air (with only the backs visible to other players) while shouting, for example, "Two! Two! Two!". At the same time they look around the room to locate and make eye contact with another player seeking to trade the same number of cards. It then becomes clear if those players wish to complete the trade: the players focus their attention on each other and the cards are physically exchanged. If at any time one party decides not to trade or their attention is drawn to another, more favoured, trading partner, this is immediately apparent. This feature of the game is difficult to reproduce in an online version where players are in different locations and communicate via messages. While safe trading transactions could be achieved by introducing trusted agents or co-opting other players to to act as notaries that manage the transaction, our preference is to preserve the peer-to-peer nature of the physical version of Pit. The approach taken here is to analyse the game in terms of commitments made by players, and to investigate mechanisms that allow these commitments to be understood and observed.

When players are advertising their desire to trade, they have no commitments to others (apart from having to obey the rules of the game). They are free to make and break eye contact until they locate a player with whom they are happy to trade and who appears to want to trade with them. At this point there is an important transition in the system. A player beginning a card exchange with another player must focus on that operation and is therefore forgoing the chance to actively seek a possibly preferred trading partner (e.g. one with a score that is further from the winning margin) and to attract his or her attention. In an electronic version of the game, a card exchange transaction may involve executing a relatively complex protocol, so each player would like to have confidence that the other party is committed to the transaction before beginning the exchange. In fact, to have complete certainty that it is safe to begin the transaction, each party A must know that the other party B is committed, that B knows that A is committed, that B knows that A knows that B knows that A is committed, ad infinitum—in other words, the trading partners must achieve *common knowledge* of their mutual commitment [13]. Another way to view this is that the two players must make a joint action to change their institutional state to one in which they must complete the trade with one another.

It has been proven that it is impossible to achieve common knowledge in a distributed system using asynchronous messages on an unreliable network [13]. However, various approximations of common knowledge are possible, e.g. making use of a "publication" multicasting primitive allows (logically) "time-stamped common knowledge" to be achieved [14]. Although we do not take an epistemological viewpoint of distributed systems in this paper, we rely on the properties of the reliable group communication mechanism presented in Section 2. This is similar to the notion of publication in the above-cited research, but does not expose logical timestamps to the application layer.

Our reliable group communication operations are applied to the Pit scenario as follows. Each player follows the same protocol, which depends on the player's state. For much of the game, and particularly when an agent is in the *Advertising* state, normal asynchronous FIPA-style messaging is used. However, this paper addresses one particular state transition in which reliable multicasting has a valuable role to play: the transition from state *SeekingPartner*(P) (meaning that the player is seeking to establish a trading session with another player P) to state *TradingWith*(P) (meaning that the player has agreed with player P to begin trading their advertised cards). A player enters state *SeekingPartner*(P) after identifying a player P that is advertising the same number of cards as itself and with whom it wishes to trade. It then begins the protocol that is shown in Figure 1 as a sequence diagram in an extended version[2] of UML 2.0 [15].

A brief summary of the notation is as follows. The operators in the boxed regions are: opt, meaning an optional section; loop—the "(*)" means there is no lower or upper limit to the number of iterations; par, meaning parallel composition by arbitrary interleaving of the interactions in the subsections of the box; alt, meaning a guarded choice of the interactions in the subregions, with the guard written in square brackets; and nondet, meaning a non-deterministic choice that is not under the control of the agent[3].

The protocol assumes that for each pair of players there is a group, and that the agent infrastructure only allows those players to join that group. In practice these groups will only exist if they are needed and associated channels are created. A player A attempts to "catch the eye" of another player B by connecting to a channel for the group $\{A, B\}$ (A could also send a standard asynchronous unicast message of invitation to the other player, but this is not depicted due to space constraints).

Upon connection, the channel sends the current list of group members to A as a *members* message, and this is repeated when the membership changes, e.g. if A was the only member initially and then B joins. If B joins the group before a timeout period, A submits the statement *att*(A, N, B), meaning "A agrees to trade N cards with B", to the channel. For the two players to know that each other is committed to trading, they must each have submitted matching *att* statements to the group. If neither player has crashed or dropped off the network, these messages will eventually be published by the channel and received by each player. However, if a player wishes to withdraw its agreement before receiving the agreement of the other, it can submit a *cancelled(att(. . .))* message to its channel. This is where the virtually synchronous property of the channels come into play: all *members*, *att* and *cancelled* messages will be received in the same order by both players. A cancellation is only deemed valid if it is received before the other player's agreement arrives, and virtual synchrony guarantees that both players agree on the validity of any cancellation publications.

Finally, if player A observes its own and player B's *att* statements without observing any cancellations or a notification of B leaving the group in between, then it changes to state *TradingWith*(B) and begins to follow a separate trading protocol[4]. However, it is important to note that virtual synchrony only guarantees *logically* simultaneous receipt of messages, not real-time synchrony. The trading protocol must therefore be designed with an initial phase that verifies that both agents have reached the *TradingWith*(. . .) state, just as the illustrated protocol begins by waiting until both players have joined the group.

---

[2] The extensions are: (i) The identification of the state of a lifeline, written in square brackets under the lifeline name and role, and a notation (appearing at the bottom of the diagram) for a state change action; (ii) the introduction of the nondet interaction type described in the main text above.

[3] This requires a branching time semantics whereas UML 2.0 sequence diagrams have trace-based semantics, but we don't address this issue.

[4] A discussion of possible trading protocols is beyond the scope of this paper.

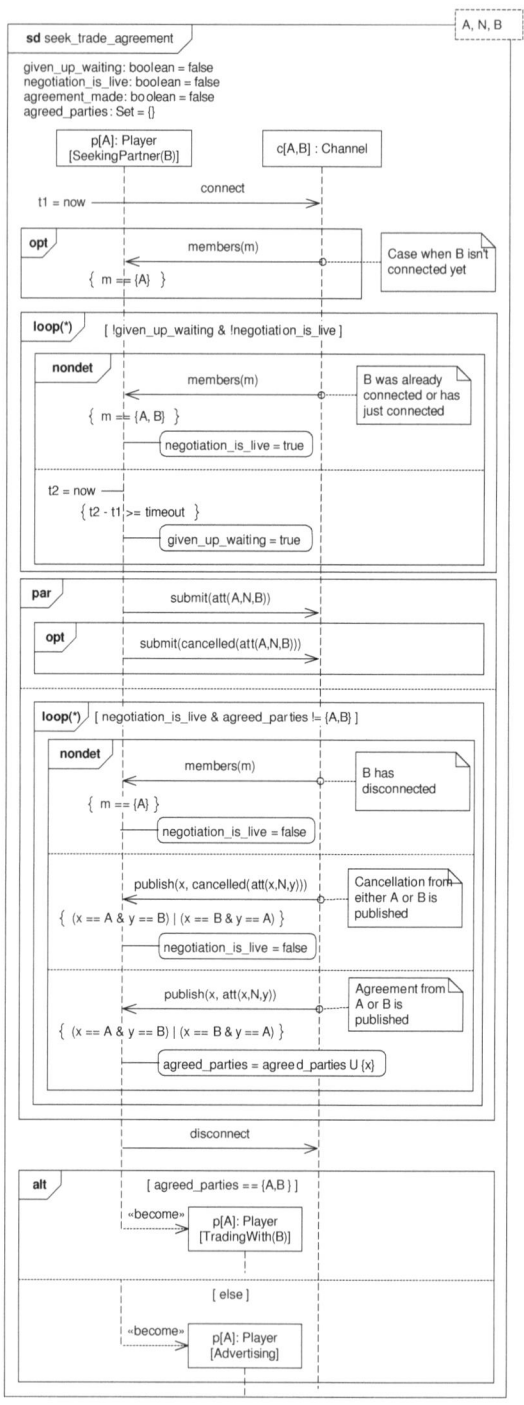

Fig. 1. The "seek trade agreement" protocol

If the protocol in Figure 1 ends without both players agreeing, player A will return to the (previous) *Advertising* state and its associated protocol.

The use of virtually synchronous group multicasting ensures that the two players have a consistent view of the outcome of the negotiation, and therefore they each know that it is safe to change state and begin the card trading protocol. However, this assumes that each player believes that the other is correctly following the protocol. In an open system, such a belief can only be justified by appealing to the rules of the society in which the agent exists. The rules of Pit should be defined to ensure that the submission of an agree to trade (*att*) statement is only done with the intent of subsequently changing state if the other player also agrees to trade. The act of submitting an *att* statement should therefore be treated as having the secondary effect (within the institution of Pit) of making a conditional commitment to change to the *TradingWith*(B) state in the appropriate circumstances. In the next section we show how this can be formalised, and demonstrate that the use of the publication mechanism allows the conditional part of this commitment to be defined in a way that guarantees that both agents have a common understanding of when each other becomes committed to the trade.

4   Publication as an Institutional Action in Pit

Following the path set by researchers of electronic institutions [10] we seek an understanding of Pit as a social interaction governed by norms, permissions, obligations, commitments, etc. In this section, a preliminary analysis of the "seek trade agreement" scenario in Figure 1 is presented, showing how the submission of an *att* statement to the channel can be defined to imply the performance of an institutional action: making a commitment to change to the *TradingWith*(...) state if both players' *att* messages are published with no intervening *cancelled* message. Based on the formalism of Verdicchio and Colombetti [16,17] for modelling commitments, agent communication and institutional action, we model the publication mechanism and the institutional meaning of an *att* submission.

4.1   Verdicchio and Colombetti's Formal Model

Verdicchio and Colombetti use a temporal logic $\text{CTL}^{\pm}$, based on CTL^{*} [18]. The semantics of $\text{CTL}^{\pm}$ assumes that time is discrete, with potentially many possible next states for any given state, i.e. agents' choices and the nondeterminism of the environment are represented by a future-branching tree of states. Standard temporal primitive and derived modal operators are used, and these can be applied in the future direction (when adorned with a superscript '+') or the past (similarly indicated by a '−'). The operators include X (the next/previous state), F (eventually), G (always) and U (until)[5]. The until operator is a binary operator meaning that the formula on its left will remain true for a (possibly empty) sequence of states, followed by a state in which the formula on its right holds. In addition, the path quantifiers A (for all paths) and E (there exists

---

[5] The presentation here uses the original notation of Verdicchio and Colombetti. In recent work [17] they use mnemonic names for temporal operators, e.g. SomeFut (sometime in the future) for F^{+}.

a path) are used to constrain the set of possible paths through time that contain a given state.

The occurrence of an event e in a state is modelled by the truth of the proposition $Happ(e)$ in that state. There is assumed to be a unique constant e to represent each distinct event, and this uniqueness constraint is represented by the following axiom:

$$Happ(e) \rightarrow \mathsf{X}^- \mathsf{G}^- \neg Happ(e) \wedge \mathsf{AX}^+ \mathsf{G}^+ \neg Happ(e)$$

Other axioms are used to constrain the 'physics' of action, but are not presented here.

Events have types, represented by logical terms such as $rain$ (it rains) or $inform(a, b, \phi)$ (a informs agent b of statement ϕ, where ϕ is a statement in an agent content language represented as a term). The type of an event is represented by a proposition of the form $EvType(e, t)$. The following abbreviation is defined:

$$Happ(e, t) =_{\text{def}} EvType(e, t) \wedge Happ(e)$$

Some events represent actions that are brought about by an agent. The following predicates and abbreviations are used to represent actions:

$Actor(a, e)$: agent a is an actor of event e

$Done(e, a, t) =_{\text{def}} EvType(e, t) \wedge Actor(e, a) \wedge Happ(e)$

$Done(a, t) =_{\text{def}} \exists e\, Done(e, a, t)$

to which we add:

$Happ_t(t) =_{\text{def}} \exists e\, EvType(e, t) \wedge Happ(e)$

The formalism also includes a number of predicates used to represent the existence and state of commitments between agents. $Comm(e, a, b, \tau)$ means that event e has brought about a commitment between debtor a and creditor b to the truth of the $\text{CTL}^{\pm}$ formula τ (which is encoded here as a term). Action types $mc(a, b, \tau)$ and $cc(e, a, b, \tau)$ are defined to represent making and cancelling a commitment, and axioms are used to define the meaning of these. In particular, the performance by agent a of an action $mc(a, b, \tau)$ implies that in all possible futures $Comm(e, a, b, \tau)$ holds forever or until an act of cancelling the commitment is done, in which case $Comm(e, a, b, \tau)$ ceases to be true[6]. Temporal formulae are used to define the notion of fulfilment and violation of a commitment, represented by the predicates $Fulf(e, a, b, \tau)$ and $Viol(e, a, b, \tau)$ respectively. The definition for fulfilment is:

$$Fulf(e, a, b, \tau) =_{\text{def}} Comm(e, a, b, \tau) \wedge \mathsf{AF}^-(Happ(e) \wedge \lfloor \tau \rfloor)$$

where '$\lfloor . \rfloor$' represents the mapping from a term encoding a temporal formula to the formula itself. This definition says that to determine the satisfaction of τ as a commitment, τ should be evaluated in the (possibly prior) state in which the event e—the making of the commitment—was performed.

---

[6] A counterintuitive feature of this formalism is that a commitment is modelled as continuing to exist (in an inactive state) even after it has been fulfilled.

Within an institution, acts of one type (e.g. raising one's hand during an auction) can be deemed to "count as" an action of another type (e.g. offering to buy the item being auctioned at the current price). This type of institutional fact is declared by asserting within the theory defining an institution a proposition of the form $CountsAs(t, t')$, where the meaning of the predicate $CountsAs$ is given by the following axiom[7]:

$$Done(e, a, t) \land CountsAs(t, t') \rightarrow Done(e, a, t')$$

The left hand side can include additional conjuncts testing for logical possibility and authorisation, but for the sake of brevity we do not discuss that here.

4.2 Modelling the Publication Mechanism

In our Pit protocol we consider the submission of an *att* statement to the channel as making a commitment to trade under certain conditions. To define this formally we must first model the publication mechanism using $CTL^{\pm}$. We use the following event types to represent agents leaving or joining a group (we do not model these as actions because leaving a group may occur due to a failure that is not brought about by an agent itself):

$join\_group(a, g)$

$leave\_group(a, g)$

The following predicates are used to model group membership and agents' views of group membership:

$member(a, g)$: agent a is a member of group g

$member\_in\_view(a, g, b)$: a is a member of g in b's current local view

These action types represent agents submitting and observing publications, and observing group membership changes:

$submit(\phi, g)$

$observe\_pub(e, a, \phi, g)$

$observe\_join\_group(e, a, g)$

$observe\_leave\_group(e, a, g)$

where ϕ is a statement to be published (represented as a term), g is a group name and e is the event that is being observed—either the submission of a publication or an agent joining or leaving the group. If more than one agent joins or leaves a group in a single state, this is modelled as separate but concurrent events.

$CTL^{\pm}$ axioms are used to define the meanings of the event and action types and the constraints on the publication mechanism; here we only present a sample:

$\neg member(a, g) \rightarrow \neg Happ_t(leave\_group(a, g))$

---

[7] An alternative and more complex treatment of the notion of "counting as" is given by Jones and Parent [19].

$CountsAs(submit(att(a, n, b), \{a, b\}),$
$\quad mc(a, b, ((Done(a, observe\_pub(-, b, att(b, n, a), \{a, b\}))$
$\qquad \wedge (\neg Done(a, observe\_pub(-, a, cancelled(a, n, b), \{a, b\}))$
$\qquad \mathsf{U}^-$
$\qquad Done(a, observe\_pub(-, a, att(a, n, b), \{a, b\}))))$
$\qquad \vee$
$\qquad (Done(a, observe\_pub(-, a, att(a, n, b), \{a, b\}))$
$\qquad \wedge (\neg Done(a, observe\_pub(-, b, cancelled(b, n, a), \{a, b\}))$
$\qquad \mathsf{U}^-$
$\qquad Done(a, observe\_pub(-, b, att(b, n, a), \{a, b\}))))))$
$\qquad \mathsf{S}^+$
$\qquad Done(a, change\_state(SeekingPartner(b), TradingWith(b), pit))))$

Fig. 2. The institutional meaning of submitting an agreement to trade

$\neg member(a, g) \wedge Happ_t(join\_group(a, g)) \rightarrow \mathsf{AX}^+ member(a, g)$
$\neg member(a, g) \wedge \neg Happ_t(join\_group(a, g)) \rightarrow \mathsf{AX}^+ \neg member(a, g)$
$Done(a, observe\_join\_group(-, b, g)) \rightarrow member\_in\_view(b, g, a)$
$Done(a, observe\_pub(e, -, -, -)) \rightarrow$
$\quad \mathsf{X}^- \mathsf{G}^- \neg Done(a, observe\_pub(e, -, -, -)) \wedge$
$\quad \mathsf{AX}^+ \mathsf{G}^+ \neg Done(a, observe\_pub(e, -, -, -))$

where, following Verdicchio and Colombetti, '$-$' is an abbreviation for an existentially quantified variable different from any other.

Three other important axioms (not shown here for reasons of space) state that a group member will observe its own publication unless a group membership change is observed first (the atomic delivery property), all group members observe a publication if any of them does, but the global order of these observations is not constrained, and any two group members observe any pair of observations in the same relative order.

4.3 Modelling the Trading Commitment in Pit

In the Pit protocol in Figure 1 the agents communicate by submitting *att* and *cancelled* statements to the channel to be published. In this section we define the act of submitting an *att* statement for publication as making a commitment to change state if the appropriate conditions apply. To do this, we must first define another action type: *change_state(s, s', inst)*. This represents the act of changing from state s to state s' in institution *inst*. The institutional meaning of submitting an *att* message to the channel can now be defined as shown in Figure 2. The binary operator S^+, meaning "as soon as $\langle LHS \rangle$ then $\langle RHS \rangle$", is defined by Verdicchio and Colombetti as follows:

$$\phi \, \mathsf{S}^+ \psi =_{\text{def}} (\phi \rightarrow \psi) \wedge (\mathsf{X}^+(\phi \rightarrow \psi)) \, \mathsf{W}^+ \phi$$

where W^+ is the future version of the usual "weak until" operator:

$$\phi \, \mathsf{W}^+ \psi =_{\text{def}} \mathsf{G}^+ \phi \vee \phi \, \mathsf{U}^+ \psi$$

The declaration in Figure 2 states that the act of submitting an *att* statement for publication counts as making a commitment that whenever a publication from one of the two agents is observed, if when looking backwards to find the matching publication from the other agent no cancellation of that publication has occurred more recently, then a change of state from *SeekingPartner(b)* to *TradingWith(b)* will be performed. While this might look complicated as a way of modelling the game of Pit (if one were just looking for a way of implementing Pit specifically), we believe this is exactly the type of explicit representation of commitments that will be useful in building agent-based e-commerce systems in general.

Analysing the axioms defining the properties of publication, together with the definition of fulfilment in Section 4.1, it is possible to infer[8] that if one of the two negotiating agents is committed to changing state then (eventually) they both are. The reasoning is as follows. Suppose agent a has observed the publication of an an *att* message from b, with a later publication of a matching *att* message from itself (in a state s say), and no *cancelled* publication was observed in between, then it can conclude that it has become commited to change to state *TradingWith(b)* in state s. It can also conclude that agent b saw (or will see) the same sequence of publications (leading to a state s' say) and therefore that b became (or will become) commited to change state to *TradingWith(a)* at s'. What a cannot determine is the precise time at which agent b reaches state s', however, we cannot hope to achieve perfect synchronisation in a distributed system.

This type of reasoning allows the protocol to be verified to lead to joint commitments between a and b to change state to a new phase of interaction: trading cards with each other.

5   Related Work

Section 2 discussed some prior work on group communication in multi-agent systems. In particular, this paper extends the work of Busetta et al. [5] by considering the use of group communication channels that implement reliable multicasting.

Cheriton and Skeen [21] have presented some limitations of the use of causally and totally ordered (agreed order) multicasting as a generic mechanism for solving a variety of distributed computing problems. These limitations are: (i) messages can be delivered out of order from the application viewpoint if there are causal relationships unknown to the multicasting infrastructure, e.g. due to out-of-channel communications or interactions with the environment; (ii) it is not possible to treat particular sequences of messages as atomic operations so that no other messages are delivered between them; (iii) there can be causal relationships between events at the application level that are not captured by the semantics of causally and totally ordered multicasting, e.g. when a particular message should only be sent if another message has not been received yet; and (iv) they lack efficiency and scalability compared to protocols directly based on application state.

The last limitation above is an important one, but we believe there is still a significant role for reliable multicasting to play within particular phases of an interaction

---

[8] How agents or specialised auditor agents could reason automatically using such axioms is a subject of subsequent research; in particular, a rule language based on $CTL^{\pm}$ that supports run-time monitoring of commitments has been developed [20].

protocol, where only a small group of agents (possibly a subset of all the participants) are involved. Furthermore, in some applications, such as Pit, interaction protocols are best described in terms of agents' individual states rather than a global state of the interaction. Our answer to the other three limitations is that designers of protocols using reliable multicasting do need to be aware of these issues, and they should not expect this technique to be a panacea. However, we believe that the problems identified can all be prevented by careful protocol design.

Paurobally et al. [22] proposed the use of *synchronisation protocols* that run in a layer between the network protocols and the interaction protocols that an agent follows. These synchronisation protocols ensure that the participants in an interation have a consistent belief in the state of the protocol. This is similar to the work discussed in this paper in that it relies on an underlying protocol layer to enable synchronisation without complicating the higher level interaction protocol.

The formal model of action and commitment used in this paper is that of Verdicchio and Colombetti [16,17], which uses the full power (and incurs the full complexity) of a CTL^*-style logic. Mallya et al. [23] have investigated a simpler temporal language, with semantics based on a timed version of CTL, in which temporal interval expressions can be used as existential and universal quantifiers of propositional formulae. They provided an analysis showing how to determine when a given commitment could be known to be fulfilled or violated.

The concept of a commitment machine [24,25] has been proposed as a high-level way of defining agent interaction protocols in terms of states that are sets of facts and (possibly conditional) commitments between agents, and the effects that actions have on facts and commitments. Modelling the institutional effect of an *att* publication using this formalism may allow a simpler and more abstract form of the "seek trade agreement" protocol to be defined.

6   Conclusion

This paper has proposed the use of reliable group communication mechanisms in multi-agent systems and demonstrated its utility in a peer-to-peer electronic trading scenario where agents may require some guarantees about the state of other agents. It has also demonstrated how a publication on a virtually synchronous group communication channel can be formally defined to count as the establishment of a commitment that is dependent on the commonly understood order of future publications—thus allowing distributed agents to have a shared understanding of each other's commitments.

As in human society, software agents should have a range of communication mechanisms with varying properties available to them. Providing agent messaging infrastructure supporting various modes of group communication will allow the declarative definition of simpler interaction protocols where agents act in a peer-to-peer manner and, for particular phases, need some guarantees about the institutional state of their peers. However, reliable group communication comes at a computational cost—for example, with JGroups, the first node to connect to a channel for a group becomes the coordinator for that group. The channel for that node is responsible (via appropriate underlying protocols) for ensuring atomic delivery and agreed order semantics for multicasts. Reliable multicasting is also unlikely to be practically scalable to larger groups of agents. Therefore, the appropriate role of this technique is for particular phases of interaction protocols where synchronised agreements are needed amongst small groups of agents, with standard asynchronous messaging used elsewhere.

Acknowledgements

The author would like to thank Marco Colombetti for sharing his ideas during a visit to the University of Otago in 2003, and Francesco Fumarola for his work evaluating the use of the JGroups toolkit in a multi-agent implementation of Pit.

References

1. Wooldridge, M., Jennings, N.R.: Intelligent agents: Theory and practice. Knowledge Engineering Review **10** (1995) 115–152
2. Finin, T., Labrou, Y., Mayfield, J.: KQML as an agent communication language. In Bradshaw, J.M., ed.: Software Agents. MIT Press (1997)
3. FIPA: FIPA ACL message representation in string specification, Foundation for Intelligent Physical Agents. http://www.fipa.org/specs/fipa00070/ (2002)
4. Kumar, S., Huber, M.J., McGee, D., Cohen, P.R., Levesque, H.J.: Semantics of agent communication languages for group interaction. In: Proceedings of the Seventeenth National Conference on Artificial Intelligence (AAAI 2000), AAAI Press / MIT Press (2000) 42–47
5. Busetta, P., Donà, A., Nori, M.: Channeled multicast for group communications. In: Proceedings of the 1st International Joint Conference on Autonomous Agents and Multiagent Systems (AAMAS 2002), ACM Press (2002) 1280–1287
6. Birman, K.P., Joseph, T.A.: Reliable communication in the presence of failures. ACM Transactions on Computer Systems **5** (1987) 47–76
7. Dolev, D., Malki, D.: The Transis approach to high availability cluster computing. Communications of the ACM **39** (1996) 64–70
8. JGroups project home page. http://www.jgroups.org (2004)
9. Parker Brothers: Pit rules. http://www.hasbro.com/common/instruct/pit.pdf (1904)
10. Cortés, U.: Electronic institutions and agents. AgentLink News **15** (2004) 14–15 http://www.agentlink.org/newsletter/15/AL-15.pdf.
11. Purvis, M., Nowostawski, M., Cranefield, S., Oliveira, M.: Multi-agent interaction technology for peer-to-peer computing in electronic trading environments. In Zhang, C., Guesgen, H.W., Yeap, W.K., eds.: Proceedings of the 8th Pacific Rim International Conference on Artificial Intelligence. Volume 3157 of Lecture Notes In Artificial Intelligence., Springer (2004) 625–634
12. van Ditmarsch, H.: Some game theory of Pit. In Zhang, C., Guesgen, H.W., Yeap, W.K., eds.: Proceedings of the 8th Pacific Rim International Conference on Artificial Intelligence. Volume 3157 of Lecture Notes in Artificial Intelligence., Springer (2004) 946–947
13. Fagin, R., Halpern, J.Y., Moses, Y., Vardi, M.Y.: Reasoning about Knowledge. MIT Press, Cambridge, MA (1995)
14. Neiger, G., Toueg, S.: Simulating synchronized clocks and common knowledge in distributed systems. Journal of the ACM **40** (1993) 334–367
15. Object Management Group: UML 2.0 superstructure final adopted specification. Document ptc/03-08-02, http://www.omg.org/cgi-bin/doc?ptc/2003-08-02 (2003)
16. Verdicchio, M., Colombetti, M.: A logical model of social commitment for agent communication. In: Proceedings of the 2nd International Joint Conference on Autonomous Agents and Multiagent Systems (AAMAS 2003), ACM Press (2003) 528–535

17. Verdicchio, M., Colombetti, M.: A commitment-based communicative act library. In: Proceedings of the 4th International Joint Conference on Autonomous Agents and Multiagent Systems (AAMAS 2005), ACM Press (2005) 755–761 (An extended version appears in this volume).

18. Emerson, E.A., Halpern, J.Y.: "Sometimes" and "not never" revisited: On branching versus linear time temporal logic. Journal of the ACM **33** (1986) 151–178

19. Jones, A.J.I., Parent, X.: Conventional signalling acts and conversation. In Dignum, F., ed.: Advances in Agent Communication, International Workshop on Agent Communication Languages, ACL 2003. Volume 2922 of Lecture Notes in Computer Science., Springer (2004) 1–17

20. Cranefield, S.: A rule language for modelling and monitoring social expectations in multi-agent systems. In Boissier, O. et al., eds.: Coordination, Organizations, Institutions, and Norms in Multi-Agent Systems. Volume 3913 of Lecture Notes in Computer Science., Springer (2006) 246–258

21. Cheriton, D.R., Skeen, D.: Understanding the limitations of causally and totally ordered communication. Operating Systems Review **27** (1993) 44–57 (Proceedings of the 14th ACM Symposium on Operating System Principles).

22. Paurobally, S., Cunningham, J., Jennings, N.R.: Ensuring consistency in the joint beliefs of interacting agents. In: Proceedings of the 2nd International Joint Conference on Autonomous Agents and Multiagent Systems (AAMAS 2003), ACM Press (2003) 662–669

23. Mallya, A.U., Yolum, P., Singh, M.P.: Resolving commitments among autonomous agents. In Dignum, F., ed.: Advances in Agent Communication, International Workshop on Agent Communication Languages, ACL 2003. Volume 2922 of Lecture Notes in Computer Science., Springer (2004) 166–182

24. Yolum, P., Singh, M.P.: Commitment machines. In Meyer, J.-J., Tambe, M., eds.: Intelligent Agents VIII: 8th International Workshop, ATAL 2001. Volume 2333 of Lecture Notes in Computer Science., Springer (2002) 235–247

25. Winikoff, M., Liu, W., Harland, J.: Enhancing commitment machines. In Leite, J., Omicini, A., Torroni, P., Yolum, P., eds.: Declarative Agent Languages and Technologies II. Volume 3476 of Lecture Notes in Computer Science., Springer (2005) 198–220

A Fault Tolerant Agent Communication Language for Supporting Web Agent Interaction

Nicola Dragoni, Mauro Gaspari, and Davide Guidi

Dipartimento di Scienze dell'Informazione
University of Bologna, Italy

Abstract. Agent Communication Languages (ACLs) have been developed to provide a way for agents to communicate with each other supporting cooperation in Multi-Agent Systems. In the past few years many ACLs have been proposed for Multi-Agent Systems and some standards emerged such as FIPA ACL or KQML. Despite these efforts, an important issue in the research on ACLs is still open and concerns how these languages should deal with failures of agents in asynchronous Multi-Agent Systems. The Fault Tolerant ACL presented in this paper addresses this issue providing knowledge-level fault tolerant communication primitives. To illustrate the potentiality of our ACL, we show how it can be effectively used to support fault tolerant Web agent interaction in common Web Service usage scenarios.

1 Introduction

Communication among software agents is an essential property of agency [1,2]. The power of agent systems strongly depends on inter-agent communication and as agents grow more powerful, their need for communication increases [3]. Agent Communication Languages (ACLs) have been developed to provide adequate inter-agent communication mechanisms. They allow agents to effectively communicate and exchange knowledge with other agents despite differences in hardware platforms, operating systems, architectures and programming languages. In the last decade many Agent Communication Languages have been proposed for Multi-Agent Systems (MAS), incorporating specific mechanisms of agent communication. Many of these communication mechanisms are based on *speech act theory*, which has originally been developed as a basic model of human communication [4]. The more promising ACLs that have adopted the speech act theory are KQML [5] and the FIPA ACL [6]. The goal of these languages is to support high-level, human like, communication between intelligent agents, exploiting *Knowledge-Level* features rather than symbol-level ones. They should support Knowledge-Level programming of MAS [7]: agents should be concerned with the use, request and supply of knowledge and not with symbol level issues such as the reliability, synchronization of competing requests, the allocation of resources or the physical allocation of agents on a network.

Despite these efforts, an important issue in the research on ACLs is still open and concerns how to deal with possible failures of agents. This issue will become more and more important in the foreseeable future, being that agents are one of the main

F. Dignum, R. van Eijk, and R. Flores (Eds.): AC 2005/2006, LNAI 3859, pp. 273–288, 2006.
© Springer-Verlag Berlin Heidelberg 2006

building blocks of the emerging Semantic Web infrastructure. This depends on the geographically distributed nature of the Internet and on the *asynchronous* nature of many Multi-Agent Systems. Asynchronous Multi-Agent Systems on the Web are prone to the same failures that can occur in any distributed software system. An agent may become unavailable suddenly due to various reasons. The agent may die due to unexpected conditions, improper handling of exceptions and other bugs in the agent program or in the supporting environment. The machine on which the agent process is running may crash due to hardware and/or software faults or it may become unreachable as a result of a network partition. Agent communication languages should provide high-level mechanisms to deal with these events maintaining a Knowledge-Level characterization of the communication primitives.

In this paper we address this issue proposing a Fault Tolerant Agent Communication Language (FT-ACL) which deals with *crash* failures of agents. FT-ACL provides fault-tolerant versions of common conversation performatives and an anonymous interaction protocol based on fault-tolerant one-to-many requests for knowledge. Moreover FT-ACL has been designed for open architectures and deals with a dynamic set of competences and agents. In the design we give special attention to the Knowledge-Level features of the ACL primitives as in [7], presenting a set of Knowledge-Level requirements that FT-ACL satisfies. We present the ACL and we provide a few programming examples, among them a fault tolerant solutions to the well known *Contract Net* protocol.

To illustrate the potentiality of our ACL, we show how it can be effectively used to support fault tolerant Web agent interaction in common Web Service usage scenarios.

2   The Design of a Fault Tolerant ACL

The first steps towards the design of our fault tolerant ACL concern the identification of underlying failure model assumptions. These assumptions are then used in the specification of the communication primitives and of the related agents' infrastructure.

We assume a description of agents based on two levels: a *Knowledge-Level* which focuses on agents' competences and on the definition of the ACL primitives that abstracts from implementation details, and an *Architectural-Level* which specifies the agents' infrastructure showing how these competences and primitives are realized. This approach has several advantages. Firstly, this clear distinction allows to manage agents as abstract entities which operate at the Knowledge-Level executing *high level* communication primitives. All the implementation details, such as the interaction of the architectural components of an agent, synchronization and management of failures, are handled at the Architectural-Level. Secondly, it is possible to define a set of requirements that should be satisfied at the Knowledge-Level and that can be proved at the Architectural-Level.

Failure Model. The failure model we have adopted is based on a well known classification of process failures in distributed systems [8]. Following that model, we say that an agent is *faulty* in an execution if its behaviour deviates from that prescribed by the algorithm it is running; otherwise, it is *correct*. The failure model we consider is the one that deal with *crash* failures of agents in a *fully asynchronous* Multi-Agent System: a faulty agent is *crashed* if it stops prematurely and does nothing from that point on. Before stopping, however, it behaves correctly. Note that considering only crash failures is a common fault assumption in distributed systems, since several mechanisms can be used to detect more severe failures and to force a crash in case of detection.

We assume that agents communicate by asynchronous and reliable message passing, *i.e.*, whenever a message is sent it must be eventually received by the target agent [1]. The asynchrony of the system implies that there is no bound on message delay, clock drift or the time necessary to execute a step.

2.1 Knowledge-Level Description

Following the style of [7], an agent in the system has a symbolic (logical) name and a *virtual knowledge base* (VKB). The communication actions are asynchronous, allowing buffering of messages and supporting non blocking *ask* performatives. We also assume that each communication action contains information in a given knowledge representation formalism.

Let $\mathcal{A}_{\mathcal{ACL}}$ be a countable set of agent names ranged over by $\hat{a}$, $\hat{b}$, $\hat{c}$,.... Let $VKB_{\hat{a}}$ be the virtual knowledge base of agent $\hat{a}$ which can be encoded in any knowledge representation formalism; w, w', w'' will range over VKB. We adopt the following abstract syntax for communication actions: *performative*$(\hat{a}, \hat{b}, p)$ where *performative* represents the communication action, $\hat{a}$ and $\hat{b}$ are the names of the recipient agent and of the sender agent respectively, and p is the contents of the message.

Agents react to messages received from other agents and from the user. Each agent has an associated *handler function* which maps the received message into the list of communication actions which must be executed when that message is received. $H_{\hat{a}}$ will be the handler function of agent $\hat{a}$. We assume that the handler function is enclosed in the VKB of an agent. The handler function is expressed by a set of Prolog-like rules $\{r_1, r_2 \ldots, r_n\}$ having the form:

$$handler(performative(\hat{a}, \hat{b}, p)) \leftarrow body \tag{1}$$

where *body* is a sequence of literals $h_1 \wedge h_2 \ldots \wedge h_n$ in which each h_i can be a communication action, a dynamic primitive or a predicate on the VKB of the agent.

FT-ACL Primitives. FT-ACL includes a set of standard conversation performatives and supports an *anonymous interaction protocol* integrated with agent-to-agent communication. This allows an agent to perform a request of knowledge without knowing the name of the recipient agent and to continue the cooperation using agent-to-agent communication. In more detail, thanks to the anonymous interaction protocol an agent is able to:

- ask all agents in the system for some knowledge without knowing the names of the recipient agents and wait for all or some replies. This can be done by means of a performative *ask-everybody*.

---

[1] Reliable message passing can be obtaining simply using TCP.

– share its own knowledge with all the agents in the system without knowing their names. This can be done by means of the performatives *register* and *unregister*.

Moreover, FT-ACL supports a *dynamic* set of agents, allowing the creation of new agents and the termination of existing ones.

Given the failure model we have adopted, some of the primitives of current ACLs can fail when one or more target agents crash. Since we assume asynchronous communication, ACL primitives do not explicitly wait for answers. Thus it is not possible to detect that the target agent has crashed when a communication action is executed. A fault-tolerant ACL should provide mechanisms to deal with this eventuality. For example an agent that executes an ask primitive should not wait for a response if the target agent has crashed. To solve this problem we associate a failure continuation to all the communication primitives that need to deal with a failure of the target agents. Thus FT-ACL primitives allow agents to specify their reactions to unexpected crashes defining an adequate failure continuation despite the fact that they are executed asynchronously.

We use a similar mechanism to specify the agent behaviour when it receives an answer to a given request for knowledge. This functionality is usually realized adding *:reply-to* and *:reply-with* parameters to the performatives (as in KQML) or matching answers with a template of the request (as in [7]). In FT-ACL we use success continuations to specify the agent behaviour when it receives an answer to a given request or in general when the communication action succeeds. Thus the code that the agent must execute when it will receive a tell message containing the answer to a given request is specified together with the request, despite the performative is executed asynchronously.

Table 1. Primitives of FT-ACL

Standard conversation performatives:
ask-one($\hat{a}$, $\hat{b}$, p)[on_answer($body_1$) + on_fail($body_2$)]
insert($\hat{a}$, $\hat{b}$, p)[on_ack($body_1$) + on_fail($body_2$)]
tell($\hat{a}$, $\hat{b}$, p)

One-to-many performative:
ask-everybody($\hat{b}$, p)[on_answers($body_1$) + on_fail($body_2$)]

Support for anonymous interaction:
register($\hat{b}$, p)   unregister($\hat{b}$, p)
all-answers(p)

Support for creation and termination of agents:
create($\hat{b}$, w)   clone($\hat{b}$)
bye

The primitives of the language are shown in Table 1. The standard conversation performatives are a small subset of those defined in KQML and allow one-to-one agent interaction. Executing the performative *insert*, an agent $\hat{b}$ tells an agent $\hat{a}$ to insert p in its VKB. A success continuation *on_ack($body_1$)* can be associated with this primitive and is called when $\hat{a}$ has inserted p in its VKB and $\hat{b}$ has received an acknowledgement of this event. As a consequence, the program $body_1$ is executed by $\hat{b}$. Instead, if p cannot be inserted in $\hat{a}$'s VKB because $\hat{a}$ is crashed, then the failure continuation $on\_fail(body_2)$ is activated and $\hat{b}$ executes the program $body_2$. If the success continuation is missing agent $\hat{b}$ has no way to control that p is in the VKB of agent $\hat{a}$. On the other hand the stronger version of this performative, which include the success continuation, allows us to approximate common knowledge because agent $\hat{b}$ knows that agent $\hat{a}$ has added p in his VKB.

The performative *tell* is similar to the *insert* primitive, but is less restrictive: an agent $\hat{b}$ simply sends some knowledge p to an agent $\hat{a}$ without requiring any information about the success of the performative. At the moment, no continuations can be associated with this performative, although the realization of a stronger version is possible.

Executing the performative *ask-one* an agent $\hat{b}$ asks an agent $\hat{a}$ for an instantiation of p which is true in the VKB of $\hat{a}$. This performative is associated with a success continuation $on\_answer(body_1)$ which is called when $\hat{b}$ receives the reply of the agent $\hat{a}$. As a consequence, the program $body_1$ is executed by $\hat{b}$. Instead, when $\hat{a}$ cannot reply because it is crashed, the failure continuation $on\_fail(body_2)$ is called and $\hat{b}$ executes the program $body_2$.

The anonymous interaction protocol is implemented through the *ask-everybody* one-to-many performative: an agent which executes it does not need to know the names of all the agents which are interested in a query. In particular, the performative *ask-everybody* allows an agent $\hat{b}$ to ask all agents in the system which are able to deal with p for an instantiation of p which is true in their VKB. When $\hat{b}$ executes *ask-everybody*, an *ask-one* message is sent to all the agents interested in p (except $\hat{b}$). The performative is associated with the success continuation $on\_answers(body_1)$, which is called each time $\hat{b}$ receives a reply to the multicast query and it can remain active until all the replies are arrived. Instead, if no agents are able to reply because they are all crashed, then the failure continuation $on\_fail(body_2)$ is called. This success continuation remains active until it succeeds, allowing agents to realize different protocols. For example, if $\hat{b}$ wants to wait *all the answers* of the correct agents in the system which are able to deal with p, then it can do that executing the performative *ask-everybody* with

$$body_1 \overset{def}{=} body_3 \wedge all\text{-}answers(p) \wedge body_4 \tag{2}$$

where *all-answer(p)* is a boolean predicate which returns *true* if all the *correct* agents have already replied about p or *false* if there is at least one *correct* agent which has not yet replied. Therefore each reply to the multicast query of $\hat{b}$ is handled by the program $body_3$, which is executed when the success continuation $on\_answers(body_1)$ is called. Instead the program $body_4$ is executed only when the predicate all-answers(p) returns *true*, that is only when the last reply is arrived.

To show another example, consider an agent performative *ask-first($\hat{b}$, p)* which realizes the anonymous interaction protocol with the difference that $\hat{b}$ waits only for the first reply it receives and discards all the others. This performative can be easily implemented by the performative *ask-everybody* simply associating to this performative the success continuation $on\_answer(body_1)$ instead of $on\_answers(body_1)$. So, when $\hat{b}$ receives the first reply, the function $on\_answer(body_1)$ is called, the program $body_1$ is executed and then the function becomes inactive. In this way, all the other replies are discarded.

The multicast request performed by *ask-everybody* is forwarded to all the agents on the basis of agents' declarations. An agent $\hat{b}$ can declare its competences through the *register($\hat{b}$, p)* and *unregister($\hat{b}$, p)* primitives. The primitives *create*, *clone* and *bye* are provided to support an *open* and *dynamic* Multi-Agent System: new agents can be created from other agents in the system (for example to cooperate with the existing ones) and agents can leave the community when their tasks terminate. These primitives are well integrated with the anonymous interaction protocol. For example, if $\hat{d}$ is the clone of an agent $\hat{b}$ and $\hat{d}$ is able to deal with p, then the request *ask-everybody($\hat{b}$, p)* will also reach agent $\hat{d}$.

Knowledge-Level Requirements. In [7] several conditions are postulated which require a careful analysis of the underlying agent architecture in order to ensure Knowledge-Level behaviour. We recall these *Knowledge-Level Programming Requirements* below extended to deal with crashes of agents (condition (4)).

(1) The programmer should not have to handle physical addresses of agents explicitly.
(2) The programmer should not have to handle communication faults explicitly.
(3) The programmer should not have to handle starvation issues explicitly. A situation of starvation arises when an agent's primitive never gets executed despite being enabled.
(4) The programmer should not have to handle *communication deadlocks* explicitly. A communication deadlock situation occurs when two agents try to communicate, but they do not succeed; for instance because they mutually wait for each other to answer a query [9] or because an agent waits a reply of a crashed agent forever.

Our ACL has been designed taking into account the above Knowledge-Level requirements. For example, condition (4) requires that no communication deadlocks can occur using FT-ACL. To satisfy this requirement we have designed fault tolerant ask performatives avoiding agents to wait for replies of crashed agents forever. In Section 2.2 we will show how it is possible to support fault tolerant and knowledge level communication and therefore to satisfy the Knowledge-Level requirements.

Example: Specification of a Fault Tolerant Contract Net Protocol. To illustrate the expressive power of FT-ACL, we give a fault tolerant specification of the *Contract Net Protocol* [10], a protocol which allows an agent to distribute tasks among a set of agents by means of negotiation. We only model a restricted version of the protocol with a single manager agent $\hat{a}$ and a set of workers $\hat{s}_1, ..., \hat{s}_n$ with $n \geq 1$.

Moreover, we define a new agent primitive *ask-best* which allows a query to be sent to an agent of a presorted list L of agents. In particular, executing this performative a knowledge p is sent to the first agent in L. If that agent is not able to reply because it crashed, then the message is sent to the second agent in L and so on. This performative can be programmed recursively with FT-ACL as follows:

$$
\begin{aligned}
&\text{ask-best}([], \hat{a}, p)[\text{on\_answer}(body_1) + \text{on\_fail}(body_2)] = body_2 \\
&\text{ask-best}(L, \hat{a}, p)[\text{on\_answer}(body_1) + \text{on\_fail}(body_2)] = \\
&\qquad \text{ask-one}(\text{first}(L), \hat{a}, p)[\text{on\_answer}(body_1) + \text{on\_fail}(body_3)] \quad \text{and} \\
&body_3 \overset{def}{=} \text{ask-best}(\text{rest}(L), \hat{a}, p)[\text{on\_answer}(body_1) + \text{on\_fail}(body_2)]
\end{aligned}
$$

A Contract Net can be defined by the set of agents $S = \{\hat{a}, \hat{s}_1, ..., \hat{s}_n\}$ running in parallel. The handler functions are defined as follows[2]:

$H_{\hat{a}}$: handler(tell($\hat{a}$, Y , startCN)) ←
        ask-everybody($\hat{a}$, bid(task, Z))[on_answer($body_1$) + on_fail($body_2$)]
where
$body_1 \overset{def}{=}$ update(bid(`content`, `sender`)) $\wedge$
      all-answers(bid(task, Z)) $\wedge$
      best_bid(task, L) $\wedge$
      ask-best(L, $\hat{a}$, dotask(task, R))[on_answer($body_3$) + on_fail($body_4$)]
$body_2 = body_4 \overset{def}{=}$ tell(Y, $\hat{a}$, ContractNetFailed)
$body_3 \overset{def}{=}$ update(done(`content`)) $\wedge$
      tell(Y, $\hat{a}$, ContractNetOK)

$H_{\hat{s}_i}$: handler(ask-one($\hat{s}_i$, X, bid(T, Z))) ←
        bid(T, Z) $\wedge$
        tell(X, $\hat{s}_i$, bid(T, Z))

  handler(ask-one($\hat{s}_i$, X, dotask(T, R))) ←
        dotask(T, R) $\wedge$
        tell(X, $\hat{s}_i$, dotask(T, R))

The domain-specific predicates used in the handler function are defined as follows:

- *update(bid(`content`, `sender`)):* updates the agent VKB with a new bid (specified in the message bid(`content`, `sender`)).
- *best_bid(task, L):* retrieves from agent VKB a list L of agents which are able to perform a given task.
- *bid(T, Z):* stores in the variable Z a bid for the task T.
- *dotask(T, R):* instantiates variable R with the result of the execution of task T.

When the manager $\hat{a}$ receives a *startCN* message, it exploits *ask-everybody* to perform a multicast request for bids on a given task (message bid(task, Z)). Then it starts waiting for answers. If all the agents $\hat{s}_i$ interested in the task have crashed, then $body_2$ is executed and a message of *ContractNetFailed* is sent to the starter of the protocol (another agent or the user) notifying the failure. When an agent $\hat{s}_i$ receives a query, it consults its VKB (bid(T, Z) predicate) and replies with its bid (message bid(T, Z)). When $\hat{a}$ has received all the replies of the correct agents (that is, when the predicate all-answers(bid(task, Z)) returns *true*), then it exploits the fault-tolerant performative *ask-best* to send to the agent which has submitted the best bid a request for the execution of the task. The best bid is retrieved from agent VKB by means of the predicate best_bid. In this interaction succeeds, the protocol ends successfully (message Contract-NetOK in $body_3$). Otherwise, the request is sent to the second agent with the best bid

---

[2] We use the expressions `content` and `sender` to represent the content and the sender of a message respectively.

(in the list L) and so on. Only when all the agents in L dynamically becomes crashed, the protocol fails and a *ContractNetFailed* message is sent to the starter of the protocol (program $body_4$). In all the other cases FT-ACL allows the program to tolerate agent crashes.

2.2 Architectural-Level Description

We illustrate a generic agent architecture which is able to support FT-ACL. This architecture allows us to prove that the Knowledge-Level requirements hold at the Architectural Level. A generic agent is composed of three components (Figure 1): a *Knowledge-Base (KB)* component, a *Facilitator* component and a *Failure Detector* component.

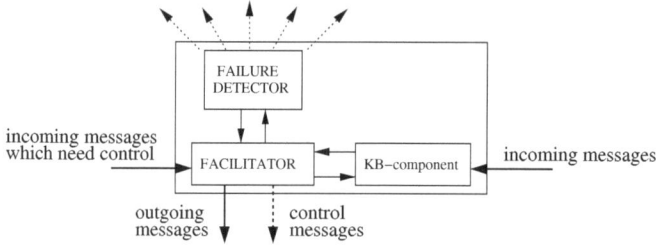

Fig. 1. Generic agent architecture which supports FT-ACL

The *KB-component* implements the VKB of an agent and its reactive behaviour. It only deals with Knowledge-Level operations and it is able to answer requests from other agents. The other two components (*Facilitator* and *Failure Detector*) allow knowledge-level and fault tolerant communication respectively. Since a detailed discussion about the *KB-component* is out of the scope of the paper, we prefer to omit it and to focus on the remaining components.

To realize the anonymous interaction protocol we exploit a *distributed facilitator service* which is hidden at the Knowledge-Level and provides mechanisms for registering capabilities of agents and delivering messages to the recipient agents. Facilitators are distributed and encapsulated in the architecture of agents. Therefore each agent has its own *facilitator component* which executes a distributed algorithm: it forwards control information to all the other local facilitators and delivers messages to their destinations. However, there is no need to have a different physical facilitator for every agent, because facilitators can also be shared between agents. Having an architecture where the kb-component and the facilitator are separated entities that work together, leads to a high level of flexibility. Note that since the facilitators are encapsulated in the agent architecture, they are not visible at the Knowledge-Level. Therefore, although facilitators deal with some low-level issues, we do not violate our Knowledge-Level requirements.

Finally, the *failure detector* component is needed to support fault tolerant communication. The concept of *unreliable failure detectors* for systems with *crash* failures has been proposed by Chandra and Toueg in [11]: since impossibility results for asynchronous systems stem from the inherent difficulty of determining whether a process has actually crashed or is only "very slow", Chandra and Toueg propose to augment the asynchronous model of computation with a model of a failure detection mechanism that can make mistakes (and therefore it is *unreliable*). Our failure detector mechanism is based on this model and is *distributed*: each agent has a local *failure detector* component which monitors a subset of the agents in the system (for example, the known agents) and maintains a list of those that it currently *suspects* to have crashed. Each failure detector component can make mistakes by erroneously adding processes to its list of suspects, *i.e.*, it can suspect that an agent $\hat{b}$ has crashed even though $\hat{b}$ is still running. If this component later believes that suspecting $\hat{b}$ was a mistake, it can remove $\hat{b}$ from its list. Thus, each module may repeatedly add and remove processes from its list of suspects. All the observations made by a local failure detector are communicated to the local facilitator, which will take them into account in all agent interactions. The failure detector component is fundamental to avoid infinite waits for replies of crashed agents (blocking the agent execution).

Note that this is a generic agent architecture: the failure detector and the facilitator components are standard for all the agents in a Multi-Agent System, while the KB-component can be instantiated with different VKBs.

Ensuring Knowledge-Level Requirements. In [12,13] a formal specification of the agent architecture and of the FT-ACL primitives has been provided. The formal approach exploits the Algebra of Actors [14], an actor-based algebra which represents a compromise between standard process algebras and the Actor model [15]. To formally express the fault tolerance of FT-ACL, an extension of the Algebra of Actors to model *crash* failures of actors and their detection has been required [13]. This extension has allowed to model a failure detector component with the following two properties:

Property 1. *If an agent $\hat{b}$ really crashes, then it is permanently suspected by every correct agent.*

Property 2. *If an agent $\hat{b}$ is correct, then it can be erroneously suspected by any correct agents.*

Property 1 guarantees that if an agent is *really* crashed, then sooner or later all the other agents in the system will permanently suspect that agent. Property 2 models the unreliability of the failure detector component stating that each correct agent can be erroneously suspected by any correct agents. Of course, each mistake of a failure detector can be dynamically corrected.

Given these properties, the formal encoding in the Algebra of Actors has been used in [12] to prove that the Knowledge-Level requirements discussed in Section 2.1 are satisfied by our ACL.

Implementation. A prototype of FT-ACL has been realized. Our objective is to provide add-on primitives for several programming languages that enable the use of agents in that particular language. We just provide a minimum common platform for agent communication, that is flexible enough to handle different high level behaviours and specializations built upon it. The modular aspect of the architecture is fully exploited in the implementation: the facilitator component is built in the Project JXTA 2.0 Super-Peer Virtual Network [16] using the Java language, while the agent code can be written in every programming language that has TCP support. Currently Java and Python are supported, while versions for Prolog and Lisp will be ready soon. The failure module has a plugin behaviour and it is currently implemented as a simple time-limit algorithm. While this method could be sufficient for a generic use, it can be overridden with a special purpose one coded for a particular context.

3   Exploiting FT-ACL in Common Web Service Usage Scenarios

We exploit FT-ACL to support Web agent interaction in an Agent-based Open Service Architecture (AOSA) [17]. We support *User Agents* which provide intelligent support and advanced services to users and *Worker Agents* which provide complex problem solving capabilities with respect to a given application domain. Capabilities of Worker Agents can be published and shared on the Web, for example by means of a set of well defined Web Services and an associated ontology. A general view of this architecture is depicted in Figure 2.

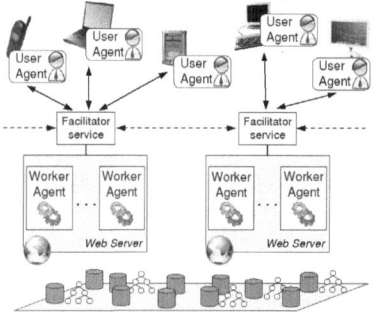

Fig. 2. An Agent-based Open Service Architecture

All the agents in the AOSA communicate each other by means of the FT-ACL primitives which subsume usual service invocation primitives. Also, the discovery facility is integrated with fault tolerant one-to-many primitives to manage multiple (non serialized) asynchronous responses.

Here we argue that, despite the fact that our ACL only provides a small set of primitives, they can be successfully used to support fault tolerant Web agent interaction in common Web Service usage scenarios. To illustrate this, we consider some of the W3C Web Service Usage Scenarios [18] and we show how they can be realized by means of our ACL. Then in Section 3.1 we show how FT-ACL can be used to realize a Travel Agent Service.

Scenario: Fire-and-Forget to a Single Receiver (S001)
Scenario definition: a sender wishes to send an unacknowledged message to a single receiver (e.g. send a stock price update every 15 minutes).

Realization: let be $\hat{a}$ a worker agent which implements the Web Service and $\hat{b}$ a generic receiver agent. Then $\hat{a}$ can send an unacknowledged message to $\hat{b}$ using the FT-ACL primitive *tell($\hat{b}$, $\hat{a}$, p)*, where p is the content of the message.

Scenario: Request/Response (S003)
Scenario definition: two parties wish to conduct electronic business by the exchange of business documents. The sending party packages one or more documents into a request message, which is then sent to the receiving party. The receiving party then processes the message contents and responds to the sending party.
Realization: this is a generic asynchronous messaging scenario which can be easily realized using the FT-ACL primitives *ask-one* and *tell*. Let be $\hat{a}$ and $\hat{b}$ the sending and receiving agent respectively. To send a request to $\hat{b}$, $\hat{a}$ can execute *ask-one($\hat{b}$, $\hat{a}$, p)[on_answer(body$_1$) + on_fail(body$_2$)]*. The receiving agent $\hat{b}$ can reply to this message using *tell($\hat{a}$, $\hat{b}$, p)*. Note that, thanks to the fault tolerance of the primitive *ask-one*, $\hat{a}$ does not wait $\hat{b}$'s reply forever, even if $\hat{b}$ is crashed. If this is the case, the failure continuation *on_fail(body$_2$)* is executed by $\hat{a}$.

Scenario: Request with Acknowledgment (S010)
Scenario definition: a sender wishes to reliably exchange data with a receiver. It wishes to be notified of the status of the data delivery to the receiver. The status may take the form of (a) the data has been successfully delivered to the receiver, or (b) some failure has occurred which prevents the successful delivery to the receiver.
Realization: this scenario can be realized by means of the FT-ACL primitive *insert*: to reliably exchange p with $\hat{b}$, an agent $\hat{a}$ can execute *insert($\hat{b}$, $\hat{a}$, p)[on_ack(body$_1$) + on_fail(body$_2$)]*. The continuations are called depending on the result of this communication: if $\hat{a}$ has reliably communicated with $\hat{b}$ then the success continuation *on_ack(body$_1$)* is called, otherwise if $\hat{b}$ is crashed the failure continuation *on_fail(body$_2$)* is called.

Scenario: Third Party Intermediary (S030)
Scenario definition: A blind auction marketplace serves as a broker between buyers and suppliers. Buyers submit their requirements to the marketplace hub, which broadcasts this information to multiple suppliers. Suppliers respond to the marketplace hub where the information is logged and ultimately delivered to the buyer.
Realization: let be $\hat{a}$ an agent buyer, $\hat{b}$ an agent broker and $S = \{\hat{s}_1, ..., \hat{s}_n | n \geq 1\}$ a set of n agent suppliers. Firstly, agent $\hat{a}$ submits its requirements to agent $\hat{b}$ using the primitive *ask-one($\hat{b}$, $\hat{a}$, p)[on_answer(body$_1$) + on_fail(body$_2$)]*, where p is the description of the requirements. When $\hat{b}$ receives this request, it forwards p to the set $S_p \subseteq S$ of agent suppliers which are able to provide p. This is a generic case of *content-based anonymous interaction* and can be realized by means of the primitive *ask-everybody($\hat{b}$, p)[on_answers(body$_1$) + on_fail(body$_2$)]*. Indeed, the set S_p of agent suppliers depends on the content p of the interaction and it is dynamically retrieved at run time. Suppliers can dynamically register and unregister their competences by means of the primitives *register* and *unregister* respectively. When an agent supplier $\hat{s}_{i_p} \in S_p, 1 \leq i_p \leq n$, receives $\hat{b}$'s request it replies using *tell($\hat{b}$, $\hat{s}_{i_p}$, p_{s_i})*. Observe that, thanks to the fault

tolerant primitive *ask-everybody*, $\hat{b}$ does not wait for replies of crashed suppliers forever, but instead sooner or later it will be able to reply to the agent buyer $\hat{a}$ using *tell($\hat{a}$, $\hat{b}$, p')*.

Scenario: Registry based Discovery (S601)

Scenario definition: Agents use a registry to discover Web Services and the interface specifications.

Realization: in our architecture the registry of Web Service specifications is distributed in the peer-to-peer network of facilitators. Each agent can dynamically update its own competences making them available to other agents by means of the primitives *register* and *unregister*. To discover a service agents can use the FT-ACL one-to-many primitives *ask-everybody* simply specifying the knowledge *p* to be discovered.

3.1   Design of a Semantic Travel Agent Service

In this example we illustrate how FT-ACL can be used in our AOSA to realize a Travel Agent Service. The purpose of the case study is to show how Knowledge-Level agents can effectively communicate to realize distributed applications exploiting existing Web Services in a context where failures are possible.

Scenario. In this scenario, a user gets the location of a Travel Agent Service (TAS) and submits to it a destination and some dates. The TAS inquiries airlines about deals and presents them to the user. We extend this scenario supporting several TASs which are *dynamically* retrieved. In this way the user can choose among several solutions provided by different TASs (which can have different intelligent behaviours).

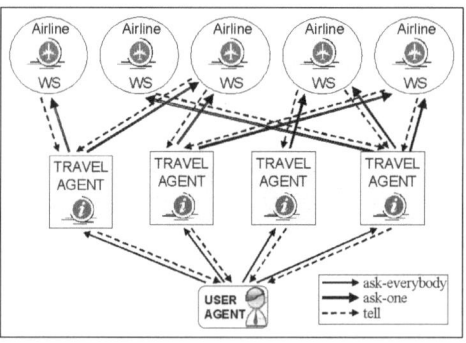

Fig. 3. Travel Agent Service Case Study

Realization. Figure 3 shows how this scenario can be realized by means of our OSA. User agents act as interface between users and the system, allowing users to specify a query and displaying the result. A TAS is implemented by a Worker agent which is able to compose available Airline Web Services (for example using AI planning techniques [19]) and to invoke the ones which are needed to solve a given query. For the sake of simplicity, we assume the existence of an ontology called *TAS_Ontology* which formally defines all the terms related to the case study.[3] To load the ontology, an agent executes the `load` routine of our AOSA specifying the URI of the ontology:

```
load(Ontology_URI)
```

New TASs can be dynamically added or removed in/from the system by means of the FT-ACL primitives *register* and *unregister* respectively. For example, the following code allows an agent to register itself as a new TAS in the system (the special term `self` represents the agent which executes a primitive):

```
register(self, Travel_Agent_Service, Travel_Agent_Code)
```

Let's suppose that a user wants to get the best combination of flights from Bologna to Tampa which satisfies his needs (prices, number of transfer airports, etc...). Let `d_start` and `d_ret` be the departure and return dates of the flight respectively. To dynamically retrieve all the TASs, the User agent simply executes:

```
ask-everybody(self, TAS(BLG,TMP,d_start,d_ret))[on_answer(
                                    find_best) + on_fail(handle_fail)]
```

where `find_best` and `handle_fail` are the functions which define the success and failure continuation respectively. For example, the function `find_best` could store all the replies of TASs and select the best one according to the user's preferences.

Thanks to the primitive `ask-everybody`, the query is sent to all the Worker agents actually registered in the system as TASs (that is, all the Worker agents which have registered the service `Travel_Agent_Service`). When a TAS receives a request, it creates a plan composing the Web Services it knows and then it executes the plan invoking the related Web Services. Note that this is possible thanks to the *agentification* of the Airline Web Services: represented as agents' competences, Web Services can be composed using AI planning techniques to solve the Worker agent's goal. After this step, the TAS replies to the User agent executing a *tell* primitive:

```
tell(UserAgentName, self, Query_solution)
```

Worker agents invoke Web Services using the *ask-one* primitive:

```
ask-one(WSName, self, par_flight)[on_answer(store_flight)
                                    + on_fail(store_fail)]
```

where `par_flight` represents the parameters of the flight, `store_flight` is the success continuation (which stores in the Worker agent VKB the result of the Web

---

[3] It would not be difficult to define such ontology, for example using OWL [20], but it would be outside the scope of this case study.

Service execution) and `store_fail` is the failure continuation. Note the importance of the failure continuation. If a Web Service in a Worker agent plan is not available, then the Worker agent must be able to calculate a new plan which does not have that Web Service. That is, the Worker agents must not wait replies forever. This is a fundamental property which guarantees *liveness* and the impossibility of *communication deadlock*.

When all the available TASs have replied[4], then the User agent selects the best solution according to the users' needs (success continuation `find_best`). Instead, if no TASs are available then the failure continuation `handle_fail` is called and executed. Note that all the agent behaviours can be programmed in a fault-tolerant way specifying the success and failure continuations for each interaction.

4 Related Work and Conclusion

The goal of developing robust multi-agent systems has been addressed in the literature in the last years [21,22,23,24] and some of the ideas presented by these authors are similar to the solution we propose in our approach. For example the idea of introducing *sentinels* to intercept exceptions [23] is similar to our facilitator level. The main difference among the two approaches is that facilitators and sentinels operate at different levels: while sentinels may still operate at Knowledge-Level, facilitators are specialized components which are directly designed to operate at a lower level. This low level characterization of facilitators (which aims to hide most low level details at the agent level) is fundamental to support Knowledge-Level agent programming [7]. The novelty of our approach is to embed some of the failure detection mechanisms in the ACL maintaining a Knowledge-Level characterization. On one hand we define a set of high-level communication primitives which are fault tolerant. On the other hand we provide a minimal interface which allows agents to deal with crash failures whenever this is necessary.

The main advantage of FT-ACL with respect to current ACLs such as KQML [5] and the FIPA ACL [6] is that we provide a set of fault-tolerant communication primitives which are well integrated at Knowledge-Level. Most of the current ACLs do not provide a clear distinction between conversation and network primitives, as these are often considered at the same level. Moreover, failures crashes and fault tolerance are often not present in the specifications. However, it is important to highlight that the main goal of FT-ACL is not to replace FIPA ACL or KQML or to become a new FIPA compliant ACL. FT-ACL primitives represent just a subset of FIPA ACL/KQML primitives and at the moment these languages are more mature. However, despite FT-ACL has a small set of primitives, it has been designed and implemented to overcome some important limitations of current ACLs, such as the integration of one-to-many performatives or the ability to support fault-tolerant communication in *open* and *dynamic* Multi-Agent Systems. Therefore, the main goal of our research in inter-agent communication is to design and realize a *core* ACL which satisfies a set of well-defined Knowledge-Level programming requirements addressing fundamental issues such as fault tolerance and anonymous interaction. From this point of view, FT-ACL can be considered an

---

[4] Note that this agent behaviour (to automatically detect and wait all the replies concerning a task despite crashes of agents) is supported by our architecture.

enhancement compared with current ACLs and, once extended with more primitives, it could be used as a valid alternative for building *real* Multi-Agent Systems.

Finally, we have also shown that FT-ACL can be used for inter-agent communication as well as for Web Service invocation. This feature has been illustrated showing how FT-ACL can support many common Web services usage scenarios and by means of a Travel Agent Service case study. This highlights a further advantage of our approach which successfully integrates different issues, such as high-level inter-agent communication and fault tolerance, in a Web based infrastructure maintaining a clean design of the architecture and a Knowledge-Level characterization.

References

1. Chaib-draa, B., Dignum, F.: Trends in agent communication language. Computational Intelligence **2**(5) (2002)
2. Singh, M.P.: Agent communication languages: Rethinking the principles. IEEE Computer **31**(12) (1998) 40–47
3. Luck, M., McBurney, P., Preist, C.: Manifesto for Agent Technology: Towards Next Generation Computing. Autonomous Agents and Multi-Agent Systems **9**(3) (2004) 203–252
4. Searle, J.: Speech Acts. Cambridge University Press (1969)
5. Finin, T., Labrou, Y., Mayfield, J.: KQML as an Agent Communication Language. In: Software Agents. MIT Press (1997) 291–316
6. FIPA: Communicative Act Library Specification. Technical Report SC00037J, Foundation for Intelligent Physical Agents (2002)
7. Gaspari, M.: Concurrency and Knowledge-Level Communication in Agent Languages. Artificial Intelligence **105**(1-2) (1998) 1–45
8. Mullender, S.: Distributed Systems. ADDISON-WESLEY (1993)
9. Singhal, M.: Deadlock Detection in Distributed Systems. IEEE Computer **22**(11) (1989) 37–48
10. Smith, R.G.: The Contract Net Protocol: High Level Communication and Control in a Distributed Problem Solver . IEEE Transactions on Computers **29**(12) (1980) 1104–1113
11. Chandra, T.D., Toueg, S.: Unreliable failure detectors for reliable distributed systems. Journal of the ACM **43**(2) (1996) 225–267
12. Dragoni, N., Gaspari, M.: Fault Tolerant Knowledge Level Communication in Open Asynchronous Multi-Agent Systems. Technical Report UBLCS-2005-10, Department of Computer Science, University of Bologna, ITALY (2005)
13. Dragoni, N., Gaspari, M.: An Object Based Algebra for Specifying A Fault Tolerant Software Architecture. Journal of Logic and Algebraic Programming (JLAP) **63** (2005) 271–297
14. Gaspari, M., Zavattaro, G.: An Algebra of Actors. In: Proceedings of IFIP Conference on Formal Methods for Open Object-based Distributed Systems (FMOODS), Kluwer Academic Publisher (1999) 3–18
15. Agha, G.: Actors: a Model of Concurrent Computation in Distributed Systems. MIT Press (1986)
16. Traversat, B., Arora, A., Abdelaziz, M., Duigou, M., Haywood, C., Hugly, J.C., Pouyoul, E., Yeager, B.: Project JXTA 2.0 Super-Peer Virtual Network. Available online: http://www.jxta.org/ (2003)
17. Dragoni, N., Gaspari, M., Guidi, D.: Integrating Knowledge-Level Agents in the (Semantic) Web: an Agent-based Open Service Architecture. In Proc. of the 18th International FLAIRS Conference, AAAI Press (2005)

18. He, H., Haas, H., Orchard, D.: Web Services Architecture Usage Scenarios. Technical Report NOTE-ws-arch-scenarios-20040211, W3C (2004)
19. Carman, M., Serafini, L., Traverso, P.: Web Service Composition as Planning. In: Proceedings of ICAPS Workshop on Planning for Web Services, Trento, Italy (2003)
20. W3C Web-Ontology Working Group: OWL Web Ontology Language Guide. (10 February 2004) W3C Recommendation.
21. Shah, N., Chao, K., Anane, R., Godwin, N.: A Flexible Approach to Exception Handling in Open Multi-agent Systems. In: Proceedings of the 2nd International Joint Conference on Autonomous Agents and Multiagent Systems (AAMAS-03) Challenges'03 Workshop. (2003) 7–10
22. Parsons, S., Klein, M.: Towards Robust Multi-Agent Systems: Handling Communication Exceptions in Double Auctions. In: 3rd International Joint Conference on Autonomous Agents and Multiagent Systems (AAMAS 2004), 19-23 August 2004, New York, NY, USA, IEEE Computer Society (2004) 1482–1483
23. Klein, M., Rodrguez-Aguilar, J.A., Dellarocas, C.: Using Domain-Independent Exception Handling Services to Enable Robust Open Multi-Agent Systems: The Case of Agent Death. Autonomous Agents and Multi-Agent Systems 7(1-2) (2003) 179–189
24. Kumar, S., Cohen, P., Levesque, H.: The Adaptive Agent Architecture: Achieving Fault-Tolerance Using Persistent Broker Teams. In: Proceedings of the Fourth International Conference on MultiAgent Systems (ICMAS-2000), Washington, DC, USA, IEEE Computer Society (2000) 159

Experiments in Selective Overhearing of Hierarchical Organizations[*]

Gery Gutnik and Gal A. Kaminka[**]

The MAVERICK Group,
Computer Science Department, Bar-Ilan University, Israel
`{gutnikg, galk}@cs.biu.ac.il`

Abstract. Lately, overhearing has gained interest in monitoring multi-agent settings. Previous investigations provided an extensive set of techniques using overhearing. However, most previous investigations rely on a problematic assumption that all inter-agent communications can be overheard. In the real-world settings, it is reasonable to assume that the available overhearing resources will be essentially limited. Thus, overhearing targets should be carefully chosen. We provide a theoretical and empirical study of selective overhearing. In particular, we focus on overhearing hierarchical organizations that are highly popular in the real-world settings. This paper first presents a theoretical approach for modelling overhearing in hierarchical organizations . Then, based on the proposed model, we present experiments in simulating conversations in hierarchical organizations, and empirically examine a set of overhearing strategies particularly suited for such organizations. Based on these extensive experiments, we are able to determine efficient overhearing strategies and isolate the parameters influencing their behavior.

1 Introduction

Recent multi-agent systems (MAS) are often built applying an *open, distributed* architecture. These systems involve various challenges of monitoring geographically-distributed and independently-built multiple agents. *Monitoring by overhearing* [1] has been found to provide a powerful monitoring technique particularly suited for open distributed MAS settings. According to this technique, an overhearing agent cooperatively monitors the exchanged communications between application agents. The overhearing agent uses these observed communications to independently assemble and infer the monitoring information on the corresponding MAS settings.

Previous investigations on overhearing have demonstrated a range of overhearing techniques. Novick and Ward [2] modelled overhearing by pilots that seek to maintain their own situational awareness. Kaminka et al. [1] developed a plan-recognition approach to overhearing in order to monitor the state of distributed agent teams. Aielo et al. [3] and Bussetta et al. [4,5] investigated an architecture that enables overhearing, so that domain experts can provide advice to problem-solving agents when necessary. Legras [6] examined the use of overhearing for maintaining organizational awareness.

---

[*] This research was supported in part by BSF Grant #2002401.
[**] Gal Kaminka is also affiliated with Carnegie Mellon University.

F. Dignum, R. van Eijk, and R. Flores (Eds.): AC 2005/2006, LNAI 3859, pp. 289–302, 2006.

Rossi and Busetta [7] applied overhearing to monitor state transitions in multi-agent settings and recognize changes in agents' social roles. Recent investigations proposed a formal approach to overhearing: our work in [8] introduced a theoretical model to over-hearing and applied it for conversation recognition, while Platon et al. [9] addressed design patterns for overhearing.

Although these previous investigations provided an extensive set of overhearing tech-niques, most rely on the ability of an overhearing agent to overhear *all* inter-agent communications. However, this assumption can be challenged both in the real-world settings and in the majority of multi-agent applications (particularly, *large-scale* MAS). Instead, we can reasonably assume that overhearing resources are essentially limited. Under the restriction of limited overhearing resources, a single overhearing agent or a team of overhearers will be able to overhear only a subset of conversations committed in monitored organizations. Consequently, efficient allocation of overhearing resources, i.e. selectivity in which agents will be overheard, is an important aspect of overhearing.

We propose a theoretical and empirical study of limited-resource overhearing in hier-archical organizations. These hierarchical organizational-structures are often associated with corporate and military organizations, which are widely spread in the real-world set-tings. This paper presents a model for overhearing hierarchical organizations providing a definition for (i) specification of conversations' characteristics in such organizations and (ii) overhearing strategies suitable for these settings. Based on the proposed model, we performed an extensive set of experiments simulating overhearing in pyramidal-hierarchical organizations. In these experiments, various centralistic overhearing strate-gies have been examined qualitatively and quantitatively.

Specifically, two overhearing strategies have been found to be efficient. The effi-ciency of overhearing strategies was measured as a percentage of optimal overhearing strategy, which can be calculated post factum (see Section 3.2). The first overhear-ing strategy addresses overhearing most important agents in multi-agent settings. This overhearing strategy assumes overhearing highly-valuable communications to be the key to efficiency. On the other hand, the second overhearing strategy proposes to over-hear agents that are less-important, but highly-communicative (i.e. involved in a large number of conversations). Here, its efficiency is based on gathering large amounts of information.

Analyzing these strategies in various configurations, we come to some interesting conclusions. The first overhearing strategy behaves as a parabolic curve with a long tail as communication activity level increases, while the second strategy maintains its linearity. Therefore, monitoring organizations, in some conditions, it is more efficient to overhear few highly-valuable conversations, while in other conditions, it is more efficient to overhear many less-valuable conversations and, thus, gather information on monitored settings due to the quantity of overheard information. In our experiments, we have also been able to examine the various factors that influence the shape and performance of these two strategies.

This paper is organized as follows. The next section presents a brief discussion of previous investigations providing the initial motivation for our work. In Section 3, we discuss in details the proposed model for overhearing hierarchical organizations, whereas Section 4 describes the set of performed experiments and their results. Section 5 concludes and presents directions for future research.

2   Background and Motivation

Work by Nowick and Ward [2] shows an early use of cooperative overhearing to model interactions between pilots and air-traffic controllers. In this model, pilots maintain mutuality of information with the controller not only by dialogue, but also by listening to the conversations of other pilots. While each pilot and controller act cooperatively, the other pilots are not necessarily collaborating on a joint task. Rather, they use overhearing to maintain their situational awareness out of their own self-interest. Similarly, Legras [6] uses overhearing as a method that allows agents to maintain organizational knowledge. In this approach, agents broadcast changes in their organizational memberships. Other agents use this information to maintain organizational awareness.

In contrast, investigations in [3,4,5] describe collaborative settings in which the overhearing agent may act on overheard messages to assist the communicating agents. The settings they describe involve communicating agents, who are engaged in problem solving. An overhearing agent monitors their conversations, and offers expert assistance if necessary.

Kaminka et al. [1] used plan recognition in overhearing a distributed team of agents, which are collaborating to carry out a specific task. Knowing the plan of this task and its steps, the monitor uses overheard messages as clues for inferring the state of different team-members. The authors presented a scalable probabilistic representation (together with associated algorithms) supporting such inference, and showed that knowledge of the conversations that take place facilitates a significant boost in accuracy.

Rossi and Busetta [7] applied overhearing to identify social roles in multi-agent settings. Initially, the authors used overhearing to monitor changes in MAS settings caused by transition from one state to another. Using a set of predefined transition rules, the monitor relies on overheard messages to follow the progress of MAS application and to determine possible faults and inconsistency. Then, the information gathered from overhearing is used to identify agent's social roles. These social roles may change over time. Thus, the monitor uses overheard messages, together with its knowledge of MAS status, to determine social roles of communicating agents at various time intervals based on a predefined set of social rules.

Finally investigations in [8,9] proposed a formal approach to overhearing. Our work in [8] introduced a comprehensive theoretical model for overhearing and applied it to one of the key steps in overhearing–conversation recognition, i.e. identifying the conversation that took place given a set of overheard messages. We developed a family of algorithms to this problem and showed their relative appropriateness for large-scale settings by analyzing their complexity. Platon et al. [9] addressed overhearing in terms of its architecture and implementation. Here, overhearing is referred as a design pattern and its various types are distinguished. In addition, the authors propose a set of implementation methods for overhearing and compare their relative strengths and weaknesses.

Most previous work assumes that *all* inter-agent communications can be overheard. However, this assumption is challenged in the real-world settings and in particular in large-scale multi-agent systems. In such settings, it is reasonable to assume that the overhearing resources are essentially limited. Therefore, it is important to be efficient, i.e. selective about which agents will be overheard, while others will not.

We focus on selective overhearing of organizations with hierarchical structure. These organizations are highly popular in real-world settings (e.g. corporate and military organizations). In such organizations, the importance of conversations varies with respect to organizational roles of their participants. Thus, our initial overhearing strategy has been to overhear agents with most important organizational roles. However, as we show later in the paper, in some conditions, this overhearing strategy performs poorly.

Therefore, the strategy of overhearing agents of most important organizational roles is insufficient. In this paper, we empirically determine a set of overhearing strategies that can be applied to efficiently overhear hierarchical organizations under the restriction of limited overhearing resources.

3   Overhearing in Hierarchical Organizations

Overhearing extracts information from *conversation systems* [8]–the set of conversations generated by an organization. Thus, conversation systems change based on the type of organization that is being overheard, and, in turn, overhearing agents must adapt their overhearing strategies to match the conversation system.

This section first describes the conversation systems expected to be generated in hierarchical organizations (Section 3.1). It then continues by proposing a number of overhearing strategies for such organizations (Section 3.2).

3.1   Modelling Conversation Systems

We define a conversation system of hierarchical organizations as a tuple (L, A, P, Λ, I, C). Some of these parameters have already been defined in [8], while others extend the previously proposed model. All of these are defined below.

Hierarchy Levels (L). The notion of hierarchy levels is an extension of our previous model. It is used to determine the relative value of various organizational roles. Thus, one agent is considered to be more valuable (in terms of conversations it commits) than another agent if and only if its hierarchy level is higher than the hierarchy level of the other agent. For each hierarchy level, we define a *value range* associated with it, i.e $\nu_{range} = [\nu_{min}(l), \nu_{max}(l)]$, $\forall l \in L$. It is used to define relation between two hierarchy levels. Thus, we will say that one hierarchy level is higher than another hierarchy level if and only if its minimum value is greater than the maximum value of the other hierarchy level, i.e. $l_1 > l_2$ where $l_1, l_2 \in L \Leftrightarrow \nu_{min}(l_1) > \nu_{max}(l_2)$.

Agents (A). A indicates the set of communicating agents in organization. As already mentioned, each communicating agent is associated with a hierarchy level, $\forall a \in A$, $\exists l \in L$ such that $L(a) = l$. The distribution of agents among hierarchy levels determines the type of hierarchical structure in organization. For instance, in pyramidal-hierarchical structure, discussed in this paper (see section 4.1), the number of agents in higher hierarchal levels is always smaller than in the lower ones.

Conversation Protocols (P). P indicates the set of conversation protocols used in a conversation system. A detailed definition of conversation protocol $p \in P$ can be found in [8]. Here, we refer only to one of its components–a set of its conversation roles, denoted by $R(p)$. For each role, we define the value of its implementation in a given conversation protocol as $\nu(r)$, $\forall r \in R(p)$.

Conversation Topics (Λ). Λ denotes the set of conversation topics. Each topic has a relative value indicated as $\nu(\lambda)$, $\forall \lambda \in \Lambda$. This value associates each conversation topic to a corresponding hierarchy level, i.e. $\forall \lambda \in \Lambda \; \exists l \in L$ such that $\nu_{min}(l) \leq \nu(\lambda) \leq \nu_{max}(l)$.

Intervals (I). An interval is a time period within the lifetime of a multi-agent system. Thus, we define I as follows: $I = \{[t_1, t_2] \mid t_1, t_2 \; time \; stamps, \; t_1 \geq 0, \; t_2 \leq lifetime, \; t_1 \leq t_2\}$.

Conversations (C). We define a conversation as a group of agents $g \in 2^A$ implementing a conversation protocol $p \in P$ on a conversation topic $\lambda \in \Lambda$ within a time interval $i \in I$. Thus, the C set can be formulated as

$$C \subseteq \{(p, g, \lambda, i) \mid p \in P, g \in 2^A, \lambda \in \Lambda, i \in I\}$$

Using this definitions, we can formulate the value of conversation for a certain communicating agent as $\nu(c, a) = \nu(\lambda) \oplus \nu(r)$ where $c = (p, g, \lambda, i)$, $a \in g$ and $r = R(a, c) \in R(p)$. Meaning that the value of conversation c for agent a (participating in it) is a function of conversation topic λ and role r (within conversation protocol p) that agent a implements. The information value of conversations distinguishes between the more important conversations and the less important ones.

A set of conversations (C), generated in hierarchical organizations, has the following characteristics:

- Conversations Distribution. Conversations distribution depends on the distribution of agents among various hierarchy levels. For instance, in pyramidal-hierarchical organizations, lower levels are the "working" levels. Thus, most conversations are held between agents in lower hierarchical levels.
- Conversation Topics. Agents communicate on topics within the scope of their organizational responsibility. Thus, agents mainly communicate on conversation topics associated with their hierarchy level or topics relatively close to it. As a result, agents of higher hierarchy levels commit conversations on more valuable topics.
- Conversation Groups. Agents communicate mostly with their peers, subordinates and their close superiors. Thus, most communications are held between agents of the same hierarchy levels or between agents in relatively close hierarchy levels.
- Conversation Roles. Mostly, agents of higher hierarchical levels implement higher-value roles in conversation protocols.

3.2   Modelling Overhearing

In this section, we present our model of overhearing organizations. Section 3.2 introduces overhearing strategies for a single overhearing agent and for teams of overhearers, whereas section 3.2 presents an evaluation technique to compare various overhearing strategies.

Overhearing Strategies. A single overhearing agent, acting in a cooperative environment, assumes some knowledge on monitored organization. An overhearing agent usually knows what agents communicate in these settings, which protocols are being used, on which topics the conversations are being held and etc. On the other hand, some information remains unknown. For instance, it does not necessarily know the complete list of conversations being held in organization at any given time.

We assume that a single overhearing agent is able to overhear all conversations held by its target agent, i.e. the communicating agent being overheard. Of course, only conversations within overhearing time interval, the time period in which the communicating agent is targeted, are being overheard.

The overhearing agent performs conversation recognition [8] for each conversation. Initially, the overhearing agent does not know the agents, protocol and topic associated with an overheard conversation. Only as the time progresses, the overhearer is able to recognize the various conversation parameters. The overhearing agent starts overhearing assuming that the conversation protocol and topic can be any of the $p \in P$ and $\lambda \in \Lambda$ respectively. Gradually, the overhearer is able to disqualify inappropriate protocols and topics until it determines the correct protocol and topic. This information, at its different stages, can be used to determine whether to continue to overhear the current agent or to find another target.

Since a single overhearing agent can only hear a small subset of conversations in a conversation system, multiple overhearing agents can be deployed to maximize coverage of the overheard conversations. However, the available overhearing resources, i.e. the number of overhearing agents, are limited. Thus, overhearing targets should be carefully chosen in order to increase the total efficiency of overhearing group.

The systematic targeting of communicating agents by an overhearing team is called *overhearing strategy*. Various strategies can be proposed: centralized vs. distributed, full vs. limited knowledge of conversation systems, various levels of collaboration between overhearing agents, etc.

We focus on centralized overhearing strategies with full information disclosure and leave investigation of other strategies for future work. Here, a central agent has knowledge of the conversation system parameters (e.g. agents' hierarchy levels, conversing agents at time t, etc.). Using this information, it directs the choice of target agents for each overhearing agent in overhearing group.

Comparing Overhearing Strategies. Each overhearing strategy may choose to overhear different target agents, and, thus, overhears different conversations. Consequently, some strategies may perform well while others perform poorly. Furthermore, the same overhearing strategy may vary in its performance under different configurations of conversation systems and overhearing resources.

Thus, contrasting overhearing strategies is important in order to determine which strategy should be applied under certain conditions. The overhearing strategies are evaluated in three steps. First, the optimal overhearing value, also referred as *optimum*, is calculated (Algorithm 1). Optimum, denoted as $\nu_{optimum}$, is the value of most efficient overhearing possible, i.e. at each time unit t overhearing the communicating agents with highest conversation values. Then, we use Algorithm 2 to calculate the strategy's *overhearing value*, denoted ν_{group}, which is the accumulative value of all overheard conversations using the specific overhearing strategy. Finally, the overhearing strategy is evaluated as a percentage of optimum, $(\nu_{group}/\nu_{optimum}) * 100$. Using this evaluation, we compare various overhearing strategies.

Algorithm 1 introduces the calculation of optimal overhearing value. For each time unit t (lines 2–8), optimum at time t is calculated and accumulated in $\nu_{optimum}$ (line 7). The optimum at time t for k overhearing agents is defined as a sum of conversation values of k agents with the highest conversation values at time t (lines 6–7). A conversation value of agent $a \in A$ at time t–denoted as $\nu_t(a)$–is the accumulative value of its conversations at time t (lines 4–5). This algorithm makes a simplifying assumption on changing overhearing targets. It assumes that a change of overhearing target by an overhearing agent is instantaneous and has no cost. This assumption is also used in other calculations.

Algorithm 1. Calculate Optimal Overhearing Value

1: $\nu_{optimum} \leftarrow 0$
2: **for all** t such that $0 \leq t \leq lifetime$ **do**
3:     $\nu_t(a) \leftarrow 0 \quad \forall a, a \in A$
4:     **for all** $c = (p, g, \lambda, i)$ such that $c \in C_t$ **do**
5:         $\nu_t(a) \leftarrow \nu_t(a) + \nu_t(c, a) \quad \forall a, a \in g$
6:     $A_{t,k} \leftarrow k$ agents in A with highest $\nu_t(a)$ values
7:     $\nu_{optimum} \leftarrow \nu_{optimum} + \nu_t(a) \quad \forall a, a \in A_{t,k}$
8: **return** $\nu_{optimum}$

Algorithm 2 presents the calculation of overhearing value for a team of k overhearers implementing specific strategy. Again, for each time unit t (lines 2–6), we calculate its overhearing value at time t and accumulate it in ν_{group} (line 6). An overhearing value at time t is defined as an accumulative conversation value of overheard agents. Thus, in lines 3–6 , for each overheard conversation, in a set of overheard conversations at time t (OC_t), its conversation value is accumulated for each participating agent that has been overheard (the OA_t parameter indicates the set of agents overheard at time t).

Algorithm 2. Calculate Group Overhearing Value

1: $\nu_{group} \leftarrow 0$
2: **for all** t such that $0 \leq t \leq lifetime$ **do**
3:     $OC_t \leftarrow$ overheard conversations at time t
4:     $OA_t \leftarrow k$ overheard agents at time t
5:     **for all** $c = (p, g, \lambda, i)$ such that $c \in OC_t$ **do**
6:         $\nu_{group} \leftarrow \nu_{group} + \nu_t(c, a) \quad \forall a, a \in g \land a \in OA_t$
7: **return** ν_{group}

---

4 Experiments

This section presents an empirical analysis of limited-resource overhearing in pyramidal-hierarchical organizations. Section 4.1 defines the experimental settings, while Section 4.2 analyzes the results of the experiments.

4.1 Experimental Settings

The experimental settings have been defined to simulate communications in pyramidal-hierarchical organizations. The number of communicating agents, i.e. $|A|$, was set to 50 simulating relatively small organizations. These simulated settings have been defined as highly hierarchical: the number of hierarchy levels ($|L|$) was set to 7. The value range for each hierarchy level was calculated as a relative portion of $[1,100]$, which was divided equally $\forall l \in L$. Agents were hyperbolically distributed among different hierarchy levels to simulate pyramidal-hierarchical structure. Thus, the number of agents, related to a hierarchy level, becomes smaller as hierarchy levels get higher.

The number of topics, i.e. $|A|$, has been set to 80. This value reflects our intuition that each agent has at least one conversation topic under its direct responsibility. The additional topics are generally common to all communicating agents. Each topic has been randomly given a value between 1 and 100 associating it with a hierarchy level.

The number of protocols was defined as 25, almost twice the number of interaction protocols specified by FIPA [10], simulating a diversity of interactions that are possible in organization. The duration of each protocol has been randomly set to a value within $\{5,10,15,20,25\}$, whereas the $lifetime$ of entire conversation system was determined to 1000. For each protocol, two roles have been defined. Their values were randomly set to one of the following combinations: $\{50,50\}$, $\{67,33\}$, $\{75,25\}$ and $\{99,1\}$. In this manner, we simulate differences in the importance of roles within the conversation. Finally, the conversation value is calculated using an accumulative function, i.e. $\nu(c,a) = \nu(\lambda) + \nu(r)$ (see Section 3.1). Thus, conversation values range from 1 to 199.

In the experiments below, we generated conversation systems and simulated their dynamic execution. These conversation systems have been statistically generated supporting the characteristics of hierarchical organizations described in Section 3.1. In each conversation system, a constant level of conversations was maintained at all time throughout the $lifetime$ of the conversation system.

Addressing certain configuration, various overhearing strategies can be compared as shown in Section 3.2. In Section 4.2, we compare proposed overhearing strategies using their evaluation values (as a percentage of optimum) in different configurations of activity levels, overhearing resources and value of information. Each evaluation is performed based on an average of 50 independent experiments committed with respect to corresponding configuration.

4.2 Results

Centralistic Overhearing Strategies. Our initial hypothesis has been that the most successful overhearing in pyramidal-hierarchical organizations (under the restriction of selectivity) can be achieved by overhearing conversations committed by most important agents. The main intuition behind this hypothesis is that most important agents commit the most valuable conversations.

Thus, our first overhearing strategy, called *MostImportantStatic*, was defined to implement this hypothesis. According to this strategy, k overhearing agents were set to overhear the k most important agents (in terms of their hierarchy level). To examine our argument, we defined an additional overhearing strategy, called *RandomStatic*, to serve as a control strategy. Here, k overhearers were set to target k random agents chosen at the beginning of the experiment.

The comparison of these two strategies is presented in Figure 1. The values on the X-axe show the activity levels of the examined conversation systems, i.e. the ratio between the number of conversations at time t ($|C_t|$) and the number of communicating agents ($|A|$), whereas the Y-axe determines the performance of compared strategies as a percentage of optimum. In results shown in Figure 1, the overhearing coverage, defined as the ratio between the number of overhearers and the number of communicating agents–$k/|A|$, was set to 30%. We can clearly see that *MostImportantStatic* strategy has been more efficient. However, both strategies perform poorly for low and medium activity levels (1%-100%)—maximum up to 70% and 40% of optimum respectively.

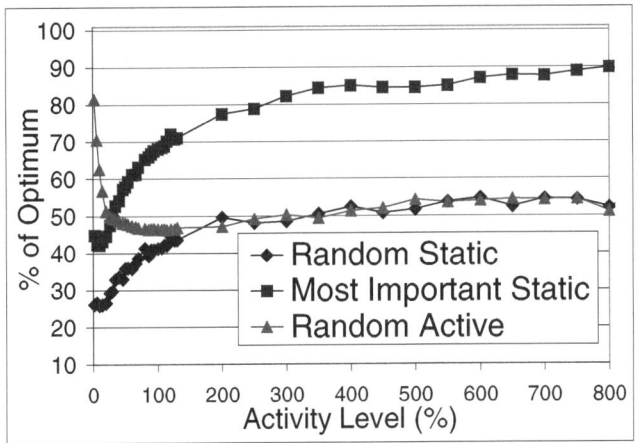

Fig. 1. Initial Overhearing Strategies

Analyzing this poor performance, we came to the conclusion that the main drawback of these strategies is that their overhearing targets are determined statically. Thus, in case that the overheard agent is idle (i.e. committing no conversations), overhearing it has zero-value. In low and medium activity levels, the probability of an agent to be idle is relatively high. In such conditions, the static strategies perform poorly. However, as the activity level grows, the probability of an agent to be idle reduces. Thus, static overhearing strategies monotonically rise as the activity level grows until the probability of an agent to be idle is close (or equal) to 0.

We developed a new overhearing strategy based on this conclusion. Similarly to *RandomStatic* strategy, *RandomActive* chooses k target agents at the beginning of the experiment. However, each time a target agent is idle, an alternative target is randomly chosen. Figure 1 shows also the performance results of this strategy. Here, we can see that at low activity levels *RandomActive* performs better than the *MostImportantStatic* strategy.

Based on the insight gained, we develop two additional strategies. The first strategy is called *MostImportantActive* strategy. It improves our initial *MostImportantStatic* strategy. The overhearing targets are determined as the k most important agents from those that are currently active. The second overhearing strategy, called *MostActive*, implements a slightly different approach. In contrast to *MostImportantActive*, *MostActive* targets k most active agents, i.e. k agents that commit the highest number of conversation at time t. Since the overhearing agent overhears all conversations committed by its target, overhearer can be efficient due to quantity of overheard conversations and not their "quality". Moreover, in pyramidal-hierarchical organizations, most conversations are held between agents of lower hierarchy levels. Thus, in fact, *MostActive* targets the less important agents. Both overhearing strategies proved to be highly efficient (Figure 2). Thus, the rest of the paper will focus on a detailed comparison of these two strategies.

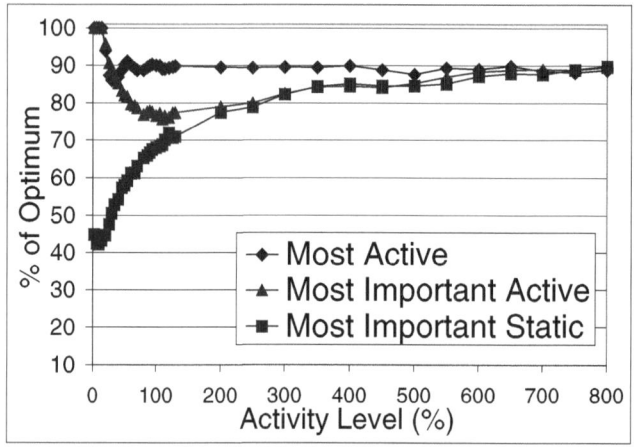

Fig. 2. Most Important vs. Most Active

Most Important Active vs. Most Active. At first, we analyzed these two strategies in various conditions of activity level maintaining the overhearing resources constant. This comparison led to a surprising result. The *MostImportantActive* strategy behaves as a parabolic curve with a long tail as the activity level increases, while *MostActive* strategy remains linear (see Figures 2, 3 and 4 for example).

This result can be explained as follows. At low activity levels, each communicating agent is either idle or involved in few conversations. Thus, overhearing important active agents is more efficient due to the higher value of their conversations. However, as the activity level grows, low-level agents become involved in more and more conversations. Consequently, at some point, overhearing a number of less-valuable conversations, committed by less important agents, becomes more efficient than overhearing a single high-value conversation of an important agent. The efficiency gap, between these strategies, becomes more significant as activity level increases and low-level agents become involved in greater number of conversations. However, at some point, the efficiency trade-off between these strategies changes. The conversation activity of high-level agents increases as well. At some point, it again becomes more efficient to overhear few conversations committed by important agents than to overhear many conversations held by low-level agents.

This surprising result implies that in monitoring organizations, an overhearer should decide when it is more efficient to target few highly-valuable communications, and when the total information, gathered from a large number of less-valuable communications, is more efficient in understanding the current status of the organization.

Value of Conversations. To understand the nature of these two strategies, we sought to isolate the parameters influencing the intersection points. As already explained above, this trade-off depends on whether it is more efficient to target small number of high-value communications or a large number of low-value conversations. Therefore, in the following experiments we changed the ratio between the low-value and the high-value conversations, i.e. the ratio between an average value of conversations in high and low hierarchy levels respectively.

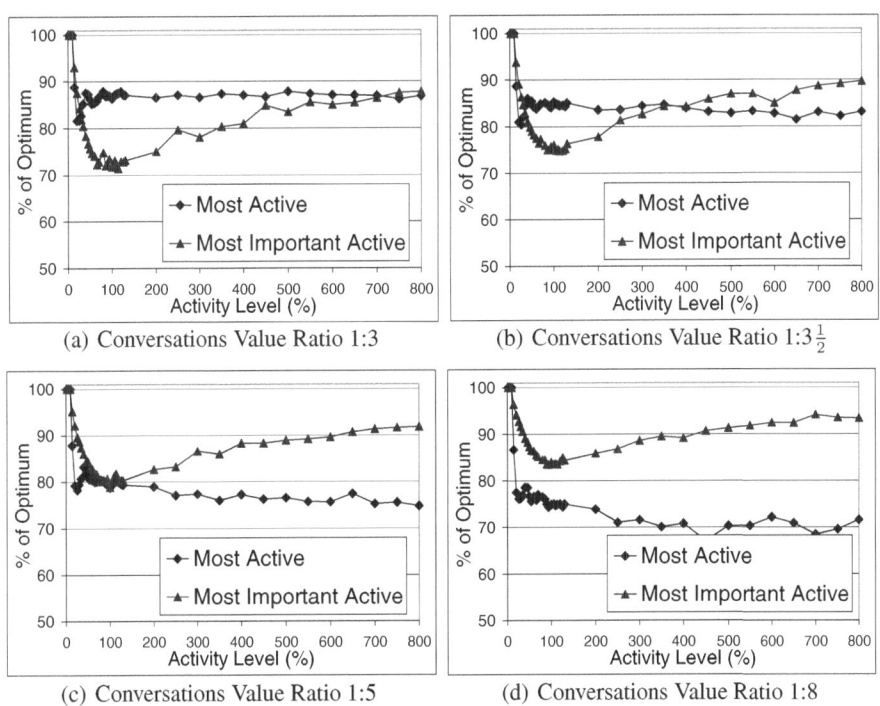

(a) Conversations Value Ratio 1:3

(b) Conversations Value Ratio 1:3½

(c) Conversations Value Ratio 1:5

(d) Conversations Value Ratio 1:8

Fig. 3. Overhearing Strategies Comparison with Respect to Conversations Value

In our experimental environment, the value of conversation ranges between 1 and 199. In average, conversations committed by agents of lowest hierarchy level are valued nearly 50, while conversations of highest-level agents value around 150 (ratio 1:3). In our experiments, we have also examined the behavior of the proposed strategies for additional ratios.

Figures 3(a-d) show the performance results of these strategies for 1:3, 1:3$\frac{1}{2}$, 1:5 and 1:8 ratios (where overhearing coverage is set to 20%). It can clearly be seen that as the ratio of conversations value increases, the *MostImportantActive* strategy improves, while the *MostActive* strategy deteriorates. At some point (Figure 3-c), the two intersection points turn into one, i.e. the two strategies intersect at the bottom of the parabola. Then, in Figure 3-d, the two graphs do not intersect at all—the *MostImportantActive* strategy remains more efficient even in its parabolic form.

Thus, in case the difference between high-level and low-level conversation values is significant, it is more efficient to target highly important agents than to overhear low-level, highly-communicative ones.

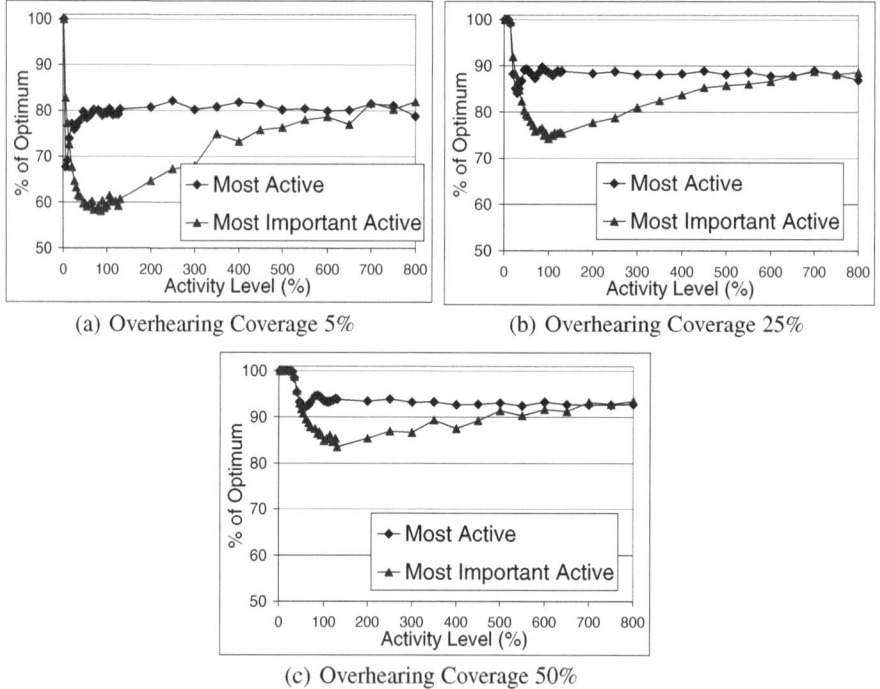

(a) Overhearing Coverage 5%   (b) Overhearing Coverage 25%

(c) Overhearing Coverage 50%

Fig. 4. Overhearing Strategies Comparison with Respect to Overhearers Number

Number of Overhearers. Finally, we examine the influence of selectivity. Figures 4(a-c) show the behavior of the proposed strategies for various levels of overhearing coverage (5%, 25% and 50%). We can see that both strategies become more efficient with higher overhearing coverage. Clearly, this conclusion is to some extent straightforward. However, an additional, less-trivial conclusion can be made. The gap between the

MostActive and the *MostImportantActive* strategies becomes less significant in larger overhearing groups. It can be seen that the parabolic curve of *MostImportantActive* graph becomes less concave. In large overhearing groups, this effect can be explained by a significant overlap in overhearing targets for both strategies.

5   Conclusions and Future Work

Lately, overhearing has become an acceptable method for monitoring multi-agent systems. Previous investigations proposed an extensive set of techniques and practises using overhearing. However, the problem of selective overhearing, under the restriction of limited overhearing resources, has not been addressed so far.

In this paper, we present an empirical study of limited-resource overhearing for hierarchically-structured organizations. Our work provides a model addressing both the characteristics of conversations in such organizations and the overhearing strategies appropriate for these settings.

Based on this model, we performed a set of experiments simulating conversations in hierarchical organizations and examined some of the proposed overhearing strategies. Analyzing the results of performed experiments, we were able to determine efficient overhearing strategies and to isolate the parameters influencing their performance. The main conclusions of our experiments can be summarized as:

1. Efficient overhearing strategies. The selective overhearing strategies of targeting k most important active agents and of targeting k most communicative agents have been found to be highly efficient.
2. Strategies Comparison. A double efficiency trade-off has been found comparing these two strategies. Thus, in some conditions, it is more efficient to overhear few highly-valuable communications, while, in other conditions, it is more efficient to target large number of less-valuable conversations.
3. Value of information. In organizations, where conversations committed by agents in high hierarchy levels are considerably more important than conversations committed in low hierarchy levels, the strategy of targeting k most important agents achieves better performance results.
4. Number of overhearers. For larger overhearing teams, both strategies perform better and the performance gap between them decreases due to the significant overlap in overheard conversations.

Currently, only centralized overhearing strategies have been concerned. Thus, in the future, we would like to examine the behavior of distributed and other overhearing strategies in these settings.

References

1. Kaminka, G., Pynadath, D., Tambe, M.: Monitoring teams by overhearing: A multi-agent plan-recognition approach. JAIR **17** (2002) 83–135
2. Novick, D., Ward, K.: Mutual beliefs of multiple conversants: A computational model of collaboration in air traffic control. In: Proceedings of AAAI-93. (1993) 196–201

3. Aiello, M., Busetta, P., Dona, A., Serafini, L.: Ontological overhearing. In: Proceedings of ATAL-01. (2001)
4. Busetta, P., Dona, A., Nori, M.: Channelled multicast for group communications. In: Proceedings of AAMAS-02. (2002)
5. Busetta, P., Serafini, L., Singh, D., Zini, F.: Extending multi-agent cooperation by overhearing. In: Proceedings of CoopIS-01. (2001)
6. Legras, F.: Using overhearing for local group formation. In: Proceedings of AAMAS-02. (2002)
7. Rossi, S., Busetta, P.: Towards monitoring of group interactions and social roles via overhearing. In: Proceedings of CIA-04, Erfurt, Germany (2004) 47–61
8. Gutnik, G., Kaminka, G.: Towards a formal approach to overhearing: Algorithms for conversation identification. In: Proceedings of AAMAS-04. (2004)
9. Platon, E., Sabouret, N., Honiden, S.: T-compound: An agent-specific design pattern and its environment. In: Proceedings of 3rd international workshop on Agent Oriented Methodologies at OOPSLA 2004. (2004) 63–74
10. FIPA: Fipa-ACL specifications, at *www.fipa.org (2005)*

Author Index

Lecture Notes in Artificial Intelligence (LNAI)